MW01092587

The Screen Censorship Companion

Exeter Studies in Film History

Series Editors:
Richard Maltby, Matthew Flinders Distinguished Emeritus
Professor of Screen Studies, Flinders University
Helen Hanson, Associate Professor in Film History at the
University of Exeter and Academic Director of the
Bill Douglas Cinema Museum
Joe Kember, Professor in Film Studies at the University of Exeter

Exeter Studies in Film History is devoted to publishing the best new scholarship on the cultural, technical and aesthetic history of cinema. The aims of the series are to reconsider established orthodoxies and to revise our understanding of cinema's past by shedding light on neglected areas in film history.

Published by University of Exeter Press in association with the Bill Douglas Centre for the History of Cinema and Popular Culture, the series includes monographs and essay collections, translations of major works written in other languages, and reprinted editions of important texts in cinema history.

Previously published titles in the series are listed at the back of this volume

The Screen Censorship Companion

Critical Explorations in the Control of Film and Screen Media

edited by
DANIEL BILTEREYST
and ERNEST MATHIJS

UNIVERSITY
of
EXETER
PRESS

First published in 2024 by
University of Exeter Press
Reed Hall, Streatham Drive
Exeter EX4 4QR
UK

www.exeterpress.co.uk

Copyright © 2024 Daniel Biltereyst, Ernest Mathijs and the contributors

The right of the various contributors to be identified as authors of this
work has been asserted by them in accordance with
the Copyright, Designs and Patents Act 1988.

Exeter Studies in Film History

ISSN 3049-7345 Print
ISSN 3049-7353 Online

A CIP record for this book is available from the British Library

https://doi.org/10.47788/YXNW9912

ISBN 978-1-80413-066-7 Hardback
ISBN 978-1-80413-067-4 ePub
ISBN 978-1-80413-068-1 PDF

Cover image: Still from *Les amants* (1958), directed by Louis Malle

Typeset in Adobe Caslon Pro by BBR Design, Sheffield
Index created by James Helling

Contents

Part 5: Disciplining Extreme Content

Illustrations

Figures

Tables

Contributors

Karina Aveyard is Associate Professor at the School of Art, Media and American Studies, University of East Anglia. She is the author of the *Historical Dictionary of Australian and New Zealand Cinema* (2018) and *The Lure of the Big Screen: Cinema in Rural Australia and the United Kingdom* (2015), and co-editor of *Watching Films: New Perspectives on Movie-Going, Exhibition and Reception* (2013) and *New Patterns in Global Television Formats* (2016).

Daniel Biltereyst is Professor in Film and Media History at Ghent University, Belgium, where he leads the Centre for Cinema and Media Studies (CIMS). Besides exploring new approaches to historical media and cinema cultures, he is engaged in work on film and screen culture as sites of censorship, controversy, public debate and audience engagement. He recently published *The Routledge Companion to New Cinema History* (2019, with R. Maltby and P. Meers), *Mapping Movie Magazines* (2020, with L. Van de Vijver), *New Perspectives on Early Cinema History* (2022, with M. Slugan), *Cinema in the Arab World: New Histories, New Approaches* (2023, with I. Elsaket and P. Meers), and a special issue on European cinema for *Cinéma & Cie* (2023, with E. Gipponi and A. Miconi).

Aydın Çam is Associate Professor at the School of Communications, Çukurova University, Turkey. He holds a BA from the Department of Communication Sciences at Marmara University and a PhD from the Media and Communication Studies programme at Galatasaray University. His research mainly focuses on New Cinema History, the cinema history of Çukurova, cinemagoing and spectatorship. Recently, he has worked on travelling cinema experiences in Taurus's highland villages, local films, and the mapping of Adana cinema history. He is also interested in cinema and space relations such as the mapping of cinematic spaces and spatial experiences. He coordinated the EU-funded project titled 'Adana Cinema Heritage'.

Mauro Giori is Associate Professor in Film Studies at the University of Milan. The majority of his research is focused on the cultural history of

Italian cinema, with a special emphasis on issues of sexuality and politics. He is co-editor of the journal *Schermi: storie e culture del cinema e dei media in Italia*. His most recent books include *Homosexuality and Italian Cinema: From the Fall of Fascism to the Years of Lead* (2017), *Rocco e i suoi fratelli: la vita amara di Luchino Visconti* (2021) and *Intorno a Luchino Visconti: dieci sguardi eccentrici* (2021). He is currently at work on a book on cinema and the extreme right-wing in Italy in the second post-war period.

Marita Eriksen Haugland holds an MA in Media and Communications from the University of Oslo. Haugland's MA thesis concerns age regulation in the video game industry and explores the differences between regulatory systems. Research interests include film, video games, censorship, media regulation, social media, audience communication and environmental issues.

Jorge Iturriaga Echeverría holds a PhD in History (Universidad Católica de Chile) and is currently Assistant Professor at Facultad de Comunicación e Imagen, Universidad de Chile. His teaching and research focus on cinema and media history, especially in regard to social reception. In 2015 he published the book *La masificación del cine en Chile 1907–1932: la conflictiva construcción de una cultura plebeya*. He leads the research project 'Film Censorship in Chile 1960–2000' and currently directs the project 'Forbidden Scenes: Analysis of Prohibited Feature Films in Chilean Dictatorship, 1973–1990'.

Karol Jóźwiak is Assistant Professor at the Culture Studies Department, University of Lodz, Poland and a visiting scholar at the University of Milan (spring semester 2023). His main research areas address issues of European transnational functioning of art and cinema in relation to memory, writing history, identity and politics in the twentieth century. Currently he supervises a research project entitled 'Philosovietism in Post-Fascist Italian Film Culture' (funded by the Polish National Research Centre), examining diplomacy between Italy and Eastern Europe during the Cold War in the field of film culture. Recent publications have appeared in *Iluminace* (2022) and the *Journal of Italian Cinema and Media Studies* (2023).

Konrad Klejsa is Professor at the Department of Film and Audio-Visual Media, University of Lodz, Poland. His research interests focus on the history of post-1945 Polish film culture, audience studies and German–Polish film cooperation (*Deutschland und Polen: filmische Grenzen und Nachbarschaften*; 2011, with S. Schahadat). Currently, he supervises the research project 'Film Distribution and Exhibition in Poland, 1945–1989', funded by the Polish National Science Centre. Recent publications include: "'It Seems to Me

That the Most Popular Films in the West Are Very Harmful to Us": Film Popularity in Poland during the Years of "High Stalinisation'", in J. Sedgwick (ed.), *Towards a Comparative Economic History of Cinema, 1930–1970* (2022); and 'Foreign Film in Poland, 1964–1975: Selection, Import and Audience', *Images: The International Journal of European Film, Performing Arts and Audiovisual Communication*, 32 (2022).

Mikołaj Kunicki is Adjunct Professor of European Cinema at Ithaca College London Center. He taught history at the University of Oxford, University of Notre Dame and University of California at Berkeley. From 2013 to 2016 he was the director of the Modern Poland programme at St Antony's College. Kunicki received his PhD in History from Stanford University in 2004. His research concentrates on communism, nationalism, authoritarianism and their relationships with popular cultures of cinema and performing arts. He is the author of *Between the Brown and the Red: Nationalism, Catholicism and Communism in Twentieth-Century Poland* (2012) as well as articles and book chapters on twentieth-century Polish and European history, cinema, nationalism and contemporary politics.

Richard Maltby is the Matthew Flinders Distinguished Emeritus Professor of Screen Studies at Flinders University, and a Fellow of the Australian Academy of the Humanities. His publications include *Decoding the Movies* (2021), *Hollywood Cinema: Second Edition* (2003, 2005), and *'Film Europe' and 'Film America': Cinema, Commerce and Cultural Exchange, 1925–1939* (1999), which won the for cinema history in 2000. He has edited eight books on the history of cinema audiences, exhibition and reception, including *Going to the Movies: Hollywood and the Social Experience of Cinema* (2007), *Explorations in New Cinema History: Approaches and Case Studies* (2011) and most recently *The Routledge Companion to New Cinema History* (2019). He is Series Editor of Exeter Studies in Film History, and the author of over fifty articles and essays. He is currently writing a history of Warner Bros for the Routledge Hollywood Centenary series.

Michael Marlatt is a disabled film archivist and current doctoral candidate in York University's Communication and Culture programme, and works as an archival accessibility consultant. His previous archival-film-related projects include the Toronto International Film Festival, CFMDC, York University, and 'Archive/Counter-Archive'. His dissertation centres on the lived experience of disability, chronic illness and neurodiversity in moving-image-preservation graduate programmes from the perspective of students and alumni. Alongside several archival conference presentations, Michael has published articles on archival accessibility for *Archival*

Outlook, *The Moving Image* and the *Journal of Film Preservation*. Michael is the co-founder and co-chair of AMIA's Accessibility Committee and is an advisor for the AMIA Pathways Fellowship.

Ernest Mathijs is Professor of Cinema and Media Studies at the University of British Columbia, Vancouver, and a lecturer and researcher at the RITCS School of Arts, Brussels. Mathijs studies the receptions of 'alternative cinema', in particular cult film and genre cinema. His essays have appeared in *Screen*, *Cinema Journal/JCMS* and the *New Review of Film and Television Studies*. His book publications include *Cult Cinema* (2011, with J. Sexton), *The Cult Film Reader* (2008, with X. Mendik), *The Cinema of David Cronenberg* (2008), *The Routledge Companion to Cult Cinema* (2019, with J. Sexton) and *The Cinema of the Low Countries* (2004). Ernest has also published on reality TV, acting and *The Lord of the Rings*. Ernest co-wrote the two-part documentary *The Quiet Revolution* (2019), and is currently writing a book on feminist actress Delphine Seyrig.

Mark McKenna is Associate Professor in the Film and Media Industries and Director of the Centre for Research in the Digital Entertainment and Media Industries at Staffordshire University. Mark's research to date has largely centred on cult and horror cinema. He is the author of *Nasty Business: The Marketing and Distribution of the Video Nasties* (2020) and *Snuff* (2023), co-editor of the Routledge collection *Horror Franchise Cinema* (2021), and author of the report *Silicon Stoke 2023: Developing Film, TV and Other Content Production in North Staffordshire*. He is currently working on his third monograph, a study of the John Milius surfing film *Big Wednesday* (1978) for the Routledge series Cinema and Youth Cultures.

Daniel Morgan is an English instructor at the Conservatoire National des Arts et Métiers in Paris and a researcher at the Université Sorbonne Nouvelle. He successfully defended his doctoral dissertation, on the representation of criminal justice in post-war French cinema, in 2018. His research has also focused on genre films and forgotten filmmakers from the period immediately before the New Wave, including André Cayatte, Maurice Cloche and Ralph Habib. A frequent translator for the journal *French Screen Studies*, his teaching and research interests include film history and historiography, censorship, propaganda, newsreels and filmed re-enactments of real events.

Julian Petley is Professor Emeritus of Journalism at Brunel University London. His many works on censorship include *Censorship: A Beginner's Guide* (2009) and *Film and Video Censorship in Modern Britain* (2011).

He was heavily involved in lobbying against the 'extreme porn' provisions of the Criminal Justice and Immigration Act 2008. He is a member of the editorial board of *Porn Studies*, and editor-in-chief of the *Journal of British Cinema and Television*. He is currently co-editing the *Routledge Companion to Censorship and Freedom of Expression*.

Fernando Ramírez Llorens is a postdoctoral fellow of the Argentine National Council for Scientific and Technical Research at the Interdisciplinary School of Advanced Social Studies (EIDAES), National University of General San Martín (UNSAM). He is Professor of Media History at the University of Buenos Aires. His research currently focuses on the political and media systems of the authoritarian states in recent history in Argentina. He is the author of *Noches de sano esparcimiento: estado, católicos y empresarios en la censura al cine en Argentina 1955–1973* (*State, Catholics and Businessmen in the Censorship of Cinema in Argentina 1955–1973*, 2016) and co-editor of *Televisión y dictaduras en el Cono Sur: apuntes para una historiografía en construcción* (*Television and Dictatorships in the Southern Cone: Notes for a Historiography under Construction*, 2021).

Viola Rühse works as the head of the Center for Image Science and course director at the University for Continuing Education Krems, Austria. She studied History of Art and German Language and Literature at the Universities of Hamburg and Vienna. She received her PhD with a dissertation on Siegfried Kracauer's film writings (*Film und Kino als Spiegel: Siegfried Kracauers Filmschriften aus Deutschland und Frankreich*, 2022). Her current themes of research in addition to film theory are modern and contemporary art and critical theory. She also works as an artist/photographer. One of her critical essays was granted the Bazon Brock Essay Award.

Daniel Sacco holds a PhD from the joint programme in Communication and Culture at York and Ryerson Universities. He has published on the films of Sam Peckinpah, Lucio Fulci, Vincent Gallo and Andrew Jarecki. His writing has appeared in *Cinephile*, *The New Review of Film and Television Studies* and *Studies in the Fantastic*. He currently teaches Screenwriting at the Toronto Film School, Yorkville University. He has recently published *Film Censorship in National Context* (2023).

İlke Şanlıer is Associate Professor at the School of Communications, Çukurova University, Turkey. She holds a BA from the Sociology Department at Boğaziçi University and a PhD from the Communication programme at Anadolu University. Her research mainly focuses on the sociology of migration and the sociology of cinema. She works on transnational politics through mediated settings, cinema and mobility, and new/local cinema history. She has a long experience of field research and ethnographic research on migrants and cinema history. She is the co-investigator for 'Topological Atlas: Mapping Contemporary Borders' (H2020-ERC) and the external expert for 'Global Asylum Governance and the European Union's Role' (ASILE), which is funded under the H2020 scheme.

Emil Sowiński is a research assistant at the Department of Film and Audio-Visual Media, University of Lodz, Poland. His research interests include the history of film culture in Poland and the economy of cinema. In 2018, he was awarded the first prize in the Professor Ewelina Nurczyńska-Fidelska Competition for the Best Master's Thesis on Polish Cinema. In the years 2018–20, Sowiński worked on the grant project 'Film Distribution and Exhibition in Poland, 1945–1989', founded by the Polish National Science Centre. Currently he supervises a research project dedicated to the film production activities of the Irzykowski Film Studio.

Elisabeth Staksrud is Professor at the Department of Media and Communication, University of Oslo and the coordinator of the EU Kids Online research network. Staksrud's research areas include research on children and media-related risk, media panics, censorship, freedom of expression and research ethics. She has written several books and articles considering the legitimacy of age-specific self-regulatory practices versus the rights of children. Her book *Children in the Online World: Risk, Regulation, Rights* (2016) deals with the balancing of media risk, problematic regulatory practices and the pressure this puts on children's participatory and provisional rights. Before returning to academia she worked for the Norwegian Board of Film Classification for seven years as a senior policy advisor and film censor.

Ben Strassfeld is currently teaching at the department of Media Studies, Queens College, CUNY, having received his PhD in Film, Television and Media from the University of Michigan in 2018. His scholarly work has appeared in *Velvet Light Trap*, *Historical Journal of Film, Radio, and Television*, *Journal of the History of Sexuality* and *Film History*. His book, *Indecent Detroit: Race, Sex, and Censorship in the Motor City*, is forthcoming from Indiana University Press.

Tomaso Subini is Professor in Film Studies at the University of Milan. Between 2014 and 2020 he has been PI of two National Interest Research Projects on the cultural history of Italian cinema. He founded and co-directed (between 2017 and 2022) the scientific journal *Schermi: storie e* *culture del cinema e dei media in Italia*, rated as 'Class A' in 2021. He recently published *Catholicism and Cinema: Modernization and Modernity* (2018, with G. della Maggiore); *La via italiana alla pornografia: cattolicesimo, sessualità e cinema (1948–1986)* (2021); and *Le Cronache di S. Matteo: il film amato e accantonato di Pier Paolo Pasolini* (2022). His research mainly focuses on Catholic Church film policy and the influence of Catholic culture on film history.

Karol Valderrama-Burgos is Associate Lecturer in Spanish Language, Literature and Culture (Ed. Focused) at the University of St Andrews. Her research interests comprise the cinemas of Colombia and Latin America, representations of gender, women filmmakers and decolonial thought. Her work has been published in English and Spanish, including in the journal *Latin American Perspectives*, in *Canaguaro Revista de Cine Colombiano* and by Emerald Publishing. Her doctoral research, funded by Colciencias (Colombia), investigated images of women in Colombian films and was adapted into a monograph in 2023. This book explores the limits of hegemonic gender norms in Colombian society through twenty-first-century films and the efforts being made to transgress those norms via cinema. Valderrama-Burgos is currently a committee member of SLAS (Society of Latin American Studies) and the co-founder of Red Cu, a research network on decolonial and queer perspectives in Latin American visual cultures.

Linda Williams is Professor in Film, Media and Rhetoric at the University of California, Berkeley. She is the author of *Figures of Desire* (1981); *Re-Vision*, a co-edited volume of feminist film criticism (1984); *Viewing Positions*, an edited volume on film spectatorship (1993); *Reinventing Film Studies* (with C. Gledhill, 2000); and *Screening Sex* (2008). In 1989 she published a study of pornographic film entitled *Hard Core: Power, Pleasure and the Frenzy of the Visible* (second edition 1999). This study of moving-image pornography looks seriously at the history and form of an enormously popular genre. She has also edited a collection of essays on pornography, *Porn Studies* (2004).

Acknowledgements

Everything has an origin idea, and in academia ideas often need time to come to fruition. The original concept of bringing together research around film and screen censorship has its origins in 2009 in Le Pré Salé. In this popular Brussels restaurant, we talked about a possible collection of texts exploring state-of-the-art research on censorship, with the intent to demonstrate how alive and how dispersed in its presence censorship of screen media is. It took us more than a decade to launch a call for papers for what became the *Screening Censorship Conference: New Histories, Perspectives, and Theories on Film and Screen Censorship* (16–17 October 2020). Due to the Covid-19 pandemic restrictions we had to rethink the conference, and it was a challenge to coordinate from Ghent and Vancouver simultaneously. We are grateful to Alexander De Man for his steady hand during the preparations and execution of the conference, and for subsequent follow-up research and logistics.

The present volume brings together a selection of research presented at this two-day online international conference about the histories and ever-changing re-emergence of strategies and practices of screen censorship, control and discipline. The editors of the volume would like to thank all the participants and contributors for sticking to deadlines, even as they, inevitably, changed along the way. We are particularly grateful to the academic keynote speakers, Professor Richard Maltby (Flinders University, Australia) and Professor Linda Williams (University of California, Berkeley, USA). A special thanks also goes to our professional keynote speakers, especially director and producer Rachel Talalay, filmmaker Manuel Mozos and film archivist and researcher Margarida Sousa (the latter both from the Cinemateca Portuguesa, Portugal).

We would also like to thank the sponsors of this conference, and in particular the members of the Digital Cinema Studies network (DICIS), the Centre for Cinema and Media Studies at the University of British Columbia (UBC) and the Centre for Cinema and Media Studies (CIMS) at Ghent University. We would like to acknowledge the support of the Fund for Scientific Research, Flanders (Fonds voor Wetenschappelijk Onderzoek, Vlaanderen). Thanks also go to Dmitri Lennikov at the UBC's

Visual Resources Centre, and to the Department of Theatre and Film's Centre for Cinema and Media Studies for their help with the hosting of the symposium's website. A special thank-you to Linda Fenton-Malloy for the website design. The website remains active, at http://www.censorship-symposium.org/index.html.

We would be amiss not to include a separate thank-you to Paul Fitzgerald and Damon Young for their care, and their curatorial and editorial management of the delivery and preparation of Linda Williams's chapter. We are honoured to be able to print it here.

Thank you to Anna Henderson at University of Exeter Press for her unwavering support and firm guidance in bringing this Companion to a successful completion, to David Hawkins for overseeing production at UEP, and to BBR Design for their expert typesetting.

Ernest owes personal thanks to Bhavan Joval, and to Dante and Albert. Daniel to Joke, Luckas, Eva and Lena.

Brussels, Ghent and Vancouver, June 2024
Daniel Biltereyst and Ernest Mathijs

Cinema, Screen Media and Censorship: An Introduction

Daniel Biltereyst and Ernest Mathijs

If only the cinema were free, it would be the eye of freedom.

Luis Buñuel

Models, Types, Mechanisms

Censorship used to be a fairly predictable topic. One of the key concepts in modern media and communication studies,[1] censorship has long been associated with ideas of repression, intolerant governments, or other strategies by powerful institutions to control the minds of powerless people. In its most caricatured form, hard censorship referred to coercive, repressive and top-down control mechanisms designed to restrict freedom of speech or undermine free artistic expression. This model of hard censorship is most clearly reflected in the way authoritarian regimes have developed a comprehensive strategy to control cinema, a medium which is arguably one of the most thoroughly censored in modern history.[2] Regimes such as those in Nazi Germany, the Soviet Union, Franco's Spain, Portugal during the Estado Novo or Communist China not only controlled the content of films through bans, cuts and alterations, but also had a much broader repertoire of censorship strategies such as infrastructural and technological censorship, control over film production, distribution, exhibition and criticism, as well as tactics to influence public discourse around (and through) films.[3]

For authoritarian regimes, cinema has been a key target because of its mass reach, its visual and emotional impact, and its perceived influence on audiences. Throughout history, cinema has also been recognized as

Daniel Biltereyst and Ernest Mathijs, "Cinema, Screen Media and Censorship: An Introduction" in: *The Screen Censorship Companion: Critical Explorations in the Control of Film and Screen Media.* University of Exeter Press (2024). © Daniel Biltereyst and Ernest Mathijs. DOI: 10.47788/RSDL4520 a powerful tool for propaganda, and as a result, cinema was scrutinized to ensure that movies complied with prescribed guidelines and did not undermine state interests. This volume on cinema and screen censorship histories contains several case studies that fit nicely with this hard censorship model. Besides the aim to make recent innovative studies on film and screen media censorship available to an international English-speaking audience, this volume intends to show the variety and changes in how censorship was and is applied, for instance in the socialist People's Republic of Poland (Chapters 3, 6 and 11), in extreme right-wing military dictatorships in Latin America (Chile in Chapter 7, Argentina in Chapter 8), in major parts of Turkey's modern history (Chapter 15), or in contemporary Communist China, which uses its market size to force foreign producers such as the Hollywood majors to (self-)censor their movies (Chapter 1).

However, authoritarian regimes did and do not have a monopoly on censorship, nor is it a thing of the past. Because cinema has often dealt with sensitive and controversial issues relating to violence, drugs, politics, religion or sexuality, films have often led to attempts to suppress or alter content so as not to offend, cause unrest or act against hegemonic cultural and social norms. This has often been the case when films are distributed to, and shown in, territories other than the ones where they are made. At the time of writing this introduction, when Hollywood applies high-tech promotion and marketing strategies to launch its 'Barbenheimer' blitz on a global scale, stories appear about *Barbie* (Greta Gerwig, 2023) facing a ban in Pakistan, Qatar, Iran, Egypt and other Muslim countries because of its pro-LGBTQ content,[4] while Christopher Nolan's R-rated *Oppenheimer* (2023) has been cut or digitally altered in several territories in Asia and the Middle East, mostly because of a scene containing images of nudity.[5] These and many other recent cases of movies, television programmes, games, filmed entertainment on VOD platforms, and other screen products facing censorship problems while travelling around the world underline that censorship is very much alive in today's polarized world, where it is seen as a means of content control and market protection, or as a tool in the global soft power battle.[6]

It would be rather short-sighted to think that censorship only occurs in authoritarian regimes or in non-Western countries where religion is closely intertwined with the legal and political system, or that it is an effect of the cross-cultural clash of ideologies between imported films and the receiving culture. The contributions to this volume will show that the practice of banning, altering or restricting the free production, distribution, exhibition and consumption of films and filmed entertainment is also practised elsewhere. Depending on the country and its specific political and cultural context, some forms of censorship also existed and exist in countries and political environments with political pluralism, competitive elections and civil liberties, and countries with constitutions that proclaim high principles of media freedom and freedom of expression. In the field of cinema in particular, most countries with a democratic political system have a long tradition of content control,[7] often at the level of the national state, as in post-war Italy (Chapter 14), but sometimes also at the regional level (Chapter 17 on Ontario, Canada) or even at the city level (Chapter 12 on Detroit, USA). Depending on prevailing cultural norms and traditions, many countries have set up censorship or regulatory bodies to screen films before they are released to determine whether the content is harmful to children or violates any laws or cultural norms (see Chapter 4 on Denmark, France, Japan, Norway and the United Kingdom). This volume also includes chapters on how extreme content such as video nasties (Chapter 16), strong depictions of sex and violence (Chapter 17 on new French extreme films), pornography, hard core and other potentially obscene fare (Chapters 18 and 19) have been received and regulated in societies where freedom of expression is a high value, and where this is countered by other principles related to societal harm and protection. Some of the chapters illustrate how, in particular historical contexts, films that dealt with politically sensitive issues, criticized the government or challenged dominant ideologies could be subject to scrutiny or suppression even in democracies. This is particularly the case for films that were perceived as a threat to national stability (e.g. Chapter 5 on the Weimar Republic in Germany) or to a country's geopolitical position and security (e.g. Chapter 2 on Italy during the Cold War).

The contributions in this book also discuss different types of control mechanisms for films consumed in cinemas or filmed entertainment shown on other screens (see, for example, Chapter 18 on censorship of films and the internet; Chapter 19 on hard core on various screens). This volume shows that censorship can be direct or indirect, explicit or implicit, visible or more subtle and very discreet in terms of structural control, internalized censorship or self-censorship. Soft and hard censorship coexist in fluid forms, with each form of control operating at different times. These mechanisms of control use different strategies, at different stages. Censorship is not only applied just before release in cinemas and on other screens; it also occurs before or during the production of films, for example through informal production censorship (e.g. Chapter 10 on Colombia) or at the distribution and export stage (e.g. Chapter 1 on Hollywood and the issue of industrial self-censorship in relation to China).

The censorship of films and filmed entertainment is not only linked to issues of governance and legal systems applying censorship, but as contributors to this volume show, it is also closely intertwined with wider political and ideological concerns, and commercial and economic interests such as market protection (e.g. Chapter 1). It is an interconnected phenomenon involving the state, the market, actors in the filmed entertainment industry, the press (see Chapter 9), as well as other societal and religious institutions,[8] and audiences.[9]

Theories, Concepts, Research

Despite its connotations with the exercise of power and the display of control mechanisms, censorship appears to be a complex, multifaceted concept with enormously changing meanings in different political, economic, social and historical contexts. The consensus about what censorship is and how it works has crumbled even further in recent decades, in theoretical, ideological and epistemological terms, especially since the 1970s and 1980s when critical approaches began to deconstruct the classical liberal view of censorship.[10] One perspective in this critical approach to censorship came from Marxist thinking on the open public sphere, on the free market of ideas, and on liberal concepts about freedom in general.

In Western liberal political thought, censorship became a key concept, constructed as opposed to the ideal of freedom. Censorship was, so to speak, the dark shadow of freedom, the other side of the coin. Censorship was what limited the ideal of freedom—particularly personal freedom, as opposed to an authority acting as a censor, using its power, intervening to control, silence or limit the freedom of expression of individuals or groups of citizens. In this liberal view, censorship was constructed as something to be avoided, to be dismantled, as something necessarily bad. The underlying idea was that legal action and political mobilization against censorship were needed to increase freedom of expression in a democratically organized society. Marxist thought has strongly criticized and deconstructed this antagonistic view of freedom versus censorship, mainly by understanding it as a liberal ideological construct. Arguing that the public sphere and the free market-place of ideas were ideological phantom or liberal ideals, critical thinking maintained that these were severely limited and that in practice certain classes and particular types of non-hegemonic social groups were excluded. In a liberal free market of ideas, many voices and opinions are marginalized, silenced or suppressed, while cultural production is considered subject to mostly hegemonic social norms and rules—in other words, censorship was part of the game or firmly rooted in the societal construct.

A major influence on critical thinking about censorship has come from Michel Foucault's writings on power and discourse, more precisely his ideas about the ability of dominant groups to shape and control knowledge production. As Matthew Bunn rightly stated, however, Foucault mostly avoided the usage of the term censorship, 'likely because the term evoked precisely the forms of juridical power'.[11] Foucault's work proposed a more sophisticated thinking about power, discourse and societal control (and censorship as part of it) that went beyond the conventional understanding of censorship as a mere restriction of freedom of expression. In his model, censorship is not 'a privilege one might possess',[12] and it goes beyond the idea of a single all-controlling authority; rather he suggests thinking about censorship as a process that operates in a network, a set of relationships that seeks to make certain words, images and discourses acceptable to other groups in order to silence, discipline and set limits on what is accepted as hegemonic. From this perspective, power means controlling the narratives and discourses that shape public perceptions. Rather than seeing power, and censorship in particular, as ostensible coercion, one can view it as a less perceptible, mostly invisible and all-pervasive process of subtle control over discourse and ideas—often leading to the internalization of hegemonic norms and to self-censorship. Rather than power emanating from an easily localizable, top-down hierarchical structure, it is embedded in the practices and discourses of different social institutions, a structure that involves a more complex relationship with the possibility of negotiation between a variety of actors. Foucault's perspective includes ideas about censorship as being productive, as it is a process of setting, testing and transgressing the boundaries of what is 'truth' and what is not.

This way of thinking has had a huge impact on scholarly work on film and screen media censorship. While traditional work in this field looked at the legal and structural underpinnings of censorship institutions and their censorial strategies and practices[13] (in some cases to legitimize censorship, as in the case of Hollywood's model of industrial self-censorship),[14] the new critical work raised other questions, using different concepts and research methods. The focus was now more on understanding the complexities of representation or the boundaries of what could be represented, linked to questions on power and the processes of negotiation about what and how something could be shown. Besides archival work carefully examining production files, internal memos, and correspondence between the censors, filmmakers, producers, pressure groups and other parties involved, and eventually oral histories, scholars examined films through careful readings or close analysis. One of the first film censorship historians who took Foucault's work on societal control and censorship as an inspiration for closely examining film censorial practices is Annette Kuhn.[15] In her pioneering social history of film censorship and sexuality in Britain between 1909 and 1925, Kuhn showed how censorship could be characterized as a struggle between a range of institutions over the nature of the new mass medium and how films could speak about sexuality. In her fascinating work, first published in 1988, Kuhn moved beyond the idea of censorship as an exclusively negative, institution-based power. Censorship was more than just repressive, or more than an act of prohibition undertaken by one specific institution (in the British case the British Board of Film Censors, or the BBFC). In her work, which was hugely inspired by feminist theories and sociologically influenced cultural studies, Kuhn insisted that the censorship process involved interactions and negotiations between various actors, including the censorship board, county councils, filmmakers and production companies, or organizations devoted to promote certain kinds of public morality. Highlighting the complexities of censorship and the making of the public sphere of cinema, Kuhn insisted that her study showed that 'various resistances and countercensorships were produced in the rivalries and alliances between them'.[16]

These more fine-grained ideas about censorship, negotiation, productivity and resistance inspired much of the work on film and screen censorship in the 1990s and until today, producing, for instance, a rich body of work on the Production Code Administration (PCA) and other types of film control on Hollywood cinema in and beyond the USA.[17] This work enabled, as Francis G. Couvares argued, 'to describe more thickly and narrate more richly the history of movie censorship'. Writing in 1992 on new research on the Hollywood internal censorship system, associated with the regimes of content regulation by the PCA, Couvares highly appreciated that these studies offered 'copious evidence of those negotiations over the boundaries of acceptable representations that are at the heart of all recent studies on censorship'.[18]

Many of the contributions to this volume are inspired by these critical perspectives on film and screen censorship—following an approach which often involves doing archival work, carefully examining and contextualizing films as socially important sites of struggle over boundaries of representation. To some extent this book's contributors adhere to what Bunn has more recently labelled New Censorship Theory,[19] or what literary historian Robert Darnton called the postmodern approach to censorship.[20] There is an effort not to overemphasize the censorial power of states or other influential institutions, while, at the same time, incorporating the importance of self-censorship, and cultural, market and other forms of impersonal, structural censorship. However, most chapters still emphasize institutions' censorial power, hence trying to avoid an all-encompassing definition of censorship.

One of the criticisms towards New Censorship scholarship is that it has become an all-pervasive, ubiquitous and inescapable phenomenon. This, as Richard Maltby writes in this volume (Chapter 1), 'endangers its heuristic potential'. Other contributors engage in discussing the danger of pushing 'the term to its limits', as Nicole Moore wrote.[21] In his contribution on French post-war cinema, censorship and criticism (Chapter 9), Daniel

Morgan refers to a certain amount of backlash against broader definitions of censorship, 'especially from researchers who have studied the systematic state censorship mechanisms imposed by authoritarian regimes: there are indeed crucial differences between them and the forms of speech regulation present in Western liberal democracies'.

In recent decades, debates about censorship have become even more sophisticated and complicated, given the expansion of the internet, social media and, more broadly, the digitization of social and political life. These fundamental changes have not only given rise to a new vocabulary for signalling new forms of controlling citizens and media professionals, such as internet service providers and social media platforms, who use their technologies for filtering, blocking, utilizing all kinds of content control, shadow banning and content moderation.[22] Digital technologies have enabled states, corporations and other powerful institutions to use ubiquitous means to enhance their control, surveillance, monitoring and censorship of citizens, users and customers. The political theoretical vocabulary now uses terms such as 'digital dictatorship' to refer to authoritarian governments such as those in China, Russia or Myanmar that use digital technologies for mass surveillance, internet censorship, social media manipulation and propaganda.[23] The use of algorithms and mass surveillance technologies, as well as fears of hate speech or harassment, are also likely to affect people's sense of self-censorship. These newer forms of censorship stand in stark contrast to a more euphoric narrative about freedom of expression associated with the internet and digital society, with stories about the internet enabling citizens to access information or exchange opinions more easily.

Another relatively recent development that has led to increased interest in today's censorship as a controversial process of representing social issues relates to debates about 'wokeness' and cancel culture.[24] Although one must be extremely careful and probably should avoid using terms related to the 'woke attitude', which is dedicated to awareness of social (in)justice and systemic discrimination, there is a lively debate linking it to censorship. In the recent culture wars, opponents have used the terms to criticize what they see as excessive activism calling for more inclusive policies in relation to race, gender, sexuality and other identity categories. The growing debates about publishers using sensitivity readers, platforms increasing their efforts to moderate content, and discussions about seeming restrictions on academic freedom are just a few examples of how issues of censorship and freedom of expression are central to contemporary social and political life. These debates raise questions about how policies that restrict freedom of expression relate to social protection against, and easy access to, digital violence and other potentially harmful material such as obscene, hardcore pornography (Chapters 18 and 19).

Structure, Chapters, Cases

This volume treats screen censorship as the attempt to limit the free expression, production, distribution, screening and reception of films and screen media. Censorship is a barometer of the state of cultures and nations. Often, censorship actions are an acute indication of how cultural concerns, be they progressive or conservative, libertarian or reactionary, are part of wider negotiations about social and individual freedoms, moral equilibrium, dignity and fairness, and the economic welfare of individuals—in this case, those who watch films, the viewers. More often than not, those viewers are not brought into these negotiations. Censorship is habitually seen as an impediment to free speech, in binary opposition to it (as Richard Maltby, in this volume, describes it), and equally frequently it is regarded as an instrument in struggles for power, in which it can serve as a tool for persuasion, discouragement, self-reflection, prosecution, policy-making, bureaucratic processing or alternative action.

This companion has screen media as its subject. Even if most of the examples and case studies come from film culture and the filmed entertainment industry, the media discussed include a wide range of distribution and access formats, from traditional theatre environments via video and digital media (VHS and DVD) to online streaming platforms such as Netflix or YouTube (e.g. Chapters 18 and 19). Archives and libraries too are part of this book's scope (e.g. Chapter 13), as their holdings, in whatever state of accessibility, form part of the collective history and memory of screen media.

The methods for investigating the screens under censorship mostly follow a historical trajectory. Chapters in this volume rely on archived documents, reports, press records, ratings, oral histories, quantifications of censorship actions across time, qualifications of decision-making processes—in short, on tangible evidence that facilitates the uncovering of how decisions about banning and blocking films are made. What these methodologies reveal, above all, is that censoring screens is an action in which multiple agents engage, with weighted interests, intentions and means. It is therefore a debate, a negotiation, a discourse; it is an uneven debate perhaps, with a tilted power balance, but a debate nonetheless.

The regions in this volume cover all continents. The opening and closing chapters emphasize Hollywood's practices and the USA's legislative context as important frames of reference for the study of filmed entertainment censorship, be they concerned with obscene materials or plain mainstream movie fare. This emphasis is not unlike that of film historiography in general, where American cinema remains a compass. This is also evidenced in how other chapters, which deal with local and regional censorship, feature American movies (be they so-called hippie films, arthouse cinema, exploitation films or auteur cinema) as their targets. This volume showcases the international scope of censorship through detailed examinations of historical censorship practices in Argentina, Canada, Chile, Colombia, Denmark, France, Germany, Italy, Japan, Norway, Poland, Sweden, Turkey, the United Kingdom and the United States.

This diversity of case studies is, we believe, an indication of the wide reach of censorship, in that nothing appears to escape its grasp, but also, and in a perhaps less sinister fashion, of censorship's contingency. With this we mean that from any present point of view it is possible, given the research tools and access to archives, to track back and explain how and why a film was censored and what the forces behind that action were so as to unveil the 'bigger picture' behind censorship, but also that at any present point, and given the multitude of agents at play, it is almost impossible to predict censorship in a general sense.

International relations, local sensitivities and negotiations

The rationale for the structuring of this volume follows a trajectory that starts with a focus on international relations, local sensitivities and negotiations. The first chapter, by Richard Maltby, sets the tone in its outline of the internalization of censorship, or self-censorship, as a most pervasive form of obedience to formal or informal demands and expectations regarding the output of media, in service of the 'monetization of cultural exchange'. The case study is that of the American MPA (Motion Pictures Association, and its differently acronymed predecessors), Hollywood's trade organization, lobby entity and spokesperson, and its efforts to 'codify' world censorship actions in order to inform (or steer) Hollywood's producers, to enhance production effectiveness. As Maltby notes, states such as China, and producers such as Marvel, with large audience potential, are increasingly playing the role of invisible 'participant' and 'negotiator' once played by the Hays Office. 'Market censorship' together with the administrative and sovereign power of 'political censorship', then, govern the proscriptions and prescriptions that make up the regulation of screen content.

Karol Jóźwiak's chapter on Italian cinema and censorship takes a different perspective on international relations, more precisely on the relations between Italy and the Soviet Union during the Cold War. Starting from the observation that in Italian post-war cinema explicit criticism of the Soviet regime was rare and that the Soviet regime was never denounced as a totalitarian state, Jóźwiak shows how Italian censorship efforts acted in support of 'philosovietism'. In his revealing historical account, the author indicates how censors made decisions (or refrained from decisions, in some cases) on films that dealt with issues involving the relationship between Italy and the

THE SCREEN CENSORSHIP COMPANION

Soviet Union. Jóźwiak uses the case of *La grande strada* (Michal Waszynski, 1947) as an example of the complications philosovietism brought to Italian film culture, and to its study.

Konrad Klejsa's chapter too takes on international relations, cinema and censorship, now by focusing on Poland in relation to the censorship of foreign films in the late 1960s and early 1970s. Klejsa's insightful contribution analyses how import restrictions, cuts, bans and demands on circulation rationed access to foreign films. Klejsa's chapter offers an alternative to studies of East European censorship because it looks not at native films, but at international arrivals. Klejsa's particular case studies investigate the censorship discussions involving Western films representing the so-called hippie subculture and underground (both avant-garde and Hollywood mainstream). While these films presented themselves as left-leaning, they were nevertheless subjected to censorship based on their representations of 'loose' Western values.

The next chapter presents a more contemporary take on the international dimension of filmed entertainment censorship. In their contribution, Elisabeth Staksrud and Marita Eriksen Haugland focus upon the cultural differences that influence how rating systems work in a series of democratic countries. In a cross-cultural comparative analysis, Staksrud and Eriksen Haugland look at more than 500 films rated between 2010 and 2015 in Denmark, France, Japan, Norway and the UK. Their research details differences in explanations for ratings and classifications by analysing the language used for these ratings. It offers a specific case study of *The Secret in Their Eyes* (Juan José Campanella, 2009) as evidence of how different rating boards can have different explanations for their evaluations, rooted in cultural usages of and impressions towards language, portrayals of sexuality and violence, and hazardous or crude situations, even when they appear to agree on some of the basics for their classifications.

Political censorship, debate and traces of resistance

The second part of this volume presents a series of chapters that deal with practices of, debates about and other acts of resistance against political censorship in four different political environments. In her quasi-micro-historical case study, Viola Rühse discusses how one singular publication, Wolfgang Petzet's *Verbotene Filme* from 1931, crystallized debates around censorship at the cusp of the Nazi takeover in Germany. The involvement of the publishing house for Petzet's book, which also published the *Frankfurter Zeitung*, as well as the engagement of eminent critical sociologist, film critic and theorist Siegfried Kracauer in *Verbotene Filme*, demonstrate not only how high the stakes were at the time, but also that film censorship was a significant political-societal battlefield. Criticism and written publications as expressions of such battle lines are, argues Rühse, of crucial significance in studying censorship.

Mikołaj Kunicki's chapter takes censorship in the People's Republic of Poland between the 1950s and 1970 as its subject. As a nation heavily dominated by Soviet Russian Stalinism, yet also known to be one of the Eastern Bloc's more liberal and politically volatile countries (until the Prague Spring of 1968 at least), Poland's system of 'film units' who were responsible for vetting film projects in conversation with the authorities created a discursive context of embedded censorship. This included what Kunicki calls an 'acculturation' of communist apparatchiks as cinephiles (if not proxy filmmakers) as well as representatives of the Catholic Church (which in Poland enjoyed relative autonomy) and filmmakers themselves, who sometimes used the system to jockey for position.

Jorge Iturriaga Echeverría's chapter focuses on censorship during the dictatorship of August Pinochet in Chile between 1973 and 1989. He outlines how the military regime immediately toughened censorship rules, enacting a new law in 1974 that explicitly mentioned Marxist ideas as a danger requiring vigilance. Whereas the Junta's overall film policy supported the capitalist free market model, its strict cultural censorship was part of the strategy used to implement a new political, economic and social model. In his thoughtful chapter, Iturriaga Echeverría concentrates specifically on films with a sexual content, and he explains how a perceived increase in these titles (and their censorship) was the result, directly and indirectly, of the Junta's policy to 'adultify' cinema culture. Faced with potential harsh restrictions on the import of material aimed at general or teen audiences, distributors chose to focus on the adult side of the business.

In neighbouring Argentina, around the same time, another military dictatorship developed a film censorship model, which was built upon two political-ideological pillars, the Catholic Church and the armed forces. In his contribution, Fernando Ramírez Llorens focuses on an abolitionist movement wishing to get rid of censorship altogether. Concentrating on this resistance movement, Ramírez Llorens analyses how discussions around the freedom of expression were often conducted in public, via press articles and other publications. Filmmakers, who often went on and off blacklists, had to carefully balance their public declarations with their intent to make movies.

Production policies and content regulation
The third part of this edited collection looks at censorship policies and practices in relation to, and from the perspective of, filmmakers, producers and other parties engaged in the filmmaking scene. In his chapter, Daniel

Morgan concentrates on post-World War II French cinema, famously criticized by New Wave critics such as François Truffaut as bland and uninteresting. Arguing that film criticism can be an instrument whose charged usage of terminology (such as the issue of 'quality') unveils attitudes towards (un)desirable properties of films, Morgan claims that post-war French films (and their activist filmmakers) were subject to censorship by having their work downgraded to the point that it has become virtually inaccessible. Leaning on the work of Michel Foucault, Morgan highlights the informal workings of censorship, more precisely the relationship between the censorial act (one of coercion and restriction of speech) and the activity of film criticism (one of speech upon speech).

The subsequent chapter discusses film censorship in Colombia between 1978 and 1993, the years of relatively stable though fractured regimes, the period of the Armed Conflict and of the rise and demise of the FOCINE agency of state-sponsored support for cinema. In their contribution, Karina Aveyard and Karol Valderrama-Burgos focus on the distinction between formal and informal forms of censorship, understood here in the relational sense, used by Foucault, as a form of negotiated power. Via three perspectives (class and economic agency, the re-evaluation of depictions of violence in previously banned films, and the representation of women in Colombian film), Aveyard and Valderrama-Burgos offer insights into the role of 'enmeshed' self-censorship, embedded within more formal arrangements.

The last chapter in this section on production, regulation and censorship looks at the censorship measures to control a particular category of cinema, namely debut films, in the People's Republic of Poland in the 1980s. In his chapter, Emil Sowiński argues that these films were especially vulnerable to censorship because of the authors' and producers' lack of preceding reputation (for better or for worse). The period under scrutiny in Sowiński's chapter covers the first half of the 1980s, and in particular the output of the Warsaw-based Irzykowski Film Studio. Through a thorough analysis of archived communication between authorities and producers, Sowiński reveals how films such as *Nadzór* (*Custody*, Wiesław Saniewski, 1983) could obtain distribution by 'mimicking' compliance with censorship demands.

Intermediality, entanglement and longitudinal approaches
The fourth section presents chapters on issues related to screen censorship from an intermedial, entangled or longitudinal perspective. Moving to North America, the contribution of Ben Strassfeld takes aim at the intersections of efforts in censorship across media, in particular cinema, literature and the performing arts, and their mutual influences on each other. Using the locale of Detroit as a case study, with a focus on the period immediately after

World War II, and through Otto Preminger's *The Moon is Blue* (1953), based on Hugh Herbert's play, Strassfeld details how pressure groups, mayoral politics and smaller censor bureaus can actively influence the availability of screen media.

Michael Marlatt's overview of the workings of the Ontario Censor Board, arguably Canada's most notorious office for censoring films between World War I and the advent of the Covid pandemic in 2020, similarly uses examples to illustrate the intents of governments, both local and federal, to control what their constituents were able to consume, enjoy and be aware of. In Marlatt's view, the survival of the archives of the Ontario Censor Board offers an opportunity to use instances of censorship as teachable materials in the study of the role of films in society—and of the prevalent political and moral battles of the period(s). Marlatt's focus is on historical examples of films fallen foul of the Ontario Censor Board.

In the following chapter, Mauro Giori and Tomaso Subini analyse the specificities of Italian censorship through a comprehensive overview of films banned, wholly or partially, rated and approved in the decades following World War II, up to the end of the 1970s, a period in which Italian culture secularized in rapid tempo, while experiencing abrupt economic changes, and also a period displaying tense political conflicts and compromises. In their quantitative analysis of censorship practices, Giori and Subini argue that, above all, the debate over censorship in Italy was, and remains, one of constant negotiation between forces on a national and regional and sometimes parish level.

In the last chapter of this part of the volume, İlke Şanlıer and Aydın Çam concentrate their analysis on film censorship in Turkey, extending the notion of cinema, in this case, to include alternative screen versions of films available via YouTube. In their 'long history' of film censorship in Turkey, they point out how tendencies towards censorship in the various governmental and commercial regimes have shaped a 'path dependency' in which contemporary attitudes and actions are inspired, steered or influenced by steps taken earlier, creating habits and routines, as it were, that are resistant to change.

Disciplining extreme content

The fifth and final part of this companion concentrates on issues of censorship in relation to extreme content such as violence, porn and hard core. In his chapter, Mark McKenna zooms in on one of the most notorious groupings of films, the British video nasties, and the moral panic surrounding their existence and visibility in the early 1980s, characterized by Margaret Thatcher's Conservative premiership. The video nasties were not

THE SCREEN CENSORSHIP COMPANION

a genre, a cycle or a movement, but their grouping together by the British press and moral campaigners as a 'threat' came at a time, McKenna argues, that saw widespread concern over the then new technologies of VCR, VHS and videotaping. The video nasties became embroiled in this discourse, and it coloured their treatment by censorship apparatuses. McKenna relies on press material, government reports and trade communications to sketch the landscape of a business (that of video sales and rentals) in full development, and he makes the case that the video nasties were as much about 'video' as about 'nastiness'.

Daniel Sacco's contribution extends this scrutiny to more recent examples of the working of the Ontario Film Review Board (the name the Ontario Censor Board adopted in the 1980s), in tandem with (and sometimes against) local and federal government agencies in Canada. Focusing on the reception and censorship of French New Extremity cinema, Sacco's chapter offers an intriguing case study of *À ma soeur* (*Fat Girl*, Catherine Breillat, 2001). Sacco shows how censorship boards were forced to acknowledge artistic merit and freedom of expression as privileged cultural concepts even if it meant allowing controversial material to be released to the public.

In the next chapter, Julian Petley focuses on censorship from the angle of online and internet media, and the legalities of accessing controversial and provocative materials. Here Petley looks at films from decades ago (which were subject to distribution-specific laws) under the cap of new regulations and political initiatives, several of which are themselves subject to battles between governing and opposition politics in turn subject to opaque intentions. In an era where the very definition of a 'screen' (its size, reach and 'place' uncertain), the materiality of 'viewing' (where and when, and towards what kind of physical sensorial activity) and 'ownership' (can one own something a company claims they are licensing but not parting ownership with?) are fuzzy, Petley's chapter asks what protections (if any) exist against sweeping interpretations of possession via covert surveillance, and what safeguards (again, if any) laws on privacy can offer.

The concluding chapter in this collection addresses the topic of 'obscenity', often defined by a cleavage between actions by viewers or producers that are deemed illegal infractions or misdemeanours, and actions seen as criminal and therefore subject to laws under that definition. Linda Williams, with Damon R. Young, distinguishes between three (or actually four) 'moments' of obscenity in the history of, mainly, US pornographic material. In her groundbreaking chapter, Williams asks the question of how and when an image or a film is considered obscene. In her historical trajectory, the 'moments' she identifies align with political and social sensitivities throughout the twentieth and into the twenty-first century. Relying on filmic materials (and indeed often controversial imagery), Williams

14

uncovers a line of argumentation around the 'visibility' of pleasure that informs much of America's fascination with 'hard core'. Williams ends her chapter with an anthropological and auto-ethnographic look at what is seen as the 'pinnacle' of obscenity and hardcore pornography in today's media landscape, namely internet porn.

In their coverage of diverse areas and with their specific foci, the chapters of *The Screen Censorship Companion* share one important purpose: to go into detail, and to not let the fog of generalization obfuscate the precise actions that make up censorship. By discussing cases, particular films, receptions, agencies, regimes and their bureaucracies, and archives and their workings, the chapters in this volume assign accountability. They also shed light to expose the underlying, often inarticulate ideological spines and cultural and moral inspirations of censorship—those elements not explicated in guidelines but evidenced through censorship actions and implications.

We hope that by offering this companion, more research into the mechanisms that determine who censors, how and why can be encouraged (and indeed funded). Work on censorship is never-ending and it is more than ever a relevant societal issue. Though many of the case studies are historically situated, the topics this volume isolates supersede time-brackets. Readers are invited to transport the concepts brought forward in this volume and apply them to current, localized instances. We hope the volume shows what a fascinating phenomenon censorship still is today, a perspective which enables us to think in more subtle terms about shifting boundaries of public morality, and social and cultural norms across time, space and ideology.

Notes

1   See for instance Sue Curry Jansen, *Censorship: The Knot That Binds Power and Knowledge* (New York: Oxford University Press, 1991); Beate Müller, 'Censorship & Cultural Regulation: Mapping the Territory', in Beate Müller (ed.), *Censorship & Cultural Regulation in the Modern Age* (Amsterdam: Rodopi, 2004): 1–31; Michael Holquist, 'Corrupt Originals: The Paradox of Censorship', *PMLA* 109.1 (1994): 14–25; Robert Post (ed.), *Censorship and Silencing: Practices of Cultural Regulation* (Los Angeles: Getty Research Institute for the History of Art and the Humanities, 1998); Lee Grieveson, 'Censorship', *Oxford Bibliographies* (Oxford: Oxford University Press, 2012/22); Betty Houchin Winfield, 'Censorship', *Oxford Bibliographies* (Oxford: Oxford University Press, 2012/23).

2   Daniel Biltereyst and Roel Vande Winkel (eds), *Silencing Cinema: Film Censorship around the World* (New York: Palgrave, 2013).

3   On Nazi Germany and censorship, see Martin Loiperdinger, 'Film Censorship in Germany', in *Silencing Cinema*, pp. 81–96. On Nazi Germany's film policy during

the Second World War in occupied countries, see Roel Vande Winkel and David Welch (eds), *Cinema and the Swastika: The International Expansion of Third Reich Cinema* (New York: Palgrave, 2007). On film censorship in the Soviet Union, see Richard Taylor, *Film Propaganda: Soviet Russia and Nazi Germany* (London: I.B. Tauris, 1998); Richard Taylor, 'Cinema Red: Political Control of Cinema in the Soviet Union', in *Silencing Cinema*, pp. 97–108. On censorship during the Spanish Franco regime, see Fátima Gil, 'Exemplary Women: The Use of Film and Censorship as a Means of Moral Indoctrination during the Franco Dictatorship in Spain', *Journal of Popular Culture* 49.4 (2016): 856–74; Jorge Díaz-Cintas, 'Film Censorship in Franco's Spain: The Transforming Power of Dubbing', *Perspectives* 27.2 (2019): 182–200; Roman Gubern-Domènec Font, *Un cine para el cadalso* (Barcelona: Editorial Euros, 1976). On Portugal, see Ana Bela Morais, 'Censored and Banned: Portuguese Films during the Government of Marcello Caetano (1968–74)', *Portuguese Studies* 32.1 (2016): 88–107. On censorship in Communist China, see Zhiwei Xiao, 'Prohibition, Politics, and Nation-Building: A History of Film Censorship in China', in *Silencing Cinema*, pp. 109–30.

4   See for instance 'Barbie Screening Halted in Pakistan's Punjab, Released with Cuts', *India Today*, 23 July 2023.

5   See, amongst other news releases, 'Topless Florence Pugh Scene in "Oppenheimer" Digitally Censored (with a CGI Black Dress) in Middle East, India', *Hollywood Reporter*, 25 July 2023.

6   See for regular updates and discussions on censorship, media freedom, freedom of expression and human rights, amongst others, organizations campaigning for free of expression like Index on Censorship (indexoncensorship.org), Freedom House (freedomhouse.org), Reporters Without Freedom (rsf.org), PEN International (pen -international.org) and Electronic Frontier Foundation (eff.org).

7   See for instance on Belgium: Daniel Biltereyst, *Verboden beelden: de verborgen geschiedenis van filmcensuur in België* (Antwerp: Houtekiet, 2020). On Britain: Annette Kuhn, *Cinema, Censorship and Sexuality 1909–1925* (London: Routledge, 2016); James C. Robertson, *The Hidden Cinema: British Film Censorship in Action 1913–1972* (London: Routledge, 2005); Julian Petley, *Film and Video in Modern Britain* (Edinburgh: Edinburgh University Press, 2011). On Canada: Pierre Hébert, Kenneth Landry and Yves Lever, *Dictionnaire de la censure au Québec: littérature et cinéma* (Anjou: Les Éditions Fides, 2006). On France: Frédéric Hervé, *Censure et cinéma dans la France des Trente Glorieuses* (Paris: Nouveau monde, 2005); Laurent Jullier, *Interdit aux moins de 18 ans* (Paris: Armand Colin, 2008); Arnaud Esquerre, *Interdire de voir: sexe, violence et liberté d'expression au cinéma* (Paris: Fayard, 2019). On post-war Italy: Alfredo Baldi, *Schermi proibiti: la censura in Italia, 1947–1988* (Venice: B&N, 2002). On the USA: e.g. Sheri Chinen Biesen, *Film Censorship: Regulating America's Screen* (New York: Columbia University Press, 2018); Francis G. Couvares (ed.), *Movie Censorship and American Culture* (Washington & London: University of Massachusetts Press, 2006); Thomas Doherty, *Pre-Code Hollywood: Sex, Immorality, and Insurrection in American Cinema, 1930–1934* (New York: Columbia University Press, 1999); Lee Grieveson, *Policing Cinema: Movies and Censorship in Early-Twentieth-Century America* (Los Angeles: University of California Press, 2004); Janet Staiger, *Bad Women: The Regulation of Female Sexuality in Early American Cinema* (Minneapolis: University of Minnesota Press, 1995). See also note 17.

8   See, for instance, on the role of the Roman Catholic Church and Catholic organizations: Daniel Biltereyst and Daniela Treveri Gennari (eds), *Moralizing Cinema: Film, Catholicism, and Power* (New York: Routledge, 2015); Gregory D. Black, *Hollywood Censored: Morality Codes, Catholics, and the Movies* (Cambridge: Cambridge University Press, 1994); Frank Walsh, *Sin and Censorship* (New Haven: Yale University Press, 1996); Gregory D. Black, *The Catholic Crusade against the Movies* (Cambridge: Cambridge University Press, 1998).

9   See for an audience perspective on film censorship: Daniel Biltereyst, 'Film Censorship in a Liberal Free Market Democracy: Strategies of Film Control and Audiences' Experiences of Censorship in Belgium', in *Silencing Cinema*, pp. 275–93; Daniela Treveri Gennari and Silvia Dibeltulo, '"It existed indeed … it was all over the papers": Memories of Film Censorship in 1950s Italy', *Participations* 14.1 (2017): 235–48.

10 See Müller, 'Censorship & Cultural Regulation'; Robert Darnton, *Censors at Work: How States Shaped Literature* (London: British Library, 2014); Matthew Bunn, 'Reimagining Repression: New Censorship Theory and After', *History and Theory* 54 (2015): 25–44; Matei Candea, 'Silencing Oneself, Silencing Others', *Terrain: anthropologie & sciences humaines* (2019): 1–14.

11 Bunn, 'Reimagining Repression', p. 37.

12 Michel Foucault, *Discipline and Punish: The Birth of the Prison* (Harmondsworth: Penguin, 1977), p. 26. See also Michel Foucault, 'Two Lectures', in *Power/Knowledge: Selected Interviews and Other Writings, 1972–1977* (New York: Pantheon, 1980), pp. 78–108.

13 Examples include: Constantin Matthéos, *La protection de la jeunesse par la censure cinématographique en France et à l'Etranger* (Paris: Pichon & Durand-Auzias, 1966); Ira H. Carmen, *Movies, Censorship, and the Law* (Ann Arbor: University of Michigan Press, 1966); Neville March Hunnings, *Film Censors and the Law* (London: George Allen & Unwin, 1967); Richard Randall, *The Censorship of the Movies: The Social and Political Control of a Mass Medium* (Madison: University of Wisconsin Press, 1968); Paul Leglise, *Histoire de la politique du cinéma français* (Paris: Pichon & Durand, 1970); Albert Montagne, *Histoire juridique des interdits cinématographiques en France (1909–2001)* (Paris: L'Harmattan, 2007).

14 See Francis G. Couvares, 'Introduction: Hollywood, Censorship, and American Culture', *American Quarterly* 44.4 (1992): 509–11.

15 Kuhn, *Cinema, Censorship and Sexuality*.

16 Kuhn, *Cinema, Censorship and Sexuality*, p. 131.

17 For reports, testimonies and scholarly work on Hollywood's internal censorship system, see Raymond Moley, *The Hays Office* (Indianapolis: The Bobbs-Merrill Company, 1945); Gerald Gardner, *The Censorship Papers: Movie Censorship Letters from the Hays Office, 1934 to 1968* (New York: Dodd Mead, 1988); Couvares, 'Introduction'; Black, *Hollywood Censored*; Richard Maltby, 'The Genesis of the Production Code', *Quarterly Review of Film and Video* 15.4 (1995): 5–32; Walsh, *Sin and Censorship*; Black, *The Catholic Crusade against the Movies*; Ruth Vasey, *The World According to Hollywood, 1918–1939* (Exeter: University of Exeter Press, 1997); Lea Jacobs, *The Wages of Sin: Censorship and the Fallen Woman Film, 1928–1942* (Berkeley: University of California Press, 1997); Doherty, *Pre-Code Hollywood*; Matthew Bernstein (ed.), *Controlling Hollywood:*

Censorship and Regulation in the Studio Era (New Brunswick: Rutgers University Press, 1999); Leonard J. Leff and Jerold L. Simmons, *The Dame in the Kimono: Hollywood, Censorship, and the Production Code* (Lexington: University Press of Kentucky, 2001); Stephen Prince, *Classical Film Violence: Designing and Regulating Brutality in Hollywood Cinema, 1930–1968* (New Brunswick: Rutgers University Press, 2003); Richard Maltby, *Hollywood Cinema* (Malden, MA: Blackwell, 2003); Thomas Doherty, *Hollywood's Censor: Joseph I. Breen and the Production Code Administration* (New York: Columbia University Press, 2007); Laura Wittern-Keller, *Freedom of the Screen: Legal Challenges to State Film Censorship, 1915–1982* (Lexington: University Press of Kentucky, 2008); Biesen, *Film Censorship.*

18 Couvares, 'Introduction', p. 515.

19 Bunn, 'Reimagining Repression'.

20 Darnton, *Censors at Work*, p. 19.

21 Nicole Moore, 'Censorship Is', *Australian Humanities Review* 54 (2013): 45.

22 David Brommel, *Regulating Free Speech in a Digital Age: Hate, Harm and the Limits of Censorship* (Cham: Springer, 2022).

23 See for instance: Vasilis Ververis, Sophia Marguel and Benjamin Fabian, 'Cross-Country Comparison of Internet Censorship: A Literature Review', *Policy & Internet* 12.4 (2020): 450–73; Andrea Kendall-Taylor, Erica Frantz and Joseph Wright, 'The Digital Dictators: How Technology Strengthens Autocracy', *Foreign Affairs* 99 (2020): 103.

24 See for instance Bart Cammaert, 'The Abnormalisation of Social Justice: The "Anti-Woke Culture War" Discourse in the UK', *Discourse & Society* 33.6 (2002): 730–43.

Part 1

International Relations, Local Sensitivities and Negotiations

1

'Forestalling Controversy':
The Production Code Administration and the Mediation of Political Censorship

Richard Maltby

> Although certain alterations have been made in the basic story, MGM
> [...] is producing *Three Comrades* in such a manner that the release
> print will embody the full spirit of Erich Remarque's original. The
> changes were for the purpose of forestalling controversy.
>
> Motion Picture Herald[1]

> One has to be careful not to over-employ the term 'censorship' because
> this would, in many cases, obscure rather than illumine history.
>
> Beate Müller[2]

In an echo of Pierre Bourdieu's essay on 'Censorship and the Imposition of
Form', the 2020 PEN report *Made in Hollywood, Censored by Beijing* argued:

> Perhaps the greatest issue with the [Chinese Communist Party's]
> censorious effect on Hollywood is how it has instantiated self-
> censorship from filmmakers aiming to anticipate and pre-empt Beijing's
> objections. This is, of course, exactly how censorship succeeds—others
> internalize it to the point where the censor actually has to do very little.
> Over time, writers and creators don't even conceive of ideas, stories, or

Richard Maltby, "'Forestalling Controversy': The Production Code Administration and the Mediation
of Political Censorship" in: *The Screen Censorship Companion: Critical Explorations in the Control of
Film and Screen Media*. University of Exeter Press (2024). © Richard Maltby. DOI: 10.47788/AJXR2557

characters that would flout the rules, because there is no point in doing so. The orthodoxies press down imperceptibly, and the parameters of the imagination are permanently circumscribed.[3]

The report, however, included a contrary observation by an unnamed Hollywood producer that such decisions over content were 'hard to distinguish [from] what happens all the time in studio politics […] merely one of the many commercial considerations that studios must take into account when developing films'.[4] Discussing the level of cooperation with Chinese authorities and the concessions made to them by the producers of *Iron Man 3* (Marvel/Paramount, 2013), Aynne Kokas offered it as an example of 'exchanging freedom of expression for market-access opportunities' and warned that Hollywood's accommodation of the Chinese market risked altering film content not only for China, but for global markets generally.[5] While not denying his intent to maximize 'the monetization of cultural exchange', Chris Fenton, an executive of DMG Entertainment, the China-based co-producer of *Iron Man 3*, countered this argument by maintaining that cultural and commercial exchange constituted a collaborative form of diplomacy and that in opening the Chinese market, 'sometimes you need to placate the host in order to be a good guest'.[6]

These diverse opinions encapsulate the competing perspectives that have long disputed how the American film industry has conducted the practice of forestalling controversy. The history of the American film industry's processes of content self-regulation and its accommodations of external forces might equally be described as histories of self-censorship or of product quality control. In what follows I discuss Classical Hollywood's Production Code as the principal historical instance of this activity before briefly considering how closely the industry's engagement with China in the 2010s echoed its predecessors' accommodation of the demands of national, state and local governments and domestic pressure groups in the 1920s and 1930s.

'Political Censorship'

In 2016 the Motion Picture Association's CEO Chris Dodd declared that 'since our founding in 1922, the MPAA has fought for the First Amendment rights of not only our moviemakers […] but the audiences, as well'. The Production Code, he added, 'allowed Hollywood writers, directors and producers to create and manage their own content rather than have the government dictate what can and cannot be shown onscreen'.[7] Although his account was wildly at odds with his predecessor Jack Valenti's 1998 description of the Code as 'an absurd manifesto [which] literally offered a list of do's and don'ts for filmmakers and performers', Dodd's assertion was much more in keeping with the way that the 'self-regulators' of the Production Code Administration understood their role.[8] He was also substantially correct to argue that from its formation the Motion Picture Producers and Distributors of America, Inc. (MPPDA) was forthrightly opposed to what it invariably referred to as 'political censorship'. Its earliest public activity was its successful campaign against the introduction of state censorship in Massachusetts in November 1922, and during the next five years it lobbied successfully to defeat all forty-five censorship bills introduced in state legislatures along with recurrent attempts to introduce federal motion picture censorship.[9] MPPDA president Will Hays repeatedly declared that 'censorship in motion pictures is [...] wrong [...] as un-American in conception as it is ineffective in execution'.[10]

Motion picture censorship was, however, an established fact, its constitutionality affirmed by the Supreme Court decision in *Mutual Film Corporation v. Industrial Commission of Ohio* in 1915.[11] Much recent writing about content regulation in Classical Hollywood cinema proceeds as if our contemporary expectations concerning freedom of speech pertained in the 1920s and 1930s, so it is worth emphasizing that in 1915 and for some considerable time after, few people argued either that the First Amendment offered protection to any form of speech that might threaten the 'peace, safety, good order, [and] health interests of the State', or that silent motion pictures should be considered as speech.[12] Legal historian David Rabban has argued that 'no group of Americans was more hostile to free speech claims before World War I than the judiciary, and no judges were more hostile than the justices on the United States Supreme Court'.[13] In this context, perhaps the most remarkable aspect of the *Mutual* case was that the company's lawyers based so much of their argument to the Court on the entirely novel claim that motion pictures were part of the press. No previous litigant had ever attacked laws licensing or restricting theatrical entertainment on free speech grounds. As the Industrial Commission of Ohio pointed out in their brief to the Court, 'it was never contemplated that the liberty of speech or liberty of the press included the theater within their scope'.[14] The Court concurred, peremptorily dismissing the idea that motion pictures, any more than the theatre, the circus or any of 'the multitudinous shows which are advertised on the billboards of our cities and towns' should be brought 'into practical and legal similitude to a free press and liberty of opinion'.[15]

Four years after the *Mutual* case, in *Schenck v. United States*, Justice Oliver Wendell Holmes famously opined that the character of every act of expression 'depends upon the circumstances in which it is done [...] The most stringent protection of free speech would not protect a man in falsely shouting fire in a theatre and causing a panic', or any other expression that might harm the public welfare.[16] While judicial attitudes to the censorship of political speech mellowed significantly after 1919, censorship 'on the ground of morality' remained uncontested.[17] Until 1925 state and local governments were, in any event, not restricted by the First Amendment and could, in consequence, pass laws restricting free speech.[18] Moreover, courts consistently expressed confidence in the 'sense and experience' of administrative officials and dismissed arguments contesting the definitional imprecision of such terms as 'immoral' or 'obscene' in censorship statutes.[19] Until the Supreme Court heard the *Miracle* case in 1952, no censorship statute was found invalid because of its vagueness. In some municipalities, there was no provision for judicial review of censors' decisions. In almost all jurisdictions, the only issue that could be brought before the courts was whether the censors had abused their discretion in applying their standards, and courts consistently refused to substitute their judgement for that of the censors.[20] The decisions of censorship boards were in practice not susceptible to effective legal challenge, since the burden of proof lay with the distributor to demonstrate that the picture in question was innocent of whatever undefined term it had been found to violate. Legal challenges to state or municipal censorship were rare before World War II and never brought by the major companies. On only six occasions in the 1930s was a decision by the New York censor board challenged in court; in all six cases, the board's decision was upheld.[21]

The geographic scope of domestic censorship also needs emphasizing. Although only seven states passed censorship legislation, somewhere between 100 and 300 municipalities established censorship procedures, including major distribution centres such as Chicago, Detroit, Dallas and Atlanta.[22] Prints used for first-run exhibition in these cities circulated in their censored form across a much wider area in subsequent runs; by the time it reached its fourth or fifth run, a print might have been further cut by two or three additional local censors. As a result, exhibition in as many as thirty of the forty-eight states was captured by 'political censorship'. At Congressional hearings in 1936, the MPPDA's General Counsel Charles Pettijohn explained that 'all positive prints of pictures are cut to conform with regulations of either State, city or local censorship groups' in seventeen of the country's thirty-one distribution centres, representing 70.6% of the industry's domestic revenue and at least 80% of the population.[23]

While many local boards were only occasionally active, city authorities could also use their power to revoke theatre licences to ban individual pictures, as the mayors of Lawrence and Holyoake and the city manager of Lowell, Massachusetts did in 1950 to prevent screenings of the Roberto Rossellini picture *Stromboli* starring Ingrid Bergman.[24] In a typical instance, the city of Waterloo, Iowa, had a three-member board of censors chosen by the mayor which acted on complaint from outside sources and recommended action to City Council.[25] Local censors were highly susceptible to pressure from civic and religious groups: in 1932 *Variety* reported that mayors in fifty towns were issuing instructions to the local chief of police to revoke the licence of an exhibitor who continued to show pictures considered distasteful to the representatives of women's clubs.[26] Others imposed their own criteria, most notoriously the racist Lloyd T. Binford, chair of the Memphis Censor Board from 1928 to 1955, who banned *Annie Get Your Gun* in 1945 because its African American performers 'had too familiar an air about them', *Curley* in 1947 because 'the South does not [...] recognize social equality between the races, even in children' and *City Lights* because Charlie Chaplin was a 'London guttersnipe' and 'a traitor to the Christian-American way of life'.[27]

Most of the industry's major foreign markets also operated under regimes of state-administered censorship, but while the MPPDA opposed political censorship in its domestic market, it recognized that it could not contest the legitimacy of the regulatory regimes of foreign governments. Just as MPAA spokesman Howard Gantman acknowledged the commercial reality of adjusting film content for different world markets and recognized 'China's right to determine what content enters their country' in 2013, the MPPDA was obliged to advise its members on the requirements of those foreign regimes and to negotiate with their representatives over the content of individual pictures.[28] As Ruth Vasey has detailed, these negotiations commonly took place under the threat of economic sanction either against the company concerned or against the American industry as a whole.[29] Writing in 1936 in the wake of MGM's decision not to film Sinclair Lewis's novel *It Can't Happen Here*, the *New York Times* Hollywood correspondent Douglas Churchill suggested that 'world censorship' was by then more important to Hollywood than the domestic variety:

> So closely are the wheels of international trade, politics, manipulation and influence enmeshed in foreign parts that American producers are as subject to the dictation of French, British and Italian censors as they would be if their headquarters were in Paris, London or Rome. [...] When a European censor decrees, 'This story conflicts with our economics, politics or national philosophy and will not be approved for exhibition,' Hollywood is forced to abandon the project. What cannot be shown in Rome or Berlin can generally not be shown in Omaha or Detroit.[30]

As the 1930s progressed, the arbitrariness and unpredictability of censorship decisions in several markets, particularly Germany and Italy, escalated and the ability of the MPPDA's representatives to protect American access to these markets diminished.

The precedent of the *Mutual* decision obliged the industry to live with existing state and municipal censorship and determined its response. That response might perhaps best be characterized as a public recognition that the industry needed a social licence to operate. That licence was substantially provided by its conformity to a set of conventional social behaviours in the content of its products, so that they would be considered 'unobjectionable' by what Hays variously called 'responsible public groups' or 'the classes that write, talk, and legislate'.[31] In practice, these conventions were demarcated by the political censorship they opposed, and their strategy was, as Hays frequently framed it, 'to obviate the necessity of censorship' by 'improving' pictures so that 'no reasonable person could claim there was any need for censorship'.[32] As the committee charged with drafting the 1927 variant of this codification, the 'Don'ts and Be Carefuls', explained, the purpose was simultaneously to eliminate the habitual condemnation of scenes and titles by censor boards and to avoid provoking further demands for censorship:

> By eliminating these scenes and titles we not only save footage and the possibility of a mutilated picture when they are eliminated but also effectively forestall the demand for further censorship and further develop the ground work for the repeal of such censorship as now exists.[33]

Hollywood's motivation was obviously commercial, rather than political, moral or ideological. Censorship of completed footage cost the industry many millions of dollars in wasted production costs and lost revenue annually, and the twin aims of the MPPDA's systems of self-regulation were to reduce this wastage and in the process secure its member companies' licence to operate their oligopoly control over the provision of entertainment.[34] The evolving system of what Hays called 'voluntary cooperation, at the source of production, with responsible public groups to the end that the standard of pictures produced shall be maintained and steadily improved'[35] was the instrument of his strategy of eliminating the need for censorship by internalizing the process.

The MPPDA strove to codify, as far as it could, the arbitrary and frequently inconsistent actions of political censors into a broadly coherent body of information with which it could advise producers. As the political situation evolved, this body of information was reconfigured as a formal Code: formal in the sense that the member companies of the MPPDA formally agreed to abide by it and accepted the existence of procedures for its application and penalties for its breach, although these penalties were never actually applied.[36] As Hays stated, the Code's purpose was to evade censorship by internalizing its actions to the point where political censors had little to do. The process of internalization, however, had generated many creative evasions and obfuscations that produced the ambiguities and 'dramas of false appearances' that were the commonplace complexities of Classical Hollywood narrative.[37] These two activities—the formal codification of external constraints and the administrative application of that Code on one hand, and the development of 'sophisticated' strategies to circumvent or evade a literalist and restrictive application of the Code on the other—were of a piece. Not only did one encourage the other, but the two commonly worked closely together to solve the problems inherent in the task of representing the sensational and the transgressive in ways that could be understood as uncontroversial. Whether this essentially commercial process is appropriately described as censorship depends to a large extent on whether the activity of censorship is taken to be defined by its effect or by the agency that performs it.

'Participants in the Processes of Production'

Most writing on Classical Hollywood's regimes of content regulation has remained innocent of post-Foucauldian scholarly discussions of censorship as a pervasive, normative and constitutive exercise of power establishing the practices that define us as social subjects. Rather, 'censorship' is used, in Janelle Reinelt's apposite phrase, as 'a common-sense catchword' employed as if its application to the subject matter is self-evident.[38] But this usage does share a significant characteristic with the recent scholarship discussed at greater length in the next section. Both, to use Robert Post's words, 'flatten distinctions among kinds of power, implicitly equating suppression of speech caused by state legal action with that caused by the market, or by the dominance of a particular discourse'.[39] As both Post and Beate Müller argue, this broadening and flattening of the concept of censorship endangers its heuristic potential.[40] In the case of Classical Hollywood, however, deployment of this flattened version of censorship still carries with it the odium of repression traditionally attached to the practice of state or religious censorship, along with the presumption, rarely if ever supported by evidence, that the Production Code's administration of product content was unwanted by audiences and opposed by producers. It is in this conceptual context that I want to reconsider the relationship between Classical Hollywood's practices of self-regulation and censorship.

What is perhaps most striking about the operation of the MPPDA's mechanisms for content regulation is the level of collaboration between the Association's officers and industry executives in pursuit of the common goal of reducing—ideally eliminating—external post-production censorship. In 1928 an MPPDA official recorded an increasing disposition on the part of studios 'to require us to give them the benefit of our own conclusions' about questionable content 'based on our better knowledge of the usual reaction of the different censors and of the points of view of different sections of public opinion'.[41] The Production Code evolved out of this disposition and could not have operated without it. The Resolution for Uniform Interpretation of the Production Code formalized this in 1930 by requiring its administrators to 'secure any facts, information or suggestions concerning the probable reception of stories or the manner in which in its opinion they may best be treated', and to provide 'such confidential advice and suggestion as experience, research and information indicate [...] that exception will be taken to the story or treatment'.[42] As Production Code Administration Director Joseph Breen insisted, he and his staff were 'regarded by producers, directors, and their staffs, as "participants in the processes of production"'.[43] They approached their task, he said, 'in the spirit of helpfulness. We like to think that we are employed by the producers *to render a service*, rather than to arbitrarily dogmatize either about the Code, or political censorship.'[44]

Breen's comments were made in a document he produced in June 1938 as part of a lengthy internal discussion within the MPPDA over the 'Jurisdiction of the PCA'. The discussion was occasioned by a combination of circumstances. The most important was the impending federal government antitrust suit against the eight major companies, which also threatened to include the MPPDA as a co-defendant because the Code's seal of approval operated as a barrier restraining access to the theatrical market. Several new types of production vying for theatrical exhibition, including advertising films, government-funded documentaries and educational films, occupied what the MPPDA referred to as a 'twilight zone' at the borders of the PCA's responsibilities, and the discussion was also affected by a series of controversies that had arisen in the previous two years over the production, cancellation or political censorship of pictures depicting the Spanish Civil War, recent German history and the possibility of fascism in the United States.[45] As part of the MPPDA's campaign against legislation proposing to introduce federal censorship, Hays circulated a selection of PCA decisions among Washington legislators in order to demonstrate the effectiveness of the Code. Instead, it disclosed that the PCA constantly addressed a far wider range of issues than those specifically included within the Code, and provoked accusations from political liberals that 'self-regulation [...] has degenerated into political censorship', particularly in relation to questions of 'industry policy' in the depiction of sensitive or controversial subject matter that might give offence to pressure groups, foreign governments or corporate interests.[46]

In March 1938, Hays' executive assistant Francis Harmon compiled a report on current PCA opinions, which found seventy references to 'political censorship' in some thirty letters, as well as recommendations on policy questions, including the characterization of President Roosevelt, the portrayal of a South American revolution and references to Boy Scouts, Pan-American Airways and the US Navy.[47] Harmon recommended that the PCA should make a clearer distinction between its administrative functions in enforcing compliance with the Production Code and its advisory functions in relation to policy questions and political censorship by addressing the two sets of issues in separate letters. In response, Breen claimed that mere advice would be insufficiently persuasive and would lead to 'a great increase in the number of deletions made by political censor boards throughout the world'. On policy matters, he argued that the PCA operated on precedent, ruling only on 'minor questions of policy' such as material depicting a member of the United States Senate as a 'heavy', and referring new questions to Hays in New York for decision.[48]

Two years earlier, Breen had written to Hays that:

> we like to think that the decisions of the PCA are, in reality, the decisions of a private judicial tribunal, duly instituted and empowered to interpret a set of fundamental laws. These decisions, even as the decisions of public courts, have the force of law for the industry and are carefully considered on adjudicating subsequent cases.[49]

In June 1938, he shifted his position to suggest that far from being 'comparable to that of a Board of Censors administering a statute adopted by a [...] governmental agency', the PCA's relationship with producers was 'actually much nearer to that confidential, sympathetic attitude which exists between a lawyer and his client than that between the judge on the bench and a litigant at the bar'. Where political censor boards functioned 'in an atmosphere of compulsion', the PCA's successful operation depended on the voluntary cooperation of member and non-member companies alike. In that spirit, he argued, member companies would frequently discuss with the PCA whether a production might lead to outcomes 'which are not felt to be for the best interests of the organized industry'. He insisted that there was 'nothing "sinister"' about balancing the short-term financial benefit that might come with the inclusion of some content against the attainment of fundamental objectives. 'The reconciliation of this inevitable conflict', he suggested, 'is one of the chief functions of this or any other worthwhile trade association.' Accepting the need to maintain the distinction between the PCA's administrative and advisory functions, he asked for enhanced procedures for obtaining 'definite rulings on policy matters' which would then serve as precedents. In particular, he sought a firmer definition of what the industry understood to be propaganda, one which distinguished between 'propaganda which is deliberately deceitful in order the better to accomplish a desired end, and propaganda—preachment, message—whatever we choose to call it, which deals honestly with a theme that we may not happen to like'.[50]

The outcome of these discussions was a document clarifying and limiting the jurisdiction of the PCA. Several types of production, including newsreels, advertising, sponsored and government films, were deemed as falling outside its authority. The Code was amended to remove several prohibitions, such as those against illegal drug traffic, miscegenation and 'scenes of actual childbirth in fact or silhouette', which were now permitted if they were 'treated within the limits of good taste'. Most importantly, the document stated unequivocally that the only question affecting the issuance of a Code Seal was whether a picture 'conforms to standards of decency, morality and fairness embodied in the Production Code', and that with regard to all other matters, including controversial subjects, 'the jurisdiction of the PCA is purely advisory':

> If the film deals with a controversial subject, but is free from that which offends decency or is listed in the Code as morally objectionable, then the sole remaining question to be decided by the Production Code Administration should not be whether the film is 'desirable' but whether the presentation deals fairly and honestly, and without deliberate deception, with the subject matter.[51]

Censorship Reimagined

In his 2015 essay 'Reimagining Repression: New Censorship Theory and After', Matthew Bunn describes the liberal conception of censorship that emerged from the Enlightenment struggle to free the expression of ideas from the authoritarian restraints of church and state. In this understanding of censorship as the negation of 'free speech', its essential elements are that it is external, coercive and repressive: censors are 'authoritative social actors, extrinsic to the communicative process, who deploy coercive force to intervene in the free exchange of ideas to repressive effect'.[52] The activities of the PCA clearly did not meet this definition of censorship: it was internal to the industry, its activities undertaken as a process of negotiation, and ultimately intended to facilitate the free circulation of the material under consideration, not its repression. It might perhaps be argued that in what he described as the 'vigorous' tone with which he urged eliminations or changes in scripts on producers, Breen performed the role of a censor.[53] As the negotiations over the PCA's jurisdiction in 1938 demonstrated, however, Breen's was a performance rather than a practice of censorship; what made it so was the absence of any legal authority for enforcement.[54]

In the final quarter of the twentieth century poststructuralist and sociological accounts of language developed an expanded conception of censorship to embrace a much broader range of practices and structures that influence the form and content of communication. Indebted to Michel Foucault's conceptions of power as diffuse and discourse as an exercise of constitutive power, what Bunn and others label 'New Censorship Theory' discards the liberal opposition of censorship and free expression and posits an account of censorship as a pervasive, structural phenomenon, undertaken by a multiplicity of social agencies and conditions as, in Judith Butler's phrase, 'the constituting norm by which the speakable is differentiated from the unspeakable'.[55] For Foucault, Butler and Bourdieu, censorship is productive: for Foucault, 'a regulated and polymorphous incitement to discourse'; for Butler, 'a way of *producing* speech, constraining in advance what will and will not become acceptable speech'; for Bourdieu, 'the structure [...] which governs expression by governing both access to expression and the form of expression'.[56] All three theorists consider the processes by which communication is made possible through a subject's internalization of restrictive structures to be censorship. In Robert Post's account of these new approaches, 'censorship establishes the practices that define us as social subjects': 'If censorship is a technique by which discursive practices are maintained, and if social life largely consists of such practices, it follows that censorship is the norm rather than the exception.'[57]

Somewhat unsurprisingly, this expansive understanding of censorship has been subject to the criticism that it is simultaneously too extensive and too limited, rendering censorship ineffective as a descriptive term by disposing of any distinction between regulatory censorship and the 'structural' or 'constitutive' censorship with which these accounts are principally concerned.[58] By disrupting the conventional liberal binary of censorship and free speech, however, New Censorship Theory exposes a much broader range of practices than the exercise of repressive state power to examination under the rubric of censorship. In Michael Holquist's assessment, a complete absence of censorship is impossible: 'Censorship *is*. One can only discriminate among its more and less repressive effects.'[59] While not acceding to Butler's encompassing assertion that 'censorship *produces* speech', Sue Curry Jansen proposes a definition that encompasses

all socially structured proscriptions or prescriptions which inhibit or prohibit dissemination of ideas, information, images and other messages through a society's channels of communication whether these obstructions are secured by political, economic, religious, or other systems of authority. It includes both overt and covert proscriptions and prescriptions.[60]

The activities of the PCA would clearly fall within Jansen's definition; indeed, they provide what might be considered as a precursor instance of Jansen's distinctive contribution to recent debates over the extent of censorship's territory: the concept of 'market censorship'. She argues that modern corporate capitalism has industrialized and commodified the production and distribution of ideas and cultural artefacts, making freedom of expression contingent on decisions made by private producers: the huge communication and technology conglomerates that comprise the modern consciousness industry. Jansen's definition of market censorship—'practices that routinely filter or restrict the production and distribution of selected ideas, perspectives, genres or cultural forms within mainstream media of communication based upon their anticipated profits and/or support for corporate values and consumerism'—could be said to apply to the activities of the PCA and its precursors. So could her suggestion that these practices are integrated into the media's organizational structures and presented as outcomes of consumer choices rather than as profit-driven managerial decisions, and her summary definition that 'market censorship refers to the conditions of production and consumption that produce cultural hegemony'.[61]

One feature that, however, at least partially distinguishes the PCA from Jansen's concept is that its activities were conducted, if not entirely in public, at least according to documented policies—the Production Code and its precursors—that were published and extensively discussed. While its commercial purpose—its 'response to profit imperatives'—was never denied or obscured, it was presented as being, and was, the outcome of what Hays called a 'voluntary cooperation [...] with responsible public groups' to maintain and improve the moral standard of pictures: it was undoubtedly the production of a cultural hegemony, but one that was publicly negotiated.

With this polyvalent enlargement of censorship's field, it is hardly surprising that Sophia Rosenfeld concludes that within cultural theory, 'there seems no longer to be any consensus about what censorship is'.[62] Critiques of New Censorship Theory all acknowledge the problem of 'flattening' and potential trivialization, but they disagree on how to apply the analytic strengths of the new scholarship without diffusing the object of their enquiry. While there is some broad acceptance that a distinction could be drawn between the normative constraints that inhibit communication and specific acts of instrumental power, there is no agreement over where the binary divide lies, or how it might best be described: between implicit and explicit forms of censorship; constitutive and regulatory censorship; official and unofficial censorship. In a review of the field, Kenji Yoshino goes so far as to diagram nine different models of censorship, with the intention of showing that 'the practice we call "censorship" actually denominates a family of very different sub-practices which it is useful—however incoherently—to disaggregate'.[63]

Literary historian Nicole Moore suggests that 'perhaps the difference between regulation by and constitution by censorship is only identifiable through ascertaining what lies on the continuum between them'. Her own account, however, privileges the state as 'the administrative and ideological horizon for censorship', arguing that other forms of restriction on speech cannot be defined as censorship when not bolstered by the sovereign power of the state. Censorship in her conception 'is about state making, not subject making'; its aim is to delimit the boundaries of legitimate communication within the state.[64] Cultural historian Robert Darnton similarly argues for the distinction between power that is monopolized by the state and power that exists everywhere else in society. Censorship, he maintains, 'is essentially political; it is wielded by the state'. In his ethnographic history of how censorship actually operated in three very different political systems— Bourbon France, British India and East Germany—Darnton emphasizes the 'complicity, collaboration, and negotiation' that pervaded the interactions of authors and censors. The French censors of the mid-eighteenth century, for example, were themselves authors, academics and men of letters, who frequently edited and corrected the spelling, grammar and stylistic flaws of the works they examined. Some worked so closely with writers that they became effectively co-authors.[65] The PCA's partnership in production was a similarly complicit negotiation. Individual writers or directors may have felt themselves censored but they were not formally or legally the authors of the studio's products, and the PCA almost invariably communicated with studio heads or their delegated producers.

The issue posed by Marvel's placating of Chinese authorities, and more generally by the American film industry's accommodation of the restrictions of foreign governments, is that such actions fall between a state's exercise of monopoly power and a company's pursuit of maximally monetized cultural exchange. Discussing the ways in which China has used its market size to influence perceptions and silence criticism abroad, William D. O'Connell suggests that in addition to banning content, China employs two tactics for exporting censorship: position reversal, which involves 'coerced apologies, retracting controversial statements, or editing content to remove undesirable or include desirable language or imagery'; and self-censorship, when foreign actors, on their own initiative, avoid engaging in controversial topics or promote positions favourable to the regime.[66] Jansen, however, resists the use of 'self-censorship' as a descriptor of this process: while the term may accurately describe the actions of individuals, it is misleading 'when the "self" doing the censoring is a multinational communication conglomerate'. As she observes, 'once creators take their creations to market, they are subject to its disciplines'.[67]

Three Comrades: A Case Study

> The history, institutions, prominent people and citizenry of all nations shall be represented fairly.
>
> *Motion Picture Production Code*[68]

Hollywood's increasingly precarious engagement with China during the 2010s has some parallels with the industry's involvement with Germany in the years surrounding the introduction of sound, not least in the disruptive effects of technological change. In the late 1920s American companies hoped to embed themselves in the potentially lucrative German market through collaborative ventures that foundered on the parties' conflicting interests and a rising German nationalism that increasingly controlled access to the market. The controversies of the later 1930s had more to do with threats to American companies' continuing presence in Germany, and to their property and employees, than with any changes required to make an individual film acceptable to German censors. The 1932 *Kontingent* law empowered censors to refuse quota permits to producers who distributed films 'detrimental to German prestige' on the world market, and the escalating unpredictability of German censorship, which in the revised law of 1934 permitted exclusions for reasons other than a film's content, destabilized attempts to service the German market.[69]

MGM's picture *Three Comrades* was controversial less because of its content than because of its author; its source material was the final novel in Erich Maria Remarque's trilogy depicting social conditions in Germany in the 1920s. Universal had filmed the earlier novels, *All Quiet on the Western Front* (published in 1929) and *The Road Back* (1931). As part of their campaign to destabilize the government of Heinrich Brüning the Nazis orchestrated riots to disrupt screenings of *All Quiet* in Berlin and elsewhere, resulting in the picture being banned.[70] By the time *The Road Back* was released in August 1937, Remarque was in exile and the Nazi government had banned his books as 'unpatriotic'. The German consul in Los Angeles, Dr Georg Gyssling, threatened the picture's cast and crew with reprisals, an action that provoked the State Department into demanding Gyssling's removal and the German ambassador issuing a formal apology.[71] Nevertheless, after several previews Universal made a number of cuts, which *Variety* suggested (and Universal denied) had been made 'as a sop to Germany'.[72]

Under Louis B. Mayer MGM was undoubtedly the most cautious of the studios in its dealings with foreign governments. As mentioned, in 1936 Mayer had notoriously decided not to produce a film version of Sinclair Lewis's anti-fascist novel *It Can't Happen Here* because of its likely exclusion from major foreign markets. The studio bought the rights to *Three Comrades* in July 1936, six months before the novel was published in English.[73] Although it was set in the late 1920s and included some 'political and controversial material fully as ticklish from an exhibition standpoint as *The Road Back*', the novel was focused on what the *New York Times* reviewer called 'one of the most poignant love stories that have been told in our time'.[74] An expurgated version was published in serial form in *Good Housekeeping* from January to May 1937, and although MGM could have had no expectation of German government approval of any version they produced, the studio may well have bought it expecting to sanitize the story's political as well as its sexual content.[75] Announced as one of the next season's 'outstanding' productions that would 'raise the standard of the screen', it was initially scheduled to co-star Robert Taylor, James Stewart and Spencer Tracy, but budgeted at the bottom end of MGM's A-feature range.[76] R.C. Sherriff completed an initial script in May 1937, and the PCA's response, which was almost entirely concerned with the amount of drinking in the story, made no mention of any political concerns.[77] The script went through a long process of revision under producer Joseph L. Mankiewicz's supervision, with F. Scott Fitzgerald and E.E. Paramore producing six drafts between September 1937 and January 1938. During this process, several scenes of political violence including one showing book-burning were added, probably at Mankiewicz's suggestion and certainly with his approval.[78]

A final script was sent to the PCA on 18 January 1938. Breen replied to Mayer four days later that while the basic story was acceptable under the Production Code, it suggested 'enormous difficulty from the standpoint of your company's distribution business in Germany and from the general standpoint of industry "good and welfare"'. The story was 'a serious indictment of the German nation and people and is certain to be violently resented by the present government of that country'.[79] Gyssling had written to Breen about *Three Comrades* on three occasions, most recently hinting at 'future difficulties', but there is no indication that he had any detailed knowledge of the script or any further contact with Breen who, having determined some months before not to 'waste any time' attempting to satisfy any of the 'very unreasonable' local consuls, merely passed the letters on to Mayer.[80] On 27 January, Breen met first with Mayer, and then with Mankiewicz and studio executives. Acknowledging the unavoidable problem created by Remarque's authorship, the meeting aimed to minimize other difficulties, agreeing as a basic premise that 'there will be nothing to indicate in any way that the story is a reflection on the Nazi government'. As was common PCA practice, Breen came to the meeting with a list of suggested changes, the major one being to set the story not in the late 1920s but in the two years immediately after the end of the war and thus remove any connection to more recent events. Several references to 'democracy' and to characters' Jewish identity were removed and the allegiances of the political clubs in the story were obscured, but Mankiewicz vehemently rejected Breen's suggestion that the story's 'heavies' be portrayed as communists.[81] The changes were incorporated to the PCA's satisfaction within a week, and the picture went into production two weeks later. In removing any overt political connotation from the picture, the PCA was fulfilling its role as a participant in the processes of production, negotiating with an entirely cooperative studio over the means of forestalling unwanted controversy. Insisting that *Three Comrades* was 'not a propaganda picture', the picture's press book asserted 'it is not political or controversial and its turbulent scenes could happen in any country'.[82] The *Motion Picture Herald* concurred, declaring that 'nothing that is shown could possibly invite prejudice or animosity'.[83]

Apart from an unenthusiastic review in *Time* which blamed Hays Office interference for removing the political content, the script revisions were almost completely successful in forestalling controversy.[84] Predictably banned in Germany's sphere of influence, *Three Comrades* encountered no constraints from any of the domestic censor boards. Despite indifferent trade reviews—*Variety* found it 'a depressing, uninspiring yarn', *Hollywood Reporter* thought its theme dated and its tragic ending 'well-nigh inexcusable'—it was MGM's fourth most profitable picture of the season, earning Loew's $2 million and returning a profit of $472,000 on a production cost of $839,000.[85] Newspaper and fan magazine commentaries were kinder than the trades, with several reviews echoing Frank Nugent's comment in the *New York Times* that the adaptation was 'faithful to the spirit and, largely, to the letter of the novel' and almost all praising Margaret Sullavan's performance, for which she was also nominated for a Best Actress Academy Award.[86]

Among censorship's complex contemporary polyvalence, the essential characteristics of the liberal understanding—that it is external, coercive and repressive—remain relevant to the term's meaningful application. So too does the distinction I made earlier between defining censorship by its effect or by the agency performing it. A further distinction can be made between who or what is censored: a person or an idea; a subject or an object. In the case of *Three Comrades*, ideas implicit in Remarque's novel or added in the script drafting were removed, as happened with every production with or without the participation of the PCA, but no individual was subject to censorship. In their dealings with MGM, the PCA acted as a mediating agent, interpreting the anticipated response of an unpredictable sovereign power and providing the studio with their best, and most cautious, advice as to how to minimize any adverse consequences. None of this was unusual: in the same period, they also advised Warner Bros and Columbia over the handling of Chinese objections to *West of Shanghai* and *Outlaws of the Orient* and French objections to *Devil's Island* and *Adventure in Sahara*.[87] Undoubtedly, the outcome of their advice brought some comfort to Consul Gyssling, but it is implausible to suggest either that Breen would have consulted him or that he would have proposed or endorsed the suggestions that Breen made to MGM. Perhaps the success of the studio's strategy was most effectively marked by a letter in *Photoplay*, in which one fan found the cause of the picture's controversy to rest in the decision to fit Robert Taylor with a chest wig.[88]

Conclusion

Discussing the cancellation of *Django Unchained*'s access to the Chinese market in 2013, Nitin Govil commented that 'Hollywood really doesn't have a problem with Chinese censorship [...] The problem it has is with Chinese unpredictability.'[89] Zhiwei Xiao similarly describes Chinese censorship in the post-Mao era as 'notoriously inconsistent, arbitrary, and unpredictable'.[90] The abstract terms in which Chinese censorship criteria are expressed—prohibiting, for instance, content that 'threatens the unity, sovereignty and territorial integrity of the state [...] disrupts social order or social stability [...] corrupts social morality, or defames the superiority of national culture'—are hardly more opaque than the comparable censorship legislation of other countries, even if, as Jessica Grimm suggests, a final clause excising any content 'opposing the spirit of the law' is 'a catch-all category for any content not explicitly captured' by those preceding it.[91] The unpredictability of Chinese censorship is, however, a feature, not a bug—an exercise of state power sustained by the opacity with which its criteria are interpreted. Censorship deliberations and decisions potentially fall within the ambit of the State Secrets Law, and as Grimm observes, any communication regarding a censorship decision could be subject to that law's penalties, which range from fines and licence revocations to life imprisonment and the death penalty.[92] Given the possible consequences, it is unsurprising that required censorship changes are most often communicated in spoken, not written, exchanges, so that producers can never be certain about what is acceptable.[93] As Julia Ya Qin has observed, the censorship system's deliberate lack of transparency is designed to provide its authorities with 'the maximum level of flexibility and efficacy' in adapting to changing political circumstance and delivering its ideological objectives of serving China's national interests and maintaining the legitimacy of the ruling party.[94] What PEN and former attorney general William Barr have called Hollywood's self-censorship and Erich Schwartzel identifies as instances of 'anticipatory censorship' on the part of American producers—such as, notoriously, the removal of an image of the Taiwanese flag from the back of Tom Cruise's bomber jacket in the 2019 poster and trailer for *Top Gun: Maverick*—can equally be understood as attempts to forestall controversy when seeking to operate in what is now the world's second-largest cinema market.[95]

In the event, however, such tactics had only limited and transitory success in securing access to this market. As Wendy Su has observed, the Chinese government's central principle in dealing with Hollywood imports has been '*Yi wo wei zhu, wei wo suo yong*': 'that all film imports must serve China's needs and national interests and should be made use of for China's gains and goals'.[96] Since 2000, it has used the popularity of Hollywood's block-busters to build its domestic market, using its quota system and control over the terms of exhibition to restrict both foreign access and profits while it developed a domestic production industry capable of meeting its needs for ideologically appropriate entertainment and, ideally, exporting Chinese culture globally.[97] From 2018, when the oversight of censorship was trans-ferred from the State Administration of Press, Publication, Radio, Film and Television to the Ministry of Propaganda, the number of Hollywood productions playing in Chinese cinemas has fallen year by year, along with their share of the Chinese box office. As diplomatic relations between the two superpowers deteriorated, Chinese companies withdrew their invest-ments in Hollywood and by 2022 several of the major studios had stopped including any Chinese revenue in their projections for a picture's earnings, since it had become 'almost impossible to factor in the whims of the Chinese government'. And, forestalling domestic controversy over 'self-censorship' and no longer able to secure a Chinese release for *Top Gun: Maverick*, Paramount reinstated the Taiwanese flag on Tom Cruise's back.[98]

Notwithstanding its ideological objection to political censorship, the industry's practical problems for the past century have been created by the arbitrariness, unpredictability and capriciousness of censors' decisions. In January 1939, the MPPDA's General Counsel Charles Pettijohn wrote a thirty-page memorandum arguing that it was time to challenge the Supreme Court's 1915 decision on *Mutual v. Ohio*. He insisted that the evidence of the previous twenty-five years showed that the actions of the state censor boards were hopelessly inconsistent, operating 'without regard to any standard, guide or criterion whatsoever [...] the net result of a quarter of a century of censorship is utter disorder, doubt and perplexity throughout the industry as to the character of films required'. By contrast, he maintained, the motion picture industry's voluntary, 'well-organized system of regulation' 'has achieved precision from the sense and experience of men educated, trained and with backgrounds of many years of practice—not political appointees but capable high salaried executives'.[99]

I am by no means seeking to deny that the PCA operated to perpetuate a cultural hegemony, nor that the environment in which it operated and which it helped to sustain was anything other than socially, culturally and politically conservative. But, hewing to Beate Müller's concern not to obscure history, I do want to argue that its activities can usefully be differentiated from 'political censorship' not only because of the difference between the compulsory actions of a legislatively established body—an instrument of the state—and the voluntary actions of a membership association, but also because of the difference in purpose of their activities. For all its constraints, its reproduction of the quirks and peculiarities of political censorship and its motivation as an agency of oligopolistic capitalism, the PCA operated as an enabling body. Purveying apparently 'decent' and uncontroversial movies may have been fundamental to Classical Hollywood's profitability and social licence to operate, but this in no way negated the fact that sensationalism and transgression remained the bread and butter of commercial entertainment. It was the job of the PCA, working collaboratively with producers, to reconcile these two positions. The PCA's dialogues with studio personnel over the Code's application often took place at a high-decibel level, but that did not stop them making adjustments of nuance in genuine negotiations in which concessions were made by both parties, and the strategic fade-outs, ellipses and political obfuscations that characterized the construction of Hollywood narratives were a direct outcome of those negotiations. Whatever the apposite descriptor of this simultaneously repressive and creative collaboration might be, it is far from certain that, when compared to the arbitrary exercise of state power, it is usefully called censorship.

Notes

1   *Motion Picture Herald*, 12 March 1938: 35.
2   Beate Müller, 'Censorship & Cultural Regulation: Mapping the Territory', in Beate Müller (ed.), *Censorship & Cultural Regulation in the Modern Age* (Amsterdam: Rodopi, 2004): 1–31 (p. 8).
3   https://pen.org/report/made-in-hollywood-censored-by-beijing/. Bourdieu argues that what he describes as structural censorship is most effective when 'the need for explicit

prohibitions, imposed and sanctioned by an institutionalised authority', is diminished by its processes and restrictions becoming internalized by its subjects: 'Censorship is never quite as perfect or as invisible as when each agent has nothing to say apart from what he is objectively authorised to say [...] he is [...] censored once and for all, through the forms of perception and expression that he has internalised and which impose their form on all his expressions.' Pierre Bourdieu, 'Censorship and the Imposition of Form,' in John P. Thompson (ed.), *Language and Symbolic Power* (Cambridge: Polity Press, 1991), pp. 137–59 (p. 138).

4   https://pen.org/report/made-in-hollywood-censored-by-beijing/.

5   Aynne Kokas, *Hollywood Made in China* (Oakland, CA: University of California Press, 2017), pp. 26, 33–34, 163.

6   Chris Fenton, *Feeding the Dragon: Inside the Trillion Dollar Dilemma Facing Hollywood, the NBA, & American Business* (New York: Post Hill Press, 2020), pp. 77, 155, 216.

7   Senator Chris Dodd, MPAA Chairman and CEO, speech at Georgia 1st Amendment Foundation 2016 Weltner Awards Banquet, Atlanta, GA, 13 October 2016, https://www.motionpictures.org/wp-content/uploads/2016/10/2016-GA-1st-Amendment-Foundation-Senator-Dodd-Remarks.pdf.

8   MPAA, 'Voluntary Movie Rating System Celebrates 30 Years of Providing Information to America's Parents', press release, 27 October 1998; Jack Vizzard, *See No Evil: Life Inside a Hollywood Censor* (New York: Simon and Schuster, 1970), p. 56.

9   Richard S. Randall, *Censorship of the Movies: The Social and Political Control of a Mass Medium* (Madison, WI: University of Wisconsin Press, 1968), p. 17. Massachusetts did, however, successfully introduce censorship in 1925 by amending a colonial-era Lord's Day observance statute to empower the state's Commissioner of Public Safety and local mayors to restrict Sunday entertainments to those considered 'in keeping with the character of the day and not inconsistent with its due observance'. The law was not overturned until 1955. *New York Times*, 7 July 1955: 29.

10   For example, Hays to Senator Hiram W. Johnson, 7 February 1929. MPPDA Digital Archive, Flinders University Library Special Collections (hereafter MPPDA Digital Archive) Record 3326, https://mppda.flinders.edu.au/records/3326. In 1928 the Association endorsed the legal challenges by Warner Bros and Fox to the state censorship of speech in sound pictures, and while these were unsuccessful, they did result in state censor boards either formally or informally avoiding the censorship of newsreels. MPPDA Digital Archive Record 519, https://mppda.flinders.edu.au/records/519; Gerald R. Butters, *Banned in Kansas: Motion Picture Censorship, 1915–1966* (Columbia, MO: University of Missouri Press, 2007), pp. 186, 226–28.

11   *Mutual Film Corporation v. Industrial Commission of Ohio*, 236 U.S. 230. *Mutual v. Ohio* was cited as a precedent in some 300 subsequent cases, including thirteen Supreme Court cases and twenty-one federal district court cases. John Wertheimer, 'Mutual Film Reviewed: The Movies, Censorship, and Free Speech in Progressive America', *American Journal of Legal History* 37.2 (1993): 158–89 (p. 177); Laura Wittern-Keller, *Freedom of the Screen: Legal Challenges to State Film Censorship: 1915–1981* (Lexington, KY: University Press of Kentucky, 2008), pp. 45–46.

12   *Buffalo Branch, Mutual Film Corporation v. Breitinger*, 250 Pa. 225, 95 A. 433 (1915), quoted in Wittern-Keller, *Freedom of the Screen*, p. 41.

13 David M. Rabban, *Free Speech in Its Forgotten Years, 1870–1920* (New York: Cambridge University Press, 1997), p. 15.

14 Fifty-one of the sixty-two pages of the Mutual company's brief to the Court was devoted to this claim. Wertheimer, 'Mutual Film Reviewed', pp. 169, 179. As Wittern-Keller notes, given the Court's hostility to free speech claims, this 'was either amazingly courageous or downright foolish'. Wittern-Keller, *Freedom of the Screen*, p. 43.

15 *Mutual Film Corporation v. Industrial Commission of Ohio*, 236 U.S. 230, at 243–44.

16 *Schenck v. United States*, 249 U.S. 47 (1919), 52. As Helen Freshwater observes, Holmes's comment has subsequently become 'a free-floating, bowdlerised one-liner [...] cut adrift of its original context' discussing the publication of pamphlets urging resistance to conscription during World War I. Helen Freshwater, *Theatre Censorship in Britain: Silencing, Censure and Suppression* (Houndmills: Palgrave Macmillan, 2009), p. 7.

17 Roger Baldwin, the founder of the American Civil Liberties Union, 1923, quoted in Rabban, *Free Speech in Its Forgotten Years*, p. 312. The ACLU did not consider silent pictures to be speech and did not involve itself substantially in challenges to state film censorship in the 1930s and 1940s, adhering instead to legal scholar Alexander Meiklejohn's distinction between public or political speech, which was protected by the First Amendment, and private speech (including commercial speech), which was protected only by the Fifth Amendment's due process clause. See Alexander Meiklejohn, *Free Speech and Its Relation to Self-Government* (New York: Harper, 1948).

18 In *Gitlow v. New York*, 268 U.S. 652 (1925), the Supreme Court ruled that the Fourteenth Amendment to the Constitution had extended the First Amendment's protections of free speech and freedom of the press to apply to state as well as federal legislation. Subsequent cases extended the incorporation of other constitutional rights into the obligations of state laws, but the issue was not raised in relation to motion picture censorship until 1952.

19 *Mutual Film Corporation v. Industrial Commission of Ohio*, 236 U.S., at 245–46.

20 'Film Censorship: An Administrative Analysis', *Columbia Law Review* 39.8 (1939): 1383–1405 (p. 1398).

21 Wittern-Keller, *Freedom of the Screen*, p. 67. As Wittern-Keller notes (p. 87), none of the cases questioned the censor's qualifications or the principle of prior restraint, and none challenged the constitutionality of the censorship laws. In total, there were only eighteen cases concerning motion picture censorship brought in state courts before World War II.

22 Estimates of how many municipal censorship bodies there were vary considerably, in part because many were largely quiescent. One 1929 estimate suggested that there were as many as 300. Wittern-Keller, *Freedom of the Screen*, p. 30. The *Motion Picture Herald* identified 'approximately 267' municipal boards operating in December 1932. Leo Meehan, 'Censorship—a Box Office Factor', *Motion Picture Herald*, 31 December 1932: 1926. In 1949 *Time* estimated there were fifty, while *Business Week* and the *New York Times* suggested seventy. *Time*, 31 October 1949: 76; *Business Week*, 3 December 1949: 23; *New York Times*, 5 February 1950: X5 (93); Theodore R. Kupferman and Philip J. O'Brien Jr, 'Motion Picture Censorship: The Memphis Blues', *Cornell Law Quarterly* 36.2 (1950–51): 273–200 (p. 276). In 1952 John L. Sanders estimated that 'perhaps 75

cities' still had censorship ordinances. John L. Sanders, 'Constitutional Law—Freedom of Speech—Motion Pictures', *North Carolina Law Review* 31.1 (1952): 103–15 (p. 103).

23 'Hearing before a Subcommittee of the Committee on Interstate and Foreign Commerce, House of Representatives, 74th Congress,' 26 March 1936 (Washington, DC: Government Printing Office: 1936), p. 453.

24 *Motion Picture Daily*, 27 February 1950: 4. Nashville, Tennessee, created a censorship board in order to ban this picture or any other 'where the producer, actor or actress has a reputation for laxity in morals'. *Variety*, 1 March 1950: 7; 'Motion Pictures and the First Amendment', *Yale Law Journal* 596 (1951): 696–719 (p. 699).

25 'Motion Pictures and the First Amendment', p. 697. In December 1932 *Variety* reported on the range of censorship practices in fifty-five cities, many of them involving the decision of a single individual and 'few having the same moral pattern on which to lay film'. 'Hot and Cold Censoring', *Variety*, 27 December 1932: 7, 26.

26 *Variety*, 2 August 1932: 7. In 1938, the chief of police in Waterbury, Connecticut, banned *Spain in Flames* because it was 'controversial, anti-Catholic, and opposed by the Knights of Columbus'. 'Film Censorship: An Administrative Analysis', p. 1404. In the waning years of the Production Code, comparable forms of what Richard Randall termed 'informal censorship', aimed at intimidating exhibitors, proliferated, with prosecutions of theatre owners and managers under local obscenity statutes increasing tenfold between 1960 and 1965. Randall, *Censorship of the Movies*, pp. 169–78; Jon Lewis, *Hollywood v. Hard Core: How the Struggle over Censorship Saved the Modern Film Industry* (New York: New York University Press, 2000), pp. 127–33.

27 https://www.memphisflyer.com/banned-in-memphis. The MPAA and the American Civil Liberties Union both hoped to make the ban on *Curley* a test case for the constitutionality of local censorship, but the Tennessee Supreme Court upheld Binford on a technicality and the Supreme Court declined to review the case. Wittern-Keller, *Freedom of the Screen*, p. 103; Whitney Strub, 'Black and White and Banned All Over: Race, Censorship and Obscenity in Postwar Memphis', *Journal of Social History* 40.3 (2007): 685–715.

28 https://pen.org/report/made-in-hollywood-censored-by-beijing/; Associated Press, 18 September 2013, https://www.petoskeynews.com/entertainment/hollywood-yielding-to-china-s-growing-film-clout/article_511e2abb-e8ef-5518-9d70-b59ffa8e2aaf.html.

29 Ruth Vasey, *The World According to Hollywood, 1919–1939* (Exeter: University of Exeter Press, 1997), pp. 158–93.

30 Douglas W. Churchill, 'Hollywood's Censor Is All the World', *New York Times*, 29 March 1936: 7, 10 (144).

31 Hays, draft, MPPDA 1932 Annual Report, Will H. Hays Papers, Indiana State Library, Indianapolis (hereafter Hays Papers).

32 Hays, quoted in *New York Times*, 25 July 1922: 18; Hays, press release, 14 January 1929, MPPDA Digital Archive Record 518, https://mppda.flinders.edu.au/records/518.

33 The Committee of the AMPP included: E.H. Allen (Educational), Paul Bern (First National), Sol Wurtzel (Fox), Will Hays, Jason Joy and Fred Beetson. The Committee's draft in May featured thirteen 'Don'ts' and twenty-three 'Be Carefuls'. In the final version, the treatment of law enforcement, the use of drugs and 'excessive or lustful kissing' were moved into the 'Be Carefuls'. MPPDA Minute Book, 29 June 1927.

MPPDA Digital Archive Records 341, 365, https://mppda.flinders.edu.au/records/341, https://mppda.flinders.edu.au/records/365.

34 In September 1932 the MPPDA claimed that the implementation of the Production Code was saving the industry $4 million annually in Chicago and the six states with active censor boards. *Variety*, 6 September 1932: 5.

35 'Will Hays on Censorship', Providence, RI, *Sunday Tribune*, 23 December 1928, MPPDA Digital Archive Record 1315, https://mppda.flinders.edu.au/records/1315.

36 The changes to Code procedure introduced in mid-1934 included the addition of a penalty clause imposing a $25,000 fine for violation of the Code's Resolution for Uniform Interpretation. Although this clause has subsequently been cited as the sanction ultimately enforcing the Code, any attempt to impose it would probably have constituted a breach of the antitrust laws, and it was never used. Richard Maltby, 'The Production Code and the Hays Office', in Tino Balio, *Grand Design: Hollywood as a Modern Business Enterprise, 1930–1939* (New York: Charles Scribner's Sons, 1993), pp. 37–72 (p. 61).

37 Martha Wolfenstein and Nathan Leites, *Movies: A Psychological Study* (Glencoe, IL: Free Press, 1950), p. 189. For discussion of this consequence, see Richard Maltby, '"A Brief Romantic Interlude": Dick and Jane Go to Three-and-a-Half Seconds of the Classical Hollywood Cinema', in *Decoding the Movies: Hollywood in the 1930s* (Exeter: University of Exeter Press, 2021), pp. 27–51.

38 Janelle Reinelt, 'The Limits of Censorship', *Theatre Research International* 32.1 (2007): 3–15 (p. 3). Examples from a long list of such usage include Gerald Gardner, *The Censorship Papers: Movie Censorship Letters from the Hays Office, 1934–1968* (New York: Dodd, Mead & Company, 1987); Gregory D. Black, *Hollywood Censored: Morality Codes, Catholics, and the Movies* (Cambridge: Cambridge University Press, 1994); Thomas Doherty, *Hollywood's Censor: Joseph I. Breen and the Production Code Administration* (New York: Columbia University Press, 2007).

39 Robert C. Post, 'Censorship and Silencing', in Robert C. Post (ed.), *Censorship and Silencing: Practices of Cultural Regulation* (Los Angeles: Getty Research Institute for the History of Art and the Humanities, 1998), pp. 1–16 (p. 4).

40 Müller, 'Censorship & Cultural Regulation', p. 1.

41 Memo, John V. Wilson to Carl E. Milliken, 23 November 1928, MPPDA Digital Archive Record 398, https://mppda.flinders.edu.au/records/398.

42 Resolution for Uniform Interpretation of the Production Code, 31 March 1930, in Richard Maltby, 'Documents on the Genesis of the Production Code', *Quarterly Review of Film and Video* 15.4 (March 1995): 33–63 (p. 56).

43 Memo, Breen, 'Code, Extra-Code and Industry Regulation in Motion Pictures: A Study of the Effects of the Production Code and Its Administration upon the Type and Content of American Motion Pictures and Certain Other Basic Industry Policies and Their Current Application', 22 June 1938, MPPDA Digital Archive Record 1192, https://mppda.flinders.edu.au/records/1192.

44 Breen to Hays, 26 March 1938, MPPDA Digital Archive Record 1196, https://mppda.flinders.edu.au/records/1196.

45 State and municipal censor boards consistently rejected most of the 'twilight zone' pictures that caused the PCA difficulties, including the semi-documentary *The Birth of a*

Baby, and two documentaries on the Spanish Civil War, *The Spanish Earth* and *Spain in Flames*, which Ohio banned because 'it was not in accord with the policy of neutrality adopted by this country' and the governor of Pennsylvania called 'pure communist propaganda'. The Legion of Decency created a new category, 'separate classification', to accommodate *The Birth of a Baby*. The New York courts upheld the censors' rejection of the picture as 'indecent', 'immoral' and tending to corrupt minors. Pennsylvania and Virginia also rejected it, although Ohio licensed it. There was much press and public criticism of the decision. The Virginia decision was overturned by a lower state court—one of only three successful challenge cases since *Mutual*. The Russian film *Professor Mamlock*, depicting Nazi persecutions, was given a Code Seal under the new interpretation of the PCA's jurisdiction, but banned in Ohio and Chicago in late 1938. As late as 1940 a Pennsylvania court upheld a ban on Louis de Rochemont's *The Ramparts We Watch* on the grounds that it might inflame resentment against German Americans.

46 Ray Norr, MPPDA Washington Bureau, quoted in Breen memo, 22 June 1938, MPPDA Digital Archive Record 1192, https://mppda.flinders.edu.au/records/1192.

47 Memo, Harmon and Milliken to Hays, 31 March 1938, MPPDA Digital Archive Record 1196, https://mppda.flinders.edu.au/records/1196.

48 Breen to Hays, 26 March 1938, MPPDA Digital Archive Record 1196, https://mppda.flinders.edu.au/records/1196.

49 Breen, letter to Hays, 6 March 1936, quoted in Raymond Moley, *The Hays Office* (Indianapolis: Bobbs-Merrill, 1945), p. 97.

50 Breen to Hays, 22 June 1938, MPPDA Digital Archive Record 1192, https://mppda.flinders.edu.au/records/1192.

51 Memo, Harmon, 25 July 1938, MPPDA Digital Archive Record 1190, https://mppda.flinders.edu.au/records/1190. In September, Breen suggested an amendment removing the words 'fairly and honestly' on the grounds that the PCA could not 'accept the responsibility of saying that the controversial matter has been <u>fairly</u> presented, without considerable study of the subject', which would involve 'a great deal of research work'. Breen to Hays, 14 September 1938, MPPDA Digital Archive Record 1216, https://mppda.flinders.edu.au/records/1216.

52 Matthew Bunn, 'Reimagining Repression: New Censorship Theory and After', *History and Theory* 54 (2015): 25–54 (p. 29).

53 See, for example, Thomas Doherty's description of Breen as *Hollywood's Censor*.

54 Breen to Hays, 22 June 1938, MPPDA Digital Archive Record 1192, https://mppda.flinders.edu.au/records/1192.

55 Judith Butler, *Excitable Speech: A Politics of the Performative* (New York: Routledge, 1997), p. 138.

56 Michel Foucault, *The History of Sexuality*, vol. 1, trans. Robert Hurley (London: Random House, 1978), p. 34; Butler, *Excitable Speech*, p. 128; Bourdieu, *Language and Symbolic Power*, 138. For an application of these ideas to film censorship, see Annette Kuhn, *Cinema, Censorship and Sexuality, 1909–1925* (London: Routledge, 1988), pp. 126–34.

57 Post, 'Censorship and Silencing', p. 2.

58 It is worth noting that the three theorists' attachment to 'censorship' as a descriptor of the processes they examine is somewhat tenuous. For the most part, Foucault avoids the term; Butler acknowledges the issues with its expansion and prefers the

term 'foreclosure'; and Bourdieu describes his use of the term as metaphorical. Judith Butler, 'Ruled Out: Vocabularies of the Censor', in *Censorship and Silencing*, pp. 247–260 (p. 255); Butler, *Excitable Speech*, pp. 138–39; Bourdieu, *Language and Symbolic Power*, p. 138.

59   Michael Holquist, 'Corrupt Originals: The Paradox of Censorship', *PMLA* 109.1 (1994): 14–25 (p. 16).

60   Sue Curry Jansen, *Censorship: The Knot That Binds Power and Knowledge* (New York: Oxford University Press, 1991), p. 221 n. 1; Butler, *Excitable Speech*, p. 128.

61   Jansen's historical account dates the concept of market censorship from the 1970s and identifies its precursors as primarily products of the Cold War. She locates the concept as a practice of 'the huge communication and technology conglomerates that comprise the modern consciousness industry' and deploys it in discussions of contemporary cultural production. Sue Curry Jansen, 'Ambiguities and Imperatives of Market Censorship: The Brief History of a Critical Concept', *Westminster Papers in Communication and Culture* 7.2 (2010): 12–30 (pp. 13–14, 19).

62   Sophia Rosenfeld, 'Writing the History of Censorship in the Age of Enlightenment', in Daniel Gordon (ed.), *Postmodernism and the Enlightenment: New Perspectives in Eighteenth-Century French Intellectual History* (London: Routledge, 2001), pp. 117–45 (p. 117, quoted in Nicole Moore, 'Censorship Is', *Australian Humanities Review* 54 (2013): 45–65 (p. 45).

63   Kenji Yoshino, 'The Eclectic Model of Censorship', *California Law Review* 88.5 (2000): 1635–55 (p. 1639).

64   Nicole Moore, 'Censorship Is', pp. 52–56.

65   Robert Darnton, *Censors at Work: How States Shaped Literature* (New York: Norton, 2015), pp. 19, 43–44, 232.

66   William D. O'Connell, 'Silencing the Crowd: China, the NBA, and Leveraging Market Size to Export Censorship', *Review of International Political Economy*, 29.4 (2002), pp. 1102–34 (p. 1116).

67   Jansen, 'Ambiguities and Imperatives of Market Censorship', p. 13.

68   Pamphlet, 'A Code to Maintain Social and Community Values in the Production of Silent, Synchronized and Talking Motion Pictures', MPPDA, 31 March 1930, MPPDA Digital Archive Record 1255, https://mppda.flinders.edu.au/records/1255.

69   Ben Urwand, *The Collaboration: Hollywood's Pact with Hitler* (Cambridge, MA: Belknap Press, 2015), pp. 48, 129.

70   The ban on the film was imposed in December 1930. It was lifted in March 1931, and a modified version was shown in Germany in September 1931 to good but not spectacular business, some protests but no violence. It was banned again after Hitler's accession to power in January 1933. Unsigned memo, 29 December 1930, *All Quiet on the Western Front* PCA file, Department of Special Collections, Margaret Herrick Library, Academy of Motion Picture Arts and Sciences, Beverly Hills, CA; Andrew Kelly, *All Quiet on the Western Front: The Story of a Film* (London: I.B. Tauris, 1998), pp. 120–27.

71   Gyssling threatened that all films that the cast and crew were associated with could be banned in Germany: 'U.S. Stops Nazis' Intimidation of Hollywood Motion Picture Stars', *Motion Picture Herald*, 19 June 1937: 16. For Gyssling's biography, see Steven

Ross, *Hitler in Los Angeles: How Jews Foiled Nazi Plots against Hollywood and America* (New York: Bloomsbury, 2017), pp. 108–29, 214–27, 336–38.

72 *Variety*, 9 June 1937: 6. Universal denied having ever discussed the picture with any official in Germany, insisting that previews had led them to add 'several romantic scenes' as well as what *Silver Screen* called 'some of the silliest slapstick comedy you ever saw'. The picture, which had been intended as the studio's 'picture of the year' despite the absence of any stars, had run heavily over schedule and budget, and Universal clearly decided that the previewed version had limited commercial appeal. Its publicity emphasized its appeal to a female audience, with newspaper adverts featuring a woman with outstretched arms and copy declaring 'Millions of women waiting—a handful of men returning! […] Not a woman in the world can afford NOT to see this picture.' Despite reviews that were consistently critical of the discordant comedy elements the picture was a box-office success, although not enough to recoup its $955,000 production cost. *Motion Picture Herald*, 24 April 1937: 17; 17 July 1937: 41; *Silver Screen*, September 1937: 63; *Boxoffice*, 26 June 1937: 86; *Motion Picture Review Digest*, 27 September 1937: 78–80.

73 *Hollywood Reporter*, 10 July 1936: 1.

74 'Metro Hesitant on Remarque's Story', *Variety*, 30 June 1937: 3; J. Donald Adams, 'Erich Remarque's New Novel', *New York Times*, 2 May 1937: Section 7:1 (45).

75 The *Good Housekeeping* version is available at https://digital.library.cornell.edu/catalog/hearth6417403_1406_001.

76 *Motion Picture Daily*, 5 May 1937: 10. *Motion Picture Herald*, 9 October 1937: 24. The picture starred Taylor, Franchot Tone, Robert Young and Margaret Sullavan.

77 Breen to L.B. Mayer, 11 May 1937, PCA *Three Comrades* file.

78 Mankiewicz had been the first secretary of the Screen Writers Guild and was one of MGM's representatives on the Executive Committee of the Hollywood branch of the Los Angeles Jewish Community Committee, which was established to combat insurgent Nazism in the city. Both he and Fitzgerald were members of the Hollywood Anti-Nazi League. Mankiewicz worked extensively on the script in its final stages. Fitzgerald's first draft script of 1 September 1938 adds no overt political content to Remarque's story. The script is reproduced in Matthew J. Bruccoli (ed.), *F. Scott Fitzgerald's Screenplay for Three Comrades by Erich Maria Remarque* (Carbondale, IL: Southern Illinois University Press, 1978). In his afterword, Bruccoli reproduces extracts from Fitzgerald's correspondence with Mankiewicz and Paramore, none of which comment on the inclusion or subsequent removal of any of the political scenes.

79 Breen to L.B. Mayer, 22 January 1938, PCA *Three Comrades* file.

80 Breen to Herron, 4 June 1937, PCA *West of Shanghai* file.

81 Memo, 'Three Comrades', n.d., PCA *Three Comrades* file. The Marxist weekly *New Masses* published an account of the meeting, emphasizing Mankiewicz's rejection of Breen's suggestion to make the thugs communists and concluding that 'an honest book and honest film artists have little chance against capitalist greed, guarded in the name of decency by the vulgarians of the Hays office'. The article also claimed (incorrectly) that Breen had discussed the script with Gyssling. 'Off-Color Remarque', *New Masses*, 15 February 1938: 10–11. It seems unlikely that Breen or any of the MGM executives would have provided the paper with this information. In his account of these events in

his 2015 book *The Collaboration*, Ben Urwand proposes that Breen's list was produced by Mayer and Gyssling after a screening of the picture. Along with many other writers on the period, Urwand consistently exaggerates Gyssling's influence, but never more so than in the suggestion that he could somehow view a picture two months before any of it had been shot. Urwand, *The Collaboration*, p. 189. Mayer did invite Gyssling to a screening in May, after the picture had been completed. Breen subsequently informed Gyssling that three further minor changes had been made, although whether they were made on the studio's initiative or at Gyssling's suggestion is not clear. Breen to Gyssling, 16 May 1938, PCA *Three Comrades* file.

82 Curiously, the press book also claimed its setting 'might be any large Central European city and the time is the present'. Quoted in Steven Ross, *Hitler in Los Angeles*, pp. 217–18.

83 *Motion Picture Herald*, 28 May 1938: 54, 57. Nevertheless, the Legion of Decency classified it B—objectionable in part. *Motion Picture Herald*, 4 June 1938: 27.

84 *Time*, 6 June 1938: 41. *Variety* reported the accusation and Mankiewicz's denial of the PCA's involvement in the studio's decision to delete sequences extraneous to the love story. *Variety*, 9 June 1938: 26.

85 *Variety*, 25 May 1938: 12; *Hollywood Reporter*, 21 May 1938; Microform Appendix to H. Mark Glancy, 'MGM Film Grosses, 1924–1948: The Eddie Mannix Ledger', *Historical Journal of Film, Radio and Television* 12.2 (1996): 127–44.

86 *New York Times*, 3 June 1938: 17.

87 For a discussion of these cases, See Vasey, *The World According to Hollywood*, pp. 175–87.

88 *Photoplay*, September 1938: 5.

89 *Django Unchained* was initially approved for release but pulled from cinemas with no explanation shortly after it had opened. Associated Press, 18 September 2013, https://www.petoskeynews.com/entertainment/hollywood-yielding-to-china-s-growing-film-clout/article_511e2abb-e8ef-5518-9d70-b59ffa8e2aaf.html.

90 Zhiwei Xiao, 'Prohibition, Politics, and Nation-Building: A History of Film Censorship in China', in Daniel Biltereyst and Roel Vande Winkel (eds), *Silencing Cinema: Film Censorship around the World* (New York: Palgrave Macmillan, 2013), p. 125.

91 *Regulations on the Administration of Films* and *Provisions on the Filing of Film Scripts* (Abstracts) and *Administration of Films*, quoted in Jessica Grimm, 'The Import of Hollywood Films in China: Censorship and Quotas', *Syracuse Journal of International Law and Commerce* 43.1 (2015): 155–89 (pp. 164–65).

92 Grimm, 'The Import of Hollywood Films in China', p. 168.

93 https://pen.org/report/made-in-hollywood-censored-by-beijing/. See also Robert Cain, 'How to Be Censored in China: A Brief Filmmaking Guide', *Indiewire*, 30 November 2011, https://www.indiewire.com/2011/11/how-to-be-censored-in-china-a-brief-filmmaking-guide-50870/; Sean O'Connor and Nicholas Armstrong, 'Directed by Hollywood, Edited by China: How China's Censorship and Influence Affect Films Worldwide', U.S.–China Economic and Security Review Commission, 28 October 2015, https://www.uscc.gov/research/directed-hollywood-edited-china-how-chinas-censorship-and-influence-affect-films-worldwide.

94 Julia Ya Qin, 'Pushing the Limits of Global Governance: Trading Rights, Censorship, and WTO Jurisprudence—A Commentary on the China-Publications Case', *Chinese Journal of International Law* 10.2 (2011): 271–322 (p. 272).

95 In a speech he made three weeks before the PEN report was released, Barr called Hollywood's 'kowtowing to the PRC [...] a massive propaganda coup for the Chinese Communist Party' and evidence of 'the film industry's submission to the CCP'. William Barr, Transcript of Attorney General Barr's Remarks on China Policy at the Gerald R. Ford Presidential Museum Grand Rapids, Michigan, 17 July 2020, https://www.justice. gov/opa/speech/transcript-attorney-general-barr-s-remarks-china-policy-gerald-r -ford-presidential-museum; Erich Schwartzel, *Red Carpet: Hollywood, China, and the Global Battle for Cultural Supremacy* (New York: Penguin Press, 2022), pp. xvi, 135.

96 Wendy Su, 'Cultural Policy and Film Industry as Negotiation of Power: The Chinese State's Role and Strategies in Its Engagement with Global Hollywood 1994–2012', *Pacific Affairs* 87.1 (2014): 93–114 (p. 101).

97 Wendy Su, 'A Brave New World? Understanding U.S.–China Coproductions: Collaboration, Conflicts, and Obstacles', *Critical Studies in Media Communication* 34.5 (2017): 480–94 (pp. 482–83).

98 Rebecca Davis, 'Inside China and Hollywood's Frayed Relationship: "We Need to Stop Trying to Keep the Status Quo, Because the Status Quo Is Gone"', *Variety*, 21 December 2021, https://variety.com/2021/film/global/china-hollywood-box-office -2022-1235140439; Michelle Toh, 'Hollywood Won't Budge for Chinese Censors Anymore. Here's What Changed', CNN Business, 8 July 2022, https://edition.cnn. com/2022/07/08/media/hollywood-china-censors-box-office-intl-hnk/index.html; Ying Zhu, *Hollywood in China: Behind the Scenes of the World's Largest Movie Market* (New York: The New Press, 2022), pp. 243–45.

99 C.C. Pettijohn and Gaylord R. Hawkins, Memorandum on the Constitutionality of the Censorship of News Reels et al, pp. 31–32, MPPDA Digital Archive Record 1199, https://mppda.flinders.edu.au/records/1199.

2

A Philosovietic Mode of Film Censorship: A Supplement to Studies of Cold War Italian Film Culture

Karol Jóźwiak

Introduction

'Anticommunism on screen doesn't work.' An anonymous article opens with this claim in the 11 February 1950 edition of the main Italian communist newspaper, *L'Unità*,[1] quite accurately uncovering one of the principles of Italian post-war cinema. Indeed, anti-communism is conspicuously absent from Italian movies. In fact, any explicit criticism of the Soviet regime is a rarity in Italian cinema from the early Cold War period. During the early Cold War, the Soviet regime was never denounced as a totalitarian state by Italian cinema, and seldom approached in a critical manner. Rare examples of films containing criticism of the Soviet Union usually faced difficulties at the level of development, censorship and distribution. Was it systemic censorship? To what extent was it the result of political pressure? Why do we know so little about this mode of censorship? In addressing those questions, I will propose the term *philosovietism*. By this I mean a positive stance towards the Soviet Union, which contributed to the legitimization of the totalitarian regime in order to maintain good relations. While the term can be pertinently applicable in the analysis of aspects of Cold War culture in the West in general, Italian film culture appears to be an exceptionally fertile ground for such a study.

Karol Jóźwiak, "A Philosovietic Mode of Film Censorship: A Supplement to Studies of Cold War Italian Film Culture" in: *The Screen Censorship Companion: Critical Explorations in the Control of Film and Screen Media*. University of Exeter Press (2024). © Karol Jóźwiak. DOI: 10.47788/HHUW8463

In this chapter I will apply the phenomenon of philosovietism to the study of political interventions in Italian film culture during the Cold War. I will argue that a philosovietic mode of film censorship existed in Italian film culture, and that its significance is yet to be acknowledged and properly framed within the already well-developed branch of research on film censorship in post-war Italy.[2] In doing so, I will apply David Forgacs's warning that talking 'simply about *the state* or *state intervention* in relation to culture can be misleading' since 'the state consisted of an ensemble of agencies and functions not all of which were necessarily coordinated with one another'.[3] Thus, as Forgacs postulates, 'in examining the operations of the state at any one time, one needs to look at the spheres of competence and interest of different agencies'.[4] In this respect, the phenomenon of philosovietism fits well into the model of research suggested by Forgacs.

At a broader level, by introducing the term philosovietism, I aim at supplementing the studies of Italian film culture. A close look at the role that Italian film culture played in different ideological and political strategies relating to the Soviet regime during the said period can reveal new knowledge which challenges the dominant categories and assumptions. It requires a shift of attention from the question of internal political battles between the left (mainly the Partito Comunista Italiano or the Italian Communist Party, henceforth referred to as PCI) and the right (Democrazia Cristiana or Christian Democracy, henceforth referred to as DC) in Cold War Italy to the external issue of the Soviet Union and different levels of bilateral diplomacy between the two states. From this perspective, the term *equidistance*, borrowed from political science, becomes quite relevant. By referring to this notion, I will argue that although during the Cold War Italy belonged to the Western Bloc, Italian film culture was at least as close to the Soviet Union as to the USA. In other words, as Italian Cold War politics were conditioned by the balancing of Soviet and American influence during the Cold War, in a similar way Italian film culture can be described by complementary paradigms of philosovietism and the containment of Soviet power (or the paradigm of the American Cold War strategy). Since several studies have focused extensively on the latter paradigm,[5] I shall concentrate on the former, which is more obscured and underestimated.

Maccartismo, or Censorship as a Figure of Speech

The political interventions in cinema in Cold War Italy are rightly associated with right-wing politics, especially DC, the main right-wing party that steadily held power for several post-war decades.[6] Italian film scholars unanimously describe Italian Cold War film culture 'in terms of containment of Soviet power and the suffocation of the left',[7] or as 'a robust anti-communism'.[8]

Those assumptions are well rooted in Italian film criticism and film history. Cinema as a shelter of an honest leftist culture against the assault of right-wing anti-communism is a topos not only of Italian film culture but also of Western cinema in general. Its most prominent example is the House Un-American Activities Committee's hearings, during 1947, and the 'witch-hunt' of presumed communists initiated by Senator Joseph McCarthy in the USA. Italian film critics almost immediately used the American template, referencing the American example in discussions on Italian films. In 1948, Umberto Barbaro denounced the first prominent case in post-war Italian film censorship, Pietro Germi's *Gioventù perduta* (1948), as an attempt to apply 'to our cinema the American "code for imbeciles"',[9] in a fight against truth. Step by step, the discussion on cinema switched focus from morality (the Hays Code referred to by Barbaro) to the ideological battle, highlighting its presumed anti-communist feature. The way censorship was described and used in public discourse reflected growing Cold War tensions.

Cinema played a crucial role in the cultural-political strategy of the PCI from early on. Already, by the end of 1947, *L'Unità* had become a platform for film directors to denounce the 'gagging of our cinema',[10] and for 'defending our cinema'.[11] As Stephen Gundle commented: 'an alliance was forged that would make the PCI into the party most identified with the interests of national filmmakers'.[12] Later, the scholar noticed that cinema was 'a decisive terrain of political and cultural conflict', described in terms of 'the battle between left and right over how society was to be reconstructed after the war'.[13] As a result, as Gianluca Fantoni claimed in his study, 'a Communist hegemony amongst film critics' was achieved by the clever PCI strategy.[14]

Essentially, leftist critics managed to successfully align the political interests of the PCI with the cause of freedom of expression in cinema, thereby, to a large extent, politically instrumentalizing the discourse on film censorship. These critics leaned on heavy-handed metaphors in order to blame a presumed anti-sovietism for the problems of Italian cinema. Most censorship was referred to as a 'clerical barbarity',[15] 'a kind of cancer',[16] 'cinematic pogroms' or 'constantly obsessed by the red menace'.[17] In the 1950s, an Italianized notion of *maccartismo* was coined by the communist press to denote the state's approach to cinema. 'McCarthyism equals fascism'[18] was the common assumption in the communist press, galvanizing as it did disgust for anti-communism. One article, 'Offensive of McCarthyism against Italian Cinema', denounced the blacklisting of directors by the right-wing press and government, but at the same time it briskly noticed that 'anti-communism has lost the battle over cinema on all fronts'.[19] The article further notes that 'anti-communism resulted in quite a bad affair, and the producers and distributors look after business rather than ideology'. In sum, on the one hand, anti-communism in cinema would be regarded as an irrational remnant of fascism, overused by those in power, instrumentalized by the DC government in the current political debate and aimed at discrediting the PCI. On the other hand, this strategy was considered a failure, an inoperative and ineffective effort. Film culture, according to the anonymous author of the article, proved altogether resistant, unfavourable to any kind of anti-communism.

Given that, what was the real impact of anti-communism on Italian film culture? The way it was addressed by the communist press of the time, and to a certain extent still is in current studies, suggests two mutually exclusive answers: it was either overwhelmingly prepotent, or it was irrelevant and fringe. Either way, a contradiction lies at the heart of how the phenomenon has been perceived.

This same contradiction seems to be one of the core problems of Italian post-war film history. Gian Piero Brunetta admits that Italian cinema 'had been reborn as a field of contradictions, and became the winning diplomatic card for Italy's rehabilitation'.[20] Describing the issue of the post-fascist remodelling of Italian cinema, he claimed that it 'was always held together by a spirit of unity, tolerance, and the will to move on and absolve directors of their ideological sins'.[21] In this context, the Soviet example was often taken as an implicit template for the reconstruction of post-fascist Italy. In his 1945 article 'Italy Needs Its Own Cinema', Carlo Lizzani refers to a key figure of Soviet social realism: 'Italy is waiting for its Gorkys', who by means of cinema will express Italy's 'collective tragedies and its new ethos, born of wartime suffering and the spirit of the struggle for liberation'. In the same vein, a takeover of the film industry in Poland by the communist totalitarian state at the time is praised by the young militant critic as 'a lesson of democratic sensibility'.[22] However, this spirit of unity and tolerance, the absolution and rehabilitation, seems to be conditioned, among other factors, by a certain consensus in regard to communism.

I suggest that the way anti-communism was approached by film critics was a part of this spirit of unity and struggle for liberation. Rather than assessing a state of affairs, the metaphors and statements regarding film censorship were consciously exaggerated, aimed at ratcheting up tensions and at stimulating militancy among left-wing critics. To a large extent film criticism became the locus of a political battle, in which the delegitimization of any criticism of communism or the Soviet regime was at stake. This was noticed at the time by the communist critics themselves. Renzo Renzi was one of the few leftist critics to abjure from some errors in the wake of de-Stalinization. Although he addressed the way film criticism In his famous article 'Released from the Vow' (which referred to the Soviet social-realist film *The Vow* (1946) made by Mikheil Chiaureli and praised by the left), he aimed at coming to terms with 'Stalin's idolatry' by Italian film critics. He acknowledged that 'the propagandistic preoccupations led to an instrumentalization of art and criticism in an excessive manner'. The criticism, notes Renzi, 'was directed towards an apology with no regard to costs, according to the principle "what is ideologically applicable is great, what is Russian, is the greatest," applied in a totalitarian way'.[23] dealt with Soviet cinema, his arguments are relevant to the broader issue of leftist criticism of early Cold War Italy. In his recent study, Gianluca Fantoni arrives at a similar conclusion, admitting that the leftist critics' 'take on both Italian cinema and neorealism was eminently political'.[24] I assume the problem of presumed anti-sovietism was instrumentalized in an excessive manner, overstating a problem that was actually minor and existed only at the fringe of debates. Most importantly though, this figure of speech covered exactly the opposite phenomenon—that is, the philosovietic aspect of film culture in post-war Italy.

Equidistanza and Cold War Italy

The hypothesis that anti-sovietism was a figure of speech coined by leftist film critics, rather than a prominent feature of post-war Italian film culture, raises the important question of whether anti-sovietism existed within the scope of right-wing politics in early Cold War Italy at all. The presumed anti-communism or anti-sovietism of DC is taken for granted, but often it is not based on facts. The implicit unilateralism of Italian policy towards the Soviet Union during the early Cold War has been questioned in studies on Cold War diplomacy.[25] Accordingly, the DC government was not necessarily interested in stimulating negative emotions towards the Soviet Union but rather aimed at instrumentalizing it in an attempt to counterbalance American influences. This strategy is referred to in terms of *equidistanza* (keeping equidistance in the bipolar world of the Cold War).

As a matter of fact, the long-standing leader of DC, Alcide De Gasperi, was far from denouncing the Soviet Union. In his speech in 1944, he referred to 'the genius of Joseph Stalin', admitting 'there is something immensely agreeable, immensely suggestive in the universalistic tendency of Russian communism',[26] which seems, according to De Gasperi, parallel to Catholicism. His successor, Giulio Andreotti, who contributed significantly to the enhancement of censorship in Italian cinema, strictly followed this approach. 'Politically I was born at the school of De Gasperi, who [...] was convinced the Soviets were objectively defenders of the peace', he declared.[27] In one of his recollections, he proudly quoted a long passage from the diaries of Andrei Gromyko, a long-standing Minister of Foreign Affairs of the Soviet Union: 'my conversations with Andreotti have always been frank and constructive', and were a 'source of great joy'.[28] When touching on the issue of de-Stalinization, the Italian statesman decisively distanced himself from the 'merciless indictment against Stalin', stating that 'today it is fashionable to judge Stalin'.[29]

Similarly, the general line of the Italian government during the early stages of the Cold War didn't provide much evidence for its anti-sovietism. On the contrary, the Italian government constantly solicited friendly relations with the Soviet authorities in the period 1944–48 due to a series of different diplomatic issues.[30] Censorship in regard to the Soviet Union was indeed implemented in Italy at that time, but quite differently from how one would expect. In his working report the Italian ambassador in Moscow, Pietro Quaroni, wrote: 'the freedom of the press to critique and to question is a nice thing, but when it comes to foreign states, a particular caution is to be applied. [...] Russia is a great country, powerful and potent, whose friendship could be useful and whose hostility could be damaging. [...] Let's have our debates internally, but at the same time let's try to be more moderate and not to say mad nonsense'. Concluding, he suggested taking 'rigorous measures against some anti-Soviet newspapers'.[31] Following this line, De Gasperi, at a press conference in 1946, expressed 'an explicit warning in regard to Russia, so the newspapers would stick to a friendly approach, which is to characterize the relationship between the two countries'.[32]

In subsequent years, when the Cold War was at its peak, the stance of De Gasperi was also considered ambivalent from the American point of view. In 1952, American reports 'tended to blame the Italian government and anti-communist parties for their alleged lack of cooperation' and 'unjustifiable, passive resistance by De Gasperi' to the adoption of measures provided by American psychological warfare.[33] The American ambassador in Rome, Clare Boothe Luce, considered a 'strongly anti-communist government' in Italy impossible.[34] In his revealing study of American psychological warfare in Italy, Mario Del Pero came to an interesting conclusion, claiming that Cold War Italian politics was 'a sort of *containment of containment* originating from the desire to safeguard Italy's equilibrium'.[35] Indeed, the anti-communist struggle was contrary to the very interests of DC as a necessary power to democratically balance the authoritarian regression pushed by the two Cold War superpowers. Rather than containing communism DC aimed at containing anti-communism, both for the particular interest of holding on to power and for safeguarding Italian autonomy and democracy.

Beyond the Pale of Censorship Historiography

The above-mentioned contexts create a useful frame to analyse some examples of censorship, which otherwise are treated as exceptional and individual cases. I hold that these cases are to be seen as part of a wider phenomenon of a philosovietic mode of film censorship. Usually, they involve minor productions by secondary filmmakers and producers, who, intentionally or not, embarked on breaking the consensual approach to the Soviet Union. Some of these productions were abandoned at the stage of concept or development, contributing to what Brunetta described as 'a map of non-existent cinema'.[36] Others were produced but censored accordingly. Many of them are hardly available today, making the phenomenon of censorship de facto far more efficient than in cases of prominent productions highlighted by mainstream criticism. That is also why the survey of these films is quite challenging. Below I give a few examples constituting the field of my ongoing research.

One group consists of films produced during the fascist period but whose post-war release was impeded. One of the most prominent and controversial examples is the case of the post-war attempt to release Roberto Rossellini's *L'uomo dalla croce* (*The Man of the Cross*, 1943). The film, produced at the demand of the fascist regime, narrates the story of the Italian Army on the eastern front during the Second World War. It presented the war with Soviet Russia as 'the crusade against the "godless ones"', depicting the Soviet soldiers and an NKVD (Naródnyy komissariát vnútrennikh del, The People's Commissariat for Internal Affairs) officer in a biased way. The request to obtain permission for the release of the film, submitted in 1950, was declined. The censorship committee justified the decision by claiming: 'the film, especially at this time, could disturb international relations with the USSR'.[37] Other lesser-known films, such as *Odessa in fiamme* (*Odessa in Flames*, Carmine Gallone, 1941) or *Ucraina rossa* (*Red Ukraine*, 1941) met a similar end.

Another group of films consists of post-war productions which, according to the censorship board, happened to contain some 'ideological errors', which put at risk 'international relations'. Mario Amendola's comedy film *I peggiori anni della nostra vita* (*The Worst Years of Our Life*, 1950) is a parody of the famous American film *The Best Years of Our Life* (William Wyler, 1946). In the Italian version, soldiers return home defeated by the Soviet Union. This light parody appeared suspicious to the censor. During the examination, the 'images of Stalin from inappropriate places' were required to be cut. In the judgement, it was claimed that such a film would 'disturb international relations with the Soviet Union and its head, and hence upset public order during the screenings'. Eventually, following philosovietic amendments, the film was released, but without permission to export it abroad.[38]

A short film by a young, militant DC supporter, Fulvio Lucisano's *Contro l'Italia* (*Against Italy*, 1954), was treated less compromisingly.[39] This documentary aimed at describing PCI activity in Italy. At the censorship examination, permission to release the film was denied since the board had noticed 'scenes contrary to the public order'. Apparently, Lucisano had some influential backing that allowed him to appeal to higher authorities. In his letter to Mario Scelba, at that time Italian Prime Minister for DC, he complained about the months-long delays at the censorship board, and about the arguments supporting the censorship board's refusal. Lucisano referred to the verbal discussion with the board's secretary, Professor Lacalamita, who admitted 'communists are all brothers, there is a need for understanding, thus the film is pointless'.[40] Despite reaching the highest political level with the backing of some very influential persons, such as Mgr Albino Galetto (head of the Catholic Cinematography Centre), the attempts to secure permission for the film's release failed. Other films, such as Giovannino Guareschi's part of *La rabbia* (*The Rage*, 1962) can be analysed as similar cases.[41]

Yet another group of films belongs to the aforementioned non-existent cinema. These were abandoned projects, some of them as a result of ostracism motivated by philosovietism. One such ostracized director is Vittorio Cottafavi who was, according to Bertrand Tavernier, 'excommunicated from neorealism by the establishment and by the conformism of political correctness'.[42] In 1952 he embarked on a film project, *Sangue sul Don* (*Blood on the Don River*), narrating the history of the Italian Army's campaign in the Soviet Union during the Second World War. The initial idea of the film was submitted to the preventive censorship board, which strongly advised against 'any polemic tone', suggesting 'for the sake of patriotism and especially in regard to foreign states, to mitigate representations of torture, Soviet spies and informers'. The preventive censorship board abstained from approval of the film and concluded: 'for a more precise judgement an examination of the screenplay is indispensable'.[43] The film never entered production and no subsequent procedure can be traced in the state archives. This abandoned project is not referenced in Italian film studies, as well as not being mentioned in studies on the work of the director.[44] Ermanno Olmi's 1960s film project *Il sergente nella neve* (*The Sergeant in the Snow*) seems to be a very similar case. The film was supposed to narrate the same war campaign, focusing especially on the fate of Italian prisoners of war lost in Russia when the war ended. Like Cottafavi, its director was associated with a non-leftist political stance. Hence, allowing Olmi to proceed with such an extremely controversial subject (Italian resentments and traumas related to the Soviet Union) was considered too delicate. Eventually, Olmi's project was abandoned. Although there is no evidence of a direct political influence, the director explicitly blamed politics for the failure of this project in an article emphatically entitled 'When the Left Impeded My Work'.[45]

La grande strada, A Case Study

Finally, one of the least-known examples of the philosovietic mode of film censorship merits detailed discussion. It concerns Michal Waszynski's film *The Great Way*, known in two parallel versions, Polish (*Wielka droga*, 1946) and Italian (*La grande strada: l'odissea di Montecassino*, 1948). It is a peculiar film, produced in Italy in the aftermath of the Second World War by a mixed Polish and Italian crew.[46] It was co-financed by the Polish Army's 2nd Corps, which was stationed at the time in Italy as a part of the Allied Forces presence. The principal aim of the film was to present the Polish perspective on the previous war to Italian and international audiences. The institutional barrier imposed by the state eventually prevented it from achieving this goal.

The film focuses on the story of the 2nd Corps of the Polish Army, from the beginning of the war to the immediate post-war period. The army was created in the wake of the German invasion of the Soviet Union in 1941. It was mainly recruited from Poles who had survived imprisonment in the Soviet gulags in Siberia. They were sent there in massive numbers during the Soviet occupation of eastern Poland as a method of de-Polonization of those territories in the period 1939–41. It was a process parallel to the extermination of the Polish intelligentsia in Katyn and other locations. Together with the 2nd Corps, a large number of former Polish political prisoners, including women and children, escaped Soviet territory, the 'inhuman land' as it was often called.[47] The army was moved from the central part of the Soviet Union through the Middle East to finally join the European war theatre in Italy in spring 1944. Its most spectacular military achievement was its noted role in the capture of Monte Cassino, as well as the liberation of the north-eastern parts of Italy, which forms the central focus of the film.

The original version of the film gave a reasonably reliable account of this history of the army, as well as the fate of Poles during the Second World War. It consisted of documentary parts, captured by the film unit during the military actions, as well as a fictional plot which was to provide the film with a coherent melodramatic story. The plot structure clearly resembles Rossellini's film *La nave bianca* (*The White Ship*, 1941), in using the story of two lovers as a frame to narrate the tragic proceedings of the war.

Inevitably, the film touched upon the negative role of the Soviet Union. The Soviet invasion of Poland in the wake of the Hitler–Stalin Pact was referred to in terms of 'stabbing Poland in the back', along with other difficult aspects of Polish–Soviet relations during the war. However, the most controversial facts at that time, such as the Katyn massacre, were not mentioned at all. *La grande strada* is the only feature film representing the Polish contribution to the battle against Nazi Germany in Italy, as well as

Figure 2.1. Still image from the film *The Great Way* (Michal Waszynski, 1946/1948). The scene shows people in Bologna cheering the Polish Army after liberating the city. This sequence, along with other major geopolitical references, was erased from the Italian version of the film. (Courtesy of National Film Archive, Audiovisual Institute)

the march of some 100,000 Poles from Siberia through the Middle East to northern Italy. Further to that, no other Polish film presented Soviet aggression in Poland until the fall of communism, almost half a century later.

However, the film has remained almost unknown. In Poland, for obvious reasons, there was no official release except for singular screenings, and even then only after the fall of communism, over forty years after its production. Since the Polish version was kept away from official distribution, the film survived intact in terms of censorship interventions. Conversely, the Italian version's release was delayed and restricted after having undergone a significant series of censorship changes (revisions), and yet the film remained 'almost unknown, released imperceptibly, seen by very few'.[48] The only trace of the film's reception is dated 1952, four years after its initial submission to the censorship board.[49] For years, the Italian version was considered lost, and then a copy was discovered in 2014.[50] Comparison of the two versions of the film shows the degrees of contention between the producers of the film and the Italian censorship board. The Italian version's plot was

Figure 2.2. The crew of the film *The Great Way* during shooting at a
film studio in Rome, 1946. The central figure sitting in the first row is
the commander of the Polish 2nd Corps, General Władysław Anders
(in the military beret), with Michal Waszynski sitting to his right
(under the camera). Author: Felicjan Maliniak. Anna Maria Anders
Collection. (Courtesy of National Film Archive, Audiovisual Institute)

significantly distorted. As such, the differences between the two versions
create a peculiar case, one that showcases the limits of what was politically
acceptable in post-war Italy—both the anti-Soviet aspects of the film as
well as its geopolitical references were eliminated.

The Polish version of the film continuously refers to Polish Lwów (now
Lviv in Ukraine), a disputed Polish-Ukrainian city annexed by the Soviet
Union in the wake of the Yalta agreement. Either by the recurrent dialogue
motif of coming back to 'our Polish Lwów', through flashbacks to pre-war
times, or via intradiegetic performances of the famous song 'Tylko we
Lwowie!' ('Only in Lwów!'), the city is one of the central focuses of the plot.
In the Italian version, the disputed city is replaced by Lublin. The latter city
was not only neutral in terms of post-war territorial changes but was also
known as the seat of the puppet government installed in Poland by Moscow
in 1944, prior to the liberation of Warsaw. It is easy to see how this change
could be taken as legitimizing the communist government in Poland.

All references to the Soviet annexation of eastern Poland after the
17 September 1939 invasion, as well as to the repressive atmosphere under

Soviet occupation, were erased in the Italian version. The Polish element of the plot is situated during the German occupation, which creates a significant incongruence in the plot as well as in the way the army's history was narrated (an illogical sudden transfer of the plot from a German concentration camp to Soviet Siberia). In order to execute this change, some sequences had to be reshot, swapping the NKVD officers and Red Army soldiers for Gestapo and Wehrmacht soldiers. A series of minor changes and erasures indicate a political motivation as well (the commander of the 2nd Corps, the final dialogue alluding to a further fight for a sovereign and independent Poland, and the shots of the liberation of Bologna and Ancona by Polish troops are absent in the Italian version). These changes made for a completely different film, and only at this stage, after eliminating any reference questionable to the interests of Italian–Soviet diplomacy, was the film made available to the public. At that time, though, in the early fifties, no one was really interested in war stories, and the film passed unnoticed by the audience.

Examination of the documents from the Italian archives adds evidence to the impediment of the film by Italian political circles, with a crucial role played by Andreotti himself, among others. The negative approach to the Soviet Union is the most feasible reason for this institutional censorship. The core of the institutional objection to the film lies in denying it the status of Italian nationality, necessary to obtain tax relief and inclusion in obligatory programming. Without this, the film was effectively excluded from commercial circulation. The efforts to release *La grande strada* continued from 1947 until 1952. A memorandum dated 12 November 1950 noticed the peculiar situation of the motion picture:

> a film produced by an Italian company, integrally shot in Italy, recognized by the Government as a film of Italian origins, is declined any governmental measures. The film is not even included in obligatory programming, which means it is treated as a foreign production, imported to Italy. Whereas, on the other hand, in order to export the film, it should undergo procedures as an Italian product.[51]

Later in the text, discerning the film's 'anti-communist attitude', the anonymous author of the memorandum wonders about 'the incomprehensible treatment of the film, from the political point of view', which 'today is of exceptional actuality'.[52] It is worth considering the 'incomprehensible treatment of the film' as a deliberate political calculation. It is probably the best cinematic example of the application of Italian politics and diplomacy with regard to the Soviet Union, as postulated by the Italian ambassador in Moscow and by De Gasperi. Since this case was outside the interests of any powerful group in Italy, no one was concerned or willing to decipher the political agenda behind this censorship. I suspect more similar examples are yet to be found and examined.

Conclusion

The problem of the relationship between Italian film culture and the Soviet Union equals that of a black box. When no one challenges a black box and its mechanism, as Bruno Latour notices, it becomes invisible with time and acquires the status of fact, 'an indisputable assertion'.[53] Opening a black box means revisiting a hidden, invisible mechanism that governs the way a certain phenomenon is understood.

Any proper assessment of the impact of philosovietism requires coming to terms with the treatment of the Soviet Union in the field of culture. This is a challenge, especially in Europe, a region that holds different, often contradictory memories and experiences concerning the role the Soviet Union played throughout the twentieth century. Currently, the polemics over history and its actual implication in the European context have been tragically updated by the war in Ukraine. It is not only a war over disputed territories but over the status of Putin's Russia in the world and its legitimacy to establish an East European order. Those claims are not dissimilar to the ones postulated by Stalin in Yalta, in 1945. Both Putin and Stalin have questioned the sovereignty of Eastern European states, reducing their status to that of a buffer zone. In the wake of the Second World War, the West went along with those unjustified claims. In today's war, the subjectivity of Eastern Europe is at stake as well. Hence, I submit to Marsha Siefert's attempt 'to give the East a place in the elaboration and critique of the concept of European Cold War Culture'.[54] In this sense, I find the philosovietic mode of film censorship to be a problem of the responsibility of film culture with regards to geopolitical and sociopolitical issues. It contributed, to a certain extent, to a legitimization of Soviet totalitarian hegemony in Eastern Europe, resulting in violence, injustice and illiberalism. Repressing representations of the negative aspects of the Soviet regime, along with suppression of any form of criticism of the same, was not only an offence to artistic freedom but a way of turning a blind eye towards totalitarianism and its victims.

Acknowledgement

This chapter was funded by the National Science Centre in Poland, under the research project: 'Philosovietism in Post-Fascist Italian Film Culture', no. UMO-2019/32/C/HS2/00536.

Notes

1   [Anon.], 'Rifiutano la propria voce a un documentario anticomunista', *L'Unità*, 11 February 1950: 2. All translations from Italian are the author's own.

2   On the censorship in Italy, see Guido Bonsaver (ed.), *Culture, Censorship and the State in Twentieth-Century Italy* (New York: Routledge, 2005); specifically on the censorship in Italian cinema, see Daniela Treveri Gennari, *Post-War Italian Cinema: American Interventions, Vatican Interests* (New York: Routledge, 2009); Tomaso Subini, *La via italiana alla pornografia: cattolicesimo, sessualità e cinema (1948–1986)* (Firenze: Le Monnier, 2021). For a more comprehensive bibliography on the subject, see Francesca Meschino, 'Bibliografia', in *Cinecensura: 100 anni di revisione cinematografica in Italia*, http://cinecensura.com/wp-content/uploads/2014/06/Bibliografia.pdf.

3   See David Forgacs, 'How Exceptional Were Culture–State Relations in Twentieth-Century Italy?', in Bonsaver, *Culture, Censorship and the State in Twentieth-Century Italy*, pp. 9–21 (p. 11).

4   Ibid., p. 12.

5   See Treveri Gennari, *Post-War Italian Cinema*.

6   Ibid.

7   Ibid., p. 15.

8   Stephen Gundle, *Between Hollywood and Moscow: The Italian Communists and the Challenge of Mass Culture, 1943–1991* (Durham & London: Duke University Press, 2000), p. 42.

9   Umberto Barbaro, 'I boy-scouts contro la verità: L'Azione Cattolica vuol fare applicare al nostro cinema l'americano "codice degli imbecilli"', *L'Unità*, 15 January 1948: 2.

10 [Anon.], 'I registi italiani denunciano l'imbavagliamento del nostro cinema', *L'Unità*, 10 December 1947: 1.

11 For a more detailed analysis of the Italian communist press debate on cinema, see Gianluca Fantoni, *Italy through the Red Lens: Italian Politics and Society in Communist Propaganda Films (1946–79)* (London: Palgrave Macmillan, 2021).

12 Gundle, *Between Hollywood and Moscow*, p. 50.

13 Ibid., pp. 195–96.

14 Fantoni, *Italy through the Red Lens*, p. 30.

15 Mino Argentieri, *La censura nel cinema italiano* (Roma: Editori Riuniti, 1974), p. 14.

16 Ibid., p. 85.

17 Franco Vigni, 'Censura a largo spettro', in Luciano De Giusti (ed.), *Storia del cinema italiano*, vol. 8: *1949/1953* (Venezia: Marsilio Edizioni, 2003), pp. 64–79 (p. 72).

18 [Anon.], 'Offensiva del maccartismo contro il cinema italiano', *Rinascita* 8–9, 17 September 1953: 3.

19 Ibid.

20 Gian Piero Brunetta, *The History of Italian cinema: A Guide to Italian Film from Its Origins to the Twenty-First Century* (Princeton: Princeton University Press, 2009), p. 109.

21 Ibid., p. 111.

22 Carlo Lizzani, 'L'Italia deve avere il suo cinema', *Politecnico*, 13 October 1945: 3.

23 Renzo Renzi, 'Sciolti dal "Giuramento"', Guido Aristarco, *Sciolti dal giuramento. Il dibattito critico-ideologico sul cinema negli anni Cinquanta* (Bari: Dedalo libri, 1981), pp. 72–80 (pp. 72–74).

24 Fantoni, *Italy through the Red Lens*, p. 21.

25 See Roberto Morozzo Della Rocca, *La politica estera italiana e l'Unione Sovietica (1944–1948)* (Roma: La Goiliardica, 1985); Mario Del Pero, 'The United States and "Psychological Warfare" in Italy, 1948–1955', *Journal of American History* 87.4 (2001): 1304–34.

26 Morozzo Della Rocca, *La politica estera italiana*, p. 19.

27 Giulio Andreotti, *L'URSS vista da vicino* (Milano: Rizzoli, 1988), p. 8.

28 Ibid., p. 12.

29 Ibid., pp. 16, 24.

30 Morozzo Della Rocca, *La politica estera italiana e l'Unione Sovietica*, pp. 13–14, 16–17.

31 Ibid, pp. 157, 88.

32 Ibid., p. 89.

33 Mario Del Pero, 'The United States and "Psychological Warfare" in Italy, 1948–1955', *Journal of American History* 87.4 (2001): 1304–34 (pp. 1316, 1317).

34 Ibid., p. 1326.

35 Ibid., p. 1333.

36 See Gian Piero Brunetta, *L'isola che non c'è: viaggi nel cinema italiano che non vedremmo mai* (Bologna: Cineteca di Bologna, 2015).

37 Archivio Revisione Cinematografica della Direzione Generale Cinema, Ministero dei Beni e delle Attività Culturali e del Turismo, Rome (henceforth ARC), in *Cinecensura database*, http://cinecensura.com/wp-content/uploads/2019/07/L_uomo-dalla-croce -2^-Edizione.pdf.

38 ARC, *I peggiori anni della nostra vita* file, in *Cinecensura database*, http://cinecensura. com/politica/i-peggiori-anni-della-nostra-vita/.

39 See Roberto Curti and Alessio Di Rocco, *Visioni proibite: i film vietati dalla censura italiana (1947–1968)* (Torino: Lindau, 2014).

40 ARC, in *Cinecensura database*, http://cinecensura.com/wp-content/uploads/2019/08/ Contro-l_Italia-Giuseppe-Bramini-1954.pdf.

41 See Tati Sanguinetti, *La rabbia: Documentary Film*, Raro Video 2008; Karol Jóźwiak, 'Pasolini-Guareschi: poetycka wściekłość i jej dalsze reperkusje', *Kwartalnik filmowy* 104.4 (2018): 45–61.

42 Bertrand Tavernier, 'Mon ami Vittorio Cottafavi', *L'Unità*, 20 December 1998: 19.

43 [Anon.], Revisione cinematografica preventiva, Archivio Centrale dello Stato, Rome (henceforth ACS), *Sangue sul Don* file, MS, 1953.

44 See Adriano Aprà, Giulio Bursi and Simone Starace (eds), *Ai poeti non si spara: Vittorio Cottafavi tra cinema e televisione* (Bologna: Cineteca di Bologna, 2010).

45 Ermanno Olmi, 'Quando la sinistra mi impediva di lavorare', *Corriere della sera*, 9 July 2005: 36. The story of this failed film production is described in Brunetta, *L'isola che non c'è*, pp. 228–29.

46 I discuss this film in detail in the article 'What Are We Fighting For? Michal Waszynski's Italian-Polish Films on the Second World War', *Journal of Italian Cinema and Media Studies* 11.3–4 (2023): 581–99.

47 It is worth mentioning that mainly thanks to the stubbornness of this army's commanders, the Soviet mass killings of Poles were brought to light and investigated

after the war. See Józef Czapski, *Inhuman Land: Searching for the Truth in Soviet Russia, 1941–1942* (New York: New York Review Books, 2018).

48 Roberto Chitti and Roberto Poppi (eds), *Dizionario del cinema italiano: dal 1945 al 1959* (Roma: Gremese Editore, 2000), p. 179.

49 Ibid.

50 Simona Casonato, 'Storia del ritrovamento della versione italiana', *Alias*, 14 November 2015: 4.

51 [Anon.], Revisione cinematografica preventiva, ACS, *La grande strada* file, MS, 1950.

52 Ibid.

53 Bruno Latour, *Science in Action: How to Follow Scientists and Engineers through Society* (Cambridge, MA: Harvard University Press, 1987), p. 23.

54 Marsha Siefert, 'East European Cold War Culture(s): Alterities, Commonalities, and Film Industries', in Anette Vowinckel, Marcus M. Payk and Thomas Lindenberger (eds), *Cold War Cultures: Perspectives on Eastern and Western European Societies* (New York: Berghan Books, 2012), pp. 23–54 (p. 24).

3

Censorship of Foreign Films in People's Poland in the Late 1960s and Early 1970s: A Case Study of Films about Hippie Subculture

Konrad Klejsa

Notwithstanding minor changes across decades, the cultural policy of the People's Republic of Poland (hereafter PRP) and other Soviet Bloc countries was characterized by the rationing of access to products made in capitalist countries.[1] If cultural texts produced in capitalist countries reached Polish audiences at all, they usually did so in limited circulation and with a significant delay. The same was true of many American and West European films related to hippie subculture, both avant-garde films created within the counterculture movement and commercial feature films produced by the Hollywood film industry.[2] This chapter will focus on the latter phenomenon: the limited presence of commercial films about hippie subculture in Polish cinemas of the late 1960s and early 1970s.

Addressing the issue of foreign film censorship in a certain territory demands attention to its specificity in relation to natively produced films. Most of all, the study of the censorship of foreign cultural texts evokes a 'basic' understanding of censorship, as actions aimed at limiting access to the specific text or part of it. While the basic sources for the study of the censorship of Polish films are transcripts of various bodies influencing

Konrad Klejsa, "Censorship of Foreign Films in People's Poland in the Late 1960s and Early 1970s: A Case Study of Films about Hippie Subculture" in: *The Screen Censorship Companion: Critical Explorations in the Control of Film and Screen Media*. University of Exeter Press (2024). © Konrad Klejsa. DOI: 10.47788/MWLP4097 the work's creation, the most important sources regarding the censorship of foreign films in the PRP are administrative decisions concerning distribution. This leads to the conclusion that research on foreign film censorship should concentrate on the activity of Główny Urząd Kontroli Prasy, Publikacji i Widowisk (the Main Office for the Control of Press, Publications and Performances, hereafter MOC).[3] However, such a study cannot be limited to this single institution only: it is also necessary to understand those principles of the functioning of the film import and distribution system that were not directly connected with the censorship office.[4] In relation to foreign cultural products, the very decision of whether 'to buy or not to buy' may bear traces of censorship thinking—although, of course, not all films which have not been released are to be considered forbidden content. Financial considerations may have played a crucial role, as the substantial problem for exchanges with capitalist states was the chronic lack of foreign currency. In practice, however, we usually have only limited data to indicate that the decision not to purchase a film was influenced by economic reasons, as the archival financial reports of the main institution responsible for film matters in the PRP of the 1960s and 1970s, Naczelny Zarząd Kinematografii (the Chief Office for Film Culture, hereafter COFC), did not detail activities that might have been considered but were not undertaken.

Structures of Foreign Film Censorship in People's Poland

To date, there has been no study analysing the censorship of foreign films in the PRP. Nor has this censorship been described by the most valuable source of knowledge about censorship in the PRP: the list of banned content, a kind of 'Bible of the MOC'. Extensive fragments of this list were handwritten clandestinely by one of the employees of the Krakow branch of the Office, and published in Great Britain after his escape to the West in 1977. A footnote to that edition is crucial to the subject matter of this chapter: there is 'no list of foreign films. The reason for this I do not know. Most probably, the list was not needed in the field offices of the MOC, since the screenings took place in the Warsaw headquarters.'[5] The author was right: data on the censorship of foreign films are available only in archival documentation, preserved in the Archive of Modern Records in Warsaw.

During the communist dictatorship, the MOC itself had a monopoly on information about censorship, publishing internal bulletins which reported on current activities. These bulletins were classified as 'strictly confidential'. With no more than 100 prints, sent directly to governmental and Party officials, they were not accessible in any library. Most of these bulletins were daily reports, describing principally 'interventions' in newspapers and magazines. Annual reports, on the other hand, usually contained quantitative data, in particular how many texts of different sorts (including films) were censored each year, and which reasons for censorship were dominant.

The MOC's approval had to be obtained for every film that was to be publicly shown in Poland. Censorship approval—referred to as a 'passport' or 'visa'—was usually valid nationwide for three years; however, it could be revoked at any time. Within the MOC, films were handled by a separate unit, the Department of Performances.[6] In 1974, it had twenty employees, about half of whom were responsible for film-related matters.[7] The rest were handling broadly defined 'stage' performances, including theatre, student cabarets or song contests, as well as radio programmes (excluding news). The MOC's regional branches did not feature a similar structure, although their employees were also sometimes charged with tasks related to film. In the 1960s and 1970s, the activity of local censorship in relation to film culture was limited to issuing permission for ephemeral prints, like programmes prepared by local film clubs.

Of particular interest are the internal bulletins (called *Przegląd*, meaning '*Review*') issued exclusively by the MOC's Department of Performances every two, three or six months from 1967 until 1976. They are a valuable source for researchers as they list all films and television programmes which were denied the permit, along with explanations for each decision written anonymously. Each newsletter ranged from thirty to seventy pages. The material in different issues is organized differently, with some bulletins beginning with a description of interventions in theatrical performances. However, a separate section on 'foreign film' appears in every *Review*.

Censorship 'interventions' were described as either 'total', when the dissemination of a particular film was prohibited wholesale, or, much more often, 'partial'. In the case of films, partial interventions were usually specified as meaning either 'interference with the image' or 'interference with the text'; the latter implied changes to the translation. Only occasionally can one come across information about the timecode of a deleted shot or the number of a modified scene. Bulletins may mention a scene, but do so in a manner reminiscent of film criticism. Typically, they use expressions like 'at some point in the first part of the film', or 'in one of the scenes towards the end of the film'.

The MOC assessments were the final stage of control of foreign films. Earlier decisions were made within the COFC, which had a monopoly not only on film production, but also on film distribution, managed by the internal unit called Centrala Wynajmu Filmów, the Film Rental Office (FRO). To serve this cause, from 1956 onwards, the FRO appointed annually an advisory body, Filmowa Rada Repertuarowa (Cinema Programming Council, CPC), which consisted of about thirty members, mainly film critics. However, the head or deputy-head of CPC was usually a member of the communist Polska Zjednoczona Partia Robotnicza (Polish United Workers' Party). The CPC members watched films either during closed screenings in Warsaw, or at foreign film festivals—the latter case was a privilege, as the PRP authorities treated travel abroad, especially to a capitalist country, as an extraordinary activity which had to be approved by various institutions. Then, the Council decided which films were to be recommended for cinema release.[8]

The CPC issued its own internal bulletin, which appeared monthly, bi-monthly, sometimes quarterly or bi-annually.[9] Each bulletin bears a similar structure. First, there is a list of all the recommended films, followed by the list of those which were rejected. Then, the register of suggested Polish titles of accepted films appears, and the list of films which the Council wishes to see in the future. Although none of this information is supplemented by any justification, they are a valuable source of data, as the list of films recommended by the CPC is quite extensive, even considering the exclusion of data from missing issues. In the years under study, around 20% of all titles with the CPC recommendation were never released in the PRP—the majority of them due to the MOC's ban.

Predominantly, films rejected by the CPC were not considered by the censorship office. However, the FRO had the right to submit a certain film to the MOC despite the Council's negative opinion of it.[10] In some cases, as the political situation changed, films which had been rejected by censors were submitted again after some time and received a positive opinion the second time around. Both the CPC and MOC also had the right to suggest distribution coverage: wide distribution with many copies, limited release across a network of film clubs, or occasional screenings at programmes organized by embassies, such as Week of French Cinema. However, even if the film was actually bought, its release might have been stopped by the MOC. In addition, even a film accepted by the censorship office could be withdrawn from distribution at any time by the decision of the Central Committee of the Communist Party.[11]

The MOC's power to challenge the CPC's recommendations produced a natural conflict between the two institutions. That conflict is attested to by the annual reports of the MOC's Department of Performances. There, the censors repeat accusations about the FRO's mismanagement: in the years prior to 1969, guided by the decisions of the CPC, the FRO bought licences for several films before they were approved by censorship. The charge was serious: in the PRP, there were heavy penalties for misappropriation of state assets, especially foreign currency. It seems, however, that the dispute between the MOC and CPC was also of a more partisan nature. In fact, several MOC reports inform that the fateful unreleased films were qualified for purchase during the CPC's trips to foreign film festivals.[12] The FRO learned a lesson from these complaints and, from 1970, MOC staff joined CPC teams abroad.[13] As it turned out, the problem of buying films which were later blocked by censors miraculously disappeared.[14]

Unlike the explanations for the CPC's recommendations, the MOC censorship notes on foreign films are partially known. Although there are no minutes of discussions and no opinions on the films which were given a permit, the *Review* includes justifications for the decisions regarding films whose release was not allowed.

Enemies of Affluent Society: Hippies, Anarchists, Perverts and Drug Addicts

Between 1968 and 1972, four counterculture-related films were not approved by the CPC: Roger Corman's *The Trip* (1967), Jack O'Connell's *Revolution* (1968), Hy Averback's *I Love You, Alice B. Toklas!* (1968) and Paul Williams's *The Revolutionary* (1970). The CPC listed two additional films—Robert Kramer's *Ice* (1970) and Ralph Bakshi's *Fritz the Cat* (1972)—as worth seeing in the future. There is no trace of these titles in the subsequent issues of the bulletin and none of these films were released in the PRP.[15]

The MOC's reports on foreign films almost always explain whether the rejection was caused by political, ideological or moral reasons—the latter sometimes being referred to as 'educational'. Among the former category of films, surprisingly many came from other Soviet Bloc countries. They included especially those which tackled the issue of reckoning with Stalinism or those which were critical of certain aspects of everyday life in a socialist state. With respect to Western films, most censorship interferences were connected to moral accusations and often ended at partial interference, for example with the cutting out of a particular scene. Not only explicit sexual content, which will be discussed later, but also scenes showing the affluence of capitalist societies were considered as a threat to public morality.

The censors of the PRP saw in American films an extension of the USA's soft power, manifested in the promise of affluence. As an internal MOC report from June 1969 described:

> American film in our conditions, when watched en masse, intensifies in the viewer the desire to possess, ignites longings and dreams to multiply one's own private property, and gives rise to a consumerist attitude to life. The flats we see are luxurious, each with a colour television, and kitchens equipped with appliances we would not even know how to use.[16]

Similar formulations are repeated in the justifications for individual films. For example, in the assessment of *The Graduate* (1967, Mike Nichols) dating from 1969, we read that the film allegedly 'advertises the luxurious conditions existing in the USA'.[17] Attention is drawn to the protagonist, who 'gets a modern sports car after graduating from high school'.

If criticisms of 'bourgeois' affluence and the rejection of welfare society were the only features of the hippie subculture, it probably could have become an ideal ally for Marxists from behind the Iron Curtain. However, the other manifestations of the hippie lifestyle, like free love, drug use and pacifism, were unacceptable to the authorities of the PRP. For example, the annual report for 1970 stated:

> the censor's reservations were aroused especially by films popularising the Maoist movement in Western countries, anarchic youth negating all order, and hippie customs and philosophy. Objections were also aroused by images or fragments of images apotheosising rape, violence and propagating sexual promiscuity and exploitation.[18]

Hippieism itself was treated as an example of the decadence and moral decay of Western societies. The activities of the leftist student movements in Western Europe were presented in a similar way. The Polish state, in which power was held by a Party built on the principles of Leninism, condemned radical factions of Marxism like Trotskyism or Maoism with particular fervour. Both hippieism and left-wing activism were described in socio-logical analyses published in Poland at that time as dangerous manifesta-tions of 'revisionism'. According to the Party's accepted interpretation, they were regarded as 'an apparently progressive phenomenon, directed against the policy of the ruling classes, but at the same time controlled by various pseudo-revolutionaries who harm the cause'.[19]

This line of thinking may be clearly seen in the justifications for censorship. For example, the 1970 American film *The Strawberry Statement*, directed by Stuart Hagmann, was stopped on the grounds of 'propagating anarchist ideology and excessively exposing the popularity of Mao Tse Tung'.[20] The views of the filmmakers could also constitute a reason for rejection. In the justification for the rejection of the film *Loin du Vietnam* (France, 1967), Claude Lelouch, Jean-Luc Godard and Alain Resnais—three of the directors of the novellas which make up the film—were described as 'bourgeois left-wing filmmakers'.[21]

As is well known, Hollywood began to produce films about Vietnam only after the conflict ended.[22] However, in many American films of the time, the subject of Vietnam appears as a secondary theme, for example through a motif of dodging the draft. Perhaps surprisingly, it is only partially correct to assume that films using this plot point would be considered beneficial from the point of view of the political interests of the PRP. A case in point is the 1969 Canadian film *Explosion*, directed by Jules Bricken, which was prevented from being screened by the MOC. Its protagonist

> decided to evade serving in the army and participating in the Vietnam War. On the surface, it would seem that this film should not raise any political objections. However, the lifestyle he leads after running away from home can only provoke disgust in the viewer for an individual who kills [...] a policeman in the performance of his duties.[23]

The murder of a law enforcement officer, even one serving the capitalist state, completely discredited the noble protagonist's motivations in the eyes of the censors.

In 1970, the censors discussed yet another non-American film with hippie themes. The justification for rejecting Johan Bergenstråhle's *Made in Sweden* (1969) clearly shows the censors' trouble with the subject: 'The film contains some positive elements, exposing modern capitalism. But that is not the point of the film. [...] The antidote to all the world's troubles is very simple: a little beauty, a lot of sex, poetry and the hippie revolution is ready.'[24] This is where the justification ends. Presumably, the ironic evaluation indicating the naivety of the narrative concept is simultaneously lined with a certain conviction of its attractiveness.

The wording 'a lot of sex' in the cited justification is rather mild when compared with the MOC's other references to erotic scenes, which are described as 'gross', 'promiscuous' or 'vulgar'. The Polish censors' attitude to sexuality is best reflected in the justification for rejecting Paul Mazursky's *Bob & Carol & Ted & Alice* (1969). 'This film', the justification reads, 'promotes the impudicity of relations between representatives of both sexes, which means crossing out the concept of shamefulness of intimate life.'[25] In the PRP, the belief that the 'personal is political', not to mention the slogans of the sexual revolution, could not be publicly manifested.

Not surprisingly, the MOC rejected the feature-length documentary which is referred to in the documentation as '*Wodstock*' (misspelling both the title of the film and the name of the town). The censors were particularly disturbed by scenes which recorded the opinions of local residents about the gathering. The authors of the *Review* seem concerned: 'There are also voices of approval, including that of the chief of police.' It is significant that this particular statement was singled out from among the many people speaking in the film.[26] Apparently, this was taken to be excessive, suggesting a leniency on the part of Western law enforcement officials towards youth culture. However, the main part of the argument is about the positive depiction of drugs, 'from marijuana to powerful hallucinatory drugs'.[27]

The censors' assessment of Miloš Forman's *Taking Off* (1971) is similar. The justification for the rejection of the film begins: 'The main accusation against the film is the filmmaker's lenient or even kind attitude to the phenomenon of drug addiction, specifically to the smoking of marijuana joints.'[28] The censor equates smoking a joint with drug addiction—had Forman made a film warning against the effects of smoking marijuana, he might have had some chance with the Polish censors. On the contrary, the film's protagonists learn that

> smoking marijuana is not a negative phenomenon. They are given a thorough lesson by a young man who has had a lot of practice in this area. After the 'lesson' an interesting card game begins—whoever loses, has to take off a part of his clothes. [...] Both the 'lesson' and the game are attended by the parents of the girl they were looking for. After a long absence, she returns home with a boy she has met in the meantime.[29]

The censorship opinion contains no further justification, as if the decision to prohibit the film's distribution was self-evident in light of the description of the 'lesson' scene.

Yet another film made in the USA by a European director, *Zabriskie Point* (1972) directed by Michelangelo Antonioni, was also banned. A significant part of the justification is taken up by a summary of the film:

> A student kills a policeman with a pistol during a riot, and then takes a long flight over desert terrain in a stolen plane. During the flight he notices a car driven by a beautiful young girl who, without her father's knowledge, has gone on a long rally over the desert roads.[30]

In this summary, the censor has made three errors. First, it is not clear on what basis it was concluded that the student in fact takes part in the student strike: admittedly, he is present at the political rally but he then leaves, bored. Second, it is not at all certain that the student kills the policeman. This is Antonioni's famous ambiguity: although the protagonist raises the gun, it is possible that the shot was fired earlier from another direction. Third, and finally, we cannot make any judgements about the family of the female protagonist—the man whom the censor considered to be the girl's father is her superior. A similar misunderstanding also applies to the erotic scenes, which were a real problem for the censor. They write: 'For more than fifteen minutes we watch not only a very naturalistic sexual close-up of the characters in the film, but at the same time we see on very close and distant planes different couples as well as groups having sexual intercourse in various configurations and arrangements.'[31]

It is noteworthy that this description refers to Antonioni's intention, which was indeed the portrayal of a monumental collective orgy scene, rather than to the poetic étude which was included in the film.[32] Nevertheless, the censor allowed the film to enter limited distribution 'after interventions in the initial part of the film and the removal of the most drastic erotic shots'.[33]

Easy Rider's Bumpy Road to Polish Screens

The source material from the period between 1968 and 1972 shows that, among English-language films with a hippie theme, the MOC considered only one other film worthy of devoting more than the most cursory consideration: *Easy Rider* (1969), directed by Dennis Hopper. From the MOC's *Review*, we know that the CPC accepted *Easy Rider* unanimously and recommended it as 'an outstanding work of art, but a profound and harrowing portrayal of the rationale of hippies and the hostility of those around them'.[34]

The justification for the decision regarding *Easy Rider* written by the censorship office employee is longer than usual. In the introduction, the author admits that the film 'departs from the previous patterns of showing the complex issues of the hippie world', as the characters 'just want to be themselves, to be different, to have the right to their own personality' and are presented as 'nice and decent boys who arouse the viewer's sincere sympathy from the first to the last shot in the film'.[35] At the end of the assessment, the censor focuses on the 'New Orleans sequence', featuring 'orgies together in the cemetery, among the tombs'.[36] This, as it will turn out later, was considered completely unacceptable. Interestingly, the censor repeatedly identifies the protagonists as hippies, even though they share only the subculture's accepting attitude to free sex and drugs. In fact, in one scene, they visit a true hippie commune and speak about it with slight contempt. However, the censor concludes:

> In portraying the hippie world, the authors of the film undoubtedly had in mind the popularization of the movement and the necessity to defend it against its increasingly numerous opponents. The apotheosis of the movement, the indication of intellectual superiority and the moral reasons expressed by the hippies led the Office to question the film as a whole.[37]

The subsequent fate of *Easy Rider* in the PRP is rather difficult to reconstruct. In 1977, the MOC rejected the state television network's request for permission to broadcast Hopper's film due, once again, to the presentation of the hippie movement in a positive light.[38] The network once again requested permission in 1979, which occasioned a memo describing *Easy Rider* as a work that was not allowed to be broadcast because it 'popularized drug addiction, contained erotic scenes taking place in a cemetery'.[39] Finally, a programming schedule shows that the film's broadcast was planned for 19 December 1981. However, this broadcast did not take place due to the imposition of martial law six days earlier. As a result, almost until Christmas, all electronic media broadcast mainly the official messages of the ruling junta. Martial law was formally in place until mid-1983, and surprisingly, it was during this period that *Easy Rider* was finally broadcast on state television on 13 May 1982.

The reasons for this decision are not known. Three explanations are possible. Perhaps it was influenced by the desire to ease social tensions by proposing an attractive television schedule, albeit one restricted solely to a pool of films which had already been purchased—after the introduction of martial law, the USA and some Western countries responded with an embargo on trade with Poland.[40] It is also possible that there was a threat of the licence expiring, which could have led to a serious charge of embezzlement of public funds being brought against the television management authorities of the time. Most likely, however, the censors agreed to the screening as American protest movements had already become history and might be used as a pretext to criticize Western culture. Therefore, Hopper's film might have been used to discredit, as one reviewer wrote immediately after the television broadcast, 'the darkest sides of the American provincial mentality. A mentality that smacks of the Middle Ages and the Inquisition.'[41] However, even in this context, *Easy Rider* still could not be fully accepted by the authorities. According to one account, the scene in the cemetery was cut out.[42] It was perhaps also significant that the film was broadcast exactly one year after the failed assassination attempt on Pope John Paul II, who was, at the time, the spiritual leader for most Poles.

Conclusion

Censorship of foreign films in the People's Republic of Poland was strongly linked to the current needs of foreign policy—subordination to the USSR and criticism of capitalism, symbolized by the USA—but also rooted in the social norms characteristic of a society in which about 90% of the citizens, including some Communist Party members, considered themselves Catholics. Films about hippieism were considered doubly dangerous: they portrayed a non-orthodox version of Marxist ideology and promoted a lifestyle deemed unacceptable by the leaders of the Communist Party. For these reasons, features about rebellious youth were a rare case of films rejected for both political-ideological and moral-educational reasons.

The analysis presented here proves that understanding the history of a country's film culture demands that attention be paid not only to the films produced within its borders, and not only to the films distributed in a given territory at a given time, but also to those films which were not released. The fact that certain films known in one country remained unknown to audiences in another creates a potential comparative context. As long as we do not examine what remained hidden from filmmakers and audiences in certain countries, our judgements about the alleged influences that some filmmakers may have had on others, and our presumptions of the audience's tastes in different countries, will remain incomplete.

Acknowledgement

Konrad Klejsa's research was made possible through a grant from the National Science Centre, Poland (2016/22/E/HS2/00135).

Notes

1   The People's Republic of Poland (or PRP) was the unsovereign state which belonged to the Soviet Union's sphere of influence from the end of the Second World War until the beginning of democratic transformations in 1989.

2   The distinction was made by David E. James, *Allegories of Cinema: American Film in the Sixties* (Princeton: Princeton University Press, 1989).

3   As the communists took power in early 1945, censorship fell under the jurisdiction of an internal unit of the Ministry of Public Security, which also issued so-called passports for film copies. The MOC, reporting directly to the Prime Minister, was established by a decree on 5 July 1946. This institution was abolished only in 1990 on the wave of democratic changes.

4   One can mention the activities of Komisja ds. Kategorii Wiekowych (Commission for Age Classification), which was appointed by the Ministry of Education and had the right to mark films with 12, 15 and 18 age restrictions.

5   Tomasz Strzyżewski, *Wielka księga cenzury PRL w dokumentach* (Warsaw: Prohibita, 2015), p. 91. This translation and all subsequent translations from Polish-language sources are my own.

6   In 1972, the name was changed to the Radio, Television and Performances Unit.

7   According to the annual report for 1974, the average age of those employed in the team was 32–35 years. All of them had higher education. Philological educational backgrounds predominated, along with a few historians and political science graduates. Warsaw, Archiwum Akt Nowych (AAN), collection 'Główny Urząd Kontroli Prasy, Publikacji i Widowisk' (MOC)—*Raport roczny* 1974, file 3301, p. 12. All subsequent archival *Raport roczny* ('Annual report') are from the MOC collection of AAN.

8   Television had its own programming committee, which will not be mentioned here.

9   Some 10% of the bulletins are probably lost to history, as they are not preserved either in the National Film Archive in Warsaw, or in the Film Museum in Lodz.

10 *Przegląd* 1 (1969), AAN, MOC, 3292, p. 20. All subsequent *Przegląd* ('*Review*') are from the MOC collection of AAN.

11 In the period under study there is a mention of one intervention of that kind. It concerned the 1966 film *Wild Angels*, directed by Roger Corman—see *Przegląd* 5 (1969), 2392, p. 250. The reasons for the ban are not revealed.

12 *Raport roczny* (1969), 3300, p. 26.

13 *Raport roczny* (1970), 3300, p. 20.

14 Ibid., p. 15.

15 See: Grzegorz Balski and Konrad Klejsa, 'Watched in PL: Database for Polish Film History', www.ogladanewprl.uni.lodz.pl (consulted on 14 February 2022).

16 AAN, MOC, *Uwagi o pewnych negatywnych tendencjach w programie artystycznym telewizji i repertuarze kin* (1969), 3292, p. 152.

17 *Przegląd* 2 (1969), 3292, p. 68. Eventually, the film was released in 1973.

18 *Raport roczny* (1970), 3300, p. 20.

19 Janusz Janicki, *Niepokoje młodzieży zachodu* (Warsaw: Iskry, 1992), p. 210.

20 *Raport roczny* (1972), 3300, p. 32. For further insights into MOC's evaluations from 1972 see: Marta Fik, 'Z archiwum GUKPPiW (rok 1972)', *Kwartalnik Filmowy* 4 (1993): 178–82.

21 *Przegląd* 3 (1968), 3291, p. 108.

22 One notable exception being the propaganda feature *Green Berets* directed by John Wayne (1968), which was not even considered by the Commission or the MOC.

23 *Przegląd* 4 (1970), 3293, p. 167.

24 Ibid., p. 166.

25 *Przegląd* 3 (1970), 3293, p. 117.

26 *Przegląd* 3 (1971), 3294, p. 66.

27 Ibid.

28 *Przegląd* 1 (1972), 3295, p. 11.

29 Ibid.

30 *Przegląd* 3 (1971), 3294, p. 70.

31 Ibid.

32 Bryan Gindoff, 'Thalberg Didn't Look Happy: With Antonioni at *Zabriskie Point*', *Film Quarterly* 1 (1970): 3–6.

33 *Przegląd* 3 (1971), 3294, p. 70. The film was not released in PRP cinemas.

34 *Przegląd* 1 (1971), 3294, p. 7.

35 Ibid.

36 Ibid., p. 8.

37 Ibid.

38 *Dzienny przegląd ingerencji*, AAN, MOC, 3584.

39 *Nota*, AAN, MOC, 3742.

40 Michał Piepiórka, 'Not Only "Teleranek": (Non)presence of Foreign Films on Polish Television during Martial Law', *Kwartalnik Filmowy* 108 (2019): 71–90 (p. 88).

41 A. Budzyński, '2x Easy Rider', *Antena* 2 (1982): 16.

42 Bogumiła Michalska, 'Teczka kartonowa z klapkami albo Skurczybyk i inni', *Kwartalnik Filmowy* 49–50 (2005): 130–46 (p. 136).

4

Sex, Drugs, Violence and/or Nudity: Differences in Film Age Rating Practices and Rationales in Denmark, France, Japan, Norway and the UK

Elisabeth Staksrud and Marita Eriksen Haugland

Introduction

What constitutes harmful film content for children and young people? In this chapter we study film rating practices in five countries—Denmark, France, Japan, Norway and the UK—comparing how they described, assessed and classified the same films over a six-year period. Our aim is to unfold what differences there are, if any, in their film age ratings. We present a comparative analysis, aiming to identify national differences in ratings, and how the national rating bodies articulate these differences through descriptions of film content.

Why is this important? In democracies, a film rating agency is one of the few (and in some countries, the only) public agencies that can evoke pre-censorship, denying certain groups in the public access to certain media content. As such, this is an often governmental, intrusive practice that needs to be considered carefully in terms of legitimacy. Yet, historically, it has been seen as a rather uncomplicated and undisputed regulatory intervention, with the agencies typically citing the protection of children from

Elisabeth Staksrud and Marita Eriksen Haugland, "Sex, Drugs, Violence and/or Nudity: Differences in Film Age Rating Practices and Rationales in Denmark, France, Japan, Norway and the UK" in: *The Screen Censorship Companion: Critical Explorations in the Control of Film and Screen Media*. University of Exeter Press (2024). © Elisabeth Staksrud and Marita Eriksen Haugland. DOI: 10.47788/FTMX2611 the (potentially) harmful effects of exposure to media content. However, what these harms would be and what kind of content might create a risk of harm is not necessarily an agreed position in research.

In the contemporary narrative, childhood is often seen as a period of danger and risk, and the concern for children's safety has increased.[1] In terms of media and risk, substantial research has been conducted through the decades on what kind of (if any) film content is harmful for children, with research pointing, for example, to aggressive behaviour in children increasing after watching violent films.[2] Much less research has been done on sexual content and harm to children.[3] In addition, the kinds of studies that would definitely prove harm and that look at the long-term effects are notoriously expensive and time-consuming, meaning that these are few and far between.[4]

In addition, age ratings for films can be seen as a product of the culture and country in which they exist, where the appropriate age rating is dependent on cultural norms.[5] This means that any difference in age rating between countries for the same film may help us to understand the cultural differences between countries regarding what is viewed as harmful to children, and how to understand and interpret media content. Comparative research on age rating can further our understanding of media lawmakers and media literacy and education, as it gives an insight into the stability of and differences between rating decisions in different countries.[6]

Furthermore, the risk and harm definitions used by the film rating agencies have implications for free speech, and may be considered a form of censorship. This is especially true if the justifications for ratings are subjective, sometimes moral, judgements, rather than objective risk of harm assessments. We know from research how moral rhetoric on child protection can lead to media policies with questionable legitimacy. Protecting children from perceived media harm can even be used as an effective 'excuse' when seeking to introduce regulation, restrictions and legislation based on other motives such as control of copyright infringement or religious objections.[7] Such processes do not only restrict children's rights to, for example, information, entertainment and participation, but also have implications for and restrict the rights of adults.[8]

Classification cultures can lead to *internal* censorship by the creative industry, where the creators/producers/directors of films change parts of their original work themselves because they know, or presume, that certain parts might not pass censorship or receive the desired classification[9]—an age classification decision can have substantial financial implications, limiting the market potential for any film.

Hence, our present research seeks to contribute to a wider body of research on the regulation of risk, and specifically on perceptions of media-related risk to children in contemporary society. We do this by first identifying all the films (504 in total) that have been rated in all countries during a six-year period (2010–15). We then analyse if and how these films have been rated differently, or not, in the five selected countries, reviewing rating rationales in their original language. Next we examine the various reasons given for the variations in rating by the rating boards themselves, by considering the twenty-seven films with the highest variability in age rating between the countries (operationalized as having four or five different ratings for the same film, ranging from 'allowed for all' to '18 years').[10] Finally, we discuss one concrete example, the rating of the film *The Secret in Their Eyes* (Campanella, 2009) to illustrate how even *similar* rationales and assessments of content can lead to different ratings between countries.

Background and Previous Research

Substantial scholarship exists in the area of film censorship and film classification, ranging from single- and multiple-volume encyclopaedias, through historical and biographical accounts, to case studies on certain countries or themes.[11] Some studies on film censorship and ratings do draw comparisons between countries, but these are typically general in their description, noting, for example, how a certain country is stricter than another, or that a given country has a certain age rating regulatory regime that differs from other countries.[12] When it comes to comparative analyses on film classification decisions and age ratings across countries and regions specifically, there have been only a few.[13] We have only identified one recent peer-reviewed paper that compares age rating decisions across several countries.[14] However, in this paper the authors rely on content measures provided by US organizations (specifically, www.kids-in-mind.com and www.screenit.com) rather than the actual national rating agencies' own assessments and reasons for giving a certain film a certain age rating.

   Against this background, we see the need to consult each of the selected country's rating bureaus, looking at age rating rationales in their original language. Specifically, we seek to identify the stated reasons related to specific film content given by national classification bodies for awarding a film a certain age rating. In doing so we also seek to control for the caveat that the film content descriptions are typically formulated from a US perspective, as stated by Price, Palsson and Gentile:

> all the measures we used are created by US-based organizations. As such the levels of each content measure may be biased toward an American perspective on cultural mores. Ideally, we would construct

content measures based on an aggregation of observations that transcend specific cultural norms.[15]

Only by reviewing the national agencies' own arguments in their own language can we control for the US bias, as 'the US places an enormous amount of weight on profanity and sex, but less weight on violence than the majority of other countries'.[16]

Rationale and Present-Day Rating Systems

Five countries are included in our comparative analysis: Denmark, France, Japan, Norway and the UK. The four European countries were chosen as we believe they represent both similarities (as Northern and Central European democracies) and differences (in terms of regulatory frameworks). Thus, one would expect that age classifications based on an evidence-based consideration of what is perceived to be harmful for children would be analogous and use comparable arguments and explanations. Nonetheless, there are known differences. Denmark and France are both anecdotally considered liberal in relation to media content regulation. Denmark abolished censorship of content for adults as early as 1969 and had a reputation for 'shocking even the French' with their films in the early days of cinema.[17] In contrast, the UK is reputed to have a system that is more restrictive than the rest of Western Europe,[18] with known examples of the film rating agencies in France and the UK classifying the same film with the same age rating but with different subsequent audience responses. For example, *9 Songs* (Winterbottom, 2004) was rated '18', causing outcry among the general public in France for being overly censorious, but there was no discussion at all in the UK.[19] Norway was chosen as a Nordic counterpart to Denmark. The Nordic countries have a long history of cooperation when it comes to ratings, but their rating decisions have not always been the same. Norway has generally been stricter (having retained the right to *ban* films, given higher ratings, and made more and/or longer cuts to the material, in addition to a general ban of pornography) than Denmark.[20] Japan was chosen as a cultural and geographical outlier. It is therefore hypothesized that if there are indeed differences between age rating outputs, Japan's ratings will reflect this because they could potentially be considered products of the culture in which they are created.

The rating systems and regulatory frameworks in effect during the period of our collected corpus differ across the selected countries. Denmark, France and Norway all have state regulation, where rating decisions are made in formal government institutions by publicly appointed servants. The examiners in Denmark and Norway mainly have relevant film and/or pedagogical expertise. In Denmark examiners must be educated in psychology or pedagogy.[21] In France, examiners are again even more diverse, with members separated into categories for 'young people' (aged 18–24), 'experts' (educated in the humanities and child psychology, representatives from the Audiovisual Superior Council (Conseil Supérieur de l'Audiovisuel, CSA), as well as large institutions within medicine, family organizations, 'administrators' (representatives of departments representing education, youth, family, interior and justice) and 'professionals' (appointed by the Department of Culture and various film organizations: critics, directors, producers, exhibitors, distributors, etc.).[22] Japan and the UK practise industry self-regulation, which is financed independently through a fee on examination.[23] In the UK, the British Board of Film Classification (BBFC) comprises a more diverse group of people: from 'journalism, media, research and marketing'.[24] In Japan the film raters are people with 'various professional backgrounds'.[25]

Which type of content is considered potentially harmful for children of different ages (providing the baseline for the rating agencies' work) is typically outlined in the agencies' internal documents and material provided for the general public, and for parental discretion in particular.[26] A summary is provided in Table 4.1.

Denmark is mainly concerned with what is 'frightening', while France mentions 'violence, sexuality, delinquent behaviour, dangerous practices'. Japan outlines eight categories: theme, language, sex, nudity, violence and cruelty, horror and menace, drug use, and criminal behaviour. Norway, like Denmark, gives weight to content that could provoke 'anxiety, arouse unrest

Table 4.1. Rating rationale as explicitly mentioned by the national film classification boards, at the time of classification (2010–2015)

Content descriptors	Denmark	France	Japan	Norway	UK
Atmosphere (frightening/anxiety-inducing content)	x		x	x	x
Violence		x	x	x	x
Sex (and sexuality)		x	x	x	x
Language			x		x
Nudity			x		x
Drug use			x		x
Other (specified as: criminal behaviour, dangerous behaviour, and offensive content relating to race, gender, religion, disability)		x	x		x

or fright' in children, but also outlines sexual and violent content—particularly the kind that 'influences children and adolescents' thoughts, ideas and attitudes'. The UK focuses on general considerations of context, theme, tone and impact, and specific considerations of discrimination, drugs, imitable behaviour, language, nudity, sex, threat and violence (all listed in alphabetical order, not indicating any category as being more important than the others). In sum, in their public assessment documentation, different agencies seem to express their own priorities when outlining how to classify and rate films based on what is considered harmful and/or unsuitable for children. How, and if, these differences are also reflected in the actual age ratings is not known.

Method

To examine possible differences between the film ratings, this study has systematically compiled lists of all the films rated in the five countries, between 1 January 2010 and 31 December 2015. Rating decisions were compared by quantitative analysis based on the full corpus of films rated in all five countries. A six-year period was selected to increase the variation in the sample and to minimize the effect of any trends that could dominate shorter periods.

Collection of rating information

The lists of age ratings for Norway and Denmark were sourced directly from the Norwegian Media Authority (Medietilsynet) and the Danish Media Council (Medierådet). Decisions were provided as lists in Excel and PDF formats respectively. Additional information needed was found in their online, searchable databases,[27] and manually edited into the list of films to be included in the study. Note that this process relies on the official lists or ratings they released. Thus, if for some reason the national rating agency had not routinely processed a film as expected, but still released it, it would not be included in our dataset.[28] The dataset for Japan was obtained through the Japanese Film Classification and Rating Committee (Eiga Rinri Kikō, EIRIN) website, by searching through their entire database (from August 2009 to the present), and subsequently downloading this to Excel using the 'Get external data' function.[29] It was further edited by manually adding extra columns translating all dates and titles into English. The BBFC and French Centre National du Cinéma et de l'Image Animée (CNC) were also contacted, but declined to release lists of their age ratings, referring to the information on their websites. As a result, their lists of age ratings were found by manually searching through their searchable databases for one film at a time.[30] As searching through all films released in a six-year period for both agencies was beyond the scope of this study, the collection of films from France and the UK was undertaken after first finding the film titles that were present in all of the other three countries, where full datasets between 2010 and 2015 had been obtained. A further complication is that the BBFC performs pre- and post-cuts of films. Pre-cuts are performed where the distributor seeks a non-committing evaluation from BBFC in a post-production phase and then decides whether to edit the film as a result of the preliminary rating. Post-cuts might happen after a rating has been given, often to make the film suitable for a younger audience for commercial reasons. For this study, the uncut versions (marked as such by the BBFC) were selected and included in the dataset. Films with the label 'extended cut' were not included unless it was specified that this was the original version. These 'extended cuts' often include *additional* material that could affect the content assessments leading to the age rating. Consequently, eight films were removed from the dataset because it proved impossible to ascertain whether the film was the exact same version as released in the other countries. It should also be noted that it is impossible to assess if pre-cut versions of films following BBFC advice also become the version distributed in other countries. As the BBFC could not answer this question and referred to the distribution companies, we contacted the distribution companies of all the films in our database with identified pre-cuts. Some did not reply, and the rest declined to answer.

Selection criteria and creation of the database

For comparisons to be made, all entries were given a column for 'English title'. These titles were obtained from the Internet Movie Database (IMDb)[31] and manually added to all datasets in order to make sure the titles did not differ in style, spelling, missing words or because of alternative titles used for the same film. English titles in the Norwegian dataset were compared with the English titles in the Danish dataset. The list of films present in both datasets was then compared against the English titles in the Japanese dataset. Comparisons were done by making sure the comparison software ignored spaces before and after values, as well as upper-case/lower-case mismatches, to ensure these differences did not exclude any films. The resulting film titles from this comparison were then looked up manually in both the French and British film rating databases. The final list of films that were rated in all five countries between 1 January 2010 and 31 December 2015 comprises 504 films.

As age classification of films is based on national regulation and legis-lation, the specific age categories/ages used for classification vary between countries. To enable comparison of similar age groups, new age categories were created, merging similar categories. For the purpose of the analysis, our study uses the following: 'Universal' (suitable for all), '7 and above', '12', '15' and '18':

- **Universal:** All five countries have a 'suitable for all' category.
- **7 and above:** A merged category that includes ages 6 and 9 in Norway, 7 in Denmark and 8 in the UK. An age class between 'Universal' and '12' is not used in Japan and France. However, for the purpose of this study, the French *'tous publics avec avertissement'* (for all audiences, but with a warning) category was coded as belonging to the '7 and above' category, as it is considered separate from a strict 'Universal' category (*'tous publics'*).
- **12:** All '12' ratings, and the '11' category used by Denmark and Norway.
- **15:** All '15' ratings, in addition to France's '16'.
- **18:** All the countries except one use this rating; Denmark does not have an '18' age class as the country does not rate films intended for adults.

In some countries, and for some categories, younger children might be allowed into cinemas if accompanied by a caretaker/adult. Moreover, all age groups assigned by the French CNC can possibly be accompanied by a warning, *'avec avertissement'*. This is used to tell the public about details of the film's content that the CNC sees as prudent to convey.[32] For the purpose of this study, we consider only the standard age classification categories and advised ages.

Results and Analysis

Our first research question is: what, if any, are the differences in age ratings for films in Denmark, France, Norway, Japan and the UK? Looking at the general distribution of the 504 films across each age class category by country (see Table 4.2), we see a substantial difference in the use of the different age categories. A unanimous assessment on age classification category occurred only for thirteen titles, 2.58% of the 504 films. One explanation for this is

Table 4.2. Number of titles in each age class (French *'avertissement'* coded as '7')

Rating	Denmark	France	Japan	Norway	UK
Universal	64 (12.70%)	380 (75.40%)	334 (66.27%)	90 (17.86%)	36 (7.14%)
7	97 (19.25%)	74 (14.68%)	–	68 (13.49%)	50 (9.92%)
12	196 (38.89%)	50 (9.92%)	95 (18.85%)	189 (37.50%)	200 (39.68%)
15	147 (29.17%)	0 (0.00%)	62 (12.30%)	155 (30.75%)	197 (39.09%)
18	–	0 (0.00%)	13 (2.58%)	2 (0.40%)	21 (4.17%)

that in the period used for the selection of cases, France gave the 'Universal' (380 films) and *'tous publics avec avertissement'* rating (74 films) to 90.08% (454 films in total). While we cannot completely exclude the possibility that this is due to a periodic variation, it is not likely. The high number of 'Universal' ratings for France corresponds to the CNC statistics for all films rated between 1 March 2006 and 28 February 2007, where 92.6% were given *'tous publics'/'tous publics avec avertissement'*. Comparing other countries, Japan also gave a high number of films 'Universal', 66.27% (334 films). In comparison, Denmark used 'Universal' for 12.70% (64 titles), Norway for 17.86% (90 titles), and interestingly, the UK only for 7.14% (36 titles). As France applied the '12' rating for only 9.92% (50 titles), and did *not once* use '15' for any of the 504 films in this dataset, it is most likely that all five countries will agree on the age rating of a film if it receives 'Universal' in all countries.

Same films, different ratings?

Similarities between the number of films rated in different categories only show part of the story. Even if two countries have the same *number* of films rated as '7', this does not mean that they are *the same* films. It is therefore necessary to see the actual percentages of films that received the same age rating between the different countries. Table 4.3 shows how 75% of the films in our study received the same age rating in Denmark and Norway, while there was agreement between France and the UK for only 7%. Compare this with the UK and Japan, which gave the same rating for 22% of the films, while France and Japan gave the same rating for 62%. Thus, our hypothesis that Japan has substantially different ratings from the other countries is not supported by our findings. Rather, based on the data it would be more correct to say that the 'most different country' in our group is France, and that the UK and France are both far more likely to agree with the Japanese raters than with each other.

Table 4.3. Similarities in ratings between countries (%) (N=504)

	Percentage with exact same classification				
	UK	France	Denmark	Norway	Japan
UK		7	54	49	22
France			13	18	62
Denmark				75	22
Norway					27
Japan					

Actual overlap in terms of percentages getting the same rating still only gives us part of the whole picture. Another way of looking at similarities and differences between countries is to consider to what degree their assessments correlate. This is useful in order to see to what extent there are systematic similarities or differences—correlations—between the countries' ratings. So, for instance, even if two countries rarely conclude with the same age rating of any film, it could be that they still have similar assessments; for example, one country might systematically rate a type of film '7', while the other country for the same type of film would always use the '11' rating. In this way they could be said to have similar assessments, even if their conclusion is different. In order to check for potential correlations, we used SPSS to analyse the correlation between the countries in the ratings of the 504 films, as shown in Table 4.4. As the analysis shows, the weakest correlation is found when comparing Japan to Denmark (r=0.270) and Norway (r=0.281) respectively. The correlation between France and the UK is also quite weak (r=0.301). The strongest correlation is between Norway and Denmark (r=0.846). This is particularly interesting, as Denmark does not have the '18' rating.

The reason for France and Japan's high usage of the 'Universal' category could originate from these two countries not having an age class for seven-year-olds, combined with the other three countries employing this age class where France and Japan used 'Universal'. To test if this was the case, the age groups for 'Universal' and '7' were combined. Table 4.5 gives an overview of the level of agreement in rating decisions by how many different ratings have been used for the exact same films combining all five countries. Bearing in mind our choice of coding the French '*avertissement*' as equivalent to the '7' rating, and that this might have influenced the distribution of films in the different categories, we also present the differences in rating when '*avertissement*' is considered as a 'Universal' category. As we can see, this

Table 4.4. Correlations of agreements between countries on film rating (N=504)

Correlations	British age group rating	Norwegian age group rating	French age group rating	Danish age group rating	Japanese age group rating
British	1	0.461*	0.301*	0.452*	0.517*
Norwegian	0.461*	1	0.307*	0.846*	0.281*
French	0.301*	0.307*	1	0.318*	0.447*
Danish	0.452*	0.846*	0.318*	1	0.270*
Japanese	0.517*	0.281*	0.447*	0.270*	1

* Correlation is significant at the 0.01 level (2-tailed).

Table 4.5. Overview of rating agreement between
countries, in actual numbers and percentage

	1 (no differences in rating)	2 (two different ratings)	3 (three different ratings)	4 (four different ratings)	5 (five different ratings)
5 ratings (*'avertissement'* coded as '7')	13 (2.58%)	223 (44.25%)	226 (44.84%)	41 (8.13%)	1 (0.20%)
5 ratings (*'avertissement'* coded as 'Universal')	13 (2.58%)	241 (47.82%)	223 (44.25%)	26 (5.16%)	1 (0.20%)
3 ratings ('Universal', '12', '15') ('18' coded as '15' and '7' as 'Universal')	66 (13.10%)	272 (53.97%)	166 (32.94%)		

makes a minor difference in the overall distribution of agreements of rating. Finally, as Denmark does not have the '18' category, we present the distribution with three main ratings: 'Universal' (including '7'), '12' and '15' (including '18'). Even with this limited scale, one-third of the films (166) received ratings in all three categories. France and Japan found a greater number of films suitable for children under the age of twelve than the UK, Denmark and Norway. Combining 'Universal' with '7', and '15' with '18' still only produced agreement on the age rating in all five countries for just 13.10% of the films (66 titles).

In sum, the results of the comparative analysis show how France stands out with its usage of the 'Universal', or 'suitable for all', category for 90.08% of films, while Japan also viewed a high number of films as 'suitable for all' audiences (66.27%). The UK, Denmark and Norway gave far fewer films the age rating of 'Universal', even with the age classes for 'Universal' and '7' combined. These three countries are quite similar in their usage of the other three age rating classes. However, the UK used the '12' and '15' age classes slightly more and 'Universal' slightly less than Denmark and Norway, suggesting that a greater number of films are viewed as unsuitable for an audience younger than twelve in the UK than in Denmark and Norway. Regarding differences and similarities between countries, the UK and France stand out as the least similar, and only agreed on the age rating for 7% of the films. The greatest overlap is between Denmark and Norway (75%) and France and Japan (62%). In terms of correlations, the least agreement exists between the two Scandinavian countries versus Japan, followed by France versus the UK. The most agreement is found between Norway and Denmark.

Exploring How Age Raters Assess Film Content: Sex, Language, Violence and More

We can explore the rationale for differences in age rating practices by looking into the five rating agencies' assessments for each film in order to identify possible cultural differences in what is viewed as harmful or unsuitable for children. Through this approach we also continue the work done by Price, Palsson and Gentile in trying to address the limitations of previous studies, where only US content descriptors were used. Importantly, Price, Palsson and Gentile consider rating rationales linked to a limited spectrum of content (sex, violence and language). However, as shown through looking at the agencies' own arguments, and as described in Table 4.1, nudity, 'atmosphere' and drugs are also important reasons for classifying films into a given age category.

For this part of the analysis we have made a sub-selection to consider the films with the greatest variability in age rating—that is, ranging from 'Universal' to '15' or '18'. These films were selected to give an insight into the types of content the five rating agencies differ on, which, again, is assumed will help explain the differences in age ratings overall. Only one film, *American Reunion* (Hurwitz & Schlossberg, 2010), received a different rating in each one of the five countries represented in our analysis (see also Table 4.5). In addition, twenty-seven films (5.6% of the total) received four different ratings across the five countries. These twenty-seven films were chosen for further analysis. The distribution of titles for these films in the different categories is presented in Table 4.6. As shown, the UK used the two highest age categories for all twenty-seven films, while France, Japan and Norway used the 'Universal' category for some of the same titles (and in the case of France, for *all* of them). Japan and Norway stand out as using almost all of the age classification categories available, while Denmark considered most to be suitable for '7 and above' (20 titles) and seven titles for '12 and above'.

Table 4.6. Number of titles in each age class for the twenty-seven films with the most variability in age ratings by country

Age classification	UK	Denmark	France	Japan	Norway
Universal	–	–	27	7	4
7	–	20	–	–	5
12	–	7	–	13	17
15	25	–	–	4	1
18	2	–	–	3	–
Total number of films	27	27	27	27	27

Using the general assessment of types of content, as presented by the classification boards themselves (see Table 4.1), we created seven content categories used as rationales for various age ratings: *atmosphere*, *violence*, *sex*, *nudity*, *language*, *drugs*, and a collected category *other*, as explained in Table 4.7. Next, using the descriptions in their original language, we analysed and categorized all descriptions from the five classification boards of the twenty-seven films (135 descriptions in total). When doing so we specifically examined how the film classification boards clarified and argued for the given age classification of each film individually, pointing to film content.

Figure 4.1 gives an overview of how different content descriptors have been used by the national film classification agencies when describing the film. Note that one film can have several different content descriptors (e.g. sex *and* bad language *and* violence). It shows how some topics, such as language as a specific content linked to age classification decisions, are more prevalent in the UK (cited for all of the films) than in the other countries (cited for five films in Denmark, three in Japan in Norway and for none in France), pointing to a potential difference in assessment of what

Table 4.7. Content categories used as the rationale for various age ratings

Atmosphere	Having a mood or an atmosphere that can be disturbing or threatening for children. This category also contains arguments connected to emotional scenes and themes (e.g. implied domestic violence, people acting aggressively, shouting and arguing without actual physical altercations, people being frightened or extremely sad, acting dramatically and suffering from illness).
Violence	Containing violence and/or other forms of physical damage or injuries (also includes suicides, depictions of domestic violence, dismemberment, blood and images of dead bodies). Rape, as sexual violence, is coded as both violence and sex.
Sex	Containing depictions/actions, language and/or themes of a sexual nature. This includes sexual humour, innuendo and characters talking about sex. Rape, as sexual violence, is coded as both violence and sex.
Nudity	Containing depictions of nudity (includes artworks and similar).
Language	Containing words that are viewed as offensive and/or containing discriminatory language.
Drugs	Depicting drugs, drug use and/or themes connected to drugs (including tobacco and alcohol). This includes characters referencing drug use or behaving differently under the influence of drugs, even if the drugs themselves are not depicted.
Other	Containing actions that are viewed as dangerous and/or depictions that can be seen as encouraging risky behaviour, depictions of discriminatory behaviour, crude pranks/humour and antisocial behaviour. This category is also used for reasons that do not fit in any other category.

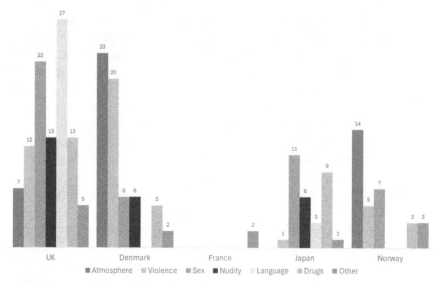

Figure 4.1. Content reasons cited for age classification, by country

is considered to be harmful for children, or alternatively, what is considered bad language. Similarly, the term 'atmosphere' is the most frequent explanation used in Danish and Norwegian for age rating decisions but is not used at all in France and Japan. This is not surprising, given that both Denmark and Norway specifically mention 'frightening atmosphere' as an important consideration when rating films. None of the countries explain *why* a certain film is given a 'Universal' rating. This means that France became almost absent from further analysis of the descriptions, as it gave *all* of the twenty-seven selected films a 'Universal' rating. Only for two of the twenty-seven films (*Ted 2* (MacFarlane, 2015) and *Jackass 3D* (Tremaine, 2010)) did France give a note or warning, stating that these films contain scenes that can be offensive and/or vulgar to younger viewers, although no details were given about the nature of the offensive or vulgar content.

So what about the 'classic' categories of content classification—violence, sex and nudity? When it comes to *violence*, Denmark cites this for 20 of the 27 films, substantially more than the other countries, followed by 12 in the UK. Given the strong correlation in rating practices between Norway and Denmark (see Table 4.4), agreeing in 75% of the cases of the whole population of films, it is interesting that violence is only referred to in five cases in Norway. France and Japan do not mention violence as a rating rationale at all.

Sex as a content descriptor explaining age classifications occurs most often in the UK, related to 22 of the 27 films, compared to 11 in Japan, 6 in Denmark and 7 in Norway. This substantial difference in how classifiers seem to view and evaluate content, not agreeing on what is perceived to be 'sexual', is interesting and merits further research. Interestingly, in Japan films said to contain 'sexual dialogue' or 'indirect depiction of sex' have all been rated '12' or higher. Price, Palsson and Gentile also made this observation, seeing Japan as part of a group of Asian countries who place 'a fairly large weight on sex relative to all other countries'.[33] This can be explained by Japan's strict obscenity law, further supported by Gerow who noted that, even though the weight placed on violence has become greater since a surge in youth crime in the late 1990s (adding the 'PG12' category as a result), EIRIN is mainly concerned with 'sexual obscenity'.[34] This might also explain why two of the three films rated '18' by the Japanese can be described as US 'teen sex comedies' (*Neighbors* (Stoller, 2014) and *American Reunion* (Hurwitz & Schlossberg, 2010)). The third film that falls into the '18' category is *The Kids Are All Right* (Cholodenko, 2010) which the examiners explain as containing 'strong scenes of a sexual nature, as well as minors using drugs'. Thus, there seem to be some surprising similarities between the assessments of sexual content between the UK and the Japanese rating agencies (although some previous research has argued that because the Japanese rating agency was established during the US occupation of Japan after the Second World War, it might have some Western influences, though Japanese culture is generally seen as stricter on sex than US culture).[35]

Nudity as a rationale for age classification is predominantly used in the UK. Half of the films (13 titles) were described as depicting nudity by the BBFC (UK) compared to 6 titles in Japan and Denmark and none in Norway and France.

Language as harmful content is particularly interesting. While this is a less important issue in the other countries, mentioned in relation to three films in Japan and with no mentions at all in Denmark and Norway, it is given as the reason for the high age classification ('15' or '18') for *all* of the films in the UK.

As for *drugs*, the UK and Japan are similar in pointing to drugs as a reason for their '13' and '9' age ratings, respectively. The number is lower in Denmark and Norway, where drugs are only mentioned in the arguments for 5 and 3 titles, respectively.

Finally, some of the 135 descriptions that contained additional assessments of content-related arguments for age classifications were not covered by the main content categories as described above. This *other* category includes the film *Jackass 3D* (Tremaine, 2010), where all countries except France cited dangerous stunts as part of the reason for not allowing a 'Universal' rating. Furthermore, this film was cited as depicting 'vomit' in the UK, 'vomit and excrement' in Denmark, and 'excrement, pranks and vomiting' in Japan.

The *other* category was further used in the UK for 'crude humour'—two characters who are having a secret love affair and later find out they are half-brother and -sister, verbal references to suicide, and 'carer is shown to come from a poor area of the city where his life was lacking direction'— while Norway used it twice more for 'crude humour' and Denmark once for 'intense driving'. In sum, while assessing age rating we considered France to be the 'most different country' in our group, and while this is also the case when it comes to content assessment and rationales, we note how the UK in particular stands out as being substantially different than the other countries on what, and how much, they assess as being problematic content for children.

Same Reason, Different Rating: The Case of *The Secret in Their Eyes*

Given some of the similarities in the base content descriptors, one would perhaps expect that when two countries cite the same types of content as a reason for any particular rating, they would also agree on what that rating should be. This does not seem to be the case. Even when excluding France for not stating a reason for the use of their 'Universal' rating, the agencies *never mentioned the same types of content or scenes as the reason for their rating for any of the twenty-seven films.* This might explain the differences in ratings. Put simply, different types of content are considered problematic for different children in different countries—and this is not dependent on their age.

As an example, the most similar descriptions can be found for the film *The Secret in Their Eyes* (Campanella, 2009). This film details a retired legal counsellor's search for closure from one of his old, unsolved homicide cases through him writing a novel about the case, leading him to also revisit an unrequited love from the past. Denmark, Japan and Norway all cited sex and violence as the reason for their rating, while the UK in addition labelled it for nudity and language. However, this did not cause the four countries to agree on the age rating. The UK gave the film an '18' certificate, Norway gave it a '15', Denmark and Japan gave it a '12' and France gave it a 'Universal'.

The agreement on content, while completely disagreeing on the age rating, helps support the conclusion that the UK gives sex and nudity content high age ratings; the description states 'a scene of sexual violence', 'the naked body of a female murder victim is discovered bloodied and bruised, with breasts and pubic hair exposed' and '[t]here is occasional use of strong language'. In contrast, Japan, which also gives high age ratings when sexual content is involved, gave the film a '12', simply giving the reason that the film contained a rape scene.[36] Denmark also mentions the rape scene as the reason for the rating, but notes, in addition, that the film contains two murders. Norway states that rape and murder are the reasons for their age rating. These two murders are not mentioned by the Japanese rating agency, which supports the notion that Denmark and the UK (and possibly also Norway, to some degree) might consider violent content as harmful or unsuitable for children more frequently than Japan, while the UK places more weight on nudity and language.

Discussion

Observing how age classifications designed to protect children of various ages are rarely questioned, or researched, we started out wondering if the perception of media effects and media harm, namely that media can *have effects* on people, and that they can *cause harm*, is culturally dependent. And if so, can these differences be identified and shown through the accrual practices of the film classification agencies? We examined this by asking: what, if any, are the differences in age ratings for films in Denmark, France, Japan, Norway and the UK? What are the rationales behind the rating decisions that are being made, and how do they differ? Our findings in an analysis of the classification of 504 unique films rated in all five countries showed that the countries only agreed on thirteen titles (2.6%). We hypothesized that Japan, as the cultural outlier, would have the most substantial difference in rating compared to the other countries. Our analysis showed that while the weakest correlation exists between Japan and the Scandinavian countries Denmark (r=0.270) and Norway (r=0.281), a similar correlation (r=0.301) exists between France and the UK, making both countries far more likely to agree with, for example, the Japanese, than with each other. The strongest correlation was found between Norway and Denmark (r=0.846), something that is not surprising given their similarities not just in culture, but also language. Looking at actual agreement in age rating, we found that 75% of the films received the same age rating in Denmark and Norway, while there was actual agreement between France and the UK for only 7%. Meanwhile, the UK and Japan gave the same rating for 22% of the films, while France and Japan gave the same rating for 62%. Based on the data, it would be more correct to say that the 'most different country' in our group is France.

Analysing the rating rationales behind the twenty-seven films with the highest variability in age rating between the countries (operationalized as receiving four or five different ratings for the same film), we found that the countries differ in what they consider harmful for children. Japan and Norway stand out as using almost all of the age classification categories available, Denmark considered most to be suitable for '7 and above' (20 films), while the UK rated all '15 or above'. This, again, is comparable to France, where all the same films were rated as 'allowed for all' ('Universal').

When it comes to assessment of film content, the categorization of 'language' as harmful is particularly striking. The UK places substantial emphasis on this when considering suitability and harm, while it is rarely, if at all, mentioned by the classification agencies in the four other countries. Our findings are in line with Price et al.,[14] who note how in some contexts an enormous amount of weight is placed on 'profanity and sex' when considering age ratings. However, as our findings show, this is not the case for all the countries.

Our study was motivated by the observation that in democracies, film rating agencies can evoke pre-censorship, denying certain groups in the public access to certain media content, thus making it imperative to understand and qualify their practices and legitimacy. As the results show, there are substantial differences between countries in how film rating agencies identify and assess film content, what they consider to merit higher or different age ratings, and what kind of content they believe may create a risk of harm for children below a particular age. Further research should look into how raters themselves view content, and the balance and understanding of moral considerations versus risk of harm assessments.

Our study also reveals substantial differences in how rating agencies— acting on behalf of entire countries—recognize and evaluate types of media content. This suggests the possibility of significant, identifiable, and systematic variations between countries and cultures in the way media content in general, and films in particular, are interpreted.

Finally, as we know that classification cultures can lead to internal censorship by the creative industry, because they know or presume that certain parts may not pass censorship or receive the desired classification, we recommend considering how some countries' subjective assessment of risk of harm towards minors, also representing a substantial market, might have severe implications for the final cut of a film.

Conclusion

Our research has sought to contribute to a wider body of research on regulation of risk, and specifically, perceptions of media-related risk to children in contemporary society. From our findings we present the following:

1. The countries differ substantially when assessing and providing justification for the appropriate age classification/age limit for films.
2. The countries differ substantially in what types of content they argue as being harmful for children.
3. The countries differ in what types of content they evaluate as meriting adult ratings.

4. Even when the countries agree on what types of potentially harmful content exist in a film, they do not agree on the age rating.

In sum, different types of content are considered problematic for different children—more based on the country they live in than on their age and development stage. And in this lies the realization that the subjective interpretive gaze of the audience will also be found in censors and regulators.

Acknowledgement

The authors would like to thank Kjartan Ólafsson and Jørgen Kirksæther for insightful comments, and Idunn Bathen Nonstad for editorial assistance.

Notes

1   See: David Buckingham, *The Material Child: Growing up in Consumer Culture* (Cambridge: Polity, 2011); Sonia M. Livingstone, *Children and the Internet: Great Expectations, Challenging Realities* (Cambridge: Polity, 2009); Elisabeth Staksrud, *Children in the Online World: Risk, Regulation, Rights* (New York: Routledge, 2016).

2   Craig A. Anderson et al., 'The Influence of Media Violence on Youth', *Psychological Science in the Public Interest* 4.3 (2003): 81–110; W. James Potter, *On Media Violence* (Thousand Oaks, CA: Sage, 1999); Brad J. Bushman and L. Rowell Huesmann, 'Short-Term and Long-Term Effects of Violent Media on Aggression in Children and Adults', *Archives of Pediatrics & Adolescent Medicine* 160.4 (2006): 348–52; Douglas A. Gentile, Sarah Coyne and David A. Walsh, 'Media Violence, Physical Aggression, and Relational Aggression in School Age Children: A Short-Term Longitudinal Study', *Aggressive Behavior* 37.2 (2011): 193–206 (p. 193); Barbara Krahé et al., 'Desensitization to Media Violence: Links with Habitual Media Violence Exposure, Aggressive Cognitions, and Aggressive Behavior', *Journal of Personality and Social Psychology* 100.4 (2011): 630–46; Douglas A. Gentile, *Media Violence and Children: A Complete Guide for Parents and Professionals* (Westport, CT: Praeger, 2003).

3   Enid Gruber and Joel W. Grube, 'Adolescent Sexuality and the Media: A Review of Current Knowledge and Implications', *Western Journal of Medicine* 172.3 (2000): 210–14; Jane D. Brown et al., 'Sexy Media Matter: Exposure to Sexual Content in Music, Movies, Television, and Magazines Predicts Black and White Adolescents' Sexual Behavior', *Pediatrics* 117.4 (2006): 1018–27 (p. 1018); Jennings Bryant and Steven C. Rockwell, 'Effects of Massive Exposure to Sexually Oriented Prime-Time Television Programming on Adolescents' Moral Judgment', in Dolf Zillman, Jennings Bryant and Aletha C. Huston (eds), *Media, Children, and the Family: Social Scientific, Psychodynamic, and Clinical Perspectives* (Hillsdale, NJ: Lawrence Erlbaum Associates, 1994), pp. 183–95; Jane D. Brown, 'Media and Sexuality', in Robin Nabi and Mary Beth Oliver (eds), *The Sage Handbook of Media Processes and Effects* (Los Angeles: Sage, 2009), pp. 409–22; Aletha C. Huston, Ellen Wartella and Edward Donnerstein, *Measuring the Effects of Sexual Content in the Media: A Report to the Kaiser Family Foundation* (Menlo Park, CA: Henry J. Kaiser Family Foundation, 1998).

4   Philip French and Julian Petley, *Censoring the Moving Image* (Seagull Books, 2007).

5   Alan S. Reid, 'Online Protection of the Child within Europe', *International Review of Law, Computers & Technology* 23.3 (2009): 217–30; Elisabeth Staksrud, 'European Principles of Protection: Convergent Media Protection in Divergent Media Cultures—Is Breastfeeding in Computer Games Sex?', *International Journal of Media & Cultural Politics* 9.3 (2013): 315–23; Jesse Graham et al., 'Cultural Differences in Moral Judgment and Behavior, across and within Societies', *Current Opinion in Psychology* 8 (2016): 125–30; Joseph Price, Craig Palsson and Doug Gentile, 'What Matters in Movie Ratings? Cross-Country Differences in How Content Influences Mature Movie Ratings', *Journal of Children and Media* 8.3 (2014): 240–52.

6   Leyla Dogruel and Sven Joeckel, 'Video Game Rating Systems in the US and Europe', *International Communication Gazette* 75.7 (2013): 672–92.

7   Elisabeth Staksrud, *Children in the Online World*; Elisabeth Staksrud, Kjartan Olafsson and Tijana Milosevic, 'Children as Crowbar? Justifying Censorship on the Grounds of Child Protection', *Nordic Journal of Human Rights* 38.2 (2020): 159–73.

8   Kirsten Drotner, 'Dangerous Media? Panic Discourses and Dilemmas of Modernity', *Paedagogica Historica* 35.3 (1999): 593–619; Anneke Meyer, 'The Moral Rhetoric of Childhood', *Childhood: A Global Journal of Child Research* 14.1 (2007): Elisabeth Staksrud and Jørgen Kirksæther, '"He who buries the little girl wins!" Moral Panics and Double Jeopardy: The Case of Rule of Rose, in Chas Critcher et al. (eds), *Moral Panics in the Contemporary World* (London: Bloomsbury Academic, 2013), pp. 145–67.

9   Andrzej Wajda, 'Two Types of Censorship', in Ruth Petrie (ed.), *Film and Censorship: The Index Reader* (London & Washington: Cassell, 1997), pp. 107–10.

10   The twenty-seven films are: *50/50* (Levine, 2011), *Albert Nobbs* (García, 2011), *American Reunion* (Hurwitz & Schlossberg, 2010), *August: Osage County* (Wells, 2013), *Boyhood* (Linklater, 2014), *Carol* (Haynes, 2015), *Eden* (Hansen-Løve, 2014), *Her* (Jonze, 2013), *Hysteria* (Wexler, 2011), *Jackass 3D* (Tremaine, 2010), *Neighbors* (Stoller, 2014), *Sils Maria* (Assayas, 2014), *Ted 2* (MacFarlane, 2015), *The Danish Girl* (Hooper, 2015), *The Great Beauty* (Sorrentino, 2013), *The Intouchables* (Nakache & Toledano, 2011), *The Judge* (Dobkin, 2014), *The Kids Are All Right* (Cholodenko, 2010), *The Secret in Their Eyes* (Campanella, 2009), *The Snows of Kilimanjaro* (Guédiguian, 2011), *This Must Be the Place* (Sorrentino, 2011), *Two Days, One Night* (Dardenne Brothers, 2014), *Vacation* (Daley & Goldstein, 2015), *Venus in Fur* (Polanski, 2013), *W.E.* (Madonna, 2011), *We're the Millers* (Thurber, 2013) and *Yves Saint Laurent* (Lespert, 2014).

11   See, for instance: Neville M. Hunnings, *Film Censors and the Law* (London: George Allen & Unwin, 1967); John Trevelyan, 'Film Censorship in Great Britain', *Screen* 11.3 (1970): 19–30; Annette Kuhn, *Cinema, Censorship and Sexuality, 1909–1925: Cinema and Society* (London: Routledge, 1988); Jonathon Green, *The Encyclopedia of Censorship* (New York: Facts on File, 1990); Jean-François Théry, *Pour en finir une bonne fois pour toutes avec la censure* (Paris: Le Cerf, 1996); Derek Jones, *Censorship: A World Encyclopedia*, vol. 1: *A–D* (London: Fitzroy Dearborn, 2001); Tanya P. Nymo, *Slibrige scener—listige knep: statens filmkontroll og den moralske orden 1913–1940* (Oslo: SAP, 2003); Jean-Pierre Krémer and Alain Pozzuoli, *Le dictionnaire de la censure* (Paris: Scali, 2007); Marjorie Heins, *Not in Front of the Children: 'Indecency', Censorship, and the Innocence of Youth* (New Brunswick, NJ: Rutgers University Press, 2007); Laikwan Pang, 'The State against

Ghosts: A Genealogy of China's Film Censorship Policy', *Screen* 52.4 (2011): 461–76; Daniel Biltereyst and Roel Vande Winkel, *Silencing Cinema: Film Censorship around the World* (London: Palgrave Macmillan, 2013).

12 See for instance Robert Klein, 'Film Censorship: The American and British Experience', *Villanova Law Review* 12.3 (1967): 419–56; Charles Goldsmith, 'Harry Potter Film Draws Stiffer European Ratings', *Wall Street Journal*, 1 June 2004: B.7; David Cooke, 'The Director's Commentary', in Edward Lamberti (ed.), *Behind the Scenes at the BBFC: Film Classification from the Silver Screen to the Digital Age* (London: British Film Institute, 2012), pp. 162–80; Joel Federman, *Media Ratings: Design, Use and Consequences* (Indiana University: Mediascope, 1996); see also Nymo, *Slibrige scener—listige knep*.

13 Jesper Bruus Pedersen, *Film og filmcensur i Norden 1965–1975: en undersøgelse af filmcensurpraksis i de fem nordiske lande* (København: Nyt fra samfundsvidenskaberne, 1976); Richard Lagercrantz, *Kontroll, granskning och censur av film: en nordisk inventering (med utblickar även mot andra länder)*, Våldsskildringsrådets skriftserie vol. 6 (Stockholm: Våldsskildringsrådet, 1993).

14 Price, Palsson and Gentile, 'What Matters in Movie Ratings?'.

15 Ibid., p. 249.

16 Ibid., p. 248.

17 See Nymo, *Slibrige scener—listige knep* and Lagercrantz, *Kontroll, granskning och censur av film*.

18 See Julian Petley, 'The Censor and the State in Britain', in Daniel Biltereyst and Roel Vande Winkel (eds), *Silencing Cinema: Film Censorship around the World* (New York: Palgrave Macmillan, 2013), pp. 149–65.

19 See Petley, 'The Censor and the State in Britain'; and Alison James, 'Smoke & Mirrors: "Songs" of Ratings Discord: Gauls Cry Censorship while Brits Play It Safe', *Variety*, 14 November 2004: 8.

20 See Nymo *Slibrige scener—listige knep*; and Kathrine Skretting, 'Filmsex og filmsensur: sengekant-filmene i skandinavia 1970–1976', *Norsk medietidsskrift* 10.1 (2003): 75–95.

21 See Lagercrantz, *Kontroll, granskning och censur av film*; and Medierådet for Børn og Unge, *Hvem vurderer og hvordan?*, n.d. [cited 30 April 2020], https://www.medieraadet. dk/medieradet/hvem-vurderer-og-hvordan.

22 AlloCiné, *Classification: mode d'emploi*, 2 June 2013 [cited 3 March 2017], http://www. allocine.fr/article/dossiers/cinema/dossier-18591917/.

23 For further information on the regulatory and/or legal frameworks for the countries represented in this analyses, see for instance 'France', in *The Encyclopedia of Censorship*, pp. 95–99; Aaron Gerow, 'JAPAN: Film', in Derek Jones (ed.), *Censorship: A World Encyclopedia*, vol. 2: *E–K* (London: Fitzroy Dearborn, 2001), pp. 1267–70; British Board of Film Classification, *BBFC Classification Guidelines*, http://web.archive. org/web/20191114161345/www.bbfc.co.uk/sites/default/files/attachments/BBFC -Classification-Guidelines.pdf; Teddy K. Petersen, 'Denmark: Since 1984', in *Censorship*, vol. 1, pp. 664–65; Bildeprogramloven, *Lov om beskyttelse av mindreårige mot skadelige bildeprogram mv.* (Norway).

24 British Board of Film Classification, *Who We Are*, n.d. [cited 6 March 2017], http:// www.bbfc.co.uk/about-bbfc/who-we-are.

25 Alex Martin, 'All Movies Subject to Rating, Even Cuts', *Japan Times*, 2 March 2010.

26 Medierådet for Børn og Unge, *Spørgsmål og svar*, n.d. [cited 15 February 2017], http://web.archive.org/web/20170210181317/www.dfi.dk/Boern_og_unge/Medieraadet-for-Boern-og-Unge/Filmvurdering/Spoergsmaal-og-svar.aspx; Centre National du Cinéma et de l'Image Animée, *Visas et classification*, n.d. [cited 3 May 2020], https://www.cnc.fr/professionnels/visas-et-classification/activite-de-la-commission-de-classification; EIRIN (Film Classification and Rating Committee), *Film Classification*, n.d. [cited 4 December 2016], https://web.archive.org/web/20161204155338/http://eirin.jp/english/008.html; Medietilsynet, *Retningslinjer: aldersklassifisering av bildeprogrammer*, 2019.

27 Medierådet for Børn og Unge, *Film og vurderinger*, n.d. [cited 30 April 2020], https://www.medieraadet.dk/medieradet/film; Medietilsynet, *Filmdatabasen*, n.d. [cited 1 June 2016], http://www.medietilsynet.no/filmdatabasen/.

28 Where the distributor chose not to obtain an evaluation from the rating authority (e.g. if they were confident they would receive the highest rating on submission), the films would get an automatic age rating of '15 and over' in Denmark and an '18' rating in Norway (Medierådet for Børn og Unge, *Film og vurderinger*; Medietilsynet, *Filmdatabasen*).

29 EIRIN (Film Classification and Rating Committee), 審査作品リスト *(Shinsa sakuhin risuto)*, n.d. [cited 1 June 2016], https://web.archive.org/web/20170210095224/http://www.eirin.jp/list/index.php.

30 British Board of Film Classification, *Search for Releases*, n.d. [cited 30 April 2020], http://www.bbfc.co.uk/search/releases; Centre National du Cinéma et de l'Image Animée, *Visas et classification: recherche par critères*, n.d. [cited 3 May 2020], https://www.cnc.fr/professionnels/visas-et-classification.

31 *Internet Movie Database (IMDb)* [cited 5 May 2020], http://www.imdb.com.

32 Centre National du Cinéma et de l'Image Animée, *Visas et classification*, n.d. [cited 3 May 2020], https://www.cnc.fr/professionnels/visas-et-classification/activite-de-la-commission-de-classification.

33 Price, Palsson and Gentile, 'What Matters in Movie Ratings?', p. 247.

34 Aaron Gerow, 'JAPAN: Film', in *Censorship*, vol. 2, pp. 1267–70. See also Jasper Sharp, *Historical Dictionary of Japanese Cinema*, Historical Dictionaries of Literature and the Arts (Lanham, MD: Rowman & Littlefield, 2011).

35 Ibid.; see also Lars-Martin Sørensen and Stephen Prince, *Censorship of Japanese Films during the American Occupation of Japan: The Cases of Yasujiro Ozu and Akira Kurosawa* (Lewiston, NY: Edwin Mellen Press, 2009); Joseph L. Anderson and Donald Richie, *The Japanese Film: Art and Industry*, expanded edn (Princeton, NJ: Princeton University Press, 1982).

36 Note that for this study, 'rape' was coded both as 'sex' and 'violence'.

Part 2

*Political Censorship, Debate
and Traces of Resistance*

5

The Last Convulsions of Democracy: Wolfgang Petzet's Pamphlet *Verbotene Filme* and the Censorship Debate at the Close of the Weimar Republic

Viola Rühse

Film developed into a mass medium during the Weimar Republic and enjoyed increasing popularity and growing social acceptance among the middle classes.[1] This development was supported by more sophisticated plots, and by a longer duration of films.[2] In addition, more prestigious performance venues that could accommodate several thousands of visitors provided an architectural attachment to high culture.[3] As a consequence, films started playing a central role in society, and their various topics challenged censorship.[4] In Germany, censorship became increasingly politically determined from the 1920s onwards.[5] In the early 1930s, in particular, it was shaped by rising nationalism and by censorship measures that were provoked by targeted actions by national socialists, such as demonstrations, for instance, against the pacifist film *All Quiet on the Western Front* (Lewis Milestone, 1930).[6] The mostly politically determined censorship measures were much discussed in the media, especially in the early 1930s. A crucial part of that discussion was the book *Verbotene Filme: eine Streitschrift* (*Banned Films: A Pamphlet*) by Wolfgang Petzet, published in the autumn of 1931 as the first comprehensive study on film censorship in the Weimar

Viola Rühse, "The Last Convulsions of Democracy: Wolfgang Petzet's Pamphlet *Verbotene Filme* and the Censorship Debate at the Close of the Weimar Republic" in: *The Screen Censorship Companion: Critical Explorations in the Control of Film and Screen Media*. University of Exeter Press (2024). © Viola Rühse. DOI: 10.47788/ODXR8776

Republic from a general rather than a purely legal perspective.[7] Petzet's publication is still used as a source of information in specialist research today. However, a more detailed analysis of his book on film censorship in the Weimar Republic is still lacking.

In *Verbotene Filme*, Petzet offers a sociological discussion for film censorship law and its amendments including how it allowed political influence and arbitrary decisions, with regard to the general state of the Republic. The book also provides an overview of the most important and significant censorship cases. Petzet further draws attention to the detrimental impact of censorship on film production. Because of its very critical approach, one reviewer aptly called the book a 'mirror of sins' of film censorship.[8] Petzet uses a special ironic style to treat the dry censorship topic in a humorous and easily readable way. The style not only showcases his experience as a writer, but also his background: as a student, he had already written poems, and after his doctorate in sociology, he worked as a journalist covering both political and cultural issues, including film.[9]

Petzet's writings on film and film censorship are influenced by Siegfried Kracauer, an important protagonist of the just-developing film criticism in the Weimar Republic. Kracauer enriched his criticism with a profound sociological approach, but its impact on German film criticism was interrupted by National Socialism. Kracauer's influence on other European film critics before 1933, such as Wolfgang Petzet, still needs to be studied in more detail.[10] *Verbotene Filme* is ideal for such a study as Petzet used Kracauer's method and figures of thought and, moreover, because the publisher involved Kracauer in the book concept. This involvement is evidenced by the previously unexamined materials held by Petzet's estate, which are very informative for the publication history of the pamphlet. The documents in the estate archives also allow insight into the internal censorship of Petzet's publication by the publisher, which is significant for the intellectual climate at the end of the Weimar Republic and the increasing right-wing forces impacting upon the cultural realm.[11]

In this chapter I will first introduce the topic of film censorship in the Weimar Republic and locate Petzet's book project within it. Next, I will describe the publisher, the author Wolfgang Petzet and the project advisor Siegfried Kracauer in more detail. Then, the content and method of the book are explored, and the influences of Kracauer and the publisher are analysed. Finally, the reception of the book will be examined. Since the topic of film censorship in the Weimar Republic is multidimensional, this chapter uses an interdisciplinary approach that combines film history, legal history and cultural history, in order to offer as vivid an insight as possible into the censorship debate at the time.

Film Censorship in the Weimar Republic

After the first announcement of the general abolition of censorship, in June 1919, film censorship was nonetheless reintroduced—ostensibly because of the flood of so-called 'Aufklärungsfilme' ('sex education films')—and specifications were added in 1920.[12] Primarily, the politically right-wing groups lobbied for film censorship because they were concerned about the political impact of cinema.[13] In the first half of the 1920s, films were indeed censored more for moral reasons, but later the censorship measures became more political.[14] Russian films in particular triggered censorship discussions, such as *Battleship Potemkin* (Броненосец Потёмкин, Sergei Eisenstein, 1925), although a political ban on Eisenstein's film was still prevented by widespread protest against it.[15]

The many harmless films of the time escaped censorship, and they provided an important distraction during socially challenging times, but they also encouraged political apathy.[16] After all, going to the movies was an affordable and popular pastime even during the economic crisis in the late 1920s and early 1930s. The Nazis too were also aware of the importance of cinema as a mass medium and tried to instrumentalize it, especially when they gained political importance in the early 1930s.[17] A case in point is *All Quiet on the Western Front* (Lewis Milestone, 1930), a film that imparted republican and pacifist values and thus conveyed the Weimar system in a particular way. The Nazis provoked bans and censorship measures against it.[18] Among other actions, they staged riots and mass demonstrations at the Berlin premiere as spontaneous outrage.[19] In addition, pressure was exerted by Reichswehr Minister Wilhelm Groener and media owner Alfred Hugenberg, whose print media began to agitate aggressively against the film.[20] To maintain domestic political peace, *All Quiet on the Western Front* was banned, thereby highlighting the political one-sidedness of film censorship.[21] The film ban was reported on the front pages of several daily newspapers and triggered a general debate on censorship.[22] The abandonment of the rule of law by the Nazis was publicly criticized, and a clear warning was given by the writer Otto Max Fromm (pseudonym: Max Wittenberg) in the *Vossische Zeitung* on 21 December 1931:

> We Republicans and peace leaders should shout it out loud: People are afraid of the streets. They're pulling back. Step by step. One day, I fear, they will reap the bloody reward. Those who are yielded to now will not be so soft-hearted. They will strike with their fists after they come to power. And then mercy to those who do not know how to maintain their authority today.[23]

Due to the extensive critical coverage of the ban in politically left-wing and liberal media, the remaining slight majority of pro-republican parliamentarians pushed for an amendment to the censorship law.[24] With the so-called 'Lex Remarque' (31 March 1931; named after the author of the book on which *All Quiet on the Western Front* is based), at least a limited re-release was granted, for certain groups of people and at closed events, later followed by a general re-release of a shortened film version.[25]

Since censorship decisions continued to be arbitrary and politically determined by the right-wing end of the spectrum, a discussion about the necessity of film censorship was conducted in various media in late spring 1931.[26] For example, Wolfgang Heine warned in the *Vossische Zeitung*, on 24 May 1931, that film censorship would no longer preserve freedom and intellectual creativity because it would undermine the Republic's foundation.[27] Additionally, in May 1931, an initiative was set up at the Schutzverband deutscher Schriftsteller (SDS, Association for the Protection of German Writers) to improve the law.[28] Film producers also criticized film censorship because due to its arbitrariness, they could not take preventive measures in advance to avoid it.

The Societäts-Verlag's Plan for a Book on Film Censorship

The Frankfurter Societäts-Druckerei, the parent publishing house of the *Frankfurter Zeitung*, which issued independent publications in addition to the newspaper, also wanted to support an end to the 'contemporary terror of censorship' with a publication about banned films.[29] The publisher's portfolio was rather diverse, but the general goal was to provide a critical overview of the current situation and to address crucial issues and new media.[30] Thus, among other pieces, several articles about the Nazi regime that had previously appeared in the *Frankfurter Zeitung* were published as a book.[31] In general, the publishing house aimed to support the Republic to 'promote understanding [...] for modern, democratic politics, i.e., politics borne by one's own responsibility'.[32] Film censorship was very well suited as a book topic at that time because, as mentioned, it had been a particularly pressing political topic for some time, and cinema had therefore become one of the political battlegrounds through which National Socialism gained influence and thereby endangered the Weimar Republic.[33]

The book was intended to provide an orientation for the general public and was therefore only 160 pages long; the publisher referred to it as a 'brochure'.[34] As indicated above, the publisher supported a sociological analysis of the censorship system and believed the deficits of the executive bodies concerning film censorship should be pointed out. The main intention was to emphasize that film censorship was inappropriate

Figure 5.1. Photo of
Wolfgang Petzet, *c.* 1933,
unknown photographer
(Source: Nana Petzet)

to the republican social order—that is, unworthy of a free people.[35] The
publishers approached Wolfgang Petzet (1896–1985) for authoring the
book at the beginning of July 1931.[36] Petzet was an old school friend of the
publishing director Eugen Claassen and had grown up in an intellectual and
culturally interested family.[37] His grandfather Georg Christian Petzet was a
journalist and historian of literature, his father Erich Petzet was a historian
of literature and worked as a senior and very distinguished librarian at the
Bavarian State Library, and his mother was a painter.[38]

Wolfgang Petzet was very versatile. He studied sociology and philosophy
in Heidelberg with Alfred Weber and Karl Jaspers. He was a member
of the politically left-wing and philosophically and culturally curious
socialist student circle around Carl Zuckmayer, Theodor Haubach, Carlo
Mierendorff and Henry Goverts.[39] Not only was Petzet already active as
a writer during his studies,[40] but after his PhD he also worked for the
Frankfurter Zeitung as an assistant for the CEO Heinrich Simon and as a
journalist until 1925.[41] He then worked as a freelance journalist and cultural
critic for various media for several years.[42] He wrote not only on politics
but also on other topics such as film.[43] Given this experience, he was well

suited thematically as an author for the book project on film censorship. In addition, as a journalist, he had learned to write quickly. He was able to write the book as requested by the publisher within a few weeks—a particularly astonishing feat given its elaborate essay style. At first, Petzet wanted to emigrate like other intellectuals such as Siegfried Kracauer, but following the book's publication he stayed in Germany.[44] After the Nazi takeover in 1933, Petzet was taken into protective custody and placed under police supervision because of his politically leftist and critical leanings. He could work as a dramatic advisor in the Munich Kammerspiele theatre but had to give up his journalistic activities in exchange. Nevertheless, he secretly attempted to support his more overtly activist friends, Mierendorff and Haubach.[45] After World War II, he was also active as a journalist, but no longer in the field of film, and he published books on art and theatre, among other things. His advanced film criticism fell into oblivion. Thus, according to media scholar Helmut Korte, Petzet is 'unjustly less well known'.[46]

Petzet's writings on film are particularly interesting because he takes up and continues a socio-critical approach introduced by Siegfried Kracauer (1889–1966). Kracauer is best known today in film studies for his two books on film written in American exile.[47] However, even as editor of the *Frankfurter Zeitung* in the Weimar Republic he was intensively involved with film issues, and about a third of his otherwise very diverse newspaper articles from the Weimar Republic period were about film.[48] In the second half of the 1920s, he developed a sociological and ideological-critical film analysis that differed markedly from that of other critics.[49] It caused a stir and though it was received favourably in France and Austria, how his contemporaries received the approach has not yet been studied in detail.[50]

Petzet exemplifies the contemporary reception of Kracauer's method. He was personally acquainted with Kracauer because the two worked together for the local section of the *Frankfurter Zeitung*. Petzet had already been influenced by Kracauer's film writings in the late 1920s.[51] For instance, in an article in 1928 Petzet criticized the unrealistic representation of the social world in films, in a similar way to Kracauer. This could have added to Petzet's suitability as an author for the publisher and their planned critical concept. Kracauer had likely suggested film censorship as a topic for a book. Due to time constraints, he could not author it himself, but he acted as an advisor to the publication.[52]

Overview of the *Verbotene Filme* Book

Petzet introduces the five main chapters of the book with a clarification, namely that the work is not directed against the censors personally and does not represent the interests of film production companies. He points out that its focus is on analysing the effects of censorship in the given general economic order.[53] Throughout the book, Petzet uses examples to explicate the workings of German censorship. In Part I, the current problems of film censorship are discussed with reference to the German film *D-Zug 13 hat Verspätung* (*Express 13*, Alfred Zeisler, 1931). Although one reviewer criticized Petzet's focus on this film, it does serve as a particularly succinct illustration of the arbitrariness and absurdity of the German censorship system. A harmless production, *D-Zug 13 hat Verspätung* obviously does not need to be censored but was nonetheless banned by the Berlin censorship board.[54] In Part II, examples offer indications of the arbitrary nature of censorship (both the law and its amendments). Contemporary reviewers appreciated Petzet's detailed analysis of legal principles and interpretations.[55] Subsequent secondary literature addressing Petzet's book often references his remarks on the 'normal moviegoer' ('*Normal-Kinobesucher*'), on behalf of whom censorship was carried out. With an ironic undertone, Petzet questions this construct as a chimera.[56]

Part III of the book examines the complicated judicial bodies involved in censorship. Petzet draws attention to the problem of mixing judicative and executive functions.[57] He describes the chairman of the supreme court of appeal as 'Janus-faced' ('*der Vorsitzende mit dem Januskopfe*') because he was both an administrative judge and a civil servant.[58] The political censorship of *All Quiet on the Western Front* dominates this chapter; it is cited frequently in secondary literature.[59] Petzet points out that the aforementioned protests

Figure 5.2. Cover of Wolfgang Petzet's *Verbotene Filme* (Source: private archive of the author)

were instigated by the Nazis and that several of the protesters had not even seen the film.[60] Petzet further notes that another republican film was banned by a republican authority, thus not only pandering to the enemies of the Republic, but also an indication of the Weimar Republic's suffering 'from a lack of courage to face itself'.[61]

Part IV deals with the effects of censorship on film production. According to Petzet, Germany's censorship situation encourages the development of 'cheesy' film stories and is an obstacle to the production of serious films.[62] In his conclusion (Part V), Petzet summarizes the censorship law as nonsensical, sinister and unjust. He argues that good, artistically and culturally valuable films should be promoted without censorship restrictions, suggesting that a full abandonment of film censorship would better fit the democratic politics of the Weimar Republic. In support of this view, Petzet refers to the theatre, which was not censored.[63] The appendix of the book contains the most important legal texts on the subject.[64]

Petzet's Method and Style

Petzet's sociological approach fitted particularly well with the editor's stipulation that the social relevance of censorship should be stressed.[65] With his doctorate in sociology, Petzet was of course particularly well suited for this.[66] Moreover, his newspaper work had trained him to reflect on immediate contemporary history. In general, the Societäts-Verlag chose authors for its publications who, like former employee Petzet, were similarly connected to the *Frankfurter Zeitung*, but who 'were able to think independently of their journalistic work in larger contexts'.[67]

The subject, however, was challenging. In one review, Rudolf Arnheim explicitly pointed to the difficult material situation caused by the 'secrecy of the censorship bodies as well as the film companies' unwillingness to make themselves unpopular by publishing censorship material'.[68] Petzet was originally supposed to finish the manuscript about six weeks after the project was first officially suggested to him, but through his daily journalistic work he was well versed in writing quickly.[69] Although he lacked the time and money for research trips, he had a supportive network to draw on.[70]

For instance, Fritz Engel, who was an external member of the highest censorship body, and the above-mentioned SDS, provided Petzet with additional PR articles that were collected at the SDS with the intention to change the law.[71] Petzet was thus able to include several important examples and arguments in his book, many of which were discussed in leftist media. Because Petzet's and the publishers' target audience was so broad (and maybe also for cautionary reasons), not many of these sources are referenced in the book. Through his contacts, Petzet also gained access to the non-public archive of the film production company Emelka in Munich, enabling him to cite examples of judgements that were otherwise inaccessible.[72] By referring to many actual censorship cases, he could point out the flimsy decisions of the censorship bodies and the loopholes that enabled political right-wing influences.

Kracauer considered Petzet's material analysis as exemplary, as it corresponded to Kracauer's own critical approach—summarized, for example, in his well-known essay 'A Minimal Demand upon Intellectuals' ('Minimalforderung an die Intellektuellen', July 1931).[73] In this programmatic text, Kracauer called for a critical perspective that focused on the concrete situation, that radically questioned facts, and that analysed their ideological use. Following Kracauer's lead, Petzet explains what hidden political effects are possible through film censorship in Germany.[74]

The sometimes very formal details and legal quibbles of the film censorship decisions presented a challenge for a book supposed to be of general interest. Yet Petzet succeeded in dealing with the difficult subject in an essayistic manner.[75] He integrated a lot of humour and irony, and even an amusing prize puzzle on censored film titles. The journalist Axel Eggebrecht appreciated this special presentation of a serious topic and stated in his review that the book was 'amusing to read in a rather distressing way'.[76] More generally, Petzet's ironic style is typical of the pamphlet ('*Streitschrift*') genre, which is mentioned in the subtitle of the book. According to Herbert Ihering, who worked as a journalist at the time, polemical and rhetorically sophisticated pamphlets were very important at this time of crisis in the early 1930s.[77]

The Influence of Siegfried Kracauer

Siegfried Kracauer not only influenced the material-saturated method adopted in *Verbotene Filme*; he also affected the content. While working on the book, Petzet studied Kracauer's articles; newspaper clippings containing them are included in the working materials for the book in the estate archives.[78] Basic statements from Kracauer's film reviews are taken up by Petzet; he elaborates on Kracauer's views on the arbitrariness of film censorship, and picks up phrases from Kracauer's articles, such as characterizing the contemporary era as the 'times of Metternich'.[79] Petzet not only shares Kracauer's concept of film realism but also includes selected examples of successful films that Kracauer also used as examples, at the request of the publisher.[80] As an advisor for the publication from its inception, Kracauer seems to be behind this request.[81]

For instance, similarly to Kracauer, Petzet criticizes the 'mean' and sensationalistic scene of the murder of a black man in the American film

Africa Speaks! (Walter Futter, 1930). According to Kracauer and Petzet, this scene should indeed have been censored.[82] Petzet's text also contains several references to Kracauer's series of articles titled 'The Little Shopgirls Go to the Movies' ('Die kleinen Ladenmädchen gehen ins Kino'), which were emblematic of Kracauer's sociological analysis and which received a lot of attention among his contemporaries.[83] In a letter to Kracauer dated 25 November 1931, Petzet mentions that he referred to this 'Little Shopgirl' series in the book: 'How do you like my film brochure; in which I, naturally, remembered the unforgotten little shop girls?'[84] Because of Kracauer's involvement in the conceptualization, his function as an advisor, and the above-mentioned similarities concerning content and method between Petzet and Kracauer, it is not surprising that Kracauer appreciated Petzet's book and tried to support it—for instance, selecting an excerpt for the *Frankfurter Zeitung* and favourably reviewing the book twice.[85]

The Influence of the Publishing House

As mentioned, the publisher proposed the book project with specific ideas in mind concerning its content. Because of the unique mission of the publishing house, Petzet was constantly reminded of the social significance of the topic during the editorial process.[86] The inclusion of this aspect helped ensure the quality of the book and was explicitly welcomed by two reviewers.[87] The publisher also demanded an exploration of censorship's consequences on film production, which was greatly appreciated.[88] In particular, the publisher wanted the current shortcomings of the Republic and its executive bodies concerning film censorship to be pointed out.[89]

However, for fear of legal consequences, the author and the publishing director Eugen Claassen also had to undertake a certain degree of self-censorship. Right at the beginning of the book,[90] Petzet emphasizes that the publication is not directed against any specific person and, obviously to avoid provocation, the title does not contain the word censorship.[91] The pamphlet genre mentioned in the subtitle underlines that the book deals with a controversial topic from a subjective point of view. As observed, Petzet himself tried to manage the tone and used a great deal of irony to express his opinion indirectly, although Claassen, who personally served as editor of the project, found some ironic passages 'too pointed' ('*zu pointiert*') and asked for corrections.[92] In addition, Claassen, together with a political advisor and two lawyers, checked the book before it was printed, requiring Petzet to smoothen out further critical and ironic statements.[93]

To give one example: any mention of the censorship of homosexuality was omitted.[94] In addition, following legal advice, Petzet was not allowed to describe the censorship authority as 'inconsistent' and its measures as 'completely inappropriate', and he was not permitted to directly criticize the 'omissions and contradictions' in censorship practice.[95] Here, one can certainly speak of the internal censorship of a (film) censorship publication—which is, of course, significant given the difficult situation of the Weimar Republic at the time. In fact, the cautious approach was also recognized in a few reviews; for instance, Rudolf Arnheim mentioned in his that a stronger self-positioning would have been appreciated.[96]

Because of the publishing house's intent to promote democratic politics, Petzet was also urged to offer a constructive ending, instead of concluding with 'the downfall of the Occident' ('*Untergang des Abendlandes*').[97] This wish was perhaps warranted in the hope of improving film censorship, a desire that could be considered realistic since there was, for example, a small pro-republican majority in the Weimar Republic government. Yet even though Petzet provided a constructive ending as requested by the publisher, he privately took a more pessimistic view of the situation, a reflection he also shared with the publishing director:

> But if it were to be worked out in all its sharpness, the result would simply be hopelessly depressing: for the demand that we must first become something like a nation is hardly something that can be done in a brochure that is supposed to have an effect from one day to the next.[98]

Petzet's personal view that no improvement was possible in the near future was also influenced by the declining socio-economic and political situation immediately preceding the book's publication in November 1931.[99] From 11 May 1931 onwards, the stock market crash led to a worsening of the financial crisis; unemployment rose steeply, and foreign investments stopped because of the rise of the Nazis.[100] This complex political situation led to an emergency decree ('*Notverordnung*') which allowed the banning of films to guarantee political order and offered the censors increased discretion in this regard.[101] Because of its timing, this decree could only be mentioned in a footnote shortly before the book was finally printed.[102] Thus, the problematic censorship legislation was further intensified instead of being abolished as Petzet and other film censorship opponents had hoped.

Marketing and Reception

Claassen invested a great deal of effort in the marketing of the book.[103] Among other things, a series of advance printings in daily newspapers and magazines was arranged—in Germany, and also in Prague and Vienna.[104] The publisher wrote advertising letters to cinema owners and other film

THE SCREEN CENSORSHIP COMPANION

business associations.[105] The book was exhibited in cinemas in Germany, and Petzet also organized a reading in a Munich cinema.[106] Well-known authors such as Thomas Mann and Bruno Frank wrote positive short statements about the book for public relations purposes, and Bruno Frank recommended it very flatteringly as follows:

> A great example for polemical writing! The material perfectly mastered, the argumentation unassailable, the lecture of calm strength, the whole highly attractive as reading—no weapon of comparable effect has ever yet been forged against the laws of cinema and their narrowly bureaucratic handling.[107]

There were numerous reviews in the trade press and daily newspapers, most of which were positive.[108] This impact certainly allows Petzet's *Verbotene Filme* to be seen as one of the most important new film books of the early 1930s. However, despite the intensive press coverage, sales were poor.[109] On the one hand, this is due to the fact that during the aggravated economic crisis, many probably found it difficult to afford books.[110] On the other hand, the authoritarian views that also determined film censorship were already too widely accepted in the general population,[111] and the initiatives against them—which included Petzet's book—were too little too late. Fittingly, Petzet wrote to Claassen on 27 October 1931: 'we seem to be fighting a losing battle'.[112]

Conclusion: An Ambitious Book Project as One of the 'Last Convulsions' of Democracy

While film censorship was intended as a socio-ethical protective measure in the Weimar Republic, it progressed into the censorship of an authoritarian state that had actually been deposed in 1918.[113] Thus, the Nazis could provoke censorship measures for *All Quiet on the Western Front* as a demonstration and consolidation of their power—and also their influence in cultural politics. This further showed the lack of political neutrality of the censorship bodies. Spring 1931 saw the deepening of the censorship debate. The Societäts-Verlag, looking to interfere in the discourse with a book project (*Verbotene Filme*), commissioned Wolfgang Petzet as an author, asking him to write on this complex topic with a deadline of just a few weeks. Nevertheless, he provided a very comprehensive study, rich in detail. Petzet took up many points of criticism from the discussions about censorship in various media at that time and pointed out the loopholes that allowed political right-wing influence. An experienced writer, he infused his discussion of a 'dry' topic with a humorous and ironic style.

The book itself shows clear traces of Siegfried Kracauer's influence on Petzet in terms of method and content. In fact, the estate materials and correspondence in other archives show that Kracauer influenced Petzet and his book intensively. Thus, the book project exemplifies Kracauer's greater impact as a film critic and intellectual in the Weimar Republic. The estate materials and archives also demonstrate the (previously unknown) existence of pressures on Petzet by the publishers, in particular through content specifications. In addition, due to a fear of legal consequences, the publisher commissioned two lawyers to review the book and Petzet consequently had to make changes to the manuscript, which led to him being criticized in some reviews for taking too liberal a view. Since Petzet's book is still frequently used as a reference work in specialist literature today, such information on the creation of *Verbotene Filme* is important for a better understanding of the book as a historical source, and, by extension, for insights into German film censorship in general.

The poor sales of an otherwise positively reviewed book must be attributed to the escalation of the economic and sociopolitical situation, and thus underline the 'political paralysis' (*'politische Paralyse'*) of the Weimar Republic.[114] Some contemporaries tried to counteract this and drew attention to Hitler's rapid expansion of power, including in the area of film censorship. Petzet's pamphlet clarifies that although the weak points of censorship law were recognized very clearly, they were not changed in spite of protests across several media.

Unfortunately, critical intellectuals such as Petzet, Claasen and Kracauer were unable to prevail against the anti-republican actions of their time, and thus the Societäts-Verlag and Petzet only captured 'the last convulsions' (*'die letzten Zuckungen'*) of democracy, unable to prevent the collapse of the state order.[115] Two years later, film censorship was put at the service of Nazi propaganda, and Nazi film control ended careers and led to a cultural impoverishment that would still be felt decades later.[116]

Notes

1   The title of this chapter is inspired by a phrase in Nikos Späth, *Das Thema hatte es in sich: die Reaktion der deutschen und amerikanischen Presse auf Erich Maria Remarques Im Westen nichts Neues: Eine vergleichende Rezeptionsstudie über Fronterlebnis- und Weltkriegserinnerung in der Weimarer Republik und den USA in den Jahren 1929 und 1930* (Göttingen: V&R Unipress, 2020), p. 319. Many thanks to Daniel Biltereyst for his helpful remarks on the first version of this chapter.

2   Helmut Korte, 'Vom Kinematographen zur nationalen Propaganda: zur Entwicklung des frühen deutschen Films', in *Film und Realität in der Weimarer Republik* (Frankfurt a.M.: Fischer Taschenbuch Verlag, 1980), pp. 13–89 (pp. 55–56).

3 Viola Rühse, 'Luxurious Cinema Palaces in the Roaring Twenties and the Twenty-First Century: Critical Analyses of Movie Theatres by Siegfried Kracauer and Their Relevance Today', *Cultural Intertexts* 10 (2020): 13–30 (p. 14).

4 Anton Kaes, 'Der Traum vom Kino: zur Filmtheorie in der Weimarer Republik', in Kunst- und Ausstellungshalle der Bundesrepublik Deutschland, Bonn and Deutsche Kinemathek Berlin (eds), *Kino der Moderne: Film in der Weimarer Republik* (Dresden: Sandstein Verlag, 2018), pp. 140–51 (p. 146).

5 Jan-Pieter Barbian, 'Filme mit Lücken: die Lichtspielzensur in der Weimarer Republik—von der sozialethischen Schutzmaßnahme zum politischen Instrument', in Uli Jung (ed.), *Der Deutsche Film: Aspekte seiner Geschichte von den Anfängen bis zur Gegenwart* (Trier: Wissenschaftlicher Verlag, 1993), pp. 51–78 (p. 53); Helmut Korte, *Der Spielfilm und das Ende der Weimarer Republik* (Göttingen: Vandenhoeck & Ruprecht, 1998), p. 99.

6 See below for more details on the targeted actions against *All Quiet on the Western Front*.

7 Wolfgang Petzet, *Verbotene Filme: eine Streitschrift* (Frankfurt a.M.: Societäts-Verlag, 1931). Books on German film censorship from a legal perspective include: Ernst Seeger, *Reichslichtspielgesetz vom 12. Mai 1920: für die Praxis erläutert* (Berlin: Heymann, 1923; a revised edition was published in 1932); Ernst Waltuch, *Filmzensur und Strafrecht* (Düren: Hamel'sche Druckerei, 1930); Eckstein published a book on film and law in 1924: Ernst Eckstein, *Deutsches Film- und Kinorecht* (Mannheim, Berlin & Leipzig: Bensheimer, 1924). In the year following the publication of Petzet's book, Herbert Veit Simon published his jurisprudential PhD thesis—Herbert Veit Simon, *Die materiellrechtlichen Voraussetzungen der Theater- und Filmzensur* (Berlin: Wolffsohn, 1932).

8 The review was published in the *Neue badische Landeszeitung* (Mannheim), and quoted in an overview of selected press reviews compiled by Eugen Claassen and sent to Wolfgang Petzet on 19 February 1932—Wolfgang Petzet, estate papers, Munich, Bavarian State Library. All translations from the German are the author's own.

9 More details on Wolfgang Petzet can be found below.

10 A first approach is made in Viola Rühse, *Siegfried Kracauers Filmschriften aus Deutschland und Frankreich* (Berlin & Boston: Walter de Gruyter, 2022), pp. 81–82.

11 Petzet's estate also contains many other valuable materials on censorship at the beginning of the 1930s that are forgotten today.

12 Richard Oswald was very influential on the 'Aufklärungsfilm' genre—see Klaus Kreimeier, 'Aufklärung, Kommerzialismus und Demokratie oder: der Bankrott des deutschen Mannes', in Hans-Michael Bock et al. (eds), *Richard Oswald: Regisseur und Produzent* (Munich: edition text + kritik, 1990), pp. 9–19.

13 Barbian, 'Filme mit Lücken', pp. 53–57.

14 Ibid., p. 53; Korte, *Der Spielfilm und das Ende der Weimarer Republik*, p. 99.

15 Ibid., p. 100.

16 Ibid., pp. 113, 121.

17 Kai Nowak, *Projektionen der Moral: Filmskandale in der Weimarer Republik* (Göttingen: Wallstein, 2015), pp. 277ff.

18 See Späth, *Das Thema hatte es in sich*, pp. 406, 446.

19 Martin Loiperdinger, 'Film Censorship in Germany: Continuity and Change through Five Political Systems', in Daniel Biltereyst and Roel Vande Winkel (eds), *Silencing*

Cinema: Film Censorship around the World (Basingstoke: Palgrave Macmillan, 2013), pp. 81–96 (p. 86).

20 Späth, *Das Thema hatte es in sich*, p. 317.

21 Petzet, *Verbotene Filme*, p. 93; see also Nowak, *Projektionen der Moral*, p. 282; Bodo Plachta, *Zensur* (Munich: Reclam, 2006), pp. 156–57.

22 Nowak, *Projektionen der Moral*, pp. 456–57.

23 'Wir Republikaner und Friedensfreunde sollten es herausschreien: Man hat Angst vor der Straße. Man weicht zurück. Schritt für Schritt. Eines Tages, fürchte ich, wird man den blutigen Lohn ernten. Diejenigen, denen man jetzt nachgibt, werden nicht so weichherzig sein. Die werden, an die Macht gelangt, mit Fäusten dreinschlagen. Und dann Gnade denen, die heute nicht verstehen, ihre Autorität zu bewahren.'—Max Wittenberg (pseudonym for Otto Max Fromm), 'Letter to the Editor', *Vossische Zeitung*, 21 December 1930.

24 Nowak, *Projektionen der Moral*, pp. 456–57, Späth, *Das Thema hatte es in sich*, p. 319.

25 Plachta, *Zensur*, p. 157.

26 For instance, film censorship was discussed in a series of articles titled 'Brauchen wir eine Filmzensur' (Engl. 'Do We Need Film Censorship?') in the *Berliner Tageblatt* in the spring of 1931 (the last article was published on 31 May 1931).

27 Wolfgang Heine, 'Soll es weiter Filmzensur geben? Sie muss fort!', *Vossische Zeitung*, 24 May 1931: 2nd supplement, p. 1.

28 *Kinematograph* editorial department, 'Die Zensoren organisieren sich', *Kinematograph* 25.111 (15 May 1931): 2.

29 '[A]ugenblicklichen Schreckensherrschaft der Zensur'—The quotation is from Siegfried Kracauer's statement on the film censorship book project, cited in the letter from Stefan Wangart to Wolfgang Petzet, 1 July 1931, Petzet, estate papers.

30 Anne-Margret Wallrath-Janssen, *Der Verlag H. Goverts im Dritten Reich* (Munich: Saur, 2007), pp. 25–27.

31 Friedrich Franz von Unruh, *National-Sozialismus* (Frankfurt a.M.: Societäts-Verlag, 1931).

32 'ich wollte Verständnis für moderne, demokratische, das heißt von eigener Verantwortung getragene Politik schaffen'—Eugen Claassen, 'Über das Verlegen', in *Eugen Claassen: von der Arbeit eines Verlegers*, edited by Reinhard Tghart, *Marbacher Magazin* 19 (1981): 1–5 (p. 4).

33 Klaus Petersen, *Zensur in der Weimarer Republik* (Stuttgart: Metzler, 1995), p. 263.

34 Letter from Stefan Wangart to Wolfgang Petzet, 1 July 1931, Petzet, estate papers.

35 Wolfgang Petzet, PR text draft for *Verbotene Filme* (*Banned Films*), Petzet, estate papers.

36 Letter from Stefan Wangart to Wolfgang Petzet, 1 July 1931, Petzet, estate papers.

37 *Eugen Claassen: von der Arbeit eines Verlegers*, p. 84.

38 Bernhard Ebneth, 'Petzet, Erich', in *Neue Deutsche Biographie* 20 (2001): 274, https://www.deutsche-biographie.de/pnd116135603.html [accessed 28 December 2022].

39 Gunther Nickel and Ulrike Weiß, *Carl Zuckmayer, 1896–1977: 'Ich wollte nur Theater machen'* (Marbach am Neckar: Deutsche Schillergesellschaft, 1996), pp. 40–41. Carlo Mierendorff was very open-minded about cinema because of its potential as a democratic mass medium and wrote a famous essay titled *Hätte ich das Kino!* (Berlin: Reiß, 1920), later trying to improve the film censorship situation. Petzet considered

dedicating the pamphlet to his old Heidelberg circle of friends because of Mierendorff's engagement—Letter from Wolfgang Petzet to Eugen Claassen, 3 September 1931, Petzet, estate papers.

40 For instance, he published poems that he wrote from 1917 until 1919 in the book *Der Vorläufer: Gedichte* (Darmstadt: Die Dachstube, 1924).

41 Birger Petersen, 'Drei Liederzyklen Wolfgang Jacobis', in Ulrich Tadday (ed.), *Wolfgang Jacobi*, MUSIK-KONZEPTE 195 (I/2022), pp. 53–67 (p. 56). Petzet's PhD thesis was published in 1929: Wolfgang Petzet, *Der Physiokratismus und die Entdeckung des wirtschaftlichen Kreislaufs* (Karlsruhe: G. Braun, 1929).

42 Petzet worked for various media such as *Ullstein Dienst*, *Frankfurter Zeitung*, *Kunstwart*, *Deutsche Filmzeitung* and *Vossische Zeitung* from 1925.

43 Wolfgang Petzet, *Theater: die Münchner Kammerspiele 1911–1975* (Munich: Kurt Desch, 1973), p. 247.

44 Ibid.

45 Ibid, pp. 247–51. Petzet published, for instance, an apolitical novella in 1943 (Wolfgang Petzet, *Inselliebe* (Munich: Arbeitsgemeinschaft für Zeitgeschichte, 1943)), and the critical poems he wrote from 1940 to 1943 were published after the war (Wolfgang Petzet, *Die Sonette des Satans* (Starnberg: Bachmair, 1947)).

46 Helmut Korte, *Der Spielfilm und das Ende der Weimarer Republik*, p. 51.

47 Siegfried Kracauer, *From Caligari to Hitler: A Psychological History of the German Film* (Princeton: Princeton University Press, 1947); Siegfried Kracauer, *Theory of Film: The Redemption of Physical Reality* (New York: Oxford University Press, 1960).

48 Viola Rühse, *Film und Kino als Spiegel: Siegfried Kracauers Filmschriften aus Deutschland und Frankreich* (Berlin/Boston: De Gruyter 2022), p. 12.

49 Ibid., pp. 65ff.

50 Ibid., pp. 81ff.

51 Helmuth Lethen, 'Einleitung: Kracauers Schauplätze der Evidenz', in Helmuth Lethen, Sabine Biebl and Johannes Moltke (eds), *Siegfried Kracauers Grenzgänge: zur Rettung des Realen* (Frankfurt & New York: Campus, 2019), pp. 1–12 (p. 1); Rühse, *Film und Kino als Spiegel*, pp. 81–82.

52 Letter from Stefan Wangart to Wolfgang Petzet, 1 July 1931, Petzet, estate papers.

53 Petzet, *Verbotene Filme*, pp. 9–11.

54 Ibid., pp. 16, 13–17; Rudolf Arnheim, 'Petzet, Kuhle Wampe, Albers', *Die Weltbühne* 13 (29 March 1932): 486–88 (p. 486).

55 Petzet, *Verbotene Filme*, pp. 19–57; see for instance Kracauer's appreciation of Petzet's precise material analysis: Siegfried Kracauer, 'Über Filmzensur', in *Kleine Schriften zum Film* (Frankfurt a.M.: Suhrkamp, 2004), vol. 6, part 2, pp. 565–67 (p. 566).

56 Petzet, *Verbotene Filme*, pp. 43–44; for references to Petzet's remarks on the 'normal moviegoer', see for instance: Korte, *Der Spielfilm und das Ende der Weimarer Republik*, p. 113; Nowak, *Projektionen der Moral*, pp. 31–32.

57 Petzet, *Verbotene Filme*, pp. 77–78. The mixing of judicative and executive functions is also seen as problematic in later literature such as Barbian, 'Filme mit Lücken', p. 58.

58 Petzet, *Verbotene Filme*, p. 78.

59 Ibid., pp. 93–101; see for instance Späth, *Das Thema hatte es in sich*, pp. 318, 320.

60 Petzet, *Verbotene Filme*, p. 97.

61 Ibid., p. 102.

62 Ibid., pp. 109–40.

63 Ibid., pp. 141–46.

64 Ibid., pp. 149–60.

65 Letter from Wolfgang Petzet to Stefan Wangart (Societäts-Verlag), 12 July 1931, Petzet, estate papers.

66 Wallrath-Janssen, *Der Verlag H. Goverts im Dritten Reich*, p. 39.

67 Claassen, 'Über das Verlegen', p. 4.

68 'Nicht leicht, das Material für eine solche Untersuchung herbeizuschaffen, bei der Geheimniskrämerei der Prüfstellen und der Unlust der Filmfirmen, sich durch Publikation von Zensurmaterial mißliebig zu machen.'—Arnheim, 'Petzet, Kuhle Wampe, Albers', p. 486. Arnheim published his book *Film als Kunst* in 1932 (Berlin: Rowohlt).

69 Letter from Stefan Wangart (Societäts-Verlag) to Wolfgang Petzet, 10 July 1931, Petzet, estate papers. Petzet worked as a freelance journalist for several newspapers such as *Kunstwart, Vossische Zeitung, Frankfurter Zeitung* and *Jugend*. Petzet finished *Verbotene Filme* and integrated his editor's feedback until the beginning of September 1931. By mid-October, some changes were made due to legal concerns, and an update due to a new law was integrated. The book was published at the end of October.

70 Petzet thanked some persons from his network at the end of his book: Petzet, *Verbotene Filme*, p. 148.

71 Letter from Wolfgang Petzet to Fritz Engel, 12 July 1931, Petzet, estate papers.

72 Letter from Wolfgang Petzet to Eugen Claassen, 22 July 1931, Petzet, estate papers; cf. Christine Kopf, '"Der Schein der Neutralität"—Institutionelle Filmzensur in der Weimarer Republik', in Thomas Koebner (ed.), *Diesseits der 'Dämonischen Leinwand': neue Perspektiven auf das späte Weimarer Kino* (Munich: edition text + kritik, 2003), pp. 57–85, https://web.archive.org/web/20160304191131/http://www.difarchiv.deutsches-filminstitut.de/news/dt2n13.htm [accessed 26 February 2022].

73 Siegfried Kracauer, 'Minimalforderung an die Intellektuellen', *Die neue Rundschau* 42.1 (July 1931): 71–75; Kracauer, 'Über Filmzensur', p. 566.

74 See also Rühse, *Film und Kino als Spiegel*, pp. 81–82.

75 Petzet was also active as a poet and playwright.

76 '[A]uf eine betrübliche Art amüsant zu lesen'—Axel Eggebrecht, 'Review of Wolfgang Petzet, *Verbotene Filme*', *Die Literarische Welt*, 27 May 1932; an excerpt is reprinted in Hans Helmut Prinzler, *Chronik des deutschen Films 1895–1994* (Stuttgart, Weimar: Metzler 1995), p. 101.

77 Herbert Ihering, 'Polemik: ein Rundfunkvortrag (1929)', in *Herbert Ihering, Filmkritiker: mit Kritiken und Aufsätzen von Herbert Ihering* (Munich: edition text + kritik 2011), pp. 82–87.

78 The newspaper clippings include, for instance: '"Im Westen nichts Neues": zum Remarque-Tonfilm', *Frankfurter Zeitung*, 7 December 1930; 'Es wird weiter verboten', *Frankfurter Zeitung*, 3 February 1931; 'Der bejubelte Fridericus Rex', *Frankfurter Zeitung*, 23 December 1930. In 1932, Petzet added another article by Kracauer, namely: '"Kuhle Wampe" verboten!', *Frankfurter Zeitung*, 5 April 1932.

79   Siegfried Kracauer, 'Es wird weiter verboten', in *Kleine Schriften zum Film*, vol. 6, part 2, pp. 449–50 (p. 449). As mentioned above, the article is also in Petzet's press clippings.

80   Petzet, *Verbotene Filme*, p. 115; Letter from the Societäts-Verlag to Wolfgang Petzet, 28 July 1931, Petzet, estate papers.

81   See, for instance, Kracauer, *Kleine Schriften zum Film*, vol. 6, part 2, pp. 392–93.

82   Petzet, *Verbotene Filme*, p. 119; Kracauer, *Kleine Schriften zum Film*, vol. 6, part 2, p. 440.

83   Petzet, *Verbotene Filme*, pp. 17 and 87 (indirect references to Kracauer's 'Little Shopgirls' series); p. 112 (direct reference to this series). See also Rühse, *Film und Kino als Spiegel*, pp. 65–104.

84   *'Wie gefällt Ihnen meine Filmbroschüre; in der ich selbstverständlich der unvergessenen kleinen Ladenmädchen gedacht?'*—Letter from Petzet to Kracauer, 25 November 1931, Petzet, estate papers.

85   Kracauer, *Kleine Schriften zum Film*, vol. 6, part 2, pp. 565–67, and vol. 6, part 3, pp. 137–38; see also the letter from Siegfried Kracauer to Wolfgang Petzet on the preprint in the *Frankfurter Zeitung* and one of the reviews, 1 December 1931, Siegfried Kracauer, estate papers, Deutsches Literaturarchiv (DLA) Marbach a.N.

86   Letter from Stefan Wangart to Wolfgang Petzet, 1 July 1931, and the letter from Eugen Claassen to Wolfgang Petzet, 26 August 1931, Petzet, estate papers.

87   Kracauer, *Kleine Schriften zum Film*, vol. 6, part 2, pp. 565–67 (p. 566); Carl Dreyfuß, 'Review of Ilja Ehrenburg, Die Traumfabrik, Wolfgang Petzet, Verbotene Filme […]', *Zeitschrift für Sozialforschung* 1 (1932): 227–28.

88   Ibid., p. 272.

89   See for instance the letter from Stefan Wangart to Wolfgang Petzet, 1 July 1931, Petzet, estate papers; and the letter from Eugen Claassen to Wolfgang Petzet 26 August 1931, Petzet, estate papers.

90   Petzet, *Verbotene Filme*, p. 9.

91   Letter from Wolfgang Petzet to Eugen Claassen, 27 August 1931, Petzet, estate papers.

92   Letter from Eugen Claassen to Petzet, 15 August 1931, Petzet, estate papers.

93   Letters from Eugen Claassen to Petzet, 16 August 1931 and 24 September 1931, Petzet, estate papers.

94   Wolfgang Petzet, typescript (TS) for *Banned Films*, Petzet, estate papers, 15; cf. Petzet *Verbotene Filme*, p. 29.

95   One undated letter from one legal advisor is preserved in Petzet, estate papers; see also Wolfgang Petzet, typescript (TS) for *Banned Films*, Petzet, estate papers, 19, cf. Petzet, *Verbotene Filme*, p. 34; Petzet, typescript (TS) for *Banned Films*, Petzet, estate papers, 23, cf. Petzet, *Verbotene Filme*, p. 40.

96   Arnheim, 'Petzet, Kuhle Wampe, Albers', p. 486; see also Dreyfuß, 'Review of Ilja Ehrenburg'; Peter Scher, 'Review of Wolfgang Petzet, *Verbotene Filme*, 1931', *Simplicissimus* 36.39 (28 December 1931): 462; and the letter from Wolfgang Petzet to Eugen Claassen, 25 December 1931, Petzet, estate papers. In contrast, Axel Eggebrecht appreciated Petzet's critical and decisive perspective: Eggebrecht, 'Review of Wolfgang Petzet, *Verbotene Filme*'.

97   Letter from the Societäts-Verlag to Wolfgang Petzet, 28 July 1931, Petzet, estate papers. The phrase alludes to Oswald Spengler's *Der Untergang des Abendlandes* (Vienna: Braumüller, 1918/22).

98 Letter from Wolfgang Petzet to Eugen Claassen, 3 September 1931, Petzet, estate papers: *'würde man es aber mit ganzer Schärfe herausarbeiten so wäre der Abschluss einfach aussichtslos deprimierend: denn mit der Forderung, wir müssten erstmal so was wie eine Nation werden, ist in einer von heute auf morgen wirken sollenden Broschüre kaum viel anzufangen.'*

99 The later publication date was partly due to the involvement of political and legal advisors. Letter from Eugen Claassen to Wolfgang Petzet, 31 October 1931, Petzet, estate papers.

100 Korte, *Der Spielfilm und das Ende der Weimarer Republik*, pp. 57–58.

101 Petersen, *Zensur in der Weimarer Republik*, pp. 260–61; Korte, *Der Spielfilm und das Ende der Weimarer Republik*, p. 98.

102 Petzet, *Verbotene Filme*, p. 160. The new emergency decree did not diminish the impact of Petzet's book; the reviews did not address this aspect. See also the letter from Wolfgang Petzet to Eugen Claassen, 13 October 1931, Petzet, estate papers.

103 The materials in the estate archives illustrate the major marketing efforts.

104 For instance, preprints were published in *Der Wiener Tag* (2 January 1931, p. 7) and *Prager Tageblatt* (3 January 1932, p. 4). Preprints in the *Deutsche Filmzeitung* and *Film-Kurier* are also mentioned in the letters between Petzet and Claassen. Letter from Eugen Claassen to Wolfgang Petzet, 24 October 1931; and from Wolfgang Petzet to Eugen Claassen, 29 November 1931, Petzet, estate papers.

105 Letter from Eugen Claassen to Wolfgang Petzet, 14 November 1931, Petzet, estate papers.

106 Letter from Eugen Claassen to Wolfgang Petzet, 27 November 1931; Wolfgang Petzet informed Eugen Claassen about his lecture in a letter dated 12 November 1931 (Petzet, estate papers).

107 *'Das Muster einer polemischen Schrift! Das Material vollkommen beherrscht, die Argumentation unangreifbar, der Vortrag von ruhiger Stärker, das Ganze als Lektüre höchst anziehend,—es ist gegen das Lichtspielgesetz und seine eng büreaukratische Handhabung noch keine gleich wirksame Waffe geschmiedet worden.'* Bruno Frank's recommendation is quoted in the overview of selected press reviews compiled by Ernst Claassen and sent to Wolfgang Petzet on 19 February 1932—Petzet, estate papers.

108 Letter from Eugen Claassen to Wolfgang Petzet, 11 December 1931, Petzet, estate papers.

109 Letter from Eugen Claassen to Wolfgang Petzet, 23 January 1932, Petzet, estate papers.

110 Petzet states 'but no one buys anything anymore' (*'aber es kauft eben überhaupt niemand mehr etwas'*)—Letter from Wolfgang Petzet to Eugen Claassen, 29 January 1932, Petzet, estate papers.

111 Korte, *Der Spielfilm und das Ende der Weimarer Republik*, p. 121.

112 *'Das wir allerdings auf einem verlorenen Posten kämpfen dürften'*—Letter from Wolfgang Petzet to Eugen Claassen, 27 January 1932, Petzet, estate papers.

113 Barbian, 'Filme mit Lücken', p. 70.

114 Nowak, *Projektionen der Moral*, p. 282.

115 Späth, *Das Thema hatte es in sich*, p. 319.

116 Barbian, 'Filme mit Lücken', p. 70; Klaus Petersen, 'Censorship and the Campaign against Foreign Influences in Film and Theater during the Weimar Republic', in John

A. McCarthy and Werner von der Ohe (eds), *Zensur und Kultur: zwischen Weimarer Klassik und Weimarer Republik mit einem Ausblick bis heute* (*Censorship and Culture: From Weimar Classicism to Weimar Republic and Beyond*) (Tübingen: Niemeyer, 1995), pp. 149–58 (p. 124); Loiperdinger, 'Film Censorship in Germany', p. 87.

6

Party Apparatchiks as Filmmakers: The Film Approval Commissions in Communist Poland, 1955–1970

Mikołaj Kunicki

Stored in a few Polish archives, the records of the Chief Board of Cinema (Naczelny Zarząd Kinematografii), which oversaw the Polish film industry during the communist period, are incomplete, inconsistent, yet fascinating and compelling. Not only do they document the history of the Polish national film industry under state socialism, but they also constitute a kaleidoscope of changing relations between the communist regime and Poland's cinematic community and artistic intelligentsia. Following the demise of Stalinism in the mid-1950s, this cohabitation became more nuanced during the long reign of Władysław Gomułka, who came to power in 1956 while riding the combined waves of social discontent, liberalization of the communist system, nationalism, and anxiety among the Party elites.[1] The political, social and cultural climate of Gomułka's era was brilliantly captured by the metaphor of 'the little stabilization'. Coined by the prominent Polish poet and playwright Tadeusz Różewicz, the term projected the discrepancy between people's expectations raised by de-Stalinization and the outcome of post-Stalinist reforms.[2] It also represented the regime's predilection for stability rather than revolutionary changes and a shift from coercive Stalinist control over society to social integration based on compliance, conformism and tacit acceptance of communist rule.

Mikołaj Kunicki, "Party Apparatchiks as Filmmakers: The Film Approval Commissions in Communist Poland, 1955–1970" in: *The Screen Censorship Companion: Critical Explorations in the Control of Film and Screen Media*. University of Exeter Press (2024). © Mikołaj Kunicki. DOI: 10.47788/SNGT2135

This chapter examines the predominant practice of censoring films in communist Poland, through an analysis of meetings of the Script Assessment Commission (Komisja Ocen Scenariuszy), abolished in 1967, and the Film Approval Commission (Komisja Kolaudacyjna). Part-government, part-industry bodies, the commissions were headed by the boss of the Polish film industry, head of the Chief Board of Cinema, and they were populated by filmmakers, Communist Party officials in charge of culture and propaganda, film critics and censors. The verdict of script assessors mandated the admission of film projects for production. Film assessors decided the future of a completed movie, whether it needed last-minute edits and was fit for release and wide distribution. From 1969 the Film Approval Commission used a scoring scale, which allocated up to fifteen points for 'general ideological assessment', fifteen points for 'general artistic assessment', five points for acting, three for camerawork, three for sound, and three for scenography/costumes. The final score placed a film into one of the following categories: 'outstanding (40–44 points)', 'valuable' (34–39 points), 'average' (27–33 points), 'weak' (19–26 points), and 'bad' (up to 18 points).[3] The chairman also had to obtain the approval of the Department of Culture of the Central Committee of the Party. In special cases, the final decision was made by members of the Politburo, the most powerful Party officials in Poland.

Prior to the meetings of the commissions, scripts and movies had to go through the internal assessment of their own film production units. Introduced in 1955 as part-artistic, part-economic enterprises, film units included directors, writers and production managers.[4] Professional censors played a secondary role in the whole process. Here, we witness the gradual erosion of institutional censorship and its replacement by what Miklós Haraszti, a Hungarian sociologist and dissident, has defined as 'a velvet prison', in which the communist state rewarded compliant artists, displayed a substantial permissiveness, and even co-opted dissent.[5] In addition, the transcripts of assessment meetings provide a rare opportunity to learn about the communist elite's cinematic taste, intellectual horizons and views on popular culture.

I argue that some of these Party officials became so immersed in discussions with members of Poland's film community that they 'became', in their own view, experts on cinema if not filmmakers. I find this 'acculturation' of communist apparatchiks both ironical and fascinating, especially because their participation in script and film approval was to enhance 'socialist film criticism', to quote the 1960 resolution of the Central Committee Secretariat of the Party about the Polish film industry.[6] At the same time, some filmmakers used commissions to defend their positions, assess their colleagues or prove their ideological credentials. The scope of my observation is limited to the period from 1955, the year of the partial de-centralization of the Polish film industry and the creation of film production units, to 1967–68, the years of the state-sponsored anti-Semitic, anti-intellectual campaign. A political watershed and one of the most significant milestones in the delegitimization of Soviet communism, the campaign affected the Polish film industry, leading to the emigration of some filmmakers of Jewish origins and the dismissal of Tadeusz Zaorski (1917–1993), the chairman of the Chief Board of Cinema and gifted broker between filmmakers and authorities. The year 1968 also marked the liquidation of eight film production units that had formed the backbone of the Polish film industry since the mid-1950s.

In its analysis, my chapter strongly opposes the Cold War construct of totalitarianism and instead reveals nuances and cracks in the regime's cultural policies and artists' responses. The treatment of the Polish cinematic community by the Communist Party stemmed from the regime's policies towards the artistic intelligentsia and oscillated between rigid dictates, mutual accommodations and negotiated autonomies. De-Stalinization, subsequent political and cultural thaw and the more repressive course of the mid-1960s did not set unitary trends. What makes the Polish case interesting for an international audience is that until the Prague Spring in Czechoslovakia in 1968, Poland had been the most liberal Soviet satellite. Its Roman Catholic Church enjoyed substantial autonomy and offered to millions of Catholic Poles an ethno-religious identity and spiritual community alternative to the secular Marxist state. The artistic intelligentsia, which included survivors of the pre-war elites, members of the wartime generation and Catholic intellectuals, enjoyed the opening of the country to Western culture and the end of socialist realism in the arts. Although Polish filmmakers could see their projects blocked by censorship at early stages, during the evaluation of scripts, they did not experience calamities such as the 1965–66 collective banning of twelve DEFA films in East Germany, or the suppression of the Czechoslovak New Wave in the aftermath of the 1968 Soviet-led invasion of Czechoslovakia. At times they could count on the goodwill of some senior communist officials and Party intellectuals who often knew filmmakers personally and could offer some protection against hardliners or, at least, tip their protégés off about decisions taken by the leadership of the Communist Party.

The transcripts of assessment meetings that I have used in my chapter testify to the complex and, at times, close relationship between filmmakers and the Party during Gomułka's years. The gatherings from the early 1960s seem to project a more relaxed and intimate atmosphere, even joviality when participants throw in jokes or bon mots, and a willingness to compromise. The meetings of the late 1960s convey tension, the desperation of filmmakers, and the growing ruthlessness of Party officials. This trajectory of mood mirrors the evolving climate of relations between the Polish artistic intelligentsia and the Gomułka regime, from high hopes raised by de-Stalinization, through complacency and low expectations brought by 'the little stabilization', to the climax of 1967–68, the years of the anti-Zionist (read 'anti-Semitic') campaign, and crackdown on the student youth and intellectuals.

Case Study: The Assessment of Kazimierz Kutz's *Silence*

Produced in 1963, Kazimierz Kutz's feature film *Milczenie* (*Silence*, 1963) is an unjustly forgotten classic of Polish art cinema, a modernist feature, which was very much in visual dialogue with the contemporary films of Michelangelo Antonioni, Ingmar Bergman and Robert Bresson. Set in post-war Poland, it is a tale of a teenage war orphan, Stach, who loses his sight after playing with explosives, and an old parish priest struck by dotage. Falsely accused of trying to murder the priest, Stach becomes the object of hatred, humiliation and ostracism from the local community. The priest, who knows the truth and commands great respect among the locals, fails to help the boy due to the combination of indecisiveness and cowardice caused by his senility. While Stach gradually learns how to live with his disability and eventually leaves the town, the priest loses his prestige among the locals and enters a lonely retirement. It is a bleak tale of intolerance and a society brutalized by war.

What makes Kutz's work particularly interesting is the paper trail left by the Script Assessment and Film Approval Commissions. The records of these meetings contain long and complex discussions that challenge the stereotypical division of oppressed filmmakers and oppressive communist censors, demonstrate the anti-clerical leanings of members of the artistic intelligentsia, and contain fascinating insights on the cinematic preferences of communist leaders. When the Film Approval Commission met in May 1963 to decide on the film's release and distribution, there was significant dissonance between filmmakers and Communist Party officials. The presence of Artur Starewicz (1917–2014), head of the Press Bureau of the Central Committee of the Party, testified to the seriousness of the matter. In fact, Starewicz voiced strong reservations about the film and questioned the decision of the Script Assessment Commission to allow its production. He anticipated vehement protests from Polish bishops, hostile reactions in small-town Poland and limited commercial success. His solution was startling: while opposing the distribution of the film in Poland, he recommended exporting it and sending it to international festivals.[7]

Figure 6.1. Frames from *Silence* (Kazimierz Kutz, 1963)

Filmmakers present at the meeting unanimously praised Kutz's film as an outstanding artistic achievement. Jerzy Pomianowski, writer and member of the film production unit Syrena, retorted that Polish cinema could not afford 'hiding outstanding movies' from Polish viewers. Director and script-writer Aleksander Ścibor-Rylski subtly cornered the communist Starewicz, emphasizing the ideological value and practical usage of Kutz's film. 'We have the opportunity to influence society in the spirit of secularization', claimed Ścibor-Rylski. 'It is an activist, wise movie, which attacks religious bigotry, ignorance and rude conduct'. At the same time, he stated that *Silence* was not an anti-Catholic film; rather it stigmatized the pressure of the Church on society and the shallowness of popular religiosity.[8]

Starewicz was not convinced. He doubted the impact of *Silence* on the Catholic masses. 'We are not going to organize any mass meetings and public discussions on it', he stated. 'What matters is the clergy, who are going to view this film as an act of war'. He also allowed himself bitter remarks about the relationship between Polish filmmakers, authorities and audiences. 'The misunderstanding between us [the Party officials] and the film community is that you [filmmakers] are fascinated by craft, and we cannot separate artistic effects from the content', he stated. 'We must treat film as a product of mass consumption which should meet the cultural needs of society'. He also referred to a recent conversation with Władysław Gomułka, the leader of the Polish Communist Party, who had complained that Polish films were pessimistic and lamented the absence of such movies as the USA's *High Noon* (Fred Zinnemann, 1952). 'The point is that films should carry an optimistic message and that the evening in a cinema should have a pleasant ending', observed Starewicz. 'The movie which we have watched today is depressing [...] and does not address the needs of wide circles of Polish society.'[9] Tadeusz Karpowicz, who oversaw the production department of the Chief Board of Cinema, objected to this opinion and illustrated his point by referring to the favourite movie of Gomułka. 'What I am going to say may strike you as a paradox, but I think that we can approach this film in the same way as we understand *High Noon*', he said. For him the cowardice of the priest showed 'the consequences of renouncing courage'.[10]

Film critic and scriptwriter Krzysztof Teodor Toeplitz aptly recapitulated the meeting by pointing out that most of the discussants sought to find a correct strategy for the distribution of the film. 'Of course, if this film enters mass distribution, it will be a dance party invitation for the episcopate', he joked. Toeplitz's conclusion deserves to be cited in full:

> We are here in an extremely convenient situation, and we will not find another such quickly. Well, in this film we expose obscurantism

[...] and we demand from the viewers answers to the issues posed in the film, and one of the issues is condemnation of obscurantism. And here everyone should answer in the affirmative because every thinking person must refer to the manifestations that this film exposes in the light of the concept of sin. If we are to have a duel [with the episcopate], we must take it in the most convenient positions.[11]

The chairman Tadeusz Zaorski sympathized with the opinions of the filmmakers. To pacify Starewicz and state censors, he recommended preliminary screenings for small audiences of ordinary viewers.[12] Kutz's film received approval for release one month after the assessment meeting. *Silence* premiered at the Venice Film Festival in 1963 and went into distribution in Poland in September of the same year. As predicted by Starewicz, it drew official protests from Polish bishops who accused the film of defaming the clergy and recommended its boycott.[13]

The Vicissitudes of Film Censorship in Gomułka's Poland

The assessment of Kutz's film captures the complexity and paradoxes of film censorship in communist Poland in the 1960s. It shows the relatively open nature of discussions that took place at the meetings of the assessment commissions. Of course, the situation could have been very different if the Party had sent someone less prone to persuasion and more ruthless than Starewicz. One can also notice the sense of solidarity among the filmmakers. Ścibor-Rylski's and Toeplitz's equilibristics to project Kutz's film as a project with a social and political mission were particularly impressive. However, I do not suggest that their passionate speeches did not contain their actual views. There was significant disdain among members of the Polish artistic intelligentsia towards Polish Catholicism, with its plebeian religiosity and conservative church leaders, for instance Cardinal Stefan Wyszyński. Some of the filmmakers who were present at the assessment of *Silence* would make long personal and political journeys. Ścibor-Rylski moved from writing socialist-realist novels in the 1950s to authoring the scripts of Andrzej Wajda's *Człowiek z marmuru* (*Man of Marble*, 1977) and *Człowiek z żelaza* (*Man of Iron*, 1981). Tadeusz Konwicki, another former literary Stalinist, would frequently submit his manuscripts straight to oppositional under-ground publishers in the 1970s and 1980s. On the other hand, the intel-lectually brilliant Toeplitz never broke away from the communist system.

The discussion of *Silence* demonstrates those features of film policy in the Soviet Bloc, and specifically Polish concerns, that Western scholars often tend to neglect or are not aware of. Let us consider Starewicz's two fears, the fact of it having a small audience (Starewicz anticipated low ticket sales due to the potential boycott of the movie by the Catholic clergy) and the protests of Polish Catholic bishops. Recent scholarship on the history of cinema and television in the Soviet Bloc highlights the impact of economic factors, and broadly defined cultures of production.[14] In addition to their criticism of 'elitist films', Starewicz and other communist officials in charge of culture were concerned with financial losses incurred by the national film industry after its 'fat' years of the late 1950s and early 1960s, when the Polish School established Poland on the cinematic map of the world and brought hard currency for the critically acclaimed movies of Andrzej Wajda, Andrzej Munk and Jerzy Kawalerowicz. Before becoming the longest-serving head of Polish cinema in 1957, Tadeusz Zaorski was an economist employed by the Ministry of Culture and Arts. He implemented the system of wages which tied filmmakers' salaries to the three categories of movie: 1) those representing high political and artistic merit; 2) those with high artistic values and social use; 3) all those that fell below the first two categories.[15]

These ideologically rigid criteria paid lip service to openly propagandist films that were produced in the Gomułka period, but also left the door open to artistic films, including the works of such individualists like Kutz and Wojciech Has, the director of *Rękopis znaleziony w Saragossie* (*The Saragossa Manuscript*, 1965). However, towards the end of his tenure as the head of the Polish film industry, Zaorski had to acknowledge that though once successful and profitable, his domain was not now yielding enough crop. 'It is not that the Script Assessment Commission does not accept [enough film scripts]', he observed in 1967. 'The problem is that the Commission does not receive interesting proposals'. Film critic Ryszard Koniczek added that the low number of submitted scripts would result in a production crisis. He recommended to Zaorski a review of all nearly completed scripts and the approval of their productions.[16]

It was not all that simple. The Polish film industry was rocked by the rebellion of several scriptwriters, who, like Jerzy Stawiński, the frequent collaborator of Wajda and Munk, wanted full recognition for their contributions to artistically and commercially successful films. But at the root of the problem were the Party's guidelines that recommended 'ideologically correct' films and strong preventive censorship. It has been estimated that throughout the 1960s the Script Assessment Commission rejected 40% of film scripts.[17] Some of these submissions were of low quality; others included materials of serious potential such as projects on the non-communist Home Army resistance movement and the Holocaust.[18] The projects that dealt with the Shoah, both scripts and finished movies, were practically eliminated in 1967–68, during the anti-Semitic campaign labelled euphemistically as 'anti-Zionist', and did not resurface until the 1980s. I will refer to the subject of censoring the Holocaust-related films in greater detail in the last part of this chapter.

I would also like to highlight a fact which often escapes the attention of film scholars working on the cinema and culture of communist Poland, namely that documentaries and shorts were more thoroughly censored than full-length feature films. This is because they were closely scrutinized by their production companies, the Documentary Film Studio and the Film Studio 'Czołówka', which was controlled by the Main Political Board of the Polish Army (Główny Zarząd Polityczny Wojska Polskiego).[19] Only a handful of documentaries were banned or withdrawn from distribution in the 1960s. The production of features demanded considerable funds for staff, equipment, shooting at locations, and so on. A banned feature film could always be shelved for later release under more favourable political circumstances, whereas a cheaply produced documentary, which aimed to catch the spirit of its time, was more prone to age quickly both in terms of its subject matter and cinematic technique. Not every banned documentary could benefit from the reversal of fortunes in the way that Jerzy Hoffman and Edward Skórzewski's *Pamiątka z Kalwarii* (*A Souvenir from Calvary*, 1958/66) did. Shot in an anthropological fashion without any commentary, the film followed the traditional Passion play performed by Polish villagers at the shrine of Kalwaria Zebrzydowska in 1958, delivering a fascinating portrayal of plebeian religiosity, depicting the emotions of the villagers as they reconstructed the last days of Christ. The documentary was quickly banned. However, six years later, during the Church–State conflict over the symbolical celebration of the Millennium of Polish statehood and Christianity, the government viewed the short more favourably, as evidence of religious fanaticism, so released it and sent it to international film festivals. *A Souvenir from Calvary* won the Grand Prize in the documentary category at Oberhausen in 1966, and a special award at the Festival dei Popoli in Florence in 1967.

The attitude of the Roman Catholic Church posed different challenges to Polish filmmakers. A predominantly Catholic country with a strong and autonomous Church—a unique case in the Soviet Bloc—Poland also experienced the parallel film censorship imposed by the Bureau of Episcopate's Commission for Film, Television, Radio and Theatre in 1957.[20] The Bureau forwarded its lists of recommended and condemned films to dioceses, which passed these suggestions on to parishes. Ironically, the verdict of Church experts often mirrored that of the Party censors. Films admonished by the Church for amorality and sexual scenes were often dubbed as pessimistic, decadent and repulsive by the Party.[21] Obviously, the Polish episcopate could not block the release of these movies or prevent their distribution, but it orchestrated their boycotts, as it did in the case of Jerzy Kawalerowicz's

Matka Joanna od aniołów (*Mother Joan of Angels*, 1961), the winner of the Special Jury Prize in Cannes in 1961.[22] These were facts not to be taken lightly by the Gomułka regime, which spent much of the 1960s fighting a cultural war against the Church. Ironically, as the assessment of *Silence* demonstrates, communist officials displayed, at times, more caution not to antagonize the Church than filmmakers who came from the ranks of the progressive intelligentsia.

Inasmuch as Starewicz's comments on Gomułka's fondness for westerns reveal the personal cinematic tastes of communist elites, they signal the classic trope of authoritarian regimes, their preference for uncomplicated movies offering mass entertainment. The Polish case also unveils genre filmmaking in the service of the party state and National Communism. Throughout the 1960s Polish film studios produced nearly 300 feature films, documentaries and TV series linked to World War II.[23] The war not only brought millions of deaths, but also transformed Poland into an ethnically homogeneous country, moved its borders westward and installed the Soviet-controlled communist regime. The Polish communists deliberately delayed closure to national mourning, magnifying a sense of victimhood and instilling fears of the German threat in society. Keen to attract young viewers to 'patriotic screens', the Polish communists endorsed the production of combat films, historical epics, westerns and TV spy series.[24]

Comrade Assessors: Party and Military Officials and Film Censorship in the 1960s

An educated man, diplomat and, in private, a long-time admirer and protector of world-renowned sculptor Magdalena Abakanowicz, Starewicz can be viewed as an eccentric and a Party moderate. He was largely responsible for the dissolution of the Script Assessment Commission, unpopular in the Polish cinema community, and its replacement with programme councils (*rady programowe*) added to film production units.[25]

Starewicz belonged to the troubleshooters team, which was formed by the Department of Culture of the Central Committee of the Party in 1959 to monitor the film industry. These 'comrades from the leadership of ideological struggle' were Gomułka's trusted lieutenants.[26] Other members included Wincenty Kraśko (1916–1976), head of the Department of Culture; Jerzy Putrament (1910–1986), writer, poet, former ambassador to France, and member of the film production unit 'Start'; and Stanisław Trepczyński (1924–2002), future diplomat and UN official. Following the passing of the 1960 resolution of the Central Committee Secretariat of the Party, which had condemned some Polish films for their pessimism and disagreement with the Party programme, Gomułka's ideological watchdogs frequently attended meetings of assessment commissions. On special occasions, it was the Party leader and his deputy, Zenon Kliszko, who made ultimate decisions about specific films, with Gomułka banning Aleksander Ford's *Ósmy dzień tygodnia* (*The Eighth Day of the Week*, 1958/83)[27] and Kliszko confirming to Jerzy Skolimowski the proscription of his *Ręce do góry* (*Hands Up!*, 1967/81/85), thereby sealing the director's decision to leave Poland.[28]

A brief glance at the list of people who assessed Kutz's *Silence* also points to the fact that script and film approval commissions were a man's world. For many years Wanda Jakubowska (1907–1998), director and head of the film production unit 'Start', and director Ewa Petelska (1920–2013) were the only female consultants occasionally invited to these meetings. The transcripts of assessment commissions show a misogynistic atmosphere riddled with sexist comments and jokes. The situation changed only in the 1970s, with more women directors, such as Barbara Sass and Agnieszka Holland, entering the male-dominated cinematic community in Poland.

The film assessment commissions also hosted senior army officers from the Main Political Board of the Polish Army. The communist military played a significant role in the production of combat dramas, lending military equipment and soldiers as extras. Often cast as military consultants advising on historical and technical matters, these officers also censored movies which depicted Polish armed forces during and after World War II. Colonel Zbigniew Załuski (1926–1978) stood out from the crowd. A historian and influential essayist close to General Mieczysław Moczar's nationalist-authoritarian faction of 'Partisans', Załuski authored many movie scripts, including portions of Yuri Ozerov's Soviet epic *Soldaty svobody* (*Soldiers of Freedom*, 1977). The leading proponent of the patriotic-Marxist fusion, he attacked auteurs associated with the Polish School, especially Andrzej Munk, for mocking military patriotism and heroism, and promoting 'the ethic of the gutter' among Polish youth.[29]

How did contacts with filmmakers and long hours spent in front of movie screens influence the ideological 'avant-garde' of the ruling party? The answers vary from case to case. Putrament's involvement in the 'Start' film production unit as well as his writer's career clearly distinguished him from Kraśko and Trepczyński, veteran party apparatchiks and the products of the system. As a student, Putrament was member of the avant-garde 'Żagary' literary group and a senior activist of the nationalist and anti-Semitic organization All-Poland Youth. In the mid-1930s, he moved away from the nationalist right to communism. Memorably portrayed as 'Gamma, the Slave of History' in *The Captive Mind* (1953), Czesław Miłosz's study of intellectuals' relationship with Stalinism, Putrament was known for his flamboyant lifestyle and unorthodox behaviour. He could attack the final, censored version of Jerzy Zarzycki's *Miasto nieujarzmione*

(*Unvanquished City*, 1950) for 'its crude, naïve, vulgar politicization' and write the sycophantic poem *Letter to Stalin*.[30] Later, while participating in script and film assessments during Gomułka's rule, he presented himself as a Party liberal, warning Kawalerowicz and Konwicki that the script of *Mother Joan of Angels* was likely to be rejected because the Party wanted to avoid a conflict with the Church.[31] He also enjoyed cultivating an image of himself as a libertine throwing sexist bon mots while evaluating *Faraon* (*Pharaoh*, Jerzy Kawalerowicz, 1966).[32]

Mild-mannered Trepczyński lacked Putrament's charisma but commanded more political influence as a high official in the Secretariat of the Central Committee of the Party, the same body which passed the notorious resolution on Polish cinema in 1960. More importantly, he was close to both Gomułka and Moczar. Always attentive to political issues, Trepczyński did not shy away from commenting on cinematic details and demonstrated good knowledge of contemporary cinema, for instance drawing comparisons between Sylwester Chęciński's *Agnieszka 46* (1964) and Luis Buñuel's *Viridiana* (1961), no small feat for a communist apparatchik.[33] While assessing Chęciński's movie, he also stuck to his own opinions rather than following the judgement of political allies such as Colonel Załuski, who vehemently attacked *Agnieszka 46* for ridiculing World War II veterans and military settlers.[34]

Out of the four Party assessors discussed in this chapter, Kraśko was the least versatile in the arts, and the most orthodox in ideological matters, ruthless and cynical. A veteran propagandist and the head of the Cultural Department of the Central Committee, he was responsible for 'killing' or 'maiming' many film projects, including Ścibor-Rylski's first script for Wajda's *Man of Marble* in 1963. 'It is not about you, but about the Party', Kraśko told the shattered Wajda, 'because this must be a Party film'.[35] He also blocked the release of Andrzej Brzozowski's short *Przy torze kolejowym* (*By the Railway Track*, 1963), the longest-banned Polish movie under communism, which would be shown to a general audience only in 1992, three years after the collapse of communism as a whole. Based on a short story from Zofia Nałkowska's *Medallions*, this étude shows the encounter between some Polish villagers and a wounded Jewess who escaped from the transport to a death camp. Faced by the indifference of the onlookers who observe her suffering for hours, the woman pleads to be killed. In the end, a young Polish man shoots her dead. While defending his movie, Brzozowski pointed out to Kraśko that Nałkowska's book was part of the state-approved reading list for secondary schools. 'When you read it, you cannot see how scary it is', replied Kraśko. 'Only when you see it on the screen, it gets shocking'.[36] Brzozowski's film violated the official heroic-martyrological narrative, which stated that Poles had selflessly helped Jews during World War II. According to Kraśko, the movie 'could be used by anti-Polish propaganda' and 'harm Polish raison d'état'.[37] Kraśko's successors in charge of the Department of Culture of the Central Committee shared this assessment or refused to confront it. At the time when many banned films were released in the late 1980s, Brzozowski's short remained blacklisted with the same annotation: 'The difficult problem of Polish–Jewish relations has been exaggerated. It does not seem right to bring the film to the screens today.'[38]

Kraśko acquired particular notoriety during the 1967–68 anti-Semitic campaign, self-described as 'anti-Zionist'. Coupled with the crackdown on the liberal intelligentsia, this ideological offensive showed the true colours of Gomułka's 'Polish road to socialism', anti-Semitism, brutal authoritarianism and populism. Kraśko was involved in banning Kazimierz Dejmek's theatrical production of *Dziady* (*The Forefathers*) by the nineteenth-century romantic Adam Mickiewicz in Warsaw in January 1968, a decision which led to the outbreak of the student rebellion.

On the film front, he distinguished himself by objecting to the release of Janusz Nasfeter's *Długa noc* (*Long Night*, 1967/89). The story of a young Pole hiding a Jew in Nazi-occupied Poland and the ring of suspicion and greed closing around them did not sit well with Kraśko. The assessment of the film was dominated by references, brought forth by Kraśko, Aleksander Ford and Krzysztof Teodor Toeplitz, to the current political situation in Poland, namely the beginning of the 'anti-Zionist' campaign in Poland following the Israeli victory in the Six-Day War in the Middle East. Seemingly distraught, both Ford and Toeplitz lamented the government's propaganda. Kraśko admitted that 'All kind of news [on the Six-Day War] that our press features lead to nothing else than to arousing anti-Semitism'. Although he declared that the Party leadership was alarmed by anti-Semitic resentment, he emphasized the necessity of avoiding those depictions of Polish–Jewish relations that would feed foreign propaganda presenting the Poles as Nazi helpers murdering the Jews.[39] Nasfeter's film, mild in its projections of Polish anti-Semitism and complicity in the Holocaust, was sacrificed because of the growing anti-Semitic propaganda in Poland. It did not premiere until 1989, the year of the collapse of communism in the country.

Among 13,000 Polish Jews who left the country as the result of the anti-Semitic campaign were people who had played an important role in the Polish film industry: director Aleksander Ford, cameramen Jerzy Lipman and Kurt Weber, production managers, and others. Tadeusz Zaorski, rector of the Lodz Film School Jerzy Toeplitz, and dean of the Film Direction Department Jerzy Bossak were all dismissed from their posts. By coincidence, the plans to reform the increasingly inefficient film industry took place amid the anti-Zionist campaign. The existing film production units were dissolved in 1968 and replaced by new ones.

One of the most striking 'cinephile' comments by censors that I have found, while working on this chapter, comes from the assessment meeting for Jerzy Passendorfer's *Dzień oczyszczenia* (*Day of Remission*, 1969) about the difficult encounter between Polish and Soviet partisans during World War II. Colonel Łokietek dismissed the objections of those attendees who criticized the director for producing an action movie. 'I am not a filmmaker, but I must admit that I really like action films. I acquired my cinematic taste while watching westerns before the war', Łokietek said. 'I also remember that I really enjoyed watching *All Quiet on the Western Front*, and I cannot simply understand why we should separate historical facts from the spirit of adventure.'[40] A World War II veteran and communist partisan, Colonel Tadeusz Maj 'Łokietek' was responsible for the murders of some forty Jews hiding in the Polish countryside during the Nazi occupation.

Conclusions

High Party dignitaries stopped attending the meetings of film assessment commissions after the fall of Gomułka in 1970. It is not that the new Edward Gierek regime did not pay attention to cinema. However, the Party state, now less authoritarian and more prone to social manipulation and consumerism, displayed different approaches towards film censorship. Several propagandists simply became scriptwriters and joined filmmakers, especially those who took pro-regime positions, as collaborators, not censors.[41] With the end of 'the long 1960s' that lasted in Poland from 1956 to 1970—that is, from the accession to power of Władysław Gomułka to his downfall—the country and its film industry experienced the partial ideological demobilization of the regime and the birth of the Cinema of Moral Anxiety (*kino moralnego niepokoju*), embodied in the early films of Krzysztof Kieślowski, Agnieszka Holland, Krzysztof Zanussi and Feliks Falk. The second flagship of Polish cinema (with the Polish School being the first) focused directly on the issues of censorship, corruption and a society in crisis. These new auteurs were less willing to play polite games with the Party and its censors than their predecessors who came from the brutalized and politically confused war generation. What also made a difference was, in my view, the devastating experience of the 1967–68 anti-Semitic campaign accompanied by the crackdown on students, followed by the invasion of Czechoslovakia.

This is the first big lesson concerning film censorship and the relationship between the communist regime and cinema community in Poland during the Gomułka era. Both filmmakers and Party officials in charge of the film industry were marked by World War II, Stalinism, and a dramatic breakaway from it around 1956. Gomułka's watchdogs who assessed films were communists, but also de-Stalinizers who received some credit of trust from members of the Polish cinematic community. To a similar extent, the filmmakers of the 1960s had the experience of socialist realism in their DNA. De-Stalinization broke these ideological constraints but did not completely wash away old habits such as, for example, the fear of authorities, conformism and doublethink. Some filmmakers were never serious adherents of communism; others could be described as sympathetic to post-Stalinist liberalizations of the system. As we have seen, both groups could find a common ground with respect to religion, especially Polish Catholicism. Here the Party officials even had to tone down the anticlericalism of filmmakers.

What constituted a bone of contention were the interconnected issues of nationalism and anti-Semitism, both directly related to Gomułka's 'Polish road to socialism', which aimed to marry ethnocentric nationalism with Marxism, and resulted in the absence of coming to terms with Polish–Jewish relations during the Holocaust. The Party proved determined to stick to its socialist-patriotic fusion, which rested on the worship of Polish heroism and martyrology, 'relegating' Jews to the status of Nazi victims and recipients of selfless Polish help. Filmmakers' attempts to challenge this dominant narrative can strike us as feeble, especially if we compare Polish movies on the Holocaust made in the 1950s and 1960s or during the entire communist period, to the output of the Czechoslovak New Wave, with movies such as *Démanty noci* (*Diamonds of the Night*, Jan Nemec, 1964), *A pátý jezdec je strach* (*The Fifth Horseman is Fear*, Zbyněk Brynych, 1965) and *Obchod na korze* (*The Shop on Main Street*, Ján Kadár and Elmar Klos, 1965). The latter was mentioned by Tadeusz Zaorski during the assessment of Nasfeter's *Long Night* as an example of negative trends in Czechoslovak cinema, which neglected Nazi crimes or 'shifted responsibility for these crimes onto other nations'. The head of the Polish film industry proudly declared: 'in our cultural policy, and, particularly, in films, there is no place for such presentation of occupation matters as in the movie *The Shop on Main Street*'.[42] The fate of Brzozowski's *By the Railway Track* fully confirms Zaorski's observation.

Notes

1   Władysław Gomułka (1905–1982) was the First Secretary of the Polish United Workers Party from 1956 to 1970. Initially viewed as a moderate—he came to power against the objections of the Soviet Union during de-Stalinization—Gomułka grew increasingly authoritarian. His 'Polish Road to Socialism' or National Communism blended ethnocentric nationalism and Marxist ideology. On Gomułka, see Anita J. Prazmowska, *Wladyslaw Gomulka: A Biography* (London: I.B. Tauris, 2015).

2   Tadeusz Różewicz, 'Świadkowie albo nasza mała stabilizacja', *Dialog* 5 (1962): 5–26.

3   Paul Coates, *The Red and the White: The Cinema of People's Poland* (London & New York: Wallflower Press, 2005), p. 79.

4   On film production units see Marcin Adamczak, Piotr Marecki and Marcin Malatyński (eds), *Restart zespołów filmowych* (*Film Units: Restart*) (Kraków & Łódź: Korporacja Ha!art, 2012).

5   Miklós Haraszti, *The Velvet Prison: Artists under State Socialism*, trans. Katalin and Stephen Landesmann (New York: Basic Books, 1987).

6   'Uchwała Sekretariatu KC w sprawie kinematografii'. Reprinted in Tadeusz Miczka and Alicja Madej (eds), *Syndrom konformizmu? Kino polskie lat sześćdziesiątych* (Katowice: Wydawnictwo Uniwersytetu Śląskiego, 1994), p. 30.

7   Archiwum Filmoteki Narodowej—Instytutu Audiowizualnego (AFINA), Komisja Kolaudacyjna (KK), A-216 poz. 1 (15 May 1963), *Milczenie*.

8   AFINA, KK, A-216 poz. 1 (15 May 1963), *Milczenie*.

9   Ibid.

10   Ibid.

11   Ibid.

12   Ibid.

13   Krzysztof Kornacki, *Kino polskie wobec katolicyzmu 1955–1970* (Gdańsk: Słowo/Obraz Terytoria, 2004), pp. 216, 386.

14   Christine E. Evans's history of Soviet television provides a thought-provoking and revisionist assessment of Soviet culture and mass media during the Brezhnev period, often described as *zastoi* (stagnation). See Christine E. Evans, *Between Truth and Time: A History of Soviet Central Television* (New Haven & London: Yale University Press, 2016). On the role of economic factors and cultures of production see Marcin Adamczak, *Obok ekranu: perspektywa badań produkcyjnych a społeczne istnienie filmu* (Poznań: Wydawnictwo Naukowe UAM, 2014); and Petr Szczepanik and Patrick Vonderau (eds), *Behind the Screen: Inside European Production Cultures* (New York: Palgrave Macmillan, 2013).

15   Anna Misiak, *Kinematograf kontrolowany: cenzura filmowa w kraju socjalistycznym i demokratycznym* (Kraków: Universitas, 2006), p. 194.

16   Archiwum Akt Nowych (AAN), Naczelny Zarząd Kinematografii (NZK), Protokoły posiedzeń z załącznikami, 1967, sygn. 1/27 (1 March 1967).

17   Ewa Gębicka, '"Obcinanie kantów", czyli polityka PZPR i państwa wobec kinematografii lat sześćdziesiątych', in Miczka and Madej (eds), *Syndrom konformizmu?*, pp. 35–57 (p. 39).

18   Piotr Zwierzchowski, *Kino nowej pamięci: obraz II wojny światowej w kinie polskim lat 60* (Bydgoszcz: Wydawnictwo Uniwersytetu Kazimierza Wielkiego, 2013), pp. 45–49.

19   The Documentary Film Studio underwent a significant metamorphosis in the 1970s, when it produced numerous feature films, including movies from Andrzej Wajda and Krzysztof Kieślowski as well as popular television miniseries.

20   During the 1970s the Commission was transformed into the Commission for Media of Social Communication, which continues to this day. However, it is an advisory body rather than a censorship office.

21   Kornacki, *Kino polskie wobec katolicyzmu 1955–1970*, pp. 31–32. Roman Polański's *Nóż w wodzie/Knife in the Water* (Roman Polański, 1962, Poland) earned condemnations from both the Church and the Department of Culture of the Central Committee.

22   Mikołaj Kunicki, 'A Church–State Conflict: Jerzy Kawalerowicz's *Mother Joan of the Angels* and the Cinematic Projections of Catholicism in Władysław Gomułka's Poland', *Iluminace: Journal of Film Theory, History, and Aesthetics* 4 (2016): 16–20.

23   Zwierzchowski, *Kino nowej pamięci*, p. 9.

24   On National Communist cinema in Poland see Mikołaj Kunicki, 'Heroism, *Raison d'état*, and National Communism: Red Nationalism in the Cinema of People's Poland', *Contemporary European History* 21 (2012): 235–56. On Polish westerns consult Mikołaj Kunicki, 'Poland's Wild West and East: Polish Westerns of the 1960s', in Dorota Ostrowska, Zsuzsanna Varga and Francesco Pitassio (eds), *Popular Cinemas in Central Europe: Film Cultures and Histories* (London & New York: I.B. Tauris, 2017), pp. 157–72. On communist responses to the phenomenon of James Bond movies see Mikołaj Kunicki, 'A Socialist 007: East European Spy Dramas in the Early James Bond Era', in Jaap Verheul (ed.), *The Cultural Life of James Bond: Spectres of 007* (Amsterdam: Amsterdam University Press, 2020), pp. 41–60.

25   Edward Zajiček, *Poza ekranem: Polska kinematografia w latach 1896–2005* (Warsaw: Stowarzyszenie Filmowców Polskich, 2009), 223. The abolition of the Script Assessment Commission proved to be a pyrrhic victory for filmmakers, as the government officials were given full powers to approve or veto scripts (Ibid., 225).

26   Misiak, *Kinematograf kontrolowany*, pp. 184–86.

27   Zajiček, *Poza ekranem*, p. 209.

28   Joanna Pogorzelska, 'Sukces jest najlepszą zemstą', *Gazeta Wyborcza* 6 (8 February 2001). While working on *Hands Up!*, Skolimowski was interrogated by the Polish security police, who tried to recruit him as an informer. Skolimowski recalled these conversations in the prologue added to the film in 1981.

29   Zbigniew Załuski, *Siedem polskich grzechów głównych* (Warsaw: Czytelnik, 1962), pp. 222–29.

30   Misiak, *Kinematograf kontrolowany*, p. 103; *Strofy o Stalinie: wiersze poetów polskich* (Warsaw: Czytelnik, 1949).

31   AFINA, Komisja Ocen Scenariuszy (KOS), A-214 poz. 142 (26 January 1960), *Matka Joanna od aniołów*.

32   AFINA, KK, A-216 poz. 80 (2 December 1965), *Faraon*.

33   Komisja Kolaudacyjna (24 March 1964), *Agnieszka 46*. Cited in Rafał Bubnicki and Andrzej Dębski (eds), *Sylwester Chęciński* (Wrocław: Wydawnictwo GAJT, 2015), p. 388.

34   Ibid.; Kunicki, 'Poland's Wild West and East', pp. 164–66. Due to criticism from military and high-ranking veterans, *Agnieszka 46* was recalled from cinemas and withdrawn from distribution.

35 AFINA, KOS, A-214 poz. 338 (30 April 1963), *Człowiek z marmuru.*

36 Cited in Joanna Preizner, 'Świadkowie: *Przy torze kolejowym* Andrzeja Brzozowskiego', *Postscriptum Polonistyczne* 5 (2010): 131–45 (p. 142).

37 Preizner, 'Świadkowie', pp. 142–43.

38 AAN, NZK, Zestawienia filmów niedopuszczonych do rozpowszechniania na mocy dekretu o stanie wojennym, 1981–87, sygn.5/74 (31 October 1987).

39 AFINA, KK, A-216, poz. 132 (15 June 1967), *Długa noc.*

40 AFINA, KK, A-344, poz. 468 (6 September 1969), *Dzień oczyszczenia.*

41 While Załuski continued a relationship with cinema until his premature death in 1978, Gierek's decade saw the rise to prominence in film and television productions of two propagandists, historian Włodzimierz T. Kowalski and journalist Ryszard Frelek—who, jointly and individually, wrote scripts for films and television productions on twentieth-century Polish history.

42 AFINA, KK, A-216, poz. 132 (15 June 1967), *Długa noc.*

7

Majors, Adults, Sex and Violence: Film Censorship under Military Dictatorship in Chile, 1973–1989

Jorge Iturriaga Echeverría

Film censorship in authoritarian regimes is most often thought of in terms of the prohibition of films, generally of a political nature, based on a supposedly coherent system of surveillance.[1] This perspective is problematic when looking at film censorship during Augusto Pinochet's dictatorship in Chile. The control enforced by the Consejo de Calificación Cinematográfica (CCC, or the Film Rating Board), housed in the Ministry of Education, centred its mission on determining which movies should only be shown to adults, with a special focus on sexual content. The CCC's (or FRB's) control over films was powerful and transformative. It did not act as a mere filter, eliminating a few bad apples, but rather took on a more sweeping role. However, this power was not always used coherently, since it resulted from a complex system that involved the board, the state, film companies and audiences, all of which were sensitive to shifting times and priorities. This chapter argues that the strong escalation of censorship under the dictatorship should not be seen only as a defensive tool against the increased eroticization of film, but also as a complement to it: hard prohibition actually brought an encouragement of risqué movies, rather than their decline. The chapter makes this argument based on the quantitative analysis

Jorge Iturriaga Echeverría, "Majors, Adults, Sex and Violence: Film Censorship under Military Dictatorship in Chile, 1973–1989" in: *The Screen Censorship Companion: Critical Explorations in the Control of Film and Screen Media*. University of Exeter Press (2024). © Jorge Iturriaga Echeverría. DOI: 10.47788/NOXF9829 of more than 5,000 rating minutes from the CCC archive, paired with a documentary analysis of other public records.

Film, Censorship and Sex under Pinochet's Dictatorship

The military coup of 11 September 1973, in which the armed forces commanded by General Augusto Pinochet overthrew the socialist government of Salvador Allende, had a strong impact on the Chilean film business. The new government quickly removed ticket price controls, reduced taxes on film imports and weakened policies to promote national cinema. The result was the 'liberation' of the film market to facilitate the return of the major Hollywood companies, which had been absent during Allende's government.[2] In terms of content control, the government toughened the rules, enacting a new law in 1974 regarding the censorship board (Decree No. 679). From that moment, the president of the board would be the Undersecretary of Education, replacing the Director of Libraries, Archives and Museums, who had been in charge of these activities from the creation of the board in 1925. The armed forces named their own representatives to the reviewer staff, and under this decree, universities lost their autonomy in exhibiting audiovisual content. 'Marxism' was explicitly mentioned as a danger requiring vigilance, and the punishment for showing material not approved by the CCC would be imprisonment. This measure far exceeded the previous penalties for violating earlier codes, which had only included fines or closure of the venue.

The state increased surveillance while simultaneously withdrawing from the responsibility for film management. In this sense, censorship can be understood as the other side of the *free market* coin. The state leveraged a new censorship regime as a mechanism to compensate/permit the opening of the film market to foreign companies. What this chapter suggests is that censorship, along with tight cultural and political control, were in fact necessary for the *free circulation* of (some) products.

This apparent paradox is very consistent with the internal dynamics of the Pinochet dictatorship, since it was a government with two 'souls': one being of nationalist-corporate leaning and the other neoliberal. Karen Donoso has pointed out that strict cultural censorship 'was part of the strategy used to implement a new political, economic, and social model'.[3] It is also noticeable that cultural control did not necessarily come from centralized coordination, like a kind of automated bureaucracy. In Chile, this is evidenced in the 1974 film censorship law which, along with upscaling surveillance, increased membership and representation on the board, in order to build broad legitimacy for its repressive agenda. The usual seven members became nineteen, in order to have enough people to work in

Figure 7.1. 'Censorship breaks records for rejected films', says the mainstream press (Source: *La Segunda*, 2 December 1974)

'parallel rooms', each one providing a balanced representation. The four represented institutions (Ministry of Education, judges, universities and parents of schoolgoing children) became six, by incorporating the Journalists' Association ('preferably critics of cinematographic and theatrical arts') and the armed forces.[4] In addition, appointment of the board members would no longer be concentrated in the hands of the President of the Republic. The previous law, from 1959, had established that the head of state directly appointed three of the seven members and another two from external shortlists. In the 1974 design, eight out of the nineteen examiners would be appointed directly by various members of the Executive Power; two would also be appointed by the government but drawn from external shortlists that were proposed by the Parents' Association. This left the remaining nine members to be appointed directly by their own institutions, which included the Supreme Court, administrators of main universities and the Journalists' Association. Of course, these were institutions in which the dictatorship strongly intervened, since truly autonomous representation or diversity did not exist. However, the point here is not one of independence, but the dictatorship's policy of alliance, particularly with film critics, in order to create a new legitimacy. Symptomatically, the most symbolic change in Decree No. 679 was the elimination of the word 'censorship' from the name of the board.

Similar dynamics of repression/opening can be found in the area of the representation of sexuality. Historian Verónica Valdivia has analysed the conservative roots of the regime, pointing out that the commercialization of the economy since the mid-1970s came to strongly contradict that tendency: 'neoliberalism and market opening made a total process of conservative restoration impossible'.[5] The author argues that the new trends in sexual matters (erotic and pornographic magazines, erotic cinemas, video stores with pornographic material, cabaret culture on national television, a massive eroticized press, topless nightclubs, massage parlours, motels, the resurgence of the miniskirt and the bikini, etc.) hindered the conservative vision of the domestic role of women—promoting, on the one hand, their role as a sexual object in the market, but also easing control over female sexuality. For film, the contradictory message regarding women was similar. Whether in the logic of the opposition between control and sex, or in the logic of their complementing one another, it is necessary to put the CCC documents in context with the trajectory of the cinematographic phenomenon.

The data for my analysis come from a self-made database, built from the film rating records of the CCC for the period 1973–89 (and supplemented by information previously collected for 1960–73).[6] Along with this repository, it relies on documentation extracted from the archives of the Ministry of Education and the Military Junta, which shed light on the internal reasoning of censorship. On this basis it is possible to present a quantitative description of the ratings of full-length films in a dictatorship, focusing on the total results, their evolution over time and the topics of the films (keywords from their titles).

Strengthening of Film Distribution

The first thing that can be noted from the size of the sample is that the dictatorship gave stability to film distribution (Figure 7.2). The number of feature films submitted to the CCC remained relatively stable (except for a significant fall in 1983), within the range of 300 to 400 productions. This trend contrasts with the performance prior to 1973. Even if the 1960s began with much higher volumes, that period ended up showing a downward movement with very unstable moments, such as the drop from 632 to 310 films from 1961 to 1965, or the fall from 490 to 173 between 1968 and 1973. Beyond the fact that the general decrease can be attributed to the rise of television, there is a concrete fact that explains the second decline: the Hollywood boycott of the Chilean socialist government over 1971–73. The dictatorship managed to recover from that considerably, offering by the end of the 1970s levels of circulated feature films equivalent to the figures of 1967–68.

This stability in distribution acquires greater prominence given that the dictatorial period was full of incidents, noted by the various players, which could have led to different results: in the economic sphere, the crisis

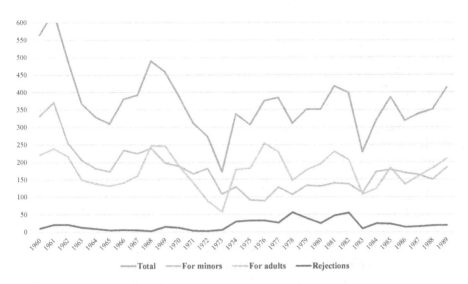

Figure 7.2. Film ratings of the Consejo de Calificación
Cinematográfica, 1960–1989, by age (Source: Rating records of
the Consejo de Calificación Cinematográfica archive)

of 1982–83; politically, the limitation of freedom of movement (curfew), restrictions on shows and intensification of censorship; and in technology, increased audiovisual competition with the appearance of colour television and home video. Indeed, the sum of these factors significantly reduced a fundamental section of the film business: the exhibition. The data from the Instituto Nacional de Estadísticas (National Statistics Institute) indicate strong decreases both in exhibition locations and in the attendance of spectators. In 1976, the metropolitan area of Santiago accounted for 99 cinemas that received more than 13 million spectators, while in 1989 there were 56 venues that received 8.1 million attendees.[7] The resulting scenario, characterized by fewer movie houses, but with the same number of films, is pretty much what the neoliberal doctrine proposes: smaller-scale activity (also more expensive) and with more disposable material (less time on exhibition). Basically, it reduced cinema to a consumer good.

Censorship as Never Seen Before

The CCC rating figures for 1973–89 show remarkable results in regard to adult ratings and movie bans. Of the 5,617 films reviewed from October 1973 to December 1989, 51.9% were rated for adults (including the categories Over 18 and Over 21) and 39.7% were authorized for minors (including the categories For Adults and Minors and Over 14). The remaining 8.4%

were rejected, approximately one out of every twelve movies reviewed by the Consejo. The severity of the period increases when we compare it with the board's performance during the three previous governments (Figure 7.3). Unlike the dictatorship, under the presidencies of Jorge Alessandri (1958–64), Eduardo Frei Montalva (1964–70) and Salvador Allende (1970–73), the CCC issued the majority of ratings for minors (56.7%, 51.9% and 60.2% respectively) and none of them exceeded a 3% rejection rate.

It is necessary to contextualize these figures. They correspond to a period, particularly the 1970s, when various transgressive genres became widespread, causing alarm in much of the film enthusiast world. Let's look at the case of Italy. Giori and Subini have quantified the ratings of the Italian censorship board from 1948 to 1976, and there is indeed a hardening in the 1970s; from 1969 onwards the number of films with restrictions (cuts or prohibition of minors) equalled and then surpassed those approved without restrictions.[8] However, it is clear that the trend started earlier, since from the mid-1960s approvals began to fall and restrictions rose significantly. This seems to be similar to the Chilean case, where the massification of transgression began in the 1960s. But clearly, not every government reacted the same way, because the numbers in Allende's period are radically different. And it is necessary to point out that the growing cinematographic boldness was not treated equally, since it seems to have an aspect more associated with

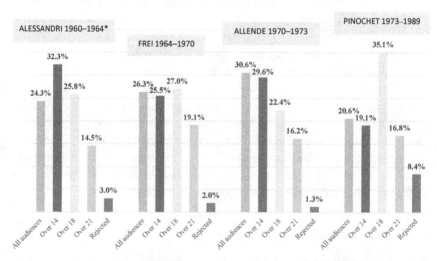

Figure 7.3. Film ratings of the Consejo de Calificación Cinematográfica under different governments, 1960–1989, by percentage of categories (Source: Rating records of Consejo de Calificación Cinematográfica archive)
* For this government the full period (1958–64) is not considered because until 1959 there were other rating categories in place.

representations of sexuality than of violence.[9] Still, going beyond the type of images portrayed, the external influence argument cannot be separated from the internal one. It is necessary to highlight that eroticization on screen is not something that *happened* to the dictatorship, but also, in part, something that it *caused*. One of the most shocking measures of the 1974 law was the elimination of the rating category 'Over 14'. So, for the Military Junta, cinema was meant to be adult.

Regarding the internal factors, it is important to note that the dictatorship projected a conservative restoration-type discourse during its early stages. The same law of 1974 indicates a desire for change when it states in its first article that 'it is necessary to adapt the legislation in force [...] to our current reality'.[10] In 1976, one of the four members of the Military Junta, Admiral José Toribio Merino, pointed out that Decree No. 679 had been issued due to 'the need to restore in Chile [...] solid moral principles necessary for Chilean morality and that they had been greatly distorted in our youth with certain types of movies'.[11] The big screen was not a minor issue for the Junta. In 1974, Augusto Pinochet himself watched *Fiddler on the Roof* (Norman Jewison, 1971) and prohibited it—thus undermining the decision of the censorship board, which had approved the film for audiences aged eighteen and older.[12] In 1985, the Junta, alerted about the possible distribution in Chile of Jean-Luc Godard's *Je vous salue, Marie* (1985), ordered the Presidential Secretary along with the CCC president to enforce its prohibition (the latter notified Customs to be aware and alerted various film distributors about the inconvenience of importing the movie).[13] Several documents suggest that, in reality, any military officer in an important position could make a recommendation to the Ministry of Education about the inconvenience of certain content. For example, in 1975 none other than Colonel Manuel Contreras, head of the Dirección de Inteligencia Nacional, DINA (National Intelligence Office), the main body of political repression by the military regime, wrote to the minister because of his concern about the CCC's authorization of the film *The Day of the Jackal* (Fred Zinnemann, 1973): 'Because this film teaches and details how to kill a president, it is suggested to you that this film must not be shown in the country'.[14] In spite of this, the CCC did not withdraw its decision in this case. Apparently, though, the political police's guardianship over the CCC was not just occasional. In 1984, we can read in the rating session minutes: 'Those with kidnappings and bombings must be authorized by the Min. of Education in coordination with the CNI.'[15] It is important to emphasize that this was not necessarily a top-down confrontation between the authorities and the board, since sometimes the CCC itself left the decision in superior hands. In 1980, for example, regarding the review of the film *Les routes du sud* (Joseph Losey, 1978, about a refugee from the Spanish Civil War), the board members stamped the following in the minutes: 'The group suggests for greater security that it is seen by an authority of the Ministry of the Interior or similar'.[16] It is no coincidence that the cited testimonies refer to films with political content, since some CCC documents show the organization's combative attitude against left-wing topics, with arguments such as 'violates the political hiatus, provided in the Decree Law No. 1,697 of 1977'.[17]

Two Very Different Periods

The severity of the dictatorial censorship ceases to have a monolithic appearance when we look at its performance year by year. The presence of two markedly different periods stands out immediately. Between 1973 and 1982 we have an extremely repressive board, while in 1983–89 all the rates of restriction dropped considerably. In the first period, the CCC issued 33.7% approvals for minors, 55.6% for adults and 10.8% rejections, while in the second the numbers were 48%, 46.8% and 5.2% respectively. These seem to be the actions of two different institutions. Rejection dropped by half, ratings for minors rose 14%, and ratings for adults dropped nearly nine points. Compared to pre-1973, the figures of the second dictatorial period are still quite high in terms of rejections; however, the ratings for adults are similar to those granted during the presidency of Eduardo Frei Montalva.

In general terms the data fit with the timeline of the dictatorship, with 1983 as the milestone during which the military government generated a certain political openness (particularly starting negotiations with the opposition), pressured by the massive eruption of protests throughout the country. However, it is necessary to shed more light on how this was reflected in film. Here we see the early development of a confrontation between the film industry and the government in censorship matters, and the existence of different positions in relation to legislative design. Aside from the undeniable areas of consensus (the dictatorship had favoured the return of the Hollywood majors, while many companies publicly expressed that political films should not be imported), the distributors did not stop raising their demands systematically. Even before the implementation of the 1974 law, businessmen Alejandro Undurraga and José Daire described it as 'an enormous danger for cinema'. They proposed structural changes such as lowering the age of maturity from eighteen to sixteen years old and eliminating the 'rejected' category or, as an alternative, allowing it only for those productions that were 'frankly pornographic or decidedly aggressive against a State, religion or the postulates of the government'.[18] The original 1974 design suffered its first setback in 1977 when the category 'Over 14' was reintroduced. When this reform was debated, the Junta members Gustavo Leigh and César Mendoza, chiefs of the air force and the police force (Carabineros) respectively, and the Minister of Education, agreed to re-establish the 'Over 14' category, against the opinion of Admiral Merino and the Minister of Justice. Leigh went further, claiming families as autonomous decision-makers: 'it is a very difficult philosophical matter to discuss as to whether it is the State that should enter to manage the family, to manage the father in his relationship with their children. [...] the government cannot be that extreme, but must educate as much as possible through censorship'.[19] The reintroduction of the teen category was a small relief for the film industry, which towards the end of the 1970s was entering an intense period of restructuring. The audiovisual entertainment ecosystem was being redefined with the sustained growth of television, the appearance of colour television in 1978, and the first arrivals of video cassettes. To reconquer movie theatre audiences, in 1980, for example, film companies began to implement half-priced ticket days. Censorship was also considered a structural factor in the crisis. In 1982, one association of companies wrote to the Ministry of Education asking for a loosening of censorship, and for a 'wider criteria in rating guidelines'. They cited as background 'the excessive competition of TV' and the social evolution that had 'achieved a wide freedom to be entertained'. Specifically, they pointed out that adults had the right to see works where 'eroticism, violence or sex scenes are justified'.[20] We have not found statements or documents explicitly sanctioning a new deal after 1983. However, it is clear that the authorities saw the issue differently from this point onwards. In that year, the government came up with a content control project for cinema, television and performing arts that, although it was never implemented, contained paradigmatic changes: the elimination of the 'Over 21' category and the creation of special theatres for 'erotic or strong content' films.[21] In fact, the film companies received the project positively. It is possible that 1983 somehow marked the dominance of a more liberal trend in censorship, or at least the will for bigger concessions to the historical demands of the business community.

Sex and Violence

To concretely outline the rating criteria during the Pinochet dictatorship, it is worth looking at the relationship between ratings and film topics that can be extracted from the movie titles. The results clearly speak of special and separated audiences for sex and for violence. Among the fifteen most common words of the 'Over 18' film titles, those related to violence predominate ('death', 'murderer', 'hell', 'kill' and 'terror'); and among the fifteen most common of the 'Over 21' group, those with a sexual connotation dominate ('woman', 'love', 'lover', 'passion', 'sin', 'sex', 'desire' and 'erotic'). This distribution shows continuity in relation to 1960–73, where in the fifteen most common words for 'Over 18' six with violent connotations predominate, and in the top 'Over 21' group, six have sexual connotations. However, the uniqueness lies in the type of sexual words, because in the dictatorship period more explicit top words appeared in 'Over 21', like 'sex' or 'erotic'. In the group of prohibited titles, meanwhile, there is clearly no continuity and one can rightly speak of an intensification of the punishment for eroticization. Between 1960 and 1973, four of the fifteen most common words in rejected films were sexual, two were associated with violence and the rest—nine—were in some way neutral. Under the dictatorship, of the fifteen most common words in rejected films, no less than ten correspond to sexual connotation, one to violence, and four are neutral. If we go over the list of eighteen words selected for each of the two topics (see footnote 9), the figures show stronger changes from one period to another. In 1960–73, violent words were rated more or less evenly between the adult and minor categories (48% versus 51%) and were barely prohibited (1%). During the dictatorship, these same eighteen words were rated in a proportion of 27%–66% for minors and adults, respectively, with a prohibition of 6%. The eighteen words with sexual connotations went from 19%–73%–8% in 1960–73, to a proportion of 12%–65%–23% in 1973–89. Hence, if violent topics went through an *adultification* (a notorious increase in adult ratings) during the dictatorship, the main change that occurred to sexual content was an increase in prohibitions.[22]

Figure 7.4. In the early 1980s it was quite common to find explicit movie posters advertising erotic cinemas in the mainstream press (Source: *La Tercera*, 3 January 1983)

These results are consistent with a noticeable concern among military authorities about sexual matters. In 1976, Admiral Merino pointed out that the 1974 law was created because of the shared diagnosis of the Junta that 'precisely there was an intent to pervert the Chilean people through cinema and television'.[23] One of the most interesting documents found in my research is a letter that the board member Colonel Patricio Araya (representative of the air force) addressed to the Minister of Education in 1982. Regarding film companies' demands for greater relaxation of censorship, the military expressed its opposition from a genuinely nationalist, corporatist and anti-liberal position. What is really striking is that the Colonel was not concerned with politics, Marxism or public order, but with sexuality. For him, cinematographic control had to be 'strengthened' in order to 'prevent eroticism and pornography from acting as solvents of moral and human values, especially of our youth'. He was particularly alarmed that some quality films 'constitute a defence of unnatural and immoral behaviours such as homosexuality and lesbianism, which are presented as phenomena of natural occurrence and acceptance', which ended up encouraging the 'exercise of an irresponsible and disordered sexuality, which can even lead to crime'.[24]

The above statements, with their defensive view of eroticism, may explain some outlooks on censorship, but also may replicate the idea of transgression as something purely external. This simplistic vision does not incorporate the role of regulation itself in eroticization. The central point is that the increase in sexual content was a response to the severity of the censorship. From early on, some company managers warned that with strict censorship there would not be enough incentive to import high-cost and 'quality cinema'.[25] In 1976, the Minister of Education himself pointed out in a Military Junta meeting that 'the system is very restrictive for certain ages and, practically, there are no shows that children under 18 can attend'.[26] So, the adultification of the cinema was not only an effect of the film companies' actions, but also of the control system. Was this not exactly what the censorship proposed: excluding minors from a large part of movie entertainment? The companies simply interpreted this message and looked to import profitable and adult material. It, of course, remains to be studied precisely what kind of sexuality was not welcomed by the censorship. A breakdown of the giant family of erotic genres must be undertaken, because, as Colonel Araya remarked, not all sexual images are the same.

Conclusion

This chapter has aimed to transcend the vision that categorizes censorship as a defensive action. Rather, it needs to be seen as a transformative tool. As Karen Donoso says, 'censorship operated as the main mechanism to make a clean slate and implement a new social order, which implied the eradication of the ideas of Marxism [...] and the incorporation of new functional categories into the capitalist economic system'.[27] In the film business that meant the adultification of movie exhibition. Ultimately, it is also not advisable to see censorship as a homogeneous, accurate and monolithic act. Although the system encouraged the exploitation of eroticism, it is clear that many of its expressions were severely filtered (a finer analysis remains to be done to determine what type of sexuality was punished).

Finally, it is not useful at all to think of censorship in the military dictatorship as an anachronism, as a device that was defeated or frustrated in the long run, given the decrease in film banning after 1983 or the spread of videocassettes. It is essential to underline that the system implemented by the military government after the 1974 law survived the dictatorship. The alliances established with the various institutions represented on the censorship board were maintained until 2003, when a new law was enacted. This persistence is, perhaps, the best way to illustrate the success of the dictatorship in managing to institutionalize a specific way of seeing culture and, in particular, the cinematographic phenomenon.

Acknowledgement

This work was supported by Agencia Nacional de Investigación y Desarrollo (ANID Fondecyt Regular n°1230934) and Facultad de Comunicación e Imagen of Universidad de Chile.

Notes

1 For an overview of the common conceptions of film censorship see Daniel Biltereyst and Roel Vande Winkel, 'Silencing Cinema: An Introduction', in Daniel Biltereyst and Roel Vande Winkel (eds), *Silencing Cinema: Film Censorship around the World* (New York: Palgrave Macmillan, 2013), pp. 1–12.

2 See Jorge Iturriaga and Karen Donoso, 'La censura cinematográfica en el primer año de la dictadura: Chile, 1974. Restauración, refundación y legitimación', *Universum* 36.2 (2021): 581–600.

3 See Karen Donoso, *Cultura y dictadura: censuras, proyectos e institucionalidad cultural en Chile, 1973–1989* (Santiago: Universidad Alberto Hurtado, 2019), p. 89. All translations from the Spanish are the author's own.

4 https://www.bcn.cl/leychile/navegar?i=6280.

5 Verónica Valdivia, '¿Las "mamitas de Chile"? Las mujeres y el sexo bajo la dictadura pinochetista', in Julio Pinto (ed.), *Mujeres: historias chilenas del siglo XX* (Santiago: LOM, 2010), p. 89.

6 The dictatorship lasted between 1973 and 1990; however, the sample does not include the year 1990 since its documents are missing from the CCC archive. The database only

considers the rating of commercial feature films—that is, short films, videos and private films were excluded. The documents contain the basic data of the rating session: date, title of the film, signature and vote of each member (occasionally information on the distributor and original language is also included). There were five rating categories: For Adults and Minors; Over 14 Years; Over 18 Years; Over 21 Years; and Rejected. To simplify the analysis, in this chapter we will combine the first and second categories (as 'for minors') and the third and fourth (as 'for adults').

7   *Compendio Estadístico* (Santiago: Instituto Nacional de Estadísticas, 1976, 1989).

8   Mauro Giori and Tomaso Subini, 'A Quantitative Analysis of Italian Film Censorship after World War II', at *Screening Censorship Conference* (Ghent, 2020).

9   The presence of eroticization is very clear when we count the keywords from the movie titles reviewed by the CCC. We selected eighteen words associated with sexuality and eighteen with violence in order to examine the evolution of their presence in 1960–73 and 1973–89. There is a decline in words associated with violence and an increase in erotic ones from one period to the other. For example, the word 'kill' dropped from 62 to 30 titles, 'devil' from 56 to 37, 'blood' from 55 to 34, 'revenge' from 52 to 35, 'gun' from 42 to 9, and 'crime' from 27 to 18 (in this topic, only the words 'police', 'violence' and 'death' significantly increased their presence). In the field of sexuality, there are notable rises in words such as 'woman' from 90 to 114, 'lover' from 49 to 57, 'sex' from 13 to 37, 'sin' from 16 to 28, 'erotic' from 3 to 19, 'ardent' from 7 to 16, 'hot' from 3 to 12 and 'schoolgirl' from 2 to 12 (in this topic, only the words 'love', 'boyfriend' and 'unmarried' clearly decreased their presence).

10   Ministerio de Educación Pública, *Decreto Ley 679*, 1 October 1974, https://www.bcn.cl/leychile/navegar?i=6280.

11   Republica de Chile, *Acta No. 277-A*.

12   Republica de Chile, Junta de Gobierno, Acta No. 7/85, 30 April 1985, https://obtienearchivo.bcn.cl/obtienearchivo?id=recursoslegales/10221.3/34907/1/acta7_1985.pdf.

13   Salamé to Underscretary of Education, 23 May 1985, Fondo Ministerio de Educación, Archivo Nacional de la Administración (hereafter Fondo Mineduc, ARNAD), vol. 50, 272.

14   See Mauricio Weibel Barahona, @mauricio_weibel, 31 May 2018, https://twitter.com/mauricio_weibel/status/1002251821363187712.

15   Minutes, n.d. [*c.* July 1984], Consejo de Calificación Cinematográfica Archive, Ministerio de Educación (hereafter CCC Archive), vol. 1984. The Central Nacional de Informaciones, CNI (National Information Agency), replaced the DINA in 1977 as the political police of the dictatorship.

16   Minutes, 8 May 1980, CCC Archive, vol. 1980.

17   Froemel to Undersecretary of Education, 7 February 1983, Fondo Mineduc, ARNAD, vol. 50, 187.

18   *Ercilla*, 16 July 1975: 41.

19   Republica de Chile, *Acta No. 277-A*.

20   Dowding to Cruz, 21 June 1982, Fondo Mineduc, ARNAD, vol. 50, 188.

21   *El Mercurio*, 21 July 1983: C1.

22   It will not be possible here to offer an in-depth study of the rejected films. However, one fact deserves to be mentioned, since it suggests a distinctive attitude of the CCC

towards the Hollywood majors: the largest number of films banned in the dictatorship are of Italian origin. Of a total of 468 feature films rejected in the period (of which we have determined via the Internet Movie Database the nationality of 400), Italy is in first place with 129 films (28%), the United States is second with 80 (17%) and France third with 47 (10%).

23   Republica de Chile, *Acta No. 277-A.*
24   Araya to Minister of Education, 30 June 1982, Fondo Mineduc, ARNAD, vol. 50, 188.
25   *Ercilla*, 19 May 1976: 41.
26   Republica de Chile, *Acta No. 277-A.*
27   Donoso, *Cultura y dictadura*, p. 41.

8

Fighting for a Free Cinema in a Country That Is Not Free: Film Censorship Abolitionism in Argentina, 1978–1983

Fernando Ramírez Llorens

Between the Catholic Nation and the Counter-Insurgency Struggle

At the end of the most recent Argentine dictatorship (1976–83), the law enabling film cuts and bans was immediately repealed and the agency in charge of prior censorship was dissolved.[1] It is only in hindsight that a full appreciation emerged of how difficult this change was at the time, more than a logical consequence of the 'return to democracy',[2] after more than fifty years of governments that arose mostly from fraud, from proscription or directly from force.[3]

However, several authors have recently warned against the assumption that the arrival of authorities elected by popular vote, the restoration of the division of powers and the enforcement of constitutional rights and guarantees have in themselves ensured an absolute break with the previous era. On the contrary, the post-dictatorship years should be thought of as transitional or post-dictatorial, because the democratic turn was hindered by the continuities of thinking that persisted after the fall of the dictatorship.[4] From this perspective, the speed and irreversibility of the change with respect to film censorship was remarkable and singular, which raises questions about the specific characteristics of the experience. My hypothesis

Fernando Ramírez Llorens, "Fighting for a Free Cinema in a Country That Is Not Free: Film Censorship Abolitionism in Argentina, 1978–1983" in: *The Screen Censorship Companion: Critical Explorations in the Control of Film and Screen Media*. University of Exeter Press (2024). © Fernando Ramírez Llorens. DOI: 10.47788/XCJE5862 in this chapter is that in the early 1980s an abolitionist attitude grew towards film censorship. For the first time in the history of the struggle against film control in Argentina, a group generated a set of ideas and a cultural policy project that rejected any kind of prohibition. This group engaged in its project most of the political parties that ran in the 1983 presidential elections, establishing the conditions of possibility to impose itself on those who defended censorship and to put an end to prohibitions.

Film censorship in Argentina in the 1960s and 1970s was supported by two fundamental pillars: the Catholic Church and the armed forces. These two key actors in the political processes of the time justified their interventions in public life on the basis of the myth of the Catholic nation and the counter-insurgency doctrine. The first concept holds that Catholicism is a constitutive element of the Argentine national identity, which enables the deployment of complementary logics of domination and conformation of authority between the state and the Church.[5] For its part, the counter-insurgency doctrine is defined as the condensation and local adaptation of the influences of the counter-revolutionary war doctrine of French origin and the US national security doctrine.[6] The counter-insurgency doctrine legitimized the tutelary role of the armed forces in the political system by proposing a total war against an internal enemy—communism—at all levels: military, but also political, economic and especially in the cultural field. Thus, Argentine state censorship advanced, Catholicized and militarized, between the defence of the national way of life and the fight against communism.

Two different strategies operationalized the myth of the Catholic nation and the counter-insurgency doctrine for film censorship: the partial (cuts) or total ban of films, and the exclusion of people (blacklists) who were forbidden to work in front of, or behind, the camera. With regard to film cuts and bans, Argentina had been home to state film censorship offices integrated with or influenced by groups of Catholic laity since the 1930s. However, it was not until the 1960s that state film censorship was developed as a process of increasing importance, instigated by moral militants from the Argentine Catholic Action. The growth of the powers of the agency took place both in dictatorships and in semi-democratic periods.[7] Finally, in 1969 the Ente de Calificación Cinematográfica (hereafter, the Ente) was created, the only agency in Argentine history that had the explicit legal power to completely prohibit the release of films (in addition to the possibility of applying cuts, a power that had formally existed since 1963). At the Ente there was a seat specifically assigned to the armed forces, so that the evaluation of films would consider not only the concerns of Catholic morality, but also those of the military who feared the spread of communism.

On the other hand, the prohibition on certain people working in the media for political reasons dates back at least to the 1940s. However, it was not until 1967, within the framework of a law to repress communism, that concrete prohibitions were legally established. This law was abolished in 1973, but since 1976 the last Argentine dictatorship had begun to draw up secret blacklists—some of which were documented and are still preserved today—that prevented certain people suspected of collaborating or sympathizing with communism from working in the media, including the cinema.[8]

The Instituto Nacional de Cinematografía (National Institute of Cinema, INC, now INCAA), the national state agency exclusively responsible for the promotion of feature film production since 1957, was the heart of the censorship network. The INC denied economic support to feature film projects whose script did not have the prior approval of the Ente, as well as to productions that incorporated blacklisted people in their casts or technical teams. This economic stifling was sufficient in the context of the Argentine film market, which had limited possibilities for profitability. In any case, it is clear that this was only the first of a series of pressure measures to which the authoritarian state could resort.

The Frustrated Opening in 1973

Since the authorization of film cuts in 1963, there have been strong movements against censorship, undertaken mainly by directors, actors and film critics. The arguments for its rejection were mainly aimed at vindicating the artistic value of films, the need for freedom in filmmaking, and the lack of suitability of the people in charge of the censorship office. However, these critical views had generally coexisted with the concession that some kind of control was in any case reasonable concerning pornography. As a result, the controversies ended up being embroiled in the discussion of what should be considered pornographic and who should administer this definition, protecting censorship as an institution from objections.[9]

This consensus against pornography operated even during the brief tenure of filmmaker Octavio Getino as head of the Ente (August to November 1973), in the context of the fall of the 1966–73 dictatorship and the electoral triumph obtained by Peronism that same year. Getino had long been one of the main promoters of the Latin American militant film movement Tercer Cine, creator (together with Fernando Solanas) of the Cine Liberación group and co-director of the then censored *La hora de los hornos* (*The Hour of the Furnaces*, Solanas & Getino, 1968). He completely abandoned the logic of censorship linked to the counter-insurgency doctrine. For example, he lifted the bans on *La chinoise* (Godard, 1967) and *Voto + fusil* (*Vote + Rifle*,

Soto, 1971), as well as approving films submitted to be rated for the first time, such as *Los traidores* (*The Traitors*, Gleyzer, 1973). Still, he took office declaring that he did not rule out the possibility of cutting or banning pornographic films, and in fact demanded the self-regulation of entrepreneurs.[10] Getino authorized films such as *Ultimo tango a Parigi* (*Last Tango in Paris*, Bertolucci, 1972), but requested cuts to *Il Decameron* (*The Decameron*, Pasolini, 1971) and banned *Africa ama* (*Africa Uncensored*, Castiglione, Castiglione & Guerrasio, 1971). The limit on eroticism was justified by the fact that the 1968 censorship law was still in force,[11] but this was also true with respect to the national security and internal order provisions established as the norm. The difference lay in the social perception of different groups regarding the value of the political and sexual content of films, and the consequent interest in mobilizing any defence for or against them. Getino was part of a movement that had fought against censorship and repression, promoting cinema as a tool for consciousness-raising and political transformation. In contrast, 'sexuality of consumption', in Getino's terms, seemed to be something that was indefensible.[12] At this point, the difference with respect to previous censors was one of degree, not of substance. This meant that the immediate reaction in the name of morality from Catholic lay groups, judicial officials and provincial governments did not meet the same resistance that a frontal attack on political cinema would have provoked. However, the subsequent escalation of repression brutally highlighted that the debate around pornography could end up becoming an excuse to consolidate a much greater network of control.

The bans of films and on people, having different origins and dynamics, were part of complementary authoritarian logics. In August 1974, the appointment of film critic Miguel Paulino Tato as head of the Ente inaugurated the most rigorous period of film bans in the name of protecting the population's morality, but also of vigilance against the advance of communism. The following month, the Argentine Anticommunist Alliance (known as the Triple A), a parapolice organization linked to the government, made public the first lists of cultural personalities who, in the name of the fight against Marxist infiltration, but notoriously also for the protection of morality and good customs, were ordered to leave the country under the threat of death.

The Public Outbreak of Abolitionism

After the military coup of 1976, the liberal newspaper *La Nación*, one of the most important and traditional in the country, maintained an editorial position of clear support for the established dictatorship, including its repressive policy. But it went beyond this support by positioning itself as a valid interlocutor with the political power, from where it intended to guide the new authoritarian government in its path.[13] Following this logic, in December 1978, an editorial note in the newspaper severely admonished the government for getting involved in a ridiculous discussion about the convenience of eliminating the teaching of modern mathematics at schools, fearing an alleged subversive potential.[14] A few days later, the cultural section of the newspaper published an extensive interview with the writer Ernesto Sábato—one of the cultural figures to whom the newspaper professed the greatest respect—in which the author took advantage of this little scandal to question the dictatorship.

It was clear to Sábato that his great intellectual prestige, together with his international projection, gave him room to intervene critically in the public debate without risking reprisals. Furthermore, his intellectual trajectory had distinguished him from both the reactionary right and the revolutionary left, which made it impossible to place him among the supporters of the dictatorship or among its declared enemies, thereby defying the binarism that sustained the repressive logic of the state. Without mentioning it, Sábato pointed to the counter-insurgency doctrine. He expressed that, in the name of the fight against any ideological enemy of the nation, 'the right-wing forces' had been enabled to carry out a 'witch hunt'. The reference to the right-wing avoided holding the armed forces directly responsible for the repression, in keeping with the editorial line of the newspaper. But the idea was clearly, insofar as it associated freedom with the capacity for dissent within democracy, to reject the possibility of the development of another type of regime in explicitly calling for the restoration of the rule of law. As Sábato expressed it: 'Woe to the nations that forget and ignore this sacred right to rebellion of their great creators.'[15] Finally, the interview established that the only censors should be judges, rejecting the possibility of the existence of any kind of prior censorship. Without making explicit references, it covered the whole repressive arc, ranging from the enforced disappearance of people to the control of the production and circulation of artistic works, including blacklists.

Sábato's concern about the topic was not new. In 1969, he had already expressed himself very critically on the sanctioning of the film censorship law. On that occasion, the magazine *Extra* organized a confrontation between the writer and the jurist Guillermo Borda, one of the ideological fathers of the state norm. Although there are strong lines of continuity with the article in *La Nación* nine years later, the comparison allows for a fuller appreciation of the evolution of Sábato's ideas after the repressive and censoring boom the country had experienced in recent years. The association between freedom of creation and democracy is absent in Sábato's reasoning in 1969. At that time the writer granted legitimacy to the official concern about pornography and considered the selection of a suitable censor a mitigating factor.[16] By comparison, in 1978 Sábato's ideas were in tune with the position of left-wing intellectual groups that began to express the need to rethink the undervaluation the Argentine intellectual field had made of democracy in previous years.[17] Censorship was an institution that responded to an authoritarian political model and should therefore be rejected *in limine*.

A few months later, in August 1979, *Clarín*—the most widely circulated newspaper of the time—published a double-page article in its cultural supplement, signed by María Elena Walsh. By then, Walsh was a very famous artist, widely acclaimed through her prolific production of songs, books and shows for children and adults. With no other political affiliation than her feminist militancy, at the time her positions were often described as liberal.[18] In any case, her work was characterized by a constant criticism of authoritarianism and conservatism. In *Clarín*, Sábato's analytical and elliptical tone was replaced by Walsh's testimonial and combative voice. The text compared the country to a kindergarten, directly associated the dictatorship with Franco's 'sad Spain', and equally directly questioned the members of the Military Junta. Walsh explicitly denounced the existence of blacklists, and knowing without a doubt that she was on the lists, she defiantly warned that she would not go into exile.

The article exhaustively detailed the main characteristics of censorship at that time. Walsh dedicated a specific reflection to cinematographic pornography, which expressed a change of perception, in tune with the impugnment of any form of censorship. She voiced her personal rejection of pornography, but at the same time defended people's freedom to watch it, and reduced it to an issue of individual taste: '[to the cinemas] the adult goes to look for it when he or she feels like it'.[19] This unprejudiced view enabled the state's tutelary role to be questioned without exception. The relationship between democracy and freedom, although also present in Walsh's text, was argued in a much more ambiguous and even contradictory way.

In any case, in spite of their significant asymmetries, both the *La Nación* and the *Clarín* texts were important, having been written by people of great prestige within the cultural field and published in the main newspapers of the country. In fact, the two articles had an important subsequent trajectory. Film critic Carlos Ferreira republished the interview with Sábato in a widely distributed book against the film censorship of the period,[20] and the writer himself included a revised version of the interview in his book *Apologías y rechazos* (*Apologies and Rejections*). Walsh's ideas were recovered by the popular magazine *Humor*, in which a few months later the author was interviewed to vindicate the text during which she continued to talk about the issues it addressed, in particular blacklists.[21] Walsh's text was reproduced on numerous further occasions—generally omitting the most controversial parts[22]—which gave it even greater forcefulness.[23] Therefore, although these were not texts that specifically analysed the situation of cinema, they served as a basis for an abolitionist perspective on film censorship.

It merits stressing that *Clarín* and *La Nación* were the newspapers closest to and at one point even literally partners of the dictatorship (an issue that goes far beyond the scope of this chapter, but which makes visible the depth of the complicity network).[24] Still, both publications gave generous space to criticisms of censorship. The showbusiness and culture journalists of both media outlets played a key role in this. For example, in 1980, Luis Gregorich, former director of the cultural supplement of *La Opinión* newspaper, made public the existence of blacklists in *Controversia*, a magazine published in Mexico by Argentinian exiles.[25] He thus joined in with the circulation of reports on the Argentine situation abroad, which the official position of the dictatorship and Gregorich's own newspaper characterized as an 'anti-Argentine campaign';[26] other media did likewise.

A Heterogeneous Panorama

Abolitionism was not the dominant position amidst the body of criticism of censorship. For example, an article published in 1981 in *La Nación* by Jaime Potenze—the most distinguished Catholic film critic of the time—conceded that some kind of exhibition control should exist, but advocated for the withdrawal of Catholic moral militancy from state censorship, arguing that lay groups had no right to impose their moral criteria on other groups. In Potenze's view, this was a clear challenge to the myth of the Catholic nation. He also highlighted the serious fissures regarding censorship that existed within Catholicism. Potenze was a lawyer and, at the time of writing the article, was defending the Argentine distributor of *Solos en la madrugada* (*Alone in the Dark*, Garci, 1978) in a lawsuit against the Ente for the cuts required to the film.[27] But he was not an abolitionist.

For its part, the film entrepreneurial sector continued with its strategy of negotiating with censorship, resigned to coexist with it.[28] In June 1981, *Humor* began to regularly publish the column *Cortes y confesión* (*Cuts and Confession*),[29] in which it reported the cuts made to films, accusing entrepreneurs of hiding information from the public, and consequently of collaborating with the Ente. Negotiation instead of confrontation was a traditional logic for the cinema business. In September, a group of producers, distributors and exhibitors submitted to the Ente a list of banned films that they demanded be authorized without cuts. Among them were films that had been banned for many years, such as *A Clockwork Orange* (Kubrick, 1971), *Looking for Mr Goodbar* (Brooks, 1977) and *La cage aux folles* (Molinaro, 1978). Months later, *Clarín* made public the 'secret list' of the requested films.[30] The very notion of secrecy highlighted the negotiating intention of the entrepreneurship. The banning of people also entered this field of negotiation. For example, the producer of the feature film *Tiro al aire* (Mario Sábato, 1980) managed to cast the renowned actor Héctor Alterio to star in the film as early as 1980, despite him being on the blacklists. Once the shooting was finished, his work ban resumed.

In November 1982, the Argentine Federation of Exhibitors insisted on the release of films retained by the Ente.[31] In a reaction, the Secretary of Public Information expressed in a harsh way the panorama presented to the government: 'Those who want controls, who are a silent majority, are as right as those who want to overthrow them, who usually have louder voices, sometimes those of some intellectuals'.[32] The statement highlighted that, beyond the public visibility of the opponents, there were still broad sectors of the population and groups with the capacity to exert pressure who, as in 1973, were pushing to maintain the bans. On the other hand, the mention of intellectuals acknowledged that abolitionism, though possibly limited to a few people, was managing to occupy the centre of the debate as the most visible position.

In fact, between 1979 and 1982, there was a succession of movements, public declarations, petitions and meetings to debate censorship that showed that the abolitionist position was growing within the field of cinema. The associations and trade unions' Directores Argentinos Cinematográficos (Argentine Film Directors, DAC), the Sociedad General de Autores de la Argentina (General Society of Authors of Argentina, known as Argentores in Spanish), the Asociación Argentina de Actores (Argentine Association of Actors, known as Actores in Spanish) and the Sindicato de la Industria Cinematográfica Argentina (Argentine Film Industry Union, SICA) formed the Committee for the Defence and Promotion of Cinema, which during the following years would carry out an intense campaign of denouncing blacklists, demanding the repeal of the censorship law, requesting the recovery of the autonomy of the INC and increasing the promotion of feature films. During 1980, the public presentation of the Argentine Movement for an Independent Cinema provided an opportunity for the scriptwriter and writer Aída Bortnik—exiled until the previous year because she was not allowed to work—to prompt: 'I would like us to reflect together on the naivety [...] that means asking, wishing, trying to fight for a free cinema in a country that is not free.'[33] Bortnik's words reiterate the association between cultural freedom and political pluralism that affirmed the unfeasibility of censorship in democracy. In 1981, some members of Actores and DAC who were on blacklists began to find column space in newspapers such as *La Prensa* and magazines such as *Humor*, using it to denounce the prohibition against them.[34] In March 1982, six important unions and associations related to cultural activities, including DAC, Actores and Argentores, joined forces to hold debate sessions. On that occasion, the film critic for *Clarín*, Jorge Miguel Couselo, reiterated the argument that was beginning to operate as a slogan in the world of cinema: that there should be no prior censorship of any kind and that the only control should be that of the justice system.

The Defenders

In a contemporary work examining readers' letters to the newspaper *La Nación* in 1981,[35] it is possible to discern a set of harmonious voices 'disenchanted with the dictatorship': readers who expressed themselves in favour of the military government and who celebrated the role played by the armed forces in the political repression, while expressing themselves openly critical in relation to a limited set of topics that they understood as unfulfilled promises by the regime. Among them, the repudiation of the relaxation of cultural control by the state took a central place. Mainly, they understood that the government was assuming a passive attitude in the face of the advance of pornographic '*destape*'.[36] The newspaper, it seemed, though editorially positioned against the bans, did not necessarily persuade its readers.

The ecclesiastical hierarchy shared the feeling that censorship had to be defended. In October 1981, Cardinal Raúl Primatesta, president of the Conferencia Episcopal Argentina (Argentine Bishops' Conference), sent a public letter to the president expressing the 'serious concern' of the Church over the 'moral permissiveness and pornography' in all media and entertainment, among which he explicitly included cinema.[37] The bishop took advantage of the opportunity to point out that immorality was once again sowing 'subversion', expressing one more time the conflation between the myth of the Catholic nation and the counter-insurgency doctrine, and the concrete possibility that in the name of the fight against pornography, a repressive role of wider powers could be enabled.

The ecclesiastical missive was a real novelty: for decades, the Bishops' Conference had not engaged itself publicly on issues of the morality of the media. The hierarchy was moving defensively, in response to an important public proclamation made a few days earlier by numerous cultural personalities and human rights activists headed by Sábato, in which the authorities were asked to 'eliminate all forms of censorship, open or concealed, practised or suggested by state bodies'.[38] The letter made it clear that the bishops understood that direct dialogue with those in power was no longer sufficient, and that they were forced to enter into public debate in order to at least avoid a diaspora in the face of the relaxation of the secular management of the Ente and the critical positions within the Church that Potenze's article had brought to light.

In this line of counter-offensive, starting in 1982 the Catholic magazine *Esquiú* began to publish regularly the column *Cine qua non*, written by Tato who, as already mentioned, was the director of the Ente during the harshest years of film banning. From this space, he would advocate the toughening of the censors' criteria, and on specific occasions he would openly criticize his successors at the state agency. The most influential figures of the Church and the most representative ones in film censorship were forced to enter the public debate so as not to yield to their detractors, showing their capacity for resistance and their willingness to fight.

The Growth of Abolitionism

In 1982, the defeat in the war against the United Kingdom opened up an opportunity due to the terminal crisis of the dictatorial regime. The most forceful action against censorship, in this context, was the March for Cinema: a mobilization on the Government House on 13 December 1982, organized by DAC, Actores and SICA. In hindsight, it is difficult to overestimate the challenges that the mobilization faced. Although protest marches were a growing phenomenon after the war, the fear of possible violent repression and subsequent reprisals was very present. In

Figure 8.1. March for Cinema in the streets of Buenos Aires, 13 December 1982
(Photo by Tito La Penna; Source: Mario Sábato's personal collection)

fact, although Argentores was part of the Committee for the Defence of Cinema, it abstained from participating; a chronicle of the time painfully pointed out the absence from the mobilization of many of the actors who had been or were still on the blacklists.[39]

The March for Cinema implied an effort to insert the demands of the Committee for the Defence of Cinema into the political agenda of the transition to democracy, together with issues such as the request for information on the disappeared and the claim for justice for state crimes, the holding of elections and the return to the rule of law, and the situation of the economy and workers. In order, the points demanded were: participation in the elaboration of a new cinematographic law project, unrestricted freedom of expression, abolition of censorship, elimination of blacklists, financial autonomy of the INC, and participation of professional and union entities in the management of the INC. The statement issued by DAC once again placed at the centre of the discussion the need for a change in the political regime in order to make cultural openness viable:

> In these obscure years, we have endured ideological persecution, bans and blacklists [...]. We know that the definitive solution to these serious problems will only be possible when the Argentinians recover our country in the popular sovereignty, the exercise of democracy and the validity of the Constitution.[40]

Two weeks later, the Comisión Episcopal para los Medios de Comunicación Social (Bishops' Commission for the Media) issued a statement calling on the government to maintain the censorship law in the face of 'an evident propaganda in favour of the modification of the law that regulates the functioning of the moral qualification agency'.[41] The document warned about the possibility of protests and disputes. In particular, the statement basically threatened to mobilize the Catholic militancy in the event of an attempt to modify the law.

In 1983, as the election climate heated up, a new group called the Interparty of Culture came into existence, made up of various cultural personalities linked to different political parties. Once again, it was a small group, to a large extent comprised by those who had been active against censorship in previous years. As had happened then, they would once again show their great capability for mobilization. One of the most outstanding achievements of the Interparty of Culture was the obtaining of the explicit commitment of the Radical, Justicialist, Christian Democrat, Intransigent, and Integration and Development Movement parties to eliminate all types of censorship, which, together, would represent 96% of the votes in the elections in October that year.

The Institutionalization of Abolition

In November 1983, after the victory of the Radical Party candidate Raúl Alfonsín in the presidential elections, the playwright Carlos Gorostiza was appointed Secretary of Culture of the Nation. Gorostiza had been on the blacklists until the last year of the dictatorship, and had participated in, among other groups, the Interparty of Culture and the Centre of Political Participation, which was a thinktank that outlined Alfonsín's political platform. Before taking office, Gorostiza publicly announced the axes of his administration. The core of his proposal was the elimination of all forms of censorship, on which he highlighted the existing agreement among parties on the issue and the support provided by the Interparty of Culture. In relation to the banning of people, he was categorical, stating that there would be no blacklists, '[neither] red, nor white, nor green [lists]'.[42] Gorostiza's emphatic assurance on this issue highlights the fact that there could still be strong uncertainties in this regard.[43] Gorostiza also announced that the film censorship law would be repealed and the Ente would be dissolved when the new government took office. In this context, he explained how the hitherto unsolvable issue of pornography would be addressed: a restricted set of special cinemas, at restrictive prices, would be set up for the projection of these films.

There was no public comment on the elimination of the blacklists. There is no reason to suppose that it could have been different: the exclusion of people had never had anyone to defend it in public—it had always been clandestine or secret. On the other hand, with respect to pornography, the reaction came from within the very government of which Gorostiza was to be a member. The following day, the appointed Minister of the Interior, Antonio Tróccoli, confronted the statements, warning that the new administration would make an 'intense prevention of pornography, vice, obscenity and eroticism'.[44] Tróccoli did not necessarily disapprove of it, but he set strict limits on the impulses for openness within Radicalism itself, and in particular, he put a strain on the abolitionist position. Gorostiza publicly acknowledged this lack of full consensus within the new government on what to do about pornography, with the intention of suggesting that an understanding between different sectors of Radicalism was possible. But he was unwittingly highlighting the important role the group of which he was a member was playing against conservative positions within the new government. Moreover, he made it clear that the abolition of censorship was driven by the field of culture, and that through this avenue some of its members had entered politics to support the change, against the position of traditional figures with their own political weight within the party and higher positions in the new government.

Figure 8.2. *Cine Libre* magazine (edited by Mario Sábato) covers the 1982 March for Cinema (Source: Historical Archive of Argentine Magazines, AHiRA)

Some of the main figures who had militated for abolitionism earlier on joined the cultural sections of the new government. Luis Brandoni, general secretary of Actores, was appointed presidential advisor. Mario Sábato, general secretary of DAC, was appointed programming manager of the state-owned television channel ATC. Aída Bortnik was also hired by ATC as an advisor. Jorge Miguel Couselo was put in charge of the Ente, with the sole mission of dissolving it. They were, as already stated, some of the voices that had advocated most loudly in previous years against blacklists, cuts and bans, associating the lack of cultural freedom with the lack of democracy.

The Consolidation of the Conquest

Shortly after the repeal of the censorship law, a counter-offensive shook the still-precarious new rating system adopted in February 1984, which was based exclusively on the protection of minors. On principle, the Catholic hierarchy explicitly rejected the elimination of the Ente, leaving vacant for two years the two seats that had been reserved for the Church in the new Comisión Asesora de Exhibiciones Cinematográficas (Advisory Commission on Cinematographic Exhibitions, CAEC).[45] In particular, the Bishops' Conference insistently warned against the advance of pornography and congratulated those who denounced films and magazines in the justice system.[46] Near the end of 1984 they would publish the episcopal document

Modesty: Defence of Human Intimacy in which, among other things, they called on Catholics to 'exercise the right to protest' against 'attacks on modesty', which in effect prompted a small mobilization in favour of film censorship.[47]

At the same time, a text by Mario Sábato published in the magazine *Cine libre* warned about these pressures and called for the defence of what had been achieved. Firstly, the text went back to the set of ideas already consolidated by abolitionism at that time: it associated censorship with dictatorship and freedom with democracy. Next, it returned to the question of pornography, showing that the issue continued to be the Achilles heel of abolitionism. Sábato began by condemning the entrepreneurs who profited from the exploitation of sex and defined them as 'our enemies', reiterating a position that brought him closer to Getino's own a decade earlier. But at the same time, he introduced the affirmation that 'the existence of a censor, of any form of censorship, is much more dangerous for the community than any pornography or immorality that can be commercialized'.[48] By ranking censorship below pornography, this argument broke the possible points of contact between them, defining a lesser and greater evil. A new position had been stated: one against pornography, but above all against censorship. The greatest threat to culture did not justify the least censorship intervention, or more precisely, the greatest threat to culture in a democracy was censorship. The article emphasized that the group of abolitionists were still mobilized, and their ideas were becoming more and more solid.

Conclusion

This chapter has aimed to understand the development and circulation of the ideas that allowed for a rapid end to the different forms of censorship immediately after the restoration of democracy in Argentina in 1983. Towards the end of the 1970s, a set of novel ideas began to circulate widely, aimed at questioning censorship without any exceptions, while associating the lack of freedom of expression with dictatorial regimes. These positions, which implicitly claimed democracy as a political regime, were growing within the world of cinema, but this did not imply that they became hegemonic. On the contrary, they coexisted with support from a broad sector that openly defended censorship and also with other critical positions that nevertheless legitimized the need for some kind of control.

The corpus of new ideas produced within the abolitionist position made it possible to develop a simple, brief, generalist, but coherent and solid cultural policy plan. In addition, there was a conscious effort to insert the issue into the political agenda of the transition to democracy, as well as to broaden the support base of the cultural policy, seeking consensus on the proposal from most of the political parties. After Alfonsín's election, this provided certainty regarding blacklists and pornography. This enabled the rapid end of censorship, even in spite of the resistant groups and the notorious differences of opinion within President Alfonsín's government team.

Overall, this development suggests that abolitionists were the group most prepared to define a cultural policy for new times, which is particularly relevant in view of what was stated in the introduction—the fact that the transition to democracy was a period plagued by uncertainties and continuities with the recent authoritarian past. Abolitionists were aware of this, and their participation in government and public debate was aimed at defending the gains achieved. The association between political authoritarianism as a cause and cultural repression as a consequence made it possible to respond to the challenge of the transition, because the call to protect what had been achieved was presented as an appeal to defend democracy.

Acknowledgement

The author wishes to dedicate this contribution to Mario Sábato (1945–2023).

Notes

1   Prior censorship is the name given to administrative censorship, carried out systematically and in advance of the release of a work (in this case, a film), to distinguish it from judicial censorship, which operates only in the event of a complaint filed by a private individual and after the work has become public (and, therefore, can be effectively known).

2   Octavio Getino, *Cine argentino: entre lo posible y lo deseable* (Buenos Aires: Ciccus, 2005); Ana Laura Lusnich, 'El Instituto Nacional de Cinematografía', in Claudio España (ed.), *Cine argentino en democracia: 1983–1993* (Buenos Aires: Fondo Nacional de las Artes, 1994), pp. 303–06. All translations from Spanish are the author's own.

3   During the twentieth century, Argentina was under dictatorship six times (1930–32, 1943–46, 1955–58, 1962–63, 1966–73 and 1976–83). Outside the dictatorial periods, until 1983 there were completely free presidential elections only in 1946 and in September 1973. In the remaining six presidential elections of the period there was proscription, persecution or harassment of important opposition candidates.

4   Claudia Feld and Marina Franco, 'Introducción', in Claudia Feld and Marina Franco (eds), *Democracia hora cero* (Buenos Aires: Fondo de Cultura Económica, 2015), pp. 9–22; Graciela Montado, *Zonas ciegas* (Buenos Aires: Fondo de Cultura Económica, 2010).

5   Roberto Di Stefano and Loris Zanatta, *Historia de la Iglesia argentina* (Buenos Aires: Grijalbo Mondadori, 2000).

6   Esteban Pontoriero, 'Represión, políticas de defensa y contrainsurgencia en la Argentina: un estado de la cuestión (1955–1976)', *Folia histórica del nordeste* 35 (2019): 145.

7   Due, among other things, to the electoral proscription of Peronism in the presidential elections of 1958 and 1963, the constitutional governments that emerged from those

elections are referred to as semi-democracies. See Marcelo Cavarozzi, *Autoritarismo y democracia* (Buenos Aires: Eudeba, 2002).

8   Full blacklists: Ministerio de Defensa, Presidencia de la Nación, *Listas negras de artistas, músicos, intelectuales y periodistas,* https://www.argentina.gob.ar/sites/default/files/listasnegras.pdf.

9   Fernando Ramírez Llorens, *Noches de sano esparcimiento: estado, católicos y empresarios en la censura al cine en Argentina 1955–1973* (Buenos Aires: Libraria, 2016).

10   Hernán Invernizzi, *Cines rigurosamente vigilados* (Buenos Aires: Capital Intelectual, 2014).

11   Octavio Getino, *Cine argentino: entre lo posible y lo deseable* (Buenos Aires: Ciccus, 2005).

12   Watch the TV interview of the time with Getino: https://youtu.be/LasdmpBRo0o.

13   Ricardo Sidicaro, *La política mirada desde arriba: las ideas del diario La Nación 1909–1989* (Buenos Aires: Siglo XXI, 1993).

14   Sidicaro, *La política mirada desde arriba,* p. 419.

15   Odile Barón Supervielle, 'Censura, libertad y disentimiento', *La Nación,* 31 December 1978: Section 3, 1–6.

16   'Censuremos la censura', *Extra* 43 (February 1969): 11–15.

17   Beatriz Sarlo, 'El campo intelectual: un espacio doblemente fracturado', in Saúl Sosnowski (ed.), *Represión y reconstrucción de una cultura: el caso argentino* (Buenos Aires: Eudeba, 2014), pp. 135–51.

18   Pujol considers that Walsh was a liberal according to the Anglo-Saxon definition of the term. Sergio Pujol, *Como la cigarra: biografía de María Elena Walsh* (Buenos Aires: Emecé, 2011).

19   María Elena Walsh, 'Desventuras en el País Jardín de infantes', *Clarín,* 16 August 1979: Section Cultura y Nación, 4–5.

20   Carlos Ferreira, *Por un cine libre* (Buenos Aires: Corregidor, 1983).

21   Mona Moncalvillo, 'Reportaje: María Elena Walsh', *Humor,* 24 December 1979: 44–48.

22   The original text defended the 'war against subversion' and thanked the dictatorship for 'maintaining social peace'; that is, for the way they had handled and continued to handle political repression. This part was omitted, for example, by Juan Carlos Cernadas Lamadrid and Ricardo Halac in *La censura, Yo fui testigo* (Buenos Aires: Perfil, 1986).

23   On the occasion of the author's death in 2011, *Clarín* republished the article as a tribute, recognizing it as one of the iconic productions of her career.

24   Marcelo Borrelli, *Por una dictadura desarrollista: Clarín frente a los años de Videla y Martínez de Hoz, 1976–1981* (Buenos Aires: Biblos, 2016); Sidicaro, *La política mirada desde arriba.*

25   Luis Gregorich, 'Las listas negras', *Controversia* 8 (September 1980): 29.

26   Daniel Gutman, *Somos derechos y humanos* (Buenos Aires: Sudamericana, 2015).

27   I would like to thank Delfina Gianibelli, who is working on this issue, for providing me this information.

28   Ramírez Llorens, *Noches de sano esparcimiento.*

29   'Cortes y confesión' is a pun on 'Corte y confección', which is a way to refer to dressmaking.

30   '40 películas y una larga espera', *Clarín,* 25 April 1982: Section Espectáculos, 1–7.

31   'Aguárdanse medidas para evitar el cierre de cines', *La Nación,* 24 November 1982: Section 2º, 1.

32 'Magdalena: "Todos tenemos buena voluntad"', *La Nación*, 26 November 1982: Section 2, 3.

33 'Para no ser socios del silencio', *Montaje*, December 1980: 6.

34 Andrés Avellaneda, *Censura, autoritarismo y cultura* (Buenos Aires: Centro editor de América Latina, 1986).

35 Paola Benassai, 'Los desencantados de la dictadura: una aproximación a las cartas de lectores del diario *La Nación* durante la transición argentina (1981)', *e-l@tina* 19.76 (2021): 25–46.

36 Tato had been removed from the management of the Ente in 1978 and, since then, the prohibitions had been somewhat relaxed. In 1979, one out of every five films submitted for grading was still banned completely. In 1980–81 that proportion was one out of ten. On the '*destape*' (uncovering) see Valeria Manzano, 'Tiempos de destape: sexo, cultura y política en la Argentina de los ochenta', *Mora* 25 (2020): 135–54; Natalia Milanesio, *Destape: Sex, Democracy, and Freedom in Postdictatorial Argentina* (Pittsburgh: University of Pittsburgh Press, 2019).

37 Raúl Primatesta, 'Carta de la Comisión permanente de la Conferencia Episcopal al Señor Presidente de la Nación, sobre el problema del permisivismo moral', 6 October 1981, https://www.episcopado.org/DOCUMENTOS/12//1981-Moral_47.htm [accessed 29 June 2021].

38 Anibal Vinelli, 'Cortes&Confesión', *Humor* 72 (November 1981): 66–67.

39 'Movilización por el cine nacional', *Heraldo del cine*, 17 December 1982: 927.

40 'Movilización por el cine nacional' p. 927.

41 Héctor Romero, Vicente Zazpe and Oscar Villena, 'Moralidad y medios de comunicación: comunicado de la Comisión Episcopal Para los Medios de Comunicación', 26 December 1982, https://episcopado.org/assetsweb/documentos/12/1982-15Moralidad_66.htm.

42 Miguel Briante, 'Carlos Gorostiza: destapar la cultura encubierta', *El Porteño*, December 1983: 42.

43 Luis Brandoni points out that a representative of Peronism in the Interparty of Culture advocated for the creation of new blacklists in case this party won the elections— against the opposition of another representative of the same party, who rejected the idea outright. Luis Brandoni, *Antes que me olvide* (Buenos Aires: Sudamericana, 2020). The testimony is consistent with the recollection of another protagonist of the time collected for this work.

44 Osvaldo Soriano, 'La autocensura de la democracia', *Humor* 118 (December 1983): 29–31.

45 Maximiliano Ekerman, *La 'transición democrática' en 35 milímetros: cine, cultura y política en la Argentina de los años ochenta (1981–1989)*, PhD dissertation, Universidad Nacional de San Martín, 2022.

46 Manzano, 'Tiempos de destape'.

47 Fernando Martín Peña, *Censura cinematográfica en Argentina: 1895–1995* (Buenos Aires, 1998).

48 Mario Sábato, 'Pornografía', *Cine libre* 7 (1984): 34. The filmmaker Mario Sábato is the son of the writer Ernesto Sábato.

Part 3

*Production Policies and
Content Regulation*

9

Censorship, Criticism and Notions of Quality in Post-War French Cinema

Daniel Morgan

Over the past forty years or so, since the emergence of postmodern perspectives on literature and history, various scholars have explored the often unclear distinctions between criticism and censorship. Few, if any, have looked specifically at the distinctions between film criticism and film censorship, or at the ways in which cinema might present differences from printed material in this respect. In this chapter, I aim to examine this question through a case study of the changing conception of 'quality' in French cinema between 1945 and 1960.

Intuitively, and according to the classic liberal framework, the concepts of censorship and criticism are easy enough to distinguish. The former is an act of coercion, implicitly coming from a position of authority, that seeks to suppress or restrict access to speech deemed undesirable. The latter is mere opinion or analysis of an existing work, however incisive or prudish it may be in its judgements: speech added upon speech. The seemingly bright line between censorship and criticism becomes blurry, however, as soon as one begins to define censorship, beginning with dictionary definitions of words like *censure* (condemnation carrying the weight of some kind of authority) or *censorious* (fault-finding, insisting on censure). It only becomes blurrier when looking at the numerous academic texts that have come to form a body of 'New Censorship Theory', starting famously with Michel Foucault's insight in *The History of Sexuality* that censorship can have constructive

Daniel Morgan, "Censorship, Criticism and Notions of Quality in Post-War French Cinema" in: *The Screen Censorship Companion: Critical Explorations in the Control of Film and Screen Media.* University of Exeter Press (2024). © Daniel Morgan. DOI: 10.47788/RFGD3515 aspects. Instead of portraying the Victorian period in England as an era of pervasive, puritanical censorship, Foucault concludes that it was actually characterized by 'a regulated and polymorphous incitement to discourse'.[1] Michael Holquist extends this reasoning in his introduction to a 1994 volume on literary censorship, focusing on the effects of censorship rather than the act itself, leading him to a conception of censorship as not only productive, but as an inevitable aspect of any speech act: 'To be for or against censorship as such is to assume a freedom no one has. Censorship *is*. One can only discriminate among its more and less repressive effects.'[2] Similarly, sociological frameworks built upon Pierre Bourdieu's work on language have sought to reframe the very notions of censorship and self-censorship.[3] Taking the title of her article from Holquist's pronouncement, Nicole Moore provides a useful overview of New Censorship scholarship, noting how this paradigm has extended the understanding of censorship so that it can be defined as 'a practice, a process, an aim [or] an effect'. She notes that censorship 'was expanded, by poststructuralist and sociological accounts of language in particular, to encompass all mechanisms of exclusion by which "the speakable is differentiated from the unspeakable"'.[4] These kinds of reasoning have also prompted a certain amount of backlash, especially from researchers who have studied the systematic state censorship mechanisms imposed by authoritarian regimes: there are indeed crucial differences between them and the forms of speech regulation present in Western liberal democracies.[5]

In this abundant academic literature, several specialists have specifically explored the murky territory lying in between censorship and criticism. Chris Baldick, in his study of the history of English literary criticism, states that 'there is no impassable gulf between censorship and criticism; the former may often be seen as the paradigm of the latter, or, so to speak, its armed wing'.[6] More recently, Robert Darnton has shown how royal literary censorship in eighteenth-century France delivered official approval in positive terms, in some ways resembling critics' blurbs on the jackets of today's books: the system aimed not only to eliminate undesirable speech but to endorse privileged publications, thus extending the hierarchy of royal power to the realm of the printed word.[7] Examining a much different context, Peter McDonald has written about how South African critics, often grounded in literary theories that could justify the role of the critic as an 'expert' or a 'guardian' of knowledge, became active participants in the apartheid state's censorship regime.[8]

How, then, do these debates, almost all referring to the censorship of printed books, apply to screen censorship? The most crucial differences between the censorship of printed and audiovisual media come down to the latter's relative complexity. Until quite recently, producing and distributing films and television programmes required considerable financial resources and involved a far greater number of people compared to books and printed material, even when one considers the efforts required to edit, print and distribute the latter. While literary censorship may take place before or after publication, and can be implemented by a variety of actors—editors, printers and authors themselves, as well as government censors—film censorship involves an even broader range of possibilities. It may occur during or after the writing of a screenplay, in post-production or even after a film's release, with censorship decisions based on text in some cases and images in others. In filmmaking, directors, screenwriters, producers and even technicians all share a degree of authorship, and their ordinary give-and-take usually includes aspects of silencing or constructive censorship. Government officials may again play a role in censoring films, but so do producers and industry bodies (such as the MPPDA's Production Code Administration in the example of Classical Hollywood), possibly acting under pressure from the state or various interest groups. Besides cuts, modifications and outright bans, the means of screen censorship also often include content warnings, age restrictions and ratings. While a production company may refuse a writer's screenplay or a director's pitch in the same way that a publisher may decide to refuse a manuscript, film censorship can also function by means of budget restrictions imposed by a producer or the refusal of public subsidies by state officials, and this financial aspect plays a much bigger role in screen censorship than in literary censorship.

Another important difference is related to the specificity of film as a medium and the perceived power of images over text. Some of this may come down to cinema's historical ability to reach broad audiences in contexts where large populations were illiterate. During the first half of the twentieth century, cinema forged a reputation as a vector for propaganda, as a particularly powerful means of persuading audiences and even influencing their behaviour. While it may have been based on dubious arguments, a certain prevailing wisdom about cinema's power over its audience can be seen in examples as diverse as the behaviourist assumptions underlying Hollywood's Production Code,[9] and Sergei Eisenstein's largely bogus claims that his editing methods were capable of inducing specific thoughts in viewers' minds.[10] These arguments about the specificity of audiovisual media may carry less weight today, when propaganda, misinformation and disinformation spread over the internet in forms that are not necessarily audiovisual, but they were widespread during much of the history of cinema and television.

Following the trend of New Censorship scholarship, a fair amount of writing on film censorship has questioned the common conception of censorship as a necessarily external, repressive force. In the introduction to her book *Cinema, Censorship and Sexuality, 1909–1925*, Annette Kuhn challenges what she refers to as the 'prohibition/institutions' model traditionally employed by scholars of film censorship. Drawing on Foucault, she aims instead to study censorship's productive aspects, to understand how it functions as an evolving set of practices and processes within a broader cultural context.[11] Following the same model, Janet Staiger not only takes an interest in the productive nature of film censorship, but suggests that censorship practices provide clues to broader social trends, as they favour the production of certain images while excluding others.[12]

The film historian Pierre Sorlin's notion of the *visible* is also interesting in this respect. Defined as 'what filmmakers aim to capture and to pass along, and what viewers accept without being astonished', this idea takes into account both censorship and self-censorship, as well as the attitudes of audiences and the ways all three of these phenomena interact.[13] For example, producers may insist on changes to a screenplay because they are convinced that the public, or a segment of the public, will disapprove, or a filmmaker may decide to avoid a subject entirely for the same reason. For Sorlin, one of the objectives of film history is therefore to locate the 'boundaries within which a society is capable of discussing its own problems', which can be teased out of films with a careful examination of their historical context.[14] Although this notion of the visible encompasses a range of production and reception practices beyond censorship, it does recall one of Nicole Moore's conclusions: 'Censorship's object is to draw the communicative boundaries of the nation; to delimit, institute and form the nation's knowledge. Censorship is about state making, not subject making.'[15] According to Moore, censorship's ultimate role within projects of nation-building has been glossed over in much New Censorship scholarship; while discussions of the productive nature of film censorship have opened new perspectives, we should not forget that film censorship also serves the purpose of setting boundaries for the topics a society can readily discuss.

Quality and Censorship in the Late 1940s

France, during the period following World War II, provides an interesting case study of murky boundaries between film censorship and film criticism. At the heart of this case lie critics' and censors' attempts to encourage 'quality' in filmmaking while discouraging films that failed to meet this standard. Just what constitutes quality cinema, however, is a complex question that frequently involves subjective value judgements: the very definition of quality underwent a crucial change in France towards the end of the 1950s.

Post-war France is particularly famous for its rich cinephile tradition, including cine-clubs, popular magazines and highbrow journals from across the political spectrum. Certainly the most celebrated example of this tradition is *Cahiers du cinéma*, the film journal staffed by the likes of François Truffaut, Éric Rohmer, Claude Chabrol and Jean-Luc Godard before they went on to become New Wave filmmakers. Today, however, the late 1940s and 1950s are also one of the least well-known and least prestigious periods in French cinema history. This lack of prestige stems largely from the influence of the *Cahiers* critics, who disliked the dominant filmmaking style in France at the time. The aesthetic preferences of the New Wave continued to dominate French film criticism, cinephilia and cinema scholarship from the 1960s to the 2000s. Histories of French cinema, written by authors from France and elsewhere, thus tend to characterize the post-war era before the New Wave as a period of stagnation: according to this logic, established veterans like Marcel Carné, Julien Duvivier, Jean Grémillon and Jean Renoir had already done most of their best work by the end of the war, while the next generation of ambitious directors had difficulty rising through the ranks of a rigid studio system that favoured experience and reliability over ambition and experimentation.[16] Despite the variety and popularity of post-war French cinema and the culture that surrounded it—viewership reached its all-time peak in 1957—this view of the era's films as academic and aesthetically uninteresting essentially formed a consensus within the scholarly community until researchers including Noël Burch, Geneviève Sellier, Ginette Vincendeau and Phil Powrie began examining questions of genre, gender and stars in 1950s French cinema.[17]

The first part of this period, immediately following the end of the war, was marked by shortages of film stock and economic difficulties for the domestic film industry, which suddenly faced competition from Hollywood after four years of being insulated during the German occupation. There has long been debate over just how much the 1946 Blum–Byrnes trade agreement, which reopened French screens to American films, harmed the French film industry; what is certain, though, is that it spurred a great deal of protest, not just among the trade unions that represented screenwriters and technicians, but also among stars and famous directors.[18] Their public objections succeeded in forcing the French government to renegotiate with the USA and obtain an extra four weeks per year when screens would be reserved for domestic films, along with an annual numerical cap on imports of American films.

Opposition to the trade agreement, especially as it initially stood, found an important forum in *L'Écran français*, a film magazine with close links to the French Communist Party, itself one of the main opponents of the accord. Although the magazine published a diversity of points of view up through 1948, when the party reorganized its publications and asserted more direct control, *L'Écran français*'s writers tended to be cheerleaders for the domestic film industry throughout the period, defending French productions and often denouncing what they saw as the bourgeois ideology of American imports. The magazine's editor-in-chief, the film distributor Jean-Pierre Barrot, was also the man who coined the term 'tradition of quality' in a 1953 edited volume on the state of the French film industry eight years after the end of the war. He used the term in order to refer to French films with certain humanistic qualities and good production values, featuring internationally recognized stars and made by highly qualified technical personnel.[19] One major implication was that craftsmanship and production values provided a blueprint for the French film industry to successfully remain competitive, both in France and abroad.[20] Of course, today, few people remember Barrot, since the term 'tradition of quality' was turned on its head and used pejoratively by François Truffaut in his 1954 breakthrough article 'A Certain Tendency of French Cinema', attacking this dominant filmmaking style that he saw as unambitious and academic.[21]

It was in this context, shortly after the end of the war, as the French film industry was grasping for ways to remain competitive in a suddenly transformed market, that the melodrama *La Route du bagne* (Léon Mathot, 1945) was censored in a particularly odd way. A costume film set in the 1860s, it features the popular star Viviane Romance as Manon, a young woman forced into prostitution by her abusive partner. She accidentally kills him and is sentenced to twenty years on a penal colony in New Caledonia. Although she is promised a reprieve if she marries an ex-convict on arrival, she begins to fall in love with the young doctor on the ship taking her to the colony. This love triangle ends in tragedy, with Manon killing herself in order to prevent a violent altercation between the two men and to avoid tearing the doctor, who is married, away from his family. The film drew a total of nearly 2.9 million viewers: a solid performance at the box office during a difficult year for both producers and theatre operators in France.[22] Since then, though it has probably not become a lost film in the full sense of the term, it has certainly been forgotten: it has never been reissued on DVD, Blu-ray or VHS, and the French national film archive in Bois d'Arcy has no copy that can be viewed by researchers.

La Route du bagne may have alluded to prostitution and represented its heroine as the victim of an unjust trial verdict—both potentially sensitive subjects at the time, at least under certain circumstances—but the film's censorship had nothing to do with these themes. Instead, it was the result of a campaign carried out by the critic Jean Derobe, better known by his pen name Jeander, who represented professional film critics on the Commission de Contrôle, the public commission established by the provisional government to censor films. Half of the commission's seats were reserved for representatives of the film industry, including one seat for critics; the other half represented the government's various ministries, with the president, also named by the government, casting the tie-breaking vote. As Jeander explains in an article written about fifteen years after the making of *La Route du bagne*, he argued in favour of an export ban on the film, claiming that it was simply too 'stupid' to favourably represent French cinema abroad.[23] In this article, he claimed to oppose most moral and political censorship, but stated that he could in good conscience cast a vote to prevent the export of movies that would harm the prestige of the national film industry. As he tells the story, to his surprise, after the film was screened before the committee, he managed to convince a majority of his colleagues to vote in favour of the export ban. Although the film did receive mostly bad reviews in the contemporary press,[24] there was more to this case than simply restricting the export of a turkey: it was actually an instance of political censorship. As explained by the film censorship scholar Frédéric Hervé, after informally conferring with members of the censorship commission, the producers of *La Route du bagne* found out the true reason their film was accused of tarnishing the image of France abroad: the star of the film, Viviane Romance, had joined a group of French stars on a publicity trip to Berlin in 1942, and the censors of 1945 were punishing her for this modest form of collaboration.[25] In 1946, the French Federation of Film Critics, on the initiative of Jeander and his colleague Georges Sadoul, a famous communist film critic and writer for *L'Écran français*, attempted to institutionalize this kind of censorship, pushing for legislative changes that would have explicitly listed quality and prestige as criteria to be taken into consideration by the censors. Under pressure from the producers, the censorship committee eventually walked back the export ban on *La Route du bagne*, and Jeander and Sadoul's proposal ran into a legislative dead end. However, this episode shows both how critics involved themselves in censorship and how they invoked criteria of quality and prestige in a way that was subjective at best and disingenuous at worst.

This incident took place within a broader context of debate over quality, selection and public funding within the French film industry. Most of the film industry professionals who protested against the Blum–Byrnes accord—and in favour of public subsidies for the film industry—wanted those subsidies to be distributed broadly, without any type of selection.[26] In 1948, lawmakers considered proposals to introduce forms of 'selective support' or tax reductions for 'quality' films, leaving the question of which films deserved that label up to a special commission; however, the idea of the commission was quashed before this first version of the law was passed, replaced by ticket revenues as the sole criterion for state support. Even as filmmakers such as Claude Autant-Lara and Jean-Paul Le Chanois, who were heavily involved in labour activism within the film industry, agitated for more favourable terms after the initial passage of the Blum–Byrnes agreement, their goal was for the national film industry to be able to produce in quantity: as the CGT union spokesman Charles Chezeau wrote in June 1946, 'We would like to remind certain advocates of quality that there is only way to achieve their goal, which is to produce a great many films.'[27] The law was revised in 1953, though, to include funding for films that 'serve the cause of French cinema', 'spread knowledge of the main themes and problems of the French Union',[28] or 'open new perspectives to cinematic art'; these decisions would be made by a jury of film professionals, critics, academics and artists, named by the Ministry of Commerce, who awarded subsidies to films after they were completed.[29] This system of selective state support came into being in part thanks to public pressure from a circle of filmmakers and critics, including André Bazin, Alexandre Astruc and Roger Leenhardt, who worked at or were close to *Cahiers du cinéma*, and saw the system established in 1948 as conferring aid to producers who took fewer risks.[30] In 1959, the system again underwent changes, as André Malraux's Culture Ministry implemented the *avance sur recettes* system, associated with the financing of New Wave films and art films that would otherwise lose money at the box office; the jury for this system awarded advances before production, based only on the submission of screenplays.[31] It is important to emphasize that the selective public subsidy system introduced in 1953, and the *avance sur recettes* that replaced it, did not constitute censorship in any traditional sense of the term. Still, the type of selection made by these juries was not only an award to deserving films, but necessarily involved exclusion, especially after the switch to allocating awards at the screenplay stage. Films with limited commercial potential, but which failed to meet the jury's definitions of quality, would have a much harder time being made.

Redefining Quality, Forcing Long-Term Change

By 1954, the notion of 'quality' was of course being turned on its head by François Truffaut and the *Cahiers du cinéma* critics. Quality went from being a notion associated with the film industry remaining successful and relevant, to being a marker of an academic style that qualified as artisanship but not as art. By the time Charles Ford published his history of post-war French cinema in 1977, a condensed version of the *Cahiers'* evaluation of most late 1940s and early 1950s filmmaking had become accepted wisdom, to the extent that Ford could write that

> Observers of French cinematic life might ask how certain artisans, whose mediocrity was obvious [...] continuously managed to make films. Mediocrity does not necessarily guarantee commercial success.

The responsibility, if there is any, lies mainly with the public authorities, who made efforts to aid the film industry, but did so without regard to quality.[32]

To its credit, in the 1950s, *Cahiers du cinéma* was a forum where complex, nuanced ideas about censorship were expressed. For instance, André Bazin, while still denouncing the inflexibility of Hollywood's Production Code, wrote about how it also had a productive side to it, honing filmmakers' creative processes. Describing the iconic image of Marilyn Monroe's dress billowing in the air over a subway grate in *The Seven Year Itch* (Billy Wilder, 1955), he wrote,

> This inspired idea could only be born in the world of a cinema with a long, rich, byzantine tradition of censorship. Inventiveness such as this presupposes an extraordinary refinement of the imagination, acquired in the struggle against the rigorous stupidity of a puritan code. Hollywood, in spite and because of the taboos that dominate it, remains the world capital of cinematic eroticism.[33]

Published in 1956, twenty years before the first volume of Foucault's *History of Sexuality*, Bazin's article essentially describes a system of productive censorship as it characterizes Wilder's reactions to the Production Code.

On the other hand, François Truffaut's ideas about censorship, while highly provocative, weren't nearly as subtle. In 'A Certain Tendency of French Cinema', Truffaut attacked an entire generation of pre-New Wave films. What is usually remembered of this article is that it laid the foundations of auteur theory through Truffaut's critique of films that he found academic, lacking in artistic vision. The substance of Truffaut's attacks on screenwriters Jean Aurenche and Pierre Bost and directors Claude Autant-Lara and Jean Delannoy can only be described as censorious, however.

While highly influential, Truffaut's views on art, and art cinema, have been reassessed as deeply conservative by some critics. While Truffaut claimed that his criticism was purely formalist and apolitical, Éric Dufour points out that his aesthetic preferences had a political side to them that was also highly reactionary.[34] Writing in one of the first issues of the journal *Jump Cut*, John Hess argues that Truffaut's conception of an auteur wasn't actually that of a director with an original, personal style, but one with a worldview in tune with Truffaut's own preferences: the films praised by Truffaut in *Cahiers du cinéma* tended to feature individualistic heroes struggling against an irredeemably corrupt universe. At the same time, Truffaut frequently maligned films that carried left-wing political messages; he especially disliked Aurenche and Bost's popular adaptations of classic literary works, which often added an anticlerical or antimilitarist angle to works of nineteenth-century fiction: in 'A Certain Tendency', he excoriated the two screenwriters for their 'marked taste for profanity and blasphemy'.[35]

Truffaut's criticism of 'tradition of quality' films was certainly censorious, but it was not censorship. Like Jeander, he disingenuously included political considerations in value judgements that he claimed were entirely aesthetic. He also went as far as to publish an off-hand provocative claim that moral censorship was 'necessary', arguing that Hollywood's censors were right to have eliminated homoerotic tendencies in the character of Philip Marlowe, and to have made most characters either good or evil, leaving little room for ambiguity.[36] Despite this, Truffaut never urged public authorities to place restrictions on films in the same way that Jeander did. The enduring success of *Cahiers du cinéma*'s 1950s criticism and the New Wave that followed it have, however, relegated large swaths of popular French cinema from the 1940s and 1950s to long-term obscurity. This includes works by directors like Claude Autant-Lara, René Clément and André Cayatte that were seen as prestigious at the time of their release, but have been largely left out of present-day retrospectives and film studies curricula.

Despite the focus in much recent censorship scholarship on market forces and self-censorship being more important than state-directed censorship mechanisms, I believe the distinction between censorship and censorious criticism is an important one. In today's popular discourse, the term 'censorship' carries a particularly strong connotation of coercion and repression. Even though criticism published in *Cahiers du cinéma* did deny audiences to 'tradition of quality' films over the long run, it did not immediately influence the boundaries of public discussion in 1950s France. Directors continued to make films in this style well into the 1960s, some of them quite successful at the box office. The long-term erasure of 'tradition of quality' films from the canon, which stemmed from the influence of the *Cahiers* critics, is an important form of silencing, but while some of the logic behind it was political, and it helped shape popular perceptions of France throughout the world, it did not in itself constitute an exercise in 'state making'.

Critical Movements to Transform Cinema

In the late 1940s, *L'Écran français* championed the French film industry and its aim of releasing 'quality' films that could stay competitive with Hollywood's output. Its critics also occasionally engaged in activities closer to the traditional, state-building conception of institutional censorship, including advocating for a cap on the number of American films that could appear in French theatres every year as well as the proposal for export bans on films that might harm French cinema's international prestige.

The *politique des auteurs* can be envisioned as a similar kind of movement that favoured certain kinds of films, while shunning certain kinds of political expression. The *Cahiers* critics were highly successful in imposing their broad vision of what art cinema should be, and this project had long-term consequences that have prevented films of which they disapproved from reaching viewers. They also advocated for cultural policies that eased the path for directors to make art films, and these policies eventually became a pillar of France's domestic film industry, and the way France sees its own filmmaking tradition with respect to the rest of the world.

In the end, asking whether or not a certain action constitutes censorship may not be a relevant question for film historians, since these actions are often part of broader movements that include multiple strategies. A variety of actors, working for the state, in the film industry or elsewhere, may take part in these movements, employing a range of actions from criticism to market regulation, from boycotts to institutional censorship. Hollywood began enforcing its Production Code in 1934 only after years of agitation by numerous pressure groups—most notably the Catholic Legion of Decency, but also other religious groups, critics, publishers, politicians and even social scientists. The Hollywood studios would never have enforced the Production Code on themselves had it not been for this public advocacy for a more 'wholesome' cinema, and for threats of government regulation.[37] The rise of socialist realism in the Soviet Union in the 1930s might be another example of a movement to transform cinema (and other arts as well), by means that could be prescriptive or proscriptive, coercive or non-coercive.

A contemporary example is the recent campaign for greater diversity in Hollywood cinema. Conservative critics have complained that new rules requiring a more diverse cast, crew or publicity team in order for films to be considered for the Academy Award for Best Picture amount to censorship.[38] While the comparison with Stalin's influence on Soviet cinema is grossly exaggerated, the new rules are designed to encourage producers, directors and screenwriters to make choices allowing for more diversity in their films, which means that they necessarily discourage the opposite choices. The rules are only one component, however, of a broader movement involving studio executives, film professionals, critics and outsiders, that affects studios' choices of films to produce and personnel to hire. While it is difficult not to see this last example through the lens of the United States' ongoing 'culture wars', post-war France provides two examples of how organized groups can try to transform the future of cinema. Criticism, censorship and combinations of the two are simply some of the tools these groups use as means to an end.

Notes

1   Michel Foucault, *The History of Sexuality*, vol. 1, trans. Robert Hurley (London: Random House, 1978), p. 34.

2   Michael Holquist, 'Introduction. Corrupt Originals: The Paradox of Censorship', *PMLA* 109.1 (1994): 14–25 (p. 16), https://doi.org/10.1632/S0030812900058363.

3   Pierre Bourdieu, *Language and Symbolic Power*, trans. Gino Raymond and Matthew Adamson (Oxford: Polity, 1992).

4   Nicole Moore, 'Censorship Is', *Australian Humanities Review* 54 (2013): 45–65; here, she quotes Judith Butler, *Excitable Speech: A Politics of the Performative* (New York & London: Routledge, 1997), pp. 137–38.

5   Moore, 'Censorship Is', p. 52.

6   Chris Baldick, *The Social Mission of English Criticism* (Oxford: Oxford University Press, 1983), pp. 8–9.

7   Robert Darnton, *Censors at Work* (New York: W.W. Norton, 2014), pp. 21–86.

8   Peter McDonald, '"That Monstrous Thing": The Critic as Censor in Apartheid South Africa', in Nicole Moore (ed.), *Censorship and the Limits of the Literary* (London: Bloomsbury, 2015), pp. 119–30.

9   Leonard J. Leff and Jerrold L. Simmons, *The Dame in the Kimono: Hollywood, Censorship, and the Production Code*, 2nd edn (Lexington: University Press of Kentucky, 2001), pp. 37–45.

10 Sergei Eisenstein, 'The Principles of the New Russian Cinema', in Richard Taylor (ed.), *Eisenstein, Writings 1922–1934* (Bloomington, IN: Indiana University Press, 1988), pp. 195–202. See also Béla Balázs, 'Flight from the Story', in Erica Carter (ed.), *Béla Balázs: Early Film Theory*, trans. Rodney Livingstone (New York: Berghahn Books, 2010), pp. 149–51.

11 Annette Kuhn, *Cinema, Censorship and Sexuality, 1909–1925* (London: Routledge, 1988), pp. 1–11.

12 Janet Staiger, *Bad Women: Regulating Sexuality in Early American Cinema* (Minneapolis: University of Minnesota Press, 1995), pp. 13–17.

13 Pierre Sorlin, *Sociologie du cinéma: ouverture pour l'histoire de demain* (Paris: Aubier Montaigne, 1977), pp. 68–72. My translation.

14 Ibid., p. 69.

15 Moore, 'Censorship Is', pp. 55–56.

16 Joël Magny, 'La chute des valeurs ou la fin des années trente', in Jean-Loup Passek (ed.), *D'un cinéma l'autre: notes sur le cinéma français des années cinquante* (Paris: Centre Georges Pompidou, 1988), pp. 56–71. Similar characterizations of post-war French cinema can be found in Alan Williams, *Republic of Images: A History of French Filmmaking* (Cambridge, MA: Harvard University Press, 1992); Pierre Billard, *L'Âge classique du cinéma français: du cinéma parlant à la Nouvelle Vague* (Paris: Flammarion, 1995); and Yann Darré, *Histoire sociale du cinéma français* (Paris: La Découverte, 2000), pp. 87–88.

17 For instance, see Phil Powrie, 'Fifteen Years of 1950s Cinema', *Studies in French Cinema* 4.1 (2004): 5–13, https://doi.org/10.1386/sfci.4.1.5/0; Gwénaëlle Le Gras and Geneviève Sellier, *Cinémas et cinéphilies populaires dans la France d'après-guerre: 1945–1958* (Paris: Nouveau Monde éditions, 2015), pp. 7–9.

18 Susan Hayward, *French National Cinema*, 2nd edn (London: Routledge, 2005), pp. 23–25.

19 Jean-Pierre Barrot, 'Une tradition de la qualité', in *Sept ans de cinéma français: 1945–1952* (Paris: Éditions du Cerf, 1953), pp. 25–37. See also Jean Montarnal, *La 'qualité française': un mythe critique?* (Paris: L'Harmattan, 2018), pp. 92–97.

20 Ibid., pp. 54–58.

21 François Truffaut, 'A Certain Tendency in French Cinema', in Barry Keith Grant (ed.), *Auteurs and Authorship: A Film Reader* (Oxford: Blackwell, 2008): pp. 9–18.

22 Simon Simsi, *Ciné-passions: le guide chiffré du cinéma en France* (Paris: Dixit, 2012), p. 10. *La Route du bagne* was the fourteenth most popular full-length feature released in France in 1945 out of a total of 131 films, including both French and foreign productions.

23 Jeander, 'Petite histoire de la censure', *Image et son* 140–41 (1961): 3–9.

24 Collected press clippings archived in *Gallica*, Bibliothèque Nationale de France, http:// ark.bnf.fr/ark:/12148/cb42684569r [accessed 1 February 2022].

25 Frédéric Hervé, *La Censure du cinéma en France à la Libération (1944–1950)* (Paris: ADHE, 2001), pp. 77–80.

26 Guillaume Vernet, 'L'hypothèse d'une "prime à la qualité" au sortir de la Seconde Guerre mondiale: discours, projets et rendez-vous manqués (1944–1948)', in Dimitri Vezyroglou (ed.), *Le Cinéma: une affaire d'État, 1945–1970* (Paris: La documentation française, 2014), pp. 73–84.

27 Charles Chezeau, 'Rien n'est dissipé!…', *Le Film français* 82 (1946): 23, cited by Vernet, 'L'hypothèse d'une "prime à la qualité"', p. 83. My translation.

28 The French Union was the new name given to France's colonial empire during the post-war Fourth Republic.

29 Article 10 of the law as passed in 1953, cited by Frédéric Gimello-Mesplomb, 'La qualité comme clef de voûte de la politique du cinéma: retour sur la genèse du régime du soutien financier sélectif à la production', in Vezyroglou (ed.), *Le cinéma*, p. 95. My translation.

30 Gimello-Mesplomb, 'La qualité comme clef de voûte de la politique du cinéma', p. 89.

31 Ibid., pp. 98–100; Hayward, *French National Cinema*, pp. 38–39.

32 Charles Ford, *Histoire du cinéma français contemporain, 1945–1977* (Paris: Éditions France-Empire, 1977), p. 117.

33 André Bazin, 'Marginal Notes on *Eroticism in the Cinema*', in *What Is Cinema?*, vol. 2, trans. Hugh Gray (Berkeley: University of California Press, 1971), pp. 169–78 (p. 172).

34 Éric Dufour, *La Valeur d'un film: philosophie du beau au cinéma* (Paris: Armand Colin, 2015), pp. 57–59.

35 John Hess, '*La politique des auteurs*, 2: Truffaut's Manifesto', *Jump Cut* 2 (1974): 20–22, http://www.ejumpcut.org/archive/onlinessays/JC02folder/auteur2.html.

36 François Truffaut, 'Aimer Fritz Lang', *Cahiers du cinéma* 31 (1954): 52–54.

37 Leff and Simmons, *The Dame in the Kimono*, pp. 34–56.

38 For example, Armond White, 'Our Sovietized Oscars', *National Review*, 11 September 2020, https://www.nationalreview.com/2020/09/academy-awards-diversity-rules -progressive-resolve-control/.

10

Hopes and Fears of Transformation: FOCINE and Informal Practices of Film Censorship in Colombia, 1978–1993

Karina Aveyard and Karol Valderrama-Burgos

Introduction

Film censorship is considered principally as a regulatory instrument of nation-states, and formalized through government agencies and institutions to control the movie consumption practices of citizens through what Foucault refers to as 'techniques of government'.[1] Acts of censorship imposed governmentally have ranged from the imposition of content ratings and restrictions on cinema admission (usually based on age), to demands to remove or edit perceived offensive scenes, through to the outright banning of some films. Representations of violence and sex have long been particular areas of public anxiety and concern. In some nation-states, films have also been censored on the basis of their political or ideological position, as was the case in Chile in the 1970s and 1980s during the presidency of Augusto Pinochet, when many films considered to positively promote Marxist or socialist ideals were banned.[2] Collectively such interventions by states are grounded in assumptions about the power of film to offend, disturb and/or subvert, and to influence human thoughts and behaviour in sustained and material ways. While such ideas have been questioned and problematized

Karina Aveyard and Karol Valderrama-Burgos, "Hopes and Fears of Transformation: FOCINE and Informal Practices of Film Censorship in Colombia, 1978–1993" in: *The Screen Censorship Companion: Critical Explorations in the Control of Film and Screen Media*. University of Exeter Press (2024). © Karina Aveyard and Karol Valderrama-Burgos. DOI: 10.47788/BEZG4529 in critical research,[3] they nevertheless continue to influence the governance of access to film content in many countries.

This chapter seeks to expand on studies of formal practices of film censorship by considering informal processes of content regulation as aligned with and enmeshed in the formal acts of states. Our case focuses on film in Colombia examined through a study of the production slate funded by the national film support body, which operated from 1978 to 1993, Compañía de Fomento Cinematográfico (FOCINE—Film Promotion Company; our translation). Without access to the processes and decision-making records of FOCINE (through documents or personnel), it is difficult to make assertions regarding the ways in which the organization interpreted its funding remit, and the extent to which there may have been an explicit institutional awareness or purpose directed towards processes of selectivity or omission of certain themes and topics. Nevertheless, there are patterns of absence and repetition that can be discerned across the slate of films financed by FOCINE, and these compel analysis in clear ways. As the public-facing and most readily accessible aspect of FOCINE's work, these films provide a different means of illuminating and evaluating some of the historical modes of content creation, and by association also regulation, of film in Colombia. Looking at the production slate closely, three social and political themes in particular emerge as significant to questions of censorship. The first relates to issues concerning class and economic agency; the second to depictions of violence that the Junta de Censura (Censorship Board) had banned in previous decades since the dictator-style government of General Gustavo Rojas Pinilla (1953–57); and the third involves the limited position and lack of agency of women in Colombian society as it existed at that time. Each of these is examined in turn in this chapter.

Our analysis is interested in the exercise of power by FOCINE as an agent of the Colombian state. However, it is also concerned with the workings of regulation more broadly, not just as formalized in modes of governmental intervention, but beyond what might be regarded as traditional forms of censorship. Here we focus on less direct and less obvious mechanisms of influence that can be discerned as also having played a substantial role in shaping the form and content of FOCINE's films. Following Foucault's notion of power as relational, our framework accords significance not just to the perspectives and workings of institutions, but to their external interfaces (in this instance filmmakers, distributors, exhibitors and audiences). In doing so, we emphasize the significance of these power relationships as a dynamic and fluid constitution of connections, rather than simply focusing the analysis on the apparatus of FOCINE as an institution and an examination of its actions. As Foucault argued, the 'fundamental point of anchorage of the [power] relationships, even if they are embodied and crystallised in an institution, is to be found outside the institution'.[4] With this in mind, we consider individual practices of self-governance and self-selection in Colombian filmmaking during the FOCINE era as having an important role in moderating and directing behaviour towards practices that can be understood as forms of censorship. These do not necessarily derive from direct exertions of state power through laws and policies, but they still work to serve the wider interests of governmentality and, in particular, its concern with the compliance of populations.[5]

Compañía de Fomento Cinematográfico (FOCINE)

While there were different and discontinuous instances of state intervention throughout the first half of the twentieth century designed to help boost production and audience engagement with Colombian film, it was only in the 1970s that state support for filmmaking was consolidated in nationally coordinated incentive programmes.[6] This began with the implementation of the contentious 1971 Ley de Sobreprecios (Surcharge Law), a stimulus plan to build a more regular and sustainable film production industry through a screen quota system. Under this scheme, the surcharge was initially applied twenty days per year and per theatre to encourage the screening of national films. Filmgoers were expected to buy their movie ticket and pay an add-on fee that funded the screening of a fifteen-minute Colombian short film prior to the feature.[7] This initiative was later followed by a more direct funding process led by FOCINE, which was established by Decree 1244 of 1978, to support and expand filmmaking activity in Colombia.[8]

The creation of FOCINE underpinned an active time for filmmaking in the country, with forty-five features, eighty-four short films and sixty-four documentaries produced over the fifteen years of its operation.[9] However, despite the hope and promise invested in the institution and its overall positive impact on production activity in Colombia, FOCINE was not successful in realizing its long-term commercial ambitions for an independent and sustainable film industry. This was attributable to several factors. The organization's criteria for the type (subject and content) of cinema it would fund was often not made clear. Commercial styles were regularly favoured and tended to produce solid financial returns. This aided the approval of film projects that were aligned with relatively safe mainstream themes, featured well-known television casts and/or were based on popular genres and aesthetics, a trend exemplified in the work of filmmaker Gustavo Nieto Roa.[10] However, at the same time, significant investments were made in many other projects that did not attract commercial interest for distribution by Cine Colombia (the country's major, multinational film-releasing organization), thus severely limiting their earnings.[11] FOCINE's financial affairs more generally also lacked rigour and transparency. The organization was beset by discontinuity, with sixteen managers over its fifteen-year history, and blighted by multiple allegations of corruption.[12] Eventually, FOCINE was declared bankrupt in 1993, after which the Colombian film industry fell into a ten-year depression.

Overall, FOCINE's projects and filmmakers were diverse and, in many ways, quite inclusive. A number of its productions are now considered important milestones in the cinema of Colombia and some have variously been accorded classic and cult status. Films such as *Pura sangre* (*Pure Blood*, Luis Ospina, 1982), *Pisingaña* (*Hopscotch*, Leopoldo Pinzón, 1986), *Rodrigo D: no futuro* (*Rodrigo D: No Future*, Víctor Gaviria, 1990) or the acclaimed *La estrategia del caracol* (*The Strategy of the Snail*, Sergio Cabrera, 1993)—to name but a few—demonstrate a breadth of approaches and aesthetics and various innovations in film form, and the development of a discernibly Colombian style of contemporary filmmaking. Further, and echoing Suárez, these movies used cinematic symbols to represent and negotiate the imaginaries of violence, a pervasive and persistent issue in the country but one that had, at that time, not widely been represented in film.[13] Despite working as isolated accounts or attempts, these films brought complex representations to what had hitherto been marginalized and unseen on screen, particularly when it came to the impact of violence in rural areas.

Class, Wealth and Power

There is much to consider within the multifaceted landscape of formal and informal power relationships between FOCINE and the filmmakers it funded. Suárez and Osorio agree that mechanisms of censorship in the FOCINE era operated in a variety of ways, and while many of these were implicit rather than explicit in their articulation, their impacts were nonetheless evident and material.[14] Specifically, Osorio refers to the opaque processes of funding selection and the non- (or limited) exhibition of films covering 'uncomfortable' themes.[15] He contends that these tacit understandings between FOCINE and its filmmakers regarding acceptable subject matter gave rise to processes of self-censorship that authors applied to themselves to avoid being discarded from FOCINE's funding scheme. This is demonstrated powerfully in the discernible shift away from the militant, revolutionary cinema that had been prominent in Latin America and Colombia in the 1960s and the 1970s but that withered under FOCINE. The FOCINE period saw notable transformations in the work of a number of leading filmmakers who in earlier decades had been engaged in producing explicitly political work. Under FOCINE, and in order to adjust and subsist in the revitalized industry, these filmmakers' socially progressive ideas were increasingly camouflaged within the familiar tropes and popular genres of fiction-based features.[16] Julianne Burton-Carvajal stresses this point in relation to renowned filmmakers Carlos Mayolo and Luis Ospina in the late 1970s and throughout the 1980s:

> In abandoning their previous documentary work in favor of their current experimentation with short fictional films, and in doing so as radicals who seek to show their work through official rather than alternative channels, they have been obliged to exchange political explicitness for irony and corrosive humor. They feel that these are effective means of reaching the larger audience to which the surcharge circuit gives them access, and that access to such a broad audience is well worth the price. They argue that the technical quality and thematic aggressiveness of their films will expose the mediocrity of current official production and contribute to its amelioration.[17]

Mayolo and Ospina are both considered leading figures in the cinema history of Colombia. They were part of the progressive filmmaking collective Grupo de Cali (The Cali Group), with fellow friends and founders Ramiro Arbeláez and Andrés Caicedo, and prominent contributors to the Gótico Tropical (Tropical Gothic) cycle of fiction films produced in Colombia from the 1970s to mid–late 1980s.[18] Their Gótico Tropical productions included the early short *Asunción* (Carlos Mayolo and Luis Ospina, 1975), and later in the 1980s the FOCINE-funded films *Pura sangre* (Luis Ospina, 1982), *Carne de tu carne* (*Flesh of Your Flesh*, Carlos Mayolo, 1983) and *La mansión de Araucaíma* (*The Araucaima Mansion*, Carlos Mayolo, 1986).

Mayolo in particular had a long-standing commitment to the political and cultural ideals of socialism, which informed his filmmaking. However, these were moderated in the fiction works mentioned above through themes of fantasy and hyper-reality, arguably rendering them more commercially and socially acceptable. This is illustrated in Mayolo's continuing interest in the figure of the vampire, which can be traced from the Gótico Tropical films right through to one of his early fictional works, *Agarrando pueblo* (*The Vampires of Poverty*, 1978). Mayolo spoke openly about using these characters to embody the bourgeois class whom he felt oppressed and exploited (or sucked the life out of) the working people of Colombia, but he avoided directly addressing this issue on screen, opting for the symbolic representation of the vampire instead.[19]

In terms of considering the power relationships governing censorship as a process of dynamic exchange and constituted in external as much as internal interactions, the recurring motif of the vampire can be understood as a process of internal adjustment by Mayolo, whereby he could continue to critique Colombian government and society, but in ways that were more palatable to a popular audience and more rewarding to the bottom line of his financiers.

Colombian Armed Conflict

For decades the depiction of the armed conflict in Colombia and the hardships and social inequalities that result from it has been one of the most overlooked or absent subjects in the nation-state's cinema. Some important films on this subject have been released in the past decade, including the documentaries *La negociación* (*The Negotiation*, Margarita Martínez, 2018) and *La impresión de una guerra* (*The Impression of War*, Camilo Restrepo, 2015). These productions were made in a period of relative calm, around the time of the 2016 Peace Agreement between the centrist government of President Juan Manuel Santos and the Fuerzas Armadas Revolucionarias de Colombia—Ejército del Pueblo, FARC-EP (Revolutionary Armed Forces of Colombia—People's Army), one of the oldest left-wing guerrillas in Colombia at that time. In the half-century prior to this, however, what was perhaps most notable is the lack of films addressing the conflict and its violence. For an issue that shaped the Colombian nation-state over such a long period and in such a profound manner, this absence suggests it was a long-standing subject that, in historical terms, few filmmakers were willing to tackle, financiers were reluctant to fund and distributors were disinclined to release. The case of one major FOCINE film that directly addressed this subject is instructive in attempting to understand the parameters and boundaries of sociopolitically acceptable representations of the internal conflict within which filmmakers of the period worked.

Cóndores no entierran todos los días (*A Man of Principle*, Francisco Norden, 1984) was important both for its depiction of the bipartisan violence in Colombia and for the way it situated this within a rural context, where the violence had such a devasting effect for many.[20] This was a story set in the 1940s to 1950s in a modest rural town, following the political career of León María Lozano (Frank Ramírez), a market cheese seller who rises to become the local Conservative Party enforcer. Along with other like-minded residents of his town, Lozano engages in various after-hours vigilante activities related to maintaining and advancing the power of Conversative politics in his town. The film positions this violence as regrettable but ultimately necessary and justified. In doing so, it condones the progress and achievement of certain 'righteous' political goals through violence and the elimination of enemies—the opposition must be killed, in this case in a very literal sense.

In the film, Lozano's Conservative political ideals are pitted against the influences of the liberal parties that were in power throughout much of Colombia (including at a national level) during the 1940s and 1950s when the film is set, and for several decades afterwards. In terms of placing the film within its production context, *Cóndores no entierran todos los días* was made and released during the period of political Conservative ascendency. This era was in many ways defined by the presidency of Belisario Betancur (1982–86), who had come to power with a resounding popular victory over the liberal factions who had previously held power for several decades. One of the decisive issues of the election was the perceived failure of liberal factions to resolve the decades-long armed conflict and deal with the severe traumas it inflicted on millions of Colombian citizens. The promotion of Conversative political principles in *Cóndores no entierran todos los días*, and the hero-like status accorded to its central character of Lozano—also evident through his symbolic role of 'Condor' as the leading 'bird' of his gang—had some very clear parallels with the election of President Betancur both in terms of chronology and ideology. Both the conception of such a project and FOCINE's decision to fund it were unprecedented in the cinema history of Colombia until that point. It is difficult to disregard the realization of this project as a set of actions that, while perhaps not expressly sought or mandated by policy, were nevertheless orientated towards the interests of governmentality as they existed at that time.

Representation and Participation of Women

The role of FOCINE in both facilitating and constraining women's participation and representation in Colombian films is a complex one. The organization arguably did much to promote the participation of women, who had previously been largely excluded from key roles both on- and off-screen.[21] In terms of management, FOCINE appointed women in senior roles, such as Isadora de Norden and María Emma Mejía.[22] The organization also supported a range of creative work made by women. Notably, they funded two major short films from the dynamic feminist media collective Cine Mujer (1978–99). *Momentos de un domingo* (*Sunday Moments*, Patricia Restrepo, 1985) and *La mirada de Myriam* (*Myriam's Gaze*, Clara Riascos, 1985) were productions that questioned and disrupted gender codes and expectations, bringing to the fore both the public and the private of a woman's world in Colombian and Latin American contexts.[23]

Cine Mujer was a vanguard in many ways for changes for women in cinema during the FOCINE period, despite its productions being relegated to smaller or select audiences in which, again, the additional issue of limited commercial distribution opportunities explicitly affected their dissemination on a wider scale.[24] The history of the collective can be traced back to the mid-1970s, before the establishment of FOCINE but when the regularization of government support for film served as a platform for the group to materialize feminist and reflexive statements in Colombian visual culture, using the benefits of state funding but without producing films *for* FOCINE's commercial interests.[25] Sara Bright and Patricia Restrepo, two of the co-founders, agree on the way in which the 1980s built a pathway for the collective to embrace a period of collaborative, even receptive and continuous work between the women of Cine Mujer—in contrast with their previous roles when working for or with male directors, and without having to prioritize fiction over documentaries, as happened with Mayolo or Ospina, for instance.[26]

While Cine Mujer worked mostly through different forms of documentary by their own choice and not out of necessity, and via video production in partnership with different entities, Goldman argues that between 1983 and 1988, their films had the tendency 'to follow a predictable formula, combining personal testimony with experts and dramatization'.[27] This format aided realism and authenticity and, with it, rendered great power and affect to Cine Mujer's stories. However, Goldman suggests it was also limiting. While not expressly prescribed by FOCINE, it was a creative mode that was acceptable to the funding body ideologically and it ensured Cine Mujer's films would remain relatively marginal, rather than finding a platform and space for expression within the commercial mainstream and thus, as Cervera Ferrer points out, breaking hierarchical paradigms of film production in Colombia.[28] Again here it is possible to discern the implicit interests of governmentality articulated in the ways Cine Mujer was able (or not) to make films with wider freedoms of creative expression. The collective also encountered problems with FOCINE's bureaucracy. Patricia Restrepo recalls how funding granted to the group in 1984 took almost a year to be released to them, eventually provided just four or five days before principal photography for the project commenced.[29] This may suggest simply some lingering loose ends related to procedure and governance, but it may equally be indicative of hesitations and a lack of confidence in giving the final green light to distinctive, influential and potentially controversial projects, such as the ones made by Cine Mujer.

Beyond Cine Mujer, FOCINE funded the first feature film directed by a woman in Colombia, Camila Loboguerrero. Her first film, *Con su música a otra parte* (*With Your Music Elsewhere*, 1984),[30] was a musical drama delving into the artistic and non-conventional dreams of the female lead when returning to Colombia from abroad; her second, *María Cano* (1990), was a biopic exploring the foundational role of María Cano, the first female Colombian political leader, who co-founded the Socialist Revolutionary

Party in the country. Not only were these the first features directed by a woman, but they also focused on women as the key narrative agents, disrupting patriarchal power relations and codes and challenging the male-dominated cinema of the time and century.

María Cano is perhaps the best known of these two films. It was a high-budget feature film that did not succeed at the box office at the time of its release but is still highly regarded historically as an important feminist work. This is due, at least in part, to its interrogation of democracy via women's leadership and its associated questioning of critical sociopolitical issues within Colombia, as well as its redefinition of the cinematic and historical agency of women.[31] The triple intersection of María Eugenia Dávila's distinguished performance as María Cano, the ground-breaking role of Loboguerrero as director during the 1980s, and the historical impact of Cano herself in Colombian society gave life to an unprecedented representation that, as Suárez and Ramírez Aissa agree, expanded the seemingly unequivocal understanding of the political leader from a critical viewpoint.[32] The film builds a multifaceted discourse of the emancipation of women that explores the human dimension of the politician. Without disregarding María's vulnerability in specific moments of her life or her occasional dependence on male figures, the film challenges gender expectations of the time and condemn injustices in the country, such as the disgraceful Masacre de las Bananeras (Banana Massacre, 1928), through the voice of a woman.

However, formulaic and canonical discourses about women within the cinema of Colombia also remained as a key part of major FOCINE productions of the time. Films like *La virgen y el fotógrafo* (*The Virgin and the Photographer*, Luis Alfredo Sánchez, 1983), *A la salida nos vemos* (*See You After School*, Carlos Palau, 1986) and *Cóndores no entierran todos los días* upheld gender stereotypes that tended not to question traditional religious and conservative values, by providing female characters that emphasized Manichean and secondary roles for women either as the submissive 'virgin' or the desirous 'whore'. Even in Carlos Mayolo's otherwise socially progressive work, stereotypical roles for women continued to be repeated. In *La mansión de Araucaíma*, Mayolo positions a woman, La Machiche (Vicky Hernández), at the centre of the story. She is mature but voluptuous and desirable, and she controls the six men of the house (from the proprietor down to the gardener) through her sexual desires and favours. It is a force that is presented as unnatural and perverted, and it creates a strong sense of foreboding in the establishing scenes. The equilibrium, such as it is, is disturbed with the arrival of a young model, Angela (Adriana Herrán), who seeks temporary refuge at the house but then finds herself unable to leave. She goes on to replicate La Machiche's sexual promiscuity with the men of the mansion. Worried she is losing her appeal, La Machiche eventually entices Angela into bed with her as well—upon which the house and the relationships that had sustained it crumble completely. Both women are punished by death: Angela by suicide in her despair, and Machiche by grief, guilt and loss of privilege, power and social status before she is eventually murdered by one of the men of the house. While this film contains elements of parody, as Mayolo suggested in an interview, the parody relies on a shared cultural understanding and acceptance of the Madonna–whore dichotomy in the Latin American context.[33]

Conclusion

Collectively, the relationships between FOCINE and its filmmakers outlined in this chapter underline the importance of regarding both formal and informal mechanisms within a broad frame of censorship analysis. The focus of our analysis here has been the external (filmmaker) side of the relationship, but one must always consider this against and as something in constant interaction with formal mechanisms of governance and control. To understand this relationship, we have drawn mostly on analysis of film texts, considering these as an illuminating and instructive series of inter-mediate points that accumulate along the linear trajectory of FOCINE's fifteen-year history of operations and its impact on film production in Colombia. Where possible, we have also drawn on direct testimonies of filmmakers to add further depth to our investigations. Across each of the three social themes identified in this chapter—class and economic agency, depictions of violence, and the position and participation of women—processes of self-censorship are suggested to have been at work during the FOCINE era. These are practices that we argue are often individually and subtly negotiated, and they constitute a process of continuous and dynamic exchange between the political commitments of filmmakers and the limita-tions of national governments, commercial markets and society.

In closing, we suggest that giving attention to more oblique and less obvious forms of content mediation, as this chapter has done, has value in opening critical research to expanded ways of comprehending the scope and scale of content regulation, in Colombia and elsewhere. It also draws attention to different cultural understandings of film and its perceived purpose. Sociopolitical ideals about what cinema 'should be' and what it 'should do' are crucial in determining *what* cinema is and *how* it functions in particular contexts.

Filmography

A la salida nos vemos, dir. by Carlos Palau (Zona A Limitada, 1986).

Agarrando pueblo, dir. by Carlos Mayolo and Luis Ospina (Luis Ospina, 1978).

Asunción, dir. by Carlos Mayolo and Luis Ospina (n.i., 1975).

Carne de tu carne, dir. by Carlos Mayolo (Zona A Limitada, 1983).

Con su música a otra parte, dir. by Camila Loboguerrero (Zona A Limitada, 1984).

Cóndores no entierran todos los días, dir. by Francisco Norden (Zona A Limitada, 1984).

La estrategia del caracol, dir. by Sergio Cabrera (n.i., 1993).

La impresión de una guerra, dir. by Camilo Restrepo (Mutokino, 2015).

La mansión de Araucaíma, dir. by Carlos Mayolo (Zona A Limitada, 1986).

La negociación, dir. by Margarita Martínez (Cine Colombia, S.A., 2018).

La virgen y el fotógrafo, dir. by Luis Alfredo Sánchez (Zona A Limitada, 1983).

María Cano, dir. by Camila Loboguerrero (Zona A Limitada, 1990).

Pisingaña, dir. by Leopoldo Pinzón (Zona A Limitada, 1986).

Pura sangre, dir. by Luis Ospina (Zona A Limitada, 1982).

Rodrigo D: no futuro, dir. by Víctor Gaviria (Zona A Limitada, 1990).

Notes

1   Regarding film censorship as a regulatory instrument, see for example Maria Fernanda Arias Osorio, 'Films That Pervert or Lift: Practices and Discourses of Film Censorship: The Case of Cali, Colombia, 1945–1955', *HistoReLo: revista de historia regional y local* 9.18 (2017): 272–312; Laura Wittern-Keller, *Freedom of the Screen: Legal Challenges to State Film Censorship, 1915–1981* (Lexington: University Press of Kentucky, 2008); Daniel Biltereyst and Roel Vande Winkel, *Silencing Cinema: Film Censorship around the World* (New York: Palgrave Macmillan, 2013). For Foucault's notion, see: Michel Foucault, *Power: Essential Works of Foucault 1954–1984*, vol. 3, trans. James D. Faubion (London: Penguin Books, 1994), p. 218.

2   For further details on Chilean film censorship, see Jorge Iturriaga and Karen Donoso Fritz, 'Cinematographic Censorship in the First Year of the Dictatorship. Chile, 1974. Restoration, Refundation and Legitimation', *Universum* 36.2 (2021): 581–600.

3   See for example Martin Barker and Julian Petley (eds), *Ill Effects: The Media/Violence Debate* (London: Routledge, 2001); Feona Attwood, Clarissa Smith and Martin Barker, '"I'm Just Curious and Still Exploring Myself": Young People and Pornography', *New Media and Society* 20.10 (2018): 3738–59.

4   Foucault, *Power*, p. 343.

5   Ibid., pp. 336–48.

6   While the first cinematograph import took place in 1907 with state help, the Ninth Law (1942) became the first official state means at national level to contribute to tax exemptions and export profits (i.e., customs taxes due to imported equipment and film material). Despite these antecedents and another state-run stimulus plan (sanctioned in the mid-1940s), there was no consistent scheme throughout the years, so filmmakers needed to find their own means of production until FOCINE's appearance. Hernando

Salcedo Silva, *Crónicas del cine colombiano, 1897–1950* (Bogotá: Carlos Valencia Editores, 1981), pp. 27–34; Hernando Martínez Pardo, 'Historia del cine colombiano', in Edna Bolkan and Rosa Coutinho (eds), *Diccionario del cine iberoamericano: España, Portugal y América* (Madrid: SGAE, 2011), https://ibermediadigital.com/ibermedia-television/contexto-historico/colombia-segun-el-diccionario-de-cine-iberoamericano/.

7   Although the Surcharge Law intended to promote filmmaking activity to solidify the industry, it also created a strong domino effect in which numerous filmmakers and exhibitors produced a myriad of low-quality short films to cash in at the expense of the screen quota. Ana María Higuita González, 'El cine documental en Colombia durante la era del sobreprecio, 1972–1978', *Historia y sociedad* 25 (2013): 107–35 (p. 109); Oswaldo Osorio, *Las muertes del cine colombiano* (Medellín: Editorial Universidad de Antioquia, 2018), pp. 74–75; Maria Czestochowa Molina Serrano, 'Cine en Colombia: historia de una industria', *Ñawi: arte diseño comunicación* 4.2 (2020): 169–80 (n.p.); Peter H. Rist, *Historical Dictionary of South American Cinema*, ed. Jon Woronoff (Plymouth: Rowman & Littlefield Publishers, 2014), p. 29.

8   Decree 1244 of 1978, 30 June, 'Por el cual se autoriza al Instituto Nacional de Radio y Televisión -Inravisión-, a la Corporación Financiera Popular y a la Compañía de Informaciones Audiovisuales para participar en la constitución de una sociedad', *Diario Oficial*, Bogotá, 24 July 1978, 35060, p. 9.

9   Jerónimo León Rivera-Betancur, 'La identidad colombiana y su representación nacional', in *El papel del cine colombiano en la escena latinoamericana* (Chía: Universidad de La Sabana, 2019), pp. 48–51; Osorio, *Las muertes del cine colombiano*, pp. 78–79.

10   Juana Suárez, *Cinembargo Colombia: ensayos críticos sobre cine y cultura* (Bogotá: Editorial Universidad del Valle, 2009), p. 98.

11   Luis Alberto Álvarez, 'Cine colombiano y FOCINE', in *Páginas de cine*, vol. 2 (Medellin: Ed. Universidad de Antioquia, 1992), pp. 23–50 (pp. 24–25). Redacción El Tiempo, 'FOCINE: la toma final', *El Tiempo*, https://www.eltiempo.com/archivo/documento/MAM-16866 [accessed 16 February 2022].

12   Oswaldo Osorio, *Por el lente de un cinéfago: antología del cine colombiano* (Medellín: UPB, 2016), p. 14; Redacción El Tiempo, 'FOCINE: la toma final'; Suárez, *Cinembargo Colombia*, p. 71.

13   Ibid., pp. 79, 87, 97.

14   Ibid., p. 79; Osorio, *Por el lente de un cinéfago*, p. 14.

15   Oswaldo Osorio, *Realidad y cine colombiano: 1990–2009* (Medellín: Editorial Universidad de Antioquia, 2010), p. 3.

16   Pedro Adrián Zuluaga, *Cine colombiano: cánones y discursos dominantes* (Bogotá: Cinemateca Distrital, IDARTES, 2013), p. 106.

17   Julianne Burton, 'The Hour of the Embers: On the Current Situation of Latin American Cinema', *Film Quarterly* 30.1 (1976): 33–44 (p. 36).

18   Juana Suárez, 'Tropical Gothic: Cinematic Dislocations of the Caribbean Imaginary in South West Colombia', *Studies in Gothic Fiction* 3.2 (2014): 24–37.

19   María Angélica Mora Buitrago (ed.), *Candilejas: revista cinema itinerante* (Tolima: Centro Cultural Universidad de Tolima, 2014), pp. 45–46, http://administrativos.ut.edu.co/images/VICEHUMANO/centro_cultural/candilejas/Candilejas4.pdf.

20 The literal translation of the title refers to 'Condors that are not buried every day', but the film was released in English under the title *A Man of Principle*.

21 Paola Arboleda Ríos and Diana Osorio Gómez, *La presencia de la mujer en el cine colombiano* (Bogotá: Ministerio de Cultura, 2003), pp. 93–109.

22 Ibid., p. 268; Redacción El Tiempo, 'FOCINE: la toma final'; Patricia Restrepo, '¿Qué es FOCINE?', *Nueva frontera* 267 (1980): 21–22.

23 Deborah Martin, *Painting, Literature and Film in Colombian Feminine Culture, 1940–2005* (Woodbridge, Suffolk & Rochester, NY: Tamesis, 2012), p. 25.

24 Lorena Cervera Ferrer, 'Towards a Latin American Feminist Cinema: The Case of Cine Mujer in Colombia', *Alphaville: Journal of Film and Screen Media* 20 (2020): 150–65 (p. 160), https://doi.org/10.33178/alpha.20.11; Suárez, *Cinembargo Colombia*, p. 115.

25 Sara Bright and Patricia Restrepo (Cine Mujer co-founders), interview with Karol Valderrama-Burgos (Leicester, 6 May 2021).

26 Ibid.

27 Ilene S. Goldman, 'Latin American Women's Alternative Film and Video', in *Visible Nations: Latin American Cinema and Video* (Minneapolis & London: University of Minnesota Press, 2000), pp. 239–62 (p. 245).

28 Cervera Ferrer, 'Towards a Latin American Feminist Cinema', p. 158.

29 Bright and Restrepo, interview.

30 The colloquial expression used for the film title suggests 'take your business [music] elsewhere'.

31 Osorio, *Las muertes del cine colombiano*, p. 81; Carlos Mario Ramírez Aissa, '*María Cano*: la endeblez de un símbolo', *Cuadernos de Filosofía Latinoamericana* 26.93 (2005): 183–93 (p. 192); Suárez, *Cinembargo Colombia*, p. 116; 'La historia de un fracaso', *Revista Semana*, n.d., https://www.semana.com/especiales/articulo/historia-fracaso/19308-3/ [accessed 18 February 2022], para 3 of 21.

32 Ramírez Aissa, '*María Cano*', p. 192; Suárez, *Cinembargo Colombia*, p. 116.

33 Mora Buitrago (ed.), *Candilejas*, p. 43.

11

State Censorship of Debut Films in the 1980s People's Republic of Poland: The Example of the Irzykowski Film Studio

Emil Sowiński

Censorship interference with filmmakers in the Polish People's Republic (or Polska Rzeczpospolita Ludowa, hereafter PRL) is closely related to political changes, especially those that took place between 1947 and 1989. Whereas the first period (1947–56) was a time when films were carefully monitored, after that, an easing of restrictions took place, related first to the death of Stalin and then to Władysław Gomułka's ascendancy to power. These political shifts also changed film culture (for instance, they resulted in the appearance of the widely known Polish Film School).[1] Subsequent interference of state authorities, in the form of the Resolution of the Central Committee Secretariat of the Polish United Workers Party (PZPR) of June 1960, prevented this trend from developing any further.[2]

As a result of this resolution, censorship interference also intensified, which then eased with another change at the highest levels of the Party when Comrade Edward Gierek (who was considered more liberal than other apparatchiks) replaced Władysław Gomułka as the First Secretary of the PZPR in 1970. Gierek's approach had two faces. While the first period can be considered liberal, after June 1976, repressions aimed at pacifying the film community were intensified. The main reason for this change

Emil Sowiński, "State Censorship of Debut Films in the 1980s People's Republic of Poland: The Example of the Irzykowski Film Studio" in: *The Screen Censorship Companion: Critical Explorations in the Control of Film and Screen Media*. University of Exeter Press (2024). © Emil Sowiński. DOI: 10.47788/SVEO2240 was the increasing involvement of artists in the activities of the emerging democratic opposition.

This chapter focuses on the first half of the next decade. It uses the case study of the Irzykowski Film Studio as a means to illustrate how the activity of censorship was managed during that politically volatile time. This Warsaw-based film studio was founded in 1981 by a group of young graduates of the Lodz Film School. It was modelled on the Hungarian Balázs Béla Studio as an institution that allowed young filmmakers to start their careers directly after graduating from film school.[3] Two events conditioned the studio's activity. The first was the living situation of young film artists. At that time, the Young Filmmakers' Circle of the Polish Filmmakers' Association, which brings together young film school graduates, included 146 filmmakers, only fourteen of whom were employed, among whom only two had permanent full-time positions. Establishing an institution for young filmmakers seemed the only way out of this crisis situation. Thus, the studio proposed by young artists was intended to be a place where filmmakers could make their first film and start a career, and perhaps above all, a company that guaranteed permanent employment, which was very important for young people (as well as the authorities) in the socialist system.

Secondly, and particularly significant for the founding of the studio, was the signing of an agreement between the Independent Self-Governing Trade Union 'Solidarity' and the socialist authorities in August 1980, which started the period of the so-called 'Carnival of Solidarity'.[4] This period experienced a blossoming of so-called underground culture, which came with a softening of direct censorship. The end of this era came with the introduction of martial law (13 December 1981), which significantly limited Polish cultural life. Martial law, however, did not affect the programme policy of the Irzykowski Film Studio. Even though it existed inside the framework of the socialist state-owned film industry, the Irzykowski Studio was much more independent than the film units (the basic organizational entities of the Polish film production system at the time) and short-film studios, and therefore unaffected by direct censorship. Despite the prevailing restrictions, the Studio continued to produce politically controversial films, thus playing a risky game with the authorities and censorship forces. This exceptional situation forms the focus of this chapter.

Organizational Structure of the Irzykowski Film Studio in the Light of the Censorship Interference System

The practices of the Irzykowski Studio must be regarded in the context of the PRL approach towards culture. Poland had to deal with internal censorship, operating within the state institutions, and external censorship in the form of the Main Office for Control (hereafter MOC), or the PZPR. Historian Zbigniew Romek writes:

> Censorship in the PRL is a whole system of institutions and people connected and cooperating with one another formally and informally. The actual and first censors were the editors, internal reviewers of publishing houses, various commissions or program committees, scientific councils, selection committees, and other bodies that planned publishing or artistic production, and assessed the works presented to them, not only from the substantive point of view, but also issued opinions on their socio-political or ideological overtones. Censorship offices sought and even demanded active participation in the process of free speech censorship from various types of institutions.[5]

Taking a closer look at the PRL film production system in the period discussed, the censorship process was multi-staged, and differed slightly depending on the type of film.[6] In the case of short films (documentaries, animations, educational films), the process usually started at the short-film studio, or in-house. The editors working in the studio's literary division assessed the finished texts and sent them to the director for approval. After that, the accepted scripts were centrally evaluated by the Programme Department of the Supreme Board of Cinematography (hereafter NZK). The clerks employed at the headquarters were therefore, directly after the editors employed by the studios, another body that could decide to reject a given project on the basis of a politically controversial topic. Further interference by censorship occurred only when the film was ready. First, the film was approved at the level of internal preview in a short-film studio, during which an official of state censorship and the owners of the studio were present. The film was then evaluated by the Artistic Evaluation Committee operating at the NZK, which decided on the distribution range (or lack of approval for distribution).

In the case of full-length live-action films, the censorship process was slightly different. Such films were created by film units. The film units were headed by an artistic director selected from a list of renowned film directors.[7] They were supported by a literary manager (usually a recognized writer or literary critic) and a production manager chosen from a group of experienced production managers. Thus, in the first stage, the evaluation of the project took place among the film authors, not the officials, whose main task was to track down the anti-socialist elements of the script. Despite this, the decision to approve the film for production belonged to the ministry official with the rank of undersecretary of state. After production, the finished film was evaluated by the ministerial Pre-Release Review Committee consisting of Party critics, writers and artistic directors of film units. And at the end of the process, the finished film was examined by the MOC, whose opinion was mandatory for the Minister of Culture and Arts who decided on the cinema exhibition licence.

This multi-stage evaluation of the film in the making was intended to prevent any future films the reception of which might be in opposition to the policies of the PZPR. With this in mind, it is interesting that the MOC always evaluated the finished film. It suggests that the PZPR trusted the cinematographic leadership and acknowledged that the internal control system was sufficient.

The main difference between the Irzykowski Film Studio and other film units was the responsibility for programme policy. An artistic manager was responsible for it in the units, while in the Studio there was a five-person Artistic Council.[8] As stated in the Studio's regulations, the Artistic Council was 'a collective, autonomous and independent body reporting directly to the Studio's members, not choosing a chairperson from among its members'.[9] One of its most important prerogatives was to accept and send the submitted project out for implementation.[10] Because of this, the council held a considerable privilege that film units did not. It is worth remembering that the artistic director of a film unit could only apply for a script to be sent to production once it had been approved by the head of cinematography.

Consequently, state censorship was not able to interfere in the decision-making process and could only make a judgement about a finished film. At this point, censors could make three decisions: allow for distribution, reject a film, or request the removal of controversial scenes or dialogues. In sum, the Irzykowski Film Studio appears to have been a small island with a democratic system on the otherwise authoritarian PRL cultural map, as it could decide on its own programme policy.

Censorship against the Films Produced by the Irzykowski Film Studio

In 1982, Colonel Leszek Adamów, a representative of the Military Council of National Salvation at the Ministry of Culture and Art,[11] demanded a list of films in preparation from the Studio's authorities. The Artistic Council complied and created such a document, but did so with a twist—it included the titles of all the films approved for production, but with especially indistinct descriptions. For example: *Sunday Pranks*, which is an image of Stalinist Poland in miniature (the characters are minors living in one of Warsaw's tenement houses, whose backyard games inspired by the communist iconosphere reflect the nature of the rules prevailing in the totalitarian regime), is described as 'a story about children's games in a

Warsaw backyard that ended tragically'.[12] The documentary *Summer Camps*, which is a courageous satire of martial law showing the phenomenon of indoctrination of children staying at summer camps by soldiers of the Polish People's Army, was described in the following words: 'a report from summer camp'.[13] It is clear from the document that military decision-makers knew relatively little about the Studio's production activities. As such, they were convinced that nothing extraordinary was happening in their subordinate film studio.

By the summer of 1983, the MOC had familiarized themselves with the Studio's finished productions. The censors were paranoid about film projects presenting the army, civic militia or prison service in a negative light, as well as attempts to show the 'Solidarity' movement in a positive light. Moreover, they were concerned about metaphorical scenes and dialogues that provoked anti-socialist associations. Out of the nineteen films produced in the years 1981–83, eleven were rejected, three were granted permission for release after recommendations had been implemented, and five were accepted in the original version (Table 11.1).

It is difficult to clearly identify specific censorship allegations against rejected films. The documents found in the National Film Archive— Audiovisual Institute merely mention the censorship's refusal to distribute them, and do not clearly explain the reasons.[14] It can be assumed that it concerned the films' political meaning. Most likely, the representatives of the MOC, after watching them, immediately decided to prohibit the films' distribution, not giving anyone any opportunity to introduce changes. Perhaps the MOC were even helpless in the face of the presented films and did not know what recommendations to make so that they could be shown to viewers. The above assumptions are confirmed by the history related to the censorship of *Summer Camps*. The film director Wojciech Maciejewski recalls:

> Preview showings of this film […] were quite an experience for me. It was evident that the film was funny and terrifying for the previewers. They asked for changes, but what changes they did not want to say, they probably thought I should know myself. In subsequent previews, they saw the same version of the film and demanded 'extensive' changes, and I asked for an indication of the place and nature of these changes.[15]

The conclusions from the analysis of this film in terms of ideologically threatening scenes do indeed confirm Maciejewski's hypothesis about the helplessness of censorship. It is difficult to find any scene in the diegetic world of the film that would be uncontroversial at the time of martial law. The main character of this ironic documentary film is a military standard

Table 11.1. State censorship of debut films produced by
the Irzykowski Film Studio during martial law

Films without censorship interference	Films approved for distribution after censorship interference	Rejected films
Dragon's Tail [*Smoczy ogon*] Michał Szczepański, 1981	*The Concert* [*Koncert*] Michał Tarkowski, 1982	*Christmas Eve* [*Wigilia*] Leszek Wosiewicz, 1982
		Still Waiting [*Jeszcze czekam*] A. Marek Drążewski, 1982
		Christmas Tree of Fear [*Choinka strachu*] Tomasz Lengren, 1982
Tenement House [*Kamienica*] Jacek Kowalczyk, 1982		*Return from the Gutenberg Galaxy* [*Powrót z galaktyki Gutenberga*] Zbigniew Kowalewski, 1983
	I Feel Great [*Czuję się świetnie*] Waldemar Szarek, 1983	*Sunday Pranks* [*Niedzielne igraszki*] Robert Gliński, 1983
Being a Human [*Być człowiekiem*] Julian Pakuła, 1983		*Summer Camps* [*Słoneczna gromada*] Wojciech Maciejewski, 1983
		The Guide [*Przewodnik*] Tomasz Zygadło, 1983
What Do You Want from Us, God [*Czego chcesz od nas Panie*] Leszek Nagrabecki, 1983	*Custody* [*Nadzór*] Wiesław Saniewski, 1983	*The Ferry* [*Prom*] Jacek Talczewski, 1983
		The Palace [*Pałac*] Jacek Siwecki, 1983
Postcard from a Journey [*Kartka z podróży*] Waldemar Dziki, 1983		*The Undefeated* [*Niepokonani*] A. Marek Drążewski, 1983
		He Has Arrived [*Jest*] Krzysztof Krauze, 1983

bearer who acts as a camp counsellor. His main task is to indoctrinate youth. A good example is the scene in which the participants of the sleepaway camp take part in a short conversation. The main character asks them: 'What does the abbreviation ZSMP stand for?' One of them answers: 'The Polish Socialist Youth Union.'—'And what does this Polish Socialist Youth Union do?'—'I don't know.'—'The Polish Socialist Youth Union is an organization of simply all our youth, Polish youth, who simply want to build our socialism and want to work well for our dear socialist homeland, who want there to be peace in our country, for our country to develop.' This scene clearly potrays the main character, through his seriousness and pride when confronted with the absurdity of his views, as a grotesque and almost amusing figure.

On the other hand, when viewing the documentary *The Concert*, which focuses on performances given by the famous bands of the 1980s,[16] censors were anxious about an animated part showing the demolition of the Palace of Culture and Science,[17] and about a shot of the young audience who showed the Victoria sign (also known as the victory or peace sign).[18] In a second musical film, *I Feel Great*,[19] the censors demanded to cut the scene in which Kora, a frontwoman of Maanam, sings a hit called 'Betrayal' ['Zdrada'], which metaphorically describes the introduction of martial law. At the end of the song, Kora suddenly goes towards the bassist and chokes him with a microphone cable. The bassist wears dark glasses, just like Wojciech Jaruzelski, the general who introduced martial law. Unsurprisingly, the director was instructed to remove the scene from the film, and changes were made to the screening copies that were shown in Warsaw cinemas. Ironically, and allegedly, in other cities, given the prohibitive costs of the censorship operation, authorities decided to screen the film in its original version.[20] Interestingly enough, *I Feel Great* has survived in an uncut version to this day.[21]

Custody—A Risky Game with Censorship

The censorship interference in the full-length debut of Wiesław Saniewski merits a separate discussion. *Custody* tells the story of Klara, who is arrested at her wedding reception for a fiscal offence. It soon transpires that she ends up in prison and is handed a life sentence (later her sentence is reduced to twenty-five years). There she gives birth to a baby, who is then taken away. Lonely and isolated, she needs to find her way around a brutal world of rules and hierarchies. The diegetic world could be described as a metaphor for the contemporary situation in Poland.

As early as September 1983, an attempt was made to submit the picture to a ministerial evaluation. In response, a letter with recommendations for changes was received. The NZK's Programme Department recommended removing the scene of the arrest of the main character during a wedding, reducing the main character's sentence from life imprisonment to at maximum fifteen years, removing the thread about the student Justyna who is convicted of distributing opposition brochures, and reducing the metaphorical shot of a sparrow dying on a red ribbon. They also recommended that the plot be set explicitly in the 1960s. The implementation of these changes was required for the production to be approved for formal evaluation.[22] A few days later, the film was re-submitted for official pre-release review, with the statement that all *possible changes* had been implemented.[23] Interestingly, despite this declaration, the film was presented to the ministerial Pre-Release Review Committee in an unchanged version.

The first and most discussed issue was the length of the sentence ruled on the main character. The artistic director of the 'Perspektywa' Film Unit, Janusz Morgenstern, had doubts: 'I don't know why this character received such a long court sentence because I imagine she would have to murder someone to get a life sentence [...]. The fact that we do not know what her crimes were weighs heavily on the entire film, which is brilliantly made, but I would advise the director to think about this.'[24] The arrest scene at the wedding also caused mixed feelings. Kazimierz Koźniewski, a writer associated with the PZPR, even advised the director to move the arrest to another day: 'I don't know whether it was impossible to wait a day or two, because such an arrest during a wedding is very brutal, and in any case, such action should be justified.'[25] The opposition of the committee members was also caused by the ambiguously defined plot setting, which in the eyes of the previewers was completely distorted by the presence of the student Justyna. Kazimierz Koźniewski said: 'I perceived these matters in such a way that this student was arrested in 1981 or 1982. It is a very important factor because the film has no subtitles and nowhere does it state in what historical era its action is set, but I assure you that if it is an arrested student, if she is accused of distributing brochures, it is 1981 or 1982.'[26]

In the stenographic record of the pre-release review session, preserved in the archive, we did not find any declaration of what would happen to the film next. However, in the documentation, a letter has been preserved which shows that the deputy Minister of Culture and Arts did not consent to its distribution.[27] It seems that the state authorities were irritated by the 'dirty' game that the film author and producer took up—that is, the false declarations of the Artistic Council and Saniewski about the changes made. In this letter, we can find an annotation confirming this thesis: 'Despite previous discussions in the NZK Programme Department, Film director W. Saniewski did not make any significant changes in the film.'[28]

What is particularly interesting is that at the same time a slightly different document was produced by the MOC, in which we can read that the film violates the provisions of the censorship act, but after the changes, it may be approved for distribution. Thus, the censorship office treated Saniewski's film somewhat more leniently than NZK's officials. The comments from the MOC mostly concerned the character of Justyna. Additionally, the official called for a change in the length of the sentence and the setting of the film's plot in the late 1960s.[29]

In February, the film director commenced his discussions with the censorship committee. Saniewski recalls that when he was going to have a discussion with the censor, he adopted a negotiation strategy:

> The censor analysed the scenes he wanted to remove. For example, he did not like the arrest at the wedding. I told him that there was no arrest there [...]. People come, they show something, a letter or ID cards, there is a cut, and then Klara is in prison. Perhaps they brought her a summons for questioning. He replied: 'You are right.' He noted my explanation, and we moved on to the next scene. He told me that showing a tube feeding Klara on a bloodstained pillow could cause a riot in prisons. I said: 'Does this mean that the film will be distributed in prisons?' He said: 'No, we will definitely not show it in prisons.' And the scene was not cut.[30]

The director of *Custody* managed to persuade the censor to leave in the remaining scenes with Justyna. Moreover, the main character's life sentence was not changed (mainly for dramatic and psychological reasons). In return, Saniewski agreed to introduce a title card that would unambiguously set the plot in the late 1960s, and to remove a fragment of the dialogue in which Justyna informs her fellow prisoners that she was detained for distributing brochures (in the exchange: 'What are you in for?'—'For brochures.'—'Are you a student?'—'Not any more', the first answer was deleted).[31] The scene with a sparrow dying on a red ribbon was also shortened. From the changes made, it can be concluded that the censor wanted the film to be devoid of any reference to the reality of martial law.

However, the meeting with a censor mentioned above did not result in the film being approved for distribution. In one of the unsigned archival memos, we can also read that Saniewski on 14 February 1984 stated that some of the changes had been made and on 25 June 1984 that all the recommendations had been implemented.[32] Therefore, archival sources paint a completely different picture from Saniewski's memoirs. In the archives, censorship appears as an unyielding institution that approves distribution only when the director agrees to introduce changes (this is also confirmed by a surviving letter signed by Saniewski of 26 June 1984, in which the director states that he has implemented all the recommendations of the censorship officials).[33] As a result, the film was approved by the Minister of Culture and Arts at the beginning of July 1984 and allowed for narrow distribution within the network of the Film Club society.[34]

Nevertheless, the distributed version of the film contains all the controversial scenes (only the aforementioned Justyna dialogue with the prisoners and the scene of the sparrow dying on the red ribbon were shortened), and a title card is introduced informing the audience that the film takes place in 1967. It can thus be assumed that the statement signed by Saniewski was a bluff, and the time that elapsed between his letter stating that all the changes had been made and the decision to accept the film (three working days)[35] means that the decision-makers did not preview the film again and took the director's word. This interpretation is supported by the fact that it was at this time that Saniewski decided to cut a twenty-minute sequence that took place after Klara's release from prison, for dramatic reasons. Therefore, the film was shorter by two acts. So, without the preview being organized, one could clearly see that significant cuts had been made. Thus, there was no reason not to believe Saniewski's declaration.

The authorities approved five copies of this version for distribution in the Film Club society network (in October 1984, distribution was extended to arthouse cinemas).[36] Of course, this had one goal: to make Saniewski's film poorly accessible but not inaccessible, so as not to create another legendary film that was banned by the authorities. Despite the limited distribution, the Ministry of Justice was concerned about the presence of *Custody* in the repertoire of arthouse cinemas. In a letter sent to the censorship office, the ministry stated that the film was biased and depicted the prison service in an unfavourable light, constituting groundless criticism of the law and the PRL system.[37] Accordingly, a request was made to suspend its distribution. In response to this call, the censorship office replied: 'It was not possible to enforce the proposed changes, as they interfered too drastically with the film, including the reduction of the sentence as an unjustified and draconian punishment, the elimination of scenes about the suicide of prisoner Justyna and the rebellion of the prisoners.'[38] This fragment clearly shows that the film that was then distributed contained controversial scenes, and the declaration signed by Saniewski on the implementation of all censorship recommendations was a bluff. This fact, of course, could not be revealed; therefore, in subsequent internal notes of the Ministry of Culture and Art, it was maintained that the director had made all the changes recommended to him by decision-makers, which resulted in the shortening of the film by more than twenty minutes.[39] An internal note from the PZPR Culture

Department also tried to prove that the Ministry of Justice was oversensitive and had misinterpreted the film's meaning.[40]

Despite these justifications, the cinema authorities responded positively to the suggestion from the Ministry of Justice to withdraw the film from distribution, probably wanting to cut off this sensitive topic as soon as possible. The film was removed from arthouse cinemas after two weeks of screening, and its further distribution was possible only and exclusively within the Film Club society network, 'with the simultaneous fulfillment of the condition to precede the screening with an appropriate commentary'.[41] Nevertheless, its brief on-screen presence did not prevent it from becoming the most popular film shown in arthouse cinemas and the Film Club network in 1985. It was seen by 132,932 viewers, which, with just 770 screenings, meant the average number of viewers per screening was 161 (as a reference point, *Indiana Jones and the Temple of Doom*, which was watched in 1985 by approximately 5.5 million people, had 166 people per screening).[42]

Conclusion

The article by Zbigniew Romek quoted near the beginning of this chapter stated that 'when a publishing house, magazine, film unit or a scientific institution did not want to fulfil the role of the first censor, the office or appropriate Party instances on its behalf sent appropriate more or less severe admonitions. And when these did not help, the institution's management was changed, and more rebellious employees were laid off.'[43] A similar fate befell the independent Irzykowski Film Studio. The number of films rejected by censorship resulted in the establishment of a special commission, whose report clearly stated that the Studio's films were anti-socialist.[44] The post-inspection conclusions stated, among other things, that NZK's Programme Department were to assess the Studio's scripts, and its director needed to be approved by the Ministry of Culture and Art.[45] These demands were implemented shortly afterwards. From July 1984, the Studio was controlled by state censorship, on the same terms as the regular film units. A year later, the position of the Artistic Council was marginalized, making it an advisory body to the director. Leszek Kwiatek, a member of the PZPR, who did not come from the film community, was appointed director and his main task was to control the Studio's programming line. The state authorities also decided to discipline the most rebellious film directors, deciding not to extend their contracts. As a result, they lost their jobs, and some of them never returned and had to take up other positions.

Acknowledgement

This work was supported by the Polish National Science Centre (no. UMO-2019/33/N/HS2/01462).

Notes

1   The Polish Film School was an informal group of young film directors and screenplay writers (among others, Andrzej Wajda, Andrzej Munk, Tadeusz Konwicki, Stanisław Różewicz, Kazimierz Kutz, Wojciech Jerzy Has, Jerzy Kawalerowicz and Stanisław Lenartowicz) active between 1956 and 1965, which embodied the generation's objections to socialist-realist art. Cf. Marek Haltof, *Polish National Cinema* (New York: Berghahn Books, 2002), pp. 73–109.

2   Marek Hatlof wrote that this Party document 'postulated making political and educational films needed in the process of "building socialism", films that reflected current problems from the socialist perspective, and works inspired by the "progressive tendencies" in Polish history'. Ibid.

3   Cf. Balázs Varga, 'Co-operation: The Organization of Studio Units in the Hungarian Film Industry of the 1950s and 1960s', in. Marcin Adamczak, Marcin Malatyński and Piotr Marecki (eds), *Film Units: Restart* (Cracow & Warsaw: ha!art, 2012), pp. 324–29.

4   The 'Solidarity' union was officially founded on 17 September 1980 and fuctioned until the introduction of martial law, i.e. 13 December 1981. In September 1981, the Union had over 10 million members, and became the largest union membership in the world and the first independent trade union in a Warsaw Pact country to be recognized by the state. The leader of the Solidarity movement, Lech Wałęsa, was a shipyard electrician by trade.

5   Zbigniew Romek, 'Kilka uwag o aktach cenzury jako źródle historycznym', *Polska 1944/45–1989: Warsztat badawczy. Studia i materiały* 6 (2004): 194. Translations from Polish are the author's own.

6   Anna Misiak, *Kinematograf kontrolowany: cenzura filmowa w kraju socjalistycznym i demokratycznym* (Cracow: Universitas, 2006).

7   In the 1980s, the heads of the film units were, among others: Andrzej Wajda ('X' Film Unit), Krzysztof Zanussi ('Tor' Film Unit), Wojciech Jerzy Has ('Rondo' Film Unit), Jerzy Kawalerowicz ('Kadr' Film Unit) and Janusz Morgenstern ('Perspektywa' Film Unit). Importantly, there were also units that dealt primarily with propaganda activities. They included: 'Profil' Film Unit (artistic director: Bohdan Poręba) and 'Iluzjon' Film Unit (artistic director: Czesław Petelski). Cf. Marcin Adamczak, 'Film Units in the People's Republic of Poland', in Adamczak, Marecki and Malatyński (eds), *Film Units: Restart*, pp. 232–70; Anna Pachnicka and Tadeusz Szczepański (eds), *Idea zespołu filmowego: historia i nowe wyzwania* (Lodz: Wydawnictwo PWSFTviT, 2014); JJarosław Grzechowiak, 'Zespół Filmowy „Iluzjon"—studium upadku', *Kwartalnik filmowy* 108 (2019): 150–69; Anna Szczepańska, *Do granic negocjacji: historia zespołu filmowego X Andrzeja Wajdy* (Cracow: Universitas, 2017).

8   The first Artistic Council (1981–84) included graduates of the Lodz Film School, i.e. Robert Gliński (in 1982 replaced by Leszek Wosiewicz), Jan Mogilnicki, Michał Tarkowski, Waldemar Dziki and Maciej Falkowski.

9   Regulations of the Irzykowski Film Studio, AAN, NZK, no. 2–109.

10 Ibid.

11 The Military Council of National Salvation was the administrative body of Poland during martial law.

12 Letter to Leszek Adamów, 23 November 1982, Narodowe Archiwum Cyfrowe [National Digital Archives], archival found: The Irzykowski Film Studio, no. 1–24.

13 Ibid.

14 The National Film Archive—Audiovisual Institute (hereafter AFINA) holds a collection of production documents for films produced by the Irzykowski Film Studio, including censorship records.

15 E-mail to Emil Sowiński, 20 September 2019.

16 The film includes scenes recorded at the Rockowisko festival in November 1981 and at a specially arranged concert by a production group in the spring of 1982.

17 The palace was 'a gift of the Soviet people to the Polish nation'. It was built in the years 1952–55 according to the design of the Soviet architect Lew Rudniew.

18 Just before the introduction of martial law, this gesture was very often used by Lech Wałęsa, the chairman of the 'Solidarity' movement and the Nobel Peace Prize winner in 1983.

19 Cf. Ewa Mazierska, 'Beyond Authenticity, Beyond Romanticism: Films About Maanam', *IASPM Journal* 1 (2017): 55–70.

20 Interview with film director Waldemar Szarek conducted by Emil Sowiński, 12 April 2020.

21 An uncensored version was aired by the Polish TVP Kultura channel on 21 April 2010.

22 Letter to the director of NZK's Programme Department, 13 December 1983, Archiwum Filmoteki Narodowej-Instytutu Audiowizualnego [Archives of the National Film Archive—Audiovisual Institute], no. S-34373.

23 Ibid.

24 Stenographic record of the session of the Pre-Release Review Committee, 27 January 1984, AFINA, no. A-344.

25 Ibid.

26 Ibid.

27 Letter to the Irzykowski Film Studio, 7 February 1984, AFINA, no. S-31373.

28 Ibid.

29 Comments on *Custody*, AFINA, no. A-344.

30 Interview with film director Wiesław Saniewski conducted by Emil Sowiński, 10 September 2021.

31 Ibid.

32 Unsigned memo regarding *Custody*, 4 March 1985, AFINA, no. A-344.

33 Letter to the Deputy Minister of Culture and Art, 26 June 1984, AFINA, no. A-344.

34 Letter to the State Film Distribution Company, 10 July 1984, AFINA, no. A-344.

35 Letter to the Deputy Minister of Culture and Art, 26 June 1984, AFINA, no. A-344.

36 Letter to the Film Distribution Company, 5 October 1984, AFINA, no. A-344.

37 Memo of the Director General at the Ministry of Justice, 4 March 1985, AAN, archival found: Main Office for Control, no. 3313.

38 Ibid.

39 Unsigned memo concerning *Custody*, no date, AFINA, no. A-344.
40 Memo concerning *Custody*, 7 March 1985, AFINA, no. A-344.
41 Ibid.
42 *Mały Rocznik Filmowy 1985* (Warsaw: Centrala Dystrybucji Filmów, 1986), p. 78.
43 Romek, 'Kilka uwag o aktach cenzury jako źródle historycznym', p. 194.
44 Report on the comprehensive audit of the activities of Irzykowski Film Studio, 21 March 1983, AAN, NZK, no. 2–109.
45 Ibid.

Part 4

*Intermediality, Entanglement and
Longitudinal Approaches*

12

Banned in Detroit: The Interconnectedness of Film, Literary and Media Censorship

Ben Strassfeld

By the time the film *The Moon Is Blue* (Otto Preminger, 1953) arrived in Detroit in July of 1953, it had already drawn significant controversy and scrutiny from local censor boards due to its risqué dialogue and story of seduction. This was in part because the film was one of the exceedingly rare examples from that era of a major American movie released without a Production Code seal. This fact, combined with a Catholic boycott campaign led by the Legion of Decency, resulted in a number of cities banning the film or delaying its release, including Minneapolis, Milwaukee and Seattle, while state censor boards in Kansas, Ohio and Maryland banned the film entirely. As for Detroit, for the film to play in the city it would first need to be approved by the Detroit Police Department's Censor Bureau, which actively inspected all movies before release, and which frequently banned films of this ilk.[1]

When it came time to decide whether to allow *The Moon Is Blue* to play in Detroit or not, the Censor Bureau was not only grappling with the film before them, but also the fact that the picture was an adaptation of a stage production which had had three separate runs in Detroit in the years prior. The issue for the Censor Bureau was that, in addition to being charged with censoring movies in Detroit, they also were responsible for censoring live theatre, meaning that the same Censor Bureau now tasked with reviewing the film version of *The Moon Is Blue* had already given their approval to the

Ben Strassfeld, "Banned in Detroit: The Interconnectedness of Film, Literary and Media Censorship" in: *The Screen Censorship Companion: Critical Explorations in the Control of Film and Screen Media.* University of Exeter Press (2024). © Ben Strassfeld. DOI: 10.47788/HBSC1824 stage production of *The Moon Is Blue*. Given this, the Detroit Censor Bureau ultimately opted against banning the film, with the Police Commissioner specifically giving as his justification: 'The stage version of the movie has appeared here three times.'[2]

This story points to the central idea I explore in this chapter, which is the importance of studying film censorship in relation with other forms of media censorship. Even as recent scholarly work on movie censorship has greatly expanded our understanding of how cinema has been regulated throughout its history by cities, states, countries and the industry itself, this work too often looks at movie censorship in isolation. The censorship of *The Moon Is Blue* in Detroit, however, and the case study I present in the rest of this chapter, illustrate the ways in which the censoring of film has always been closely tied to the censoring of all types of media and popular entertainment, including not only live theatre but also literature, comic books and adult entertainment. In particular, I will focus here on literary censorship in Detroit during the late 1940s and 1950s, pointing to how both the methods used to censor books and the books deemed in need of censorship were closely linked with various other forms of film and media censorship. As I will also show, Detroit is a particularly useful case study for thinking about censorship across media, given that, unlike most other municipal censorship boards during the twentieth century, the Censor Bureau was tasked not only with censoring movies but also all public media and entertainment in the city.

The Catholic Influence on Film and Literary Censorship

Before turning to literary censorship in Detroit, it is worth giving some brief background on the history of the Detroit Police Censor Bureau and movie censorship in Detroit. As was the case in a number of cities in the United States, during the nickelodeon and transitional eras, movies attracted a great deal of controversy and concern in Detroit over the supposed harm they were causing to children and working-class audiences. This public pressure resulted in the Detroit Police Department taking on the role of movie censor for the city in 1912. Starting then, and continuing for over a half-century to come, every film hoping to play in theatres in Detroit first had to be inspected by the police officers who made up what would come to be known as the Censor Bureau. Films would be inspected for any signs of 'indecency' and 'immorality', the standards set out by Detroit's movie censorship ordinance under which the Censor Bureau operated.[3]

To illustrate the connections between various forms of media censorship, I want to turn now to the influence of Catholics on movie censorship. As a number of scholars have explored, during the pre-Code era of the

Figure 12.1. A comic depicting the head of the National Organization for Decent Literature cleaning up news stands (Source: *Drive for Decency in Print*, 1939, p. 11)

early 1930s, in response to Hollywood making a series of risqué and racy films, Catholic leaders founded the Legion of Decency to try to reform Hollywood and the movies. In Detroit, this meant that in early 1934, the local chapter of the Legion of Decency organized a city-wide campaign to protest indecent movies, with priests using their sermons to call on parishioners to boycott immoral films, which some 350,000 local Catholics in the city pledged to do. The Detroit Legion of Decency also circulated a list of immoral films and theatres that all Catholics in the city should studiously avoid. Such efforts were mirrored in local Catholic-led movie morality campaigns happening around the country at that time. In the seemingly tidy narrative of what then followed, scholars have shown how after Hollywood adopted the Production Code midway through 1934, Catholics continued to exert influence on movie censorship both through Catholic layman Joseph Breen heading the Production Code Administration, and also through the Legion of Decency's continued surveillance of the movies in the decades ahead.[4]

But scholars have tended to ignore a central piece of this narrative, which is that after Hollywood's adoption of the Production Code, Catholic groups and leaders of this era very quickly began to target a growing perceived threat to the morals of society: indecent literature. Notably, in going after literary immorality, Catholic activists drew on what they had learned from their efforts to reform Hollywood, a fact that is illustrated through looking at the history of literary censorship in Detroit. In 1938, Catholics formed the National Organization for Decent Literature, which was something of the literary counterpart to the Legion of Decency. Detroit, which had a substantial Catholic population at that time, boasted one of the most active National Organization for Decent Literature chapters in the country. Edward Mooney, the first Archbishop of Detroit and later to be named a cardinal, helped kickstart the campaign against indecent literature in a March 1939 letter sent to the heads of every parish in the archdiocese. In it, he directed priests to sermonize about the scourge of obscene literature and called on Catholics in the city to take a pledge promising to refrain from all indecent reading material, in much the same way that priests had once called on Catholics to pledge to not go and see immoral movies. Included in the letter was a list of immoral publications of which Catholics should steer clear, again modelled after the list of indecent films prepared by the Legion of Decency. This Catholic activism ultimately spurred the Detroit Police Department's Censor Bureau in the late 1930s to begin targeting indecent literature, in addition to their existing censorial focus on movies and live theatre.[5]

Post-War Censorship of Comic Books and Paperbacks

During the Second World War, this campaign against indecent literature would largely be sidelined in the face of more immediate and pressing concerns, but it returned stronger than ever beginning in the late 1940s. This was largely due to the growing popularity of two much-maligned forms of reading that would soon become the focus for Detroit's censorship operation. The first type was comic books, which had emerged as a major target for censorship across the country during the post-war era, in the midst of a nationwide uproar over a supposed growing epidemic of juvenile delinquency. The most famous purveyor of the idea that comic books were linked to, and indeed the cause of, juvenile delinquency was psychiatrist Fredric Wertham, whose social science research arguing for this connection was published across numerous popular magazines of the day. Though rarely made explicit at the time, Wertham's work, and the attending moral panic surrounding violent and crime-laden comic books, echoed the rhetoric that had been used by critics of Hollywood in the early 1930s. In particular,

Wertham's arguments bore real similarity to those of the Payne Fund Studies, which had used social science research to claim that movies had a deleterious effect on children.[6]

In April of 1948, Detroit began its war on comic books, with Detroit's Police Commissioner announcing a ban on some thirty-six titles, most of them being crime-focused comics with titles like *Crime Exposed Comics*, *True Crime Comics* and *Gangster Comics*. Within months, the Censor Bureau had set up a system which relied on the cooperation of distributors and publishers to censor comics before their release in the city. As Censor Bureau head Herbert Case said in September of 1948, 'Ninety percent of the comic distributors and publishers cooperate with our department, with most publishers sending us advance copies of their magazines two months before publication for our approval'. The industry evidently reasoned that it was cheaper and more efficient to cooperate with the Censor Bureau rather than instigate a lengthy and expensive battle in court. This move by the comic book publishers and distributors was indicative of a larger industry-wide effort to clean up comic books in the face of increasing scrutiny and censorial activity. Eventually, these efforts would coalesce into the comic book industry adopting the self-regulatory Comics Code Authority in 1954. The comic book industry drew directly on the strategy of self-censorship adopted by Hollywood, with the Comics Code itself heavily modelled after the Production Code.[7]

With the comic book industry moving to regulate itself, the Detroit Censor Bureau soon turned its attention to another denigrated form of literature in the post-war era: paperback books. Though paperbacks had been around in various forms for decades, they exploded in popularity during the post-war era due to the way they democratized reading by offering literature to the masses at affordable prices. Paperbacks of this period came in a variety of forms, ranging from more affordable versions of literary classics to paperback-only genre books typically doling out equal measures of tawdry sex and violence. It was precisely because of paperbacks' low cost that they were targeted for censorship in Detroit, as the Censor Bureau soon set up a system for the pre-censorship of all paperbacks before they made it onto store shelves in the city. Notably, the Censor Bureau only censored paperback books, meaning that a title banned in its paperback edition might still be available in hardcover form. As a 1955 *Newsweek* article said of the elitism of this policy: 'A feature of the [Censor Bureau] is that it censors nothing but paperback books. The buyer of hardback, $3.95 books is free to ruin his morals on his own time. Critics of the Detroit Line have called this rule undemocratic—the rich can have books, the poor can't. In short, let 'em eat newspapers.'[8]

Meanwhile, the Censor Bureau's continued work regulating movie morals in Detroit drew on similar notions when it came to the perceived audience of cinema. Namely, in the 1960s the Censor Bureau gave more leeway to films playing in arthouse theatres than they did films playing in general movie theatres in the city. This system was started with the censorship of the film *The Sky Above, the Mud Below* (*Le ciel et la boue*, Pierre-Dominique Gaisseau, 1961), which was an expeditionary documentary that depicted some nudity amongst the indigenous people featured in the film. Rather than outright censoring the film, the Censor Bureau tried to have it both ways by allowing the film to play uncut in the city but only in arthouse theatres restricting admission to adults only. Said the then head of the Censor Bureau, 'If it is to be shown for general patronage, it will have to be submitted for additional censorship, and probably some scenes of unclad natives would have to be deleted'. In response, the film's distributor hired famed First Amendment attorney Ephraim S. London, who in his public comments zeroed in on the elitism of this decision by the Censor Bureau, rhetorically asking, 'Is a man more adult when he sees a film in an art theatre than when he views it at a neighborhood movie house?' For the Censor Bureau, which would expand this policy to apply to countless films in the years ahead, the important distinction was about the type of audience attracted by arthouse theatres as opposed to general movie theatres. As Patrolman Edward Marks of the Censor Bureau explained of this arthouse-only policy in 1962, 'For one thing, the price of admission is usually higher for the movies they show—about $1.50—so that the audience will be more of a select group'. Across both its literary and movie censorship operations, then, the Detroit Censor Bureau brought with it a classist notion about how indecent media needed to be kept out of reach not from the entire public at large, but rather from certain adult audiences—namely, those unable to afford a pricey hardcover book or arthouse theatre ticket.[9]

In building Detroit's system for literary censorship, police inspector Herbert Case, as head of the Detroit Censor Bureau, took inspiration from the lessons he had learned observing movie censorship efforts. He looked in particular at the example of the Legion of Decency, which, even after the adoption of the Production Code, had continued to monitor movie immorality by making its own lists of banned and objectionable films as well as, in extreme cases, organizing public boycotts of certain movies. One such example was Howard Hughes's 1943 film *The Outlaw*, which the Legion had loudly condemned for its gratuitous sexual content. While Herbert Case agreed in principle both with the notion that the film was immoral and more broadly with the Legion's mission to clean up the movies, he nevertheless criticized the Legion for the way their efforts invariably granted free publicity to controversial pictures like *The Outlaw*, only making them more alluring to the general public. As one article put it, 'Case said the result of the Legion's activities in the past has been "to obtain box office value for pictures instead of preventing their showing to the public. At least that was the result in the case of *The Outlaw*. All the furor over it built up the box office tremendously."'[10]

Given Case's views on how the Legion of Decency inadvertently spurred demand for controversial movies, the system of literary censorship in Detroit during the 1950s was designed to operate smoothly and above all silently. Paperbacks and comic books were first submitted by publishers and distributors to the Censor Bureau for inspection in advance of their distribution in the city, with the officers of the Censor Bureau reading between 90 and 125 paperbacks a month. An offending book would then be banned before it could ever make it on to bookstore shelves in the city. The goal was to make sure that news of a particular title being banned never became public knowledge, so as to avoid generating greater demand for any banned book.[11]

Meanwhile, the Censor Bureau similarly sought to operate in secrecy when it came to censoring movies before exhibition. In part they did this by trying to avoid banning movies outright. Censor Bureau head Herbert Case said in 1952, 'Generally objectionable scenes are cut. Very rarely do we ban the whole movie.' The Censor Bureau then tried to discreetly make cuts to 'indecent' movies, figuring that a complete ban on an offending film would be more likely to result in a court case and publicity. With regard to these cuts, the Bureau endeavoured to make them as invisible as possible, with Case saying that his office 'tried to make deletions in such a manner as not to mar the continuity of a story'. The result of this was that, as Case explained, 'Most of the time the public never knows a film has been cut'.[12]

Banned in Detroit

This preference for secrecy meant that the Censor Bureau worked diligently to guard their list of banned books, fearing the publicity that would result for banned titles should the list be made public. The Censor Bureau's success in keeping its banned book list secret also meant that the list itself eluded me throughout much of my time researching this topic. I eventually managed to track down a copy of the banned book list that had been published in 1957 by an experimental student newspaper at the University of Michigan, and which had found its way into the archives of the Detroit chapter of the America Civil Liberties Union. The list, which encompasses some 280 books banned between 1950 and early 1955, provides a snapshot of what literature the Censor Bureau judged in need of being kept away from the hands of the public in Detroit. Just as importantly though, when put within the context of the work of the Censor Bureau as a whole, the list points to the linkages between the priorities and practices of the Censor Bureau across all the various forms of media and popular entertainment it was tasked with regulating.[13]

One topic that landed a number of books on the Censor Bureau's banned list was any effort to deal with race, racism or the Black experience. The Censor Bureau banned at least half a dozen books that featured interracial romance as well as several protest novels by Black writers that dealt with racism and white supremacy, including Chester B. Himes's *If He Hollers Let Him Go* (1945) and William Attaway's *Blood on the Forge* (1941). Likewise, in their role as defender of movie morality in Detroit, the Censor Bureau also saw fit in 1947 to ban the film *The Burning Cross* (Walter Colmes, 1947), which was a low-budget independent picture focusing on the horrors of the vigilante violence enacted by the Ku Klux Klan against African Americans in the South during the Reconstruction Era. A similar aversion to works highlighting the impact of white supremacy also led the Censor Bureau in 1965 to go after the Concept East, a small African American-run independent legitimate theatre in Detroit. The Concept East that summer put on a production of two plays by LeRoi Jones (who would later change his name to Amiri Baraka) titled *The Toilet* (1967) and *The Slave* (1964), each dealing with the topics of race and Black nationalism. The theatre would be shut down for months after receiving multiple citations on obscenity charges from the Detroit Police. Across these examples, the Censor Bureau chose to go after works dealing with racism as well as works of political protest by Black artists. The resistance to such themes was of course part and parcel with a Detroit Police Department that was overwhelmingly white, and which had been frequently accused of brutality by African American Detroiters.[14]

The banned book list also featured dozens of works with stories centred on what might broadly be called female characters with 'loose morals'. This included numerous books in which female characters had adulterous affairs, such as John McCoy's *Love for a Stranger* (1954), Glenn Watkins's *Sinful Life* (1950) and Robert Dietrich's *The Cheat* (1954), as well as a number of books in which women engage in sex work, among them Rae Loomis's *The Marina Street Girls* (1953), Charles-Louis Philippe's *Bubu of Montparnasse* (1901), and Doug Duperrault's *Red Light Babe* (1950). The Censor Bureau's preoccupation with these topics was again reflected in their other censorial activity. For instance, films featuring female characters who trespassed across the borders of normative heterosexual romance and marriage were frequent targets for the Censor Bureau. This included the French films *The Well-Digger's Daughter* (Marcel Pagnol, 1940), *La ronde* (Max Ophüls, 1950) and *Lady Chatterley's Lover* (Marc Allégret, 1955), each of which had scenes cut entirely or trimmed significantly by the Censor Bureau due to their plots featuring adultery or premarital sex. The Censor Bureau's focus on these topics also connected with the various ways in which the Detroit Police Department regulated real women's bodies and sexualities. This included most obviously an unremitting war against sex work in the city waged by the police. More specifically within the realm of popular entertainment, the Censor Bureau also regulated all forms of live entertainment in the city, which meant they routinely scrutinized the attire worn (or not worn) by female performers in the city's burlesque and striptease venues. Altogether then, across these various arenas, the Detroit Police Censor Bureau took a keen interest in the regulation of women's bodies and sexuality.

Another form of non-normative sexuality that frequently appeared on Detroit's banned book list were works discussing the topic of homosexuality or featuring any gay or lesbian characters. Among these were the gay male coming-of-age story *Finistère* by Fritz Peters (1951), the interracial gay male romance *If This Be Sin* (originally published under the title *The Invisible Glass* in 1950) by Loren Wahl (pseudonym for Lorenzo Madalena) and *Bitter Love* by Taylor Dyson (1952), which focuses on the story of a woman who marries a gay man. Also coming under fire were lesbian pulp novels like Tereska Torrès's *Women's Barracks* (1950), Vin Packer's (a pseudonym for Marijane Meaker) *Spring Fire* (1952) and Nancy Morgan's *City of Women* (1952). Meanwhile, the same Censor Bureau also repeatedly went after films with any gay or lesbian content, as was the case with the films *Aroused* (Anton Holden, 1966) and *The Killing of Sister George* (Robert Aldrich, 1968), each of which had scenes featuring lesbian characters or sex cut from the picture. Here again, this focus on censoring representations of gay and lesbian sexuality was part of a broader campaign waged by the Censor Bureau and Detroit Police Department as a whole to regulate the activities of gay people in the city. In particular, laws against cross-dressing were frequently used by the police as a pretence to arrest queer men, while the erotic activities of gay men out in the world—including in public parks and bathrooms as well as in movie theatres—were monitored closely by police officers, who often tried to entrap gay men by flirting with them and arresting them if they reciprocated any interest.[15]

Conclusion

I would argue that any analysis of this banned book list would be incomplete without a consideration of how literary censorship in Detroit was linked with other forms of media censorship. Just as importantly, the reverse is true as well. Looked at in isolation, the Censor Bureau's ban on the anti-KKK film *The Burning Cross* might seem an interesting one-off case of race-focused censorship in Detroit. Within the context of a Censor Bureau that repeatedly targeted books and stage plays focused on racism, however, a deeper understanding begins to emerge of how race and whiteness was embedded within the whole of censorship in Detroit.

As already mentioned, the Censor Bureau is an illustrative case study for the intersections between different forms of media censorship, given that they not only censored movies but all forms of media and public entertainment in Detroit. But the same principle can apply to the whole of film and media censorship history. Rather than looking at the censorship of, for instance, Mae West films in isolation or only within the context of the pre-Code era, we might instead consider how the censorship of West's films intersected with the way in which West was also censored on the stage and on radio. In lieu of treating the Production Code as a document responding only to the concerns and interests of the film industry, we might usefully examine the Production Code in relation to the regulation of various other media, from dime novels and the penny press to burlesque and legitimate theatre. Doing so will not only give a fuller picture of the contexts in which screen cultures have long been regulated, but more broadly elucidate further the many ways in which the history of cinema has always been closely intertwined with all forms of media and popular culture.

Notes

1   Leonard J. Leff and Jerold L. Simmons, *The Dame in the Kimono: Hollywood, Censorship, and the Production Code* (Lexington: University Press of Kentucky, 2001), pp. 207–08.

2   '"Moon" OK'd Dialog Cut', *Detroit News*, 23 July 1953: 29.

3   'Detroit Police Make Rules', *Moving Picture World*, 5 August 1911: 279; 'Need Permit to Show Each Film', *Detroit Free Press*, 28 May 1912: 9.

4   '350,000 Catholics Back Clean Films', *Detroit Free Press*, 8 May 1934: 9; 'Detroit Churches Lineup Strong for Fight against Dirty Films', *Billboard*, 16 June 1934: 20. For more on the pre-Code era and the Catholic influence on the Production Code, see Thomas Doherty, *Pre-Code Hollywood: Sex, Immorality, and Insurrection in American Cinema; 1930–1934* (New York: Columbia University Press, 1999); Thomas Doherty, *Hollywood's Censor: Joseph I. Breen and the Production Code Administration* (New York: Columbia University Press, 2007); Gregory D. Black, *Hollywood Censored: Morality Codes, Catholics, and the Movies* (Cambridge: Cambridge University Press, 1996); Frank Walsh, *Sin and Censorship: The Catholic Church and the Motion Picture Industry* (New Haven: Yale University Press, 1996).

5   Thomas F. O'Connor, 'The National Organization for Decent Literature: A Phase in American Catholic Censorship', *Library Quarterly* 65.4 (1995): 395; Archbishop Edward Mooney, 21 March 1939, Edward Mooney Papers, Box 53, Folder 20, Archdiocese of Detroit Archives; *The Drive for Decency in Print: Report of the Bishops' Committee*

Sponsoring the National Organization for Decent Literature (Huntington, IN: Our Sunday Visitor Press, 1939), p. 211.

6   For more on Wertham see Bart Beaty, *Fredric Wertham and the Critique of Mass Culture* (Jackson: University Press of Mississippi, 2005).

7   Jack Schermerhorn, 'McNally Outlaws 64 Comic Books', *Detroit Free Press*, 29 April 1948: 1; 'Public and Dealers Asked to Censor Comic Books', *Detroit News*, 18 September 1948: 17. For more on the Comics Code, see Amy Kiste Nyberg, *Seal of Approval: The History of the Comics Code* (Jackson: University Press of Mississippi, 1998).

8   John Lardner, 'Let 'Em Eat Newspapers', *Newsweek*, 14 March 1955: 92. For more on the history of paperbacks in post-war America, see Kenneth C. Davis, *Two-Bit Culture: The Paperbacking of America* (Boston: Houghton Mifflin Company, 1984).

9   'Censor Ruling Faces Court Test', *Detroit News*, 3 August 1962: 3; James H. Dygert, 'Adults Only: Handy Device to Silence Film Censors', *Detroit Free Press*, 16 August 1967: 3–4; Ira Harris Carmen, *State and Local Motion Picture Censorship and Constitutional Liberties with Special Emphasis on the Communal Acceptance of Supreme Court Decision-Making*, PhD dissertation, University of Michigan, 1964, p. 418.

10 'Legion of Decency Bans Movie of *Duel in the Sun*', *Detroit News*, 21 January 1947: 12.

11 Marjorie Elaine Porter, 'PTA Opens Attack on Obscene Books', *Detroit News*, 17 November 1951: 8; James Rorty, 'The Harassed Pocket-Book Publishers', *Antioch Review* 15.4 (December 1955): 418; Lardner, 'Let 'Em Eat Newspapers', p. 92.

12 Joseph N. Hartmann, 'Pocket-Size Books Give Police Censors Biggest Headache', *Detroit News*, 29 December 1952: 12; John Finlayson, 'City's Censor Gives Movies a Good Word', *Detroit News*, 19 July 1953: 18.

13 Dave Smith, 'Detroit Renews Book Ban Despite Court's Decision', *The Michigan Journalist*, 27 March 1957: 1, 4, found in ACLU of Michigan: Metropolitan Detroit Branch Records, box 10, folder Censorship 1956–57, Walter P. Reuther Library, Wayne State University.

14 'Dezel to Fight Banning of *The Burning Cross*', *Film Daily*, 5 November 1947: 12; 'Future of 2 Theaters Periled by City Tickets', *Detroit News*, 19 August 1965: 9-B.

15 James H. Dygert, 'The Standards—And the Times that Hold Sway over Movies', *Detroit Free Press*, 13 August 1967: B-4; Ken Barnard, 'Who Killed "Sister George?"', *Detroit News*, 14 February 1969: 11-C. For more on the police harassment and entrapment of gay men in Detroit, see Tim Retzloff, *City, Suburb, and the Changing Bounds of Lesbian and Gay Life and Politics in Metropolitan Detroit, 1945–1985*, Dissertation, Yale University, 2014.

13

Splicing Back against the Censors: How Archive/Counter-Archive Saved the Ontario Board of Censors' Film Censorship Records from Destruction

Michael Marlatt

Introduction

The Ontario Board of Censors, commonly referred to as the Ontario Censor Board and later renamed the Ontario Film Review Board, was a Canadian provincial agency responsible for reviewing and censoring films to be screened in the province of Ontario.[1] The Censor Board previewed films for just over 100 years, from its formation in 1911 until its dissolution in 2019. The board created a record for each film submitted for screening in the province, kept as catalogue cards. Thousands of films were reviewed, leaving not only details on each film but also the personal notes from the censors describing material to be cut, in their own words.

This chapter will do several things. One is to provide a very brief history of the Ontario Censor Board and the problematic relationship it has had with Ontario. More importantly, however, is to highlight the need of preserving the collection. Considering the various political and social dimensions of the collection, the best place for it is not an institutional archive after all,

Michael Marlatt, "Splicing Back against the Censors: How Archive/Counter-Archive Saved the Ontario Board of Censors' Film Censorship Records from Destruction" in: *The Screen Censorship Companion: Critical Explorations in the Control of Film and Screen Media*. University of Exeter Press (2024). © Michael Marlatt. DOI: 10.47788/XLVW2388 but rather within a university's teaching collection. This chapter also argues that removing the records from their governmental context would help to hold the Ontario Censor Board's censors and the Ontario government accountable for their decisions and motivations in the censoring of films.

What Is Included within the Ontario Censor Board Collection?

The collection consists of roughly forty-three metres of material, constituting upwards of 130,000 individual records, covering the silent era until 1985. The exact earliest dates in the collection are currently undetermined but date back to at least 1922. Records are organized into several sections,

Figure 13.1. Example of the cabinets where the catalogue cards are stored (Courtesy of author)

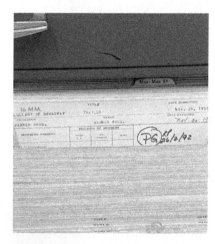

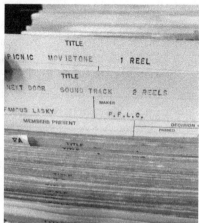

Figures 13.2 and 13.3. Examples of the collection's contents (Courtesy of author)

some by date and some by subject, then alphabetically by title in the drawers within each category (see Figures 13.1, 13.2 and 13.3). Records for trailers are also included. The primary divisions are: 'Silents' (though note that this category includes pre-Code talkies, ending at about 1934); Newsreels; 8mm/Video; Early 1930s until 1954; 1955 until 1980; and finally, 1980 to 1985.

The 'Newsreels' section is the smallest, beginning only mid-century. It appears that earlier newsreel records currently remain at the Archives of Ontario.[2] This raises the question of why the provincial archives accessioned some of the records and not the entire collection. The selection of only newsreel records from the early half of the twentieth century seems surprising. Unfortunately, restrictions of the Covid-19 pandemic of the early 2020s made consulting these records difficult. Integrating the material from the Archives of Ontario into the wider collection would be beneficial but no such donation has been offered. The '8mm/Video' section is also quite small and appears to mostly be pornographic films from the 1970s and 1980s.

The Ontario Censor Board was formed in 1911, about fifteen years after films made their debut in Canada, following the passing of the Theatres and Cinematographs Act.[3] All films screened in the province needed to be passed by the censors in order to be screened. While initially starting with feature films and newsreels, the purview would grow to eventually include such material as film trailers, pornography, avant-garde films and video art. In 1985, changes to the Ontario Censor Board resulted in a renaming to the Ontario Film Review Board.[4] This is where this particular collection ends. However, the Ontario Film Review Board itself continued to operate until the autumn of 2019, when the Conservative Ontario government, under premier Doug Ford, closed the body, determining that Ontario would now use the same ratings board as the province of British Columbia.[5]

The Problematic Past of the Ontario Censor Board

The Ontario Censor Board has an interesting and controversial history, both in how the board reviewed material but also in its perception by the public. Library and Archives Canada holds early film footage of the Ontario Censor Board not long after its formation. In 1916, in what appears to be newsreel footage, the Ontario Censor Board is shown burning 40,000 feet of banned films. In the description of the footage from Library and Archives Canada:

> The Ontario Board of Censors destroys 9 miles of nitrate film. Members of the Censor Board look on as the Toronto fire chief sets piles of film on fire. The seven men and a woman cringe back in fear as the nitrate film leaps into a blazing inferno. They wrestle each other

in a congratulatory fashion at a job well done. Shown left to right are G. Anderson, R. Wilson, and G. Burns, members of the Ontario Censor Board, as they examine the ashes and declare the burning a success.[6]

The way the censors celebrate the burning of these films, dancing and pushing each other, is almost childlike. Perhaps this playfulness is to show the audience that they were not staunch and overly serious; or perhaps they did gain that much enjoyment from burning film stock. Unfortunately, the content of these destroyed films remains a mystery. The records held by Archive/Counter-Archive only begin in the 1920s, at least four years after this footage was taken. Before 1919 only 25% of films submitted were approved by the Ontario Censor Board.[7]

The joy of film censorship depicted in the 1916 clip was certainly not universally felt. Various newspaper articles, trade journals and political cartoons critical of Ontario censorship would appear throughout the twentieth century. An early example is a two-panel comic from a 1921 issue of *The Goblin*, a student humour magazine based at the University of Toronto, titled 'Here's to the Censors!'.[8] One panel depicts a young, vibrant, dancing woman in a short, close-fitting dress evoking the period's flapper, captioned 'Aphrodite in New York'. This contrasts with the second panel, where a woman still dances but this time is old, fully clothed, sad-looking and not nearly as animated. Here the caption is '[Aphrodite] in Toronto', highlighting the difference *The Goblin* perceived between censorship in Ontario and New York. Even then members of the public could recognize how much was modified for Ontario screenings. Many newspaper and magazine articles would be published criticizing the Ontario Censor Board in subsequent years.[9]

The late 1920s saw newspaper articles addressing the work the Ontario Censor Board was doing to 'clean up' the incoming 'talkies'.[10] A focus on family films would continue into the 1930s.[11] In 1949, the Toronto Local Council of Women requested more women on the board.[12] Members were not named publicly at the time. The further digitization and studying of these records would allow researchers to note changing definitions of morality as well as representation among board members.

Information about the activities of the Ontario Censor Board was kept quite secretive until 1981.[13] This includes changes demanded, the list of banned films and the public listing of censors. None of the censors' names were released publicly until 1979.[14] The Ontario Censor Board members and film publishers themselves could not even publicly state that edits had even been made, even though most of the American films screened in Ontario in the 1940s, for example, were edited in some capacity.[15]

Even before reaching the censor's scissors, films in Ontario were shaped by the board's presence. In 1931, amendments were made for a British quota, which was still the case fifty years later in 1981. Films were charged a fee to be reviewed. In 1921 the rate was $3 per reel, or $10 per reel for an appeal.[16] Larger studios could better afford these censorship rates. British filmmakers also paid lower fees for censorship review than other foreign markets.[17] The only exception to film censorship in the province was for films produced by the National Film Board of Canada. These films were exempt because they were federally produced, therefore overriding any authority at the provincial level.[18] The provincial government's direct influence on the Ontario Censor Board was often glaring. There were certainly instances of nepotism. In 1934, Ontario premier Mitchell Hepburn appointed family friend O.J. Silverthorne to the head of the Ontario Censor Board. Silverthorne would end up becoming fairly liberal, opposing the outright banning of films but preferring them to be edited.[19] Government influence could also extend to a form of political suppression. For instance, newsreels depicting worker's rights were censored; one notable example is the banning of footage that depicted the Oshawa General Motors strike of 1937.[20] Premier Mitchell Hepburn claimed this was to 'to avoid propaganda by either side'.[21] It is important to note however that Hepburn was widely known to be staunchly anti-union.[22]

A second prominent example of provincial government interference in the banning of political films came in 1940 when Hepburn, still premier and also by then chairman of the Ontario Board of Censors appeal board, banned the March of Time series film, *Canada at War*. This banning was meant to last until after the planned federal election that year, on the grounds that the film constituted 'pure political propaganda for the Mackenzie King government'.[23] Though Hepburn and Prime Minister William Lyon Mackenzie King were both members of the Liberal Party, there was personal animosity between the two due to Mackenzie King's refusal to send the Royal Canadian Mounted Police in to shut down the previously mentioned Oshawa General Motors strike. This clear evidence of political censorship from Hepburn's time in office raises questions over what material may have been banned to less publicity. This particular banning was worldwide news, likely owing to the fact that the March of Time was a major American newsreel series published by Time Inc.[24] In its reportage, the *New York Times* article noted that 'most Canadians hate censorship'.[25]

Debates continued. Members and ratings classifications changed but the cutting and banning of films in the province continued through the century. Satires of the practice continued in a similar vein as the 1921 cartoon. For example, a political cartoon in 1984 is described by Library and Archives Canada as 'depicting an ONTARIO CENSORBOARD EDITING

BOOTH machine where rock music videos enter one side and exit the other side as classical music videos'.[26] A second political cartoon in the collection, this one undated, depicts 'three members of the Ontario Censor Board dressed in hooded robes and brandishing scissors in the air'.[27]

Things would get especially heated in the 1970s and 1980s, particularly between the Ontario Censor Board and avant-garde filmmakers, film festivals such as TIFF (Toronto International Film Festival, then known as the Festival of Festivals) and media arts organizations. Non-compliance screenings were held and even led to some arrests, as was the case for the organizers of a film festival in the Ontario city of Peterborough. The programmers arrested would be known nationwide as 'The Peterborough Four'.[28] Frequent clashes over censor actions led to bans, last-minute edits and even protests. Accusations of racist and homophobic censoring practices would lead to further protests and the creation of local community advocacy groups.

Film as a medium itself was used to criticize the Ontario Censor Board. A particularly notable example is the humorous claymation film *The Censor* (Gordon Lawson, 1980).[29] This six-minute film mocks the self-righteous outrage that the Ontario Censor Board expresses when watching and censoring film. The film being censored within the film culminates in an over-the-top sex scene where two clay figures are rolling around together all over a bedroom, eventually even swinging from a chandelier, to the 'oh dears' and utter disgust of the censors.

Issues with the Ontario Censor Board occurred as recently as 2010, when the executive director of the Images Film Festival in Toronto announced that there would need to be an 18+ rating for every screening at the festival. This was due to the festival refusing to submit work to the Ontario Censor Board as objection to government censorship, as well as lacking the funding to afford the thousands of dollars necessary for the films to even be reviewed.[30]

The Records

The physical records themselves make for interesting objects of study. While the formatting style has changed over time, each record consists of one or more standard-sized index cards containing most of the following fields: format, length, title, submission fee, date submitted, exchange (who was screening the picture), maker, date reviewed, members present, screening decision and, significantly, descriptions of section(s) that needed to be cut for approval.

A few illustrative examples are drawn from the 'Silents' section. In the case of the 1926 version of *The Great Gatsby* (Herbert Brenon), a lost film, a full ban was implemented, due, in the censor's handwritten words, to its 'salacious story emphasizing infidelity debauchery and lust'. The record does not go into further detail on the banning (see Figure 13.4).

The 1925 lost film *Fine Clothes* (John M. Stahl) provides an interesting example of an appeal (see Figures 13.5 and 13.6). This film was initially given a number of required edits. After resubmission with the necessary changes made, the Ontario Censor Board ended up condemning the film after all, feeling the plot no longer made any coherent sense. This means the film was banned by consequence of following all the requirements laid out by the Ontario Censor Board.

Records of non-lost films from the silent era are also telling, for instance the 1927 film *Wings* (William A. Wellman) (see Figure 13.7). Cuts demanded, which were written on the back of the card, include scenes of alcohol consumption, flirtation and certain intertitles. Records for non-lost films provide the opportunity to examine what films look like today in home releases versus how audiences would have seen them at the time of release.

The 1931 Universal film *Dracula* (Tod Browning) demonstrates a film passed without any edits (see Figure 13.8). The card, however, includes information for the multiple releases brought before the Ontario Censor Board, each getting approval, with the fee written on the initial record. To avoid needing to re-screen a passed film each time it was submitted for screening, new records would simply contain instructions to see the initial record. This record provides a window into the history of re-screening films in the province.

Archive/Counter-Archive's Involvement with the Collection

In 2019, a York University faculty member, Dr Kenneth Rogers, saved the collection from being discarded after the dissolvement of the Ontario Censor Board. Archive/Counter-Archive was informed about the collection and the records delivered to their York University office for temporary safekeeping. An initial plan to donate the collection to the Archives of Ontario was cancelled after learning that the physical records would likely be discarded, leaving a more suitable future for these rich materials open for discussion.

Archive/Counter-Archive is a multi-year university project partnering with Canadian universities including York University, Toronto Metropolitan University (formerly named Ryerson University), Queen's University and Concordia University. Archive/Counter-Archive also has community partners that include Canadian archives with moving-image collections. Archive/Counter-Archive defines itself as:

> a project dedicated to activating and remediating audiovisual archives created by Indigenous Peoples (First Nations, Métis, Inuit), the Black

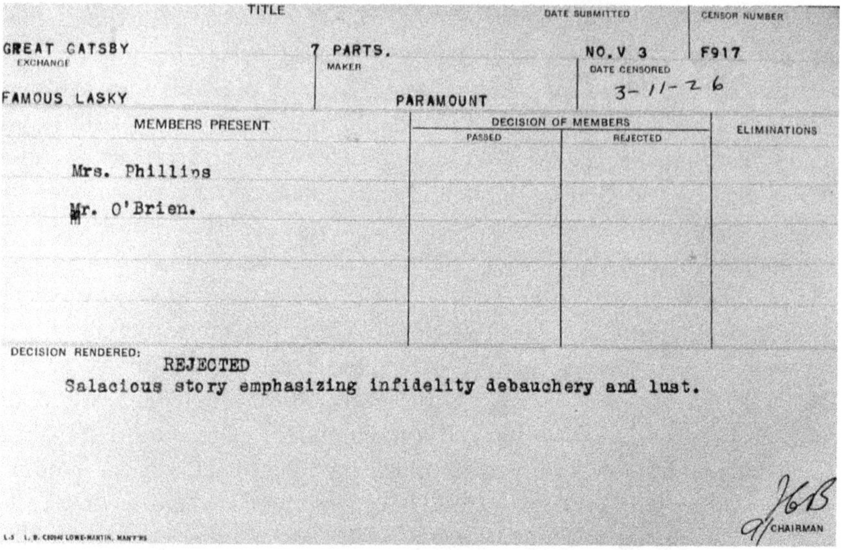

THE SCREEN CENSORSHIP COMPANION

Figure 13.4. The censor record of the rejected 1926 version of *The Great Gatsby* (Courtesy of author)

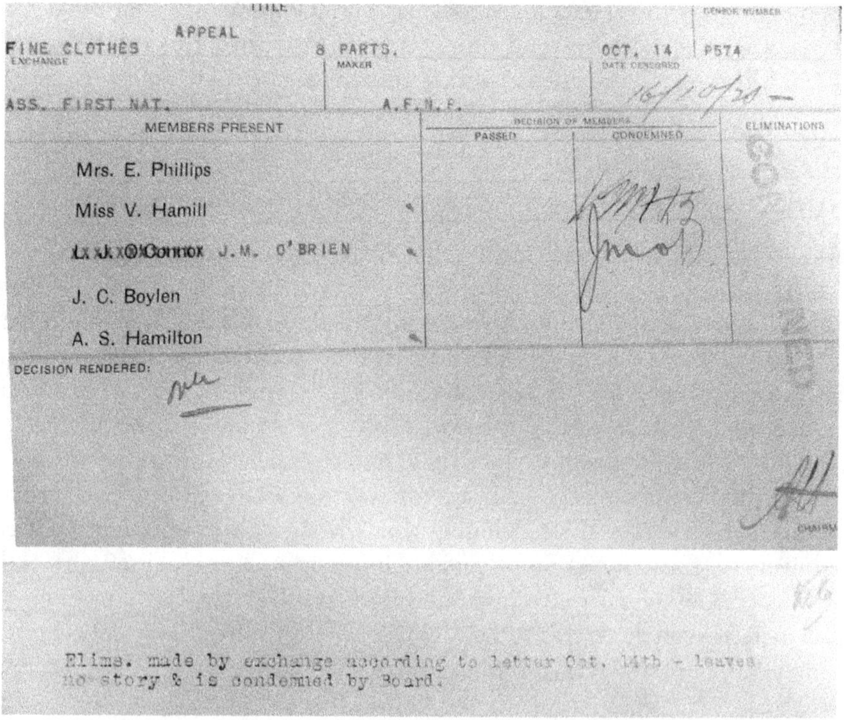

Figures 13.5 and 13.6. An appeal record for the 'condemned' film *Fine Clothes* (Courtesy of author)

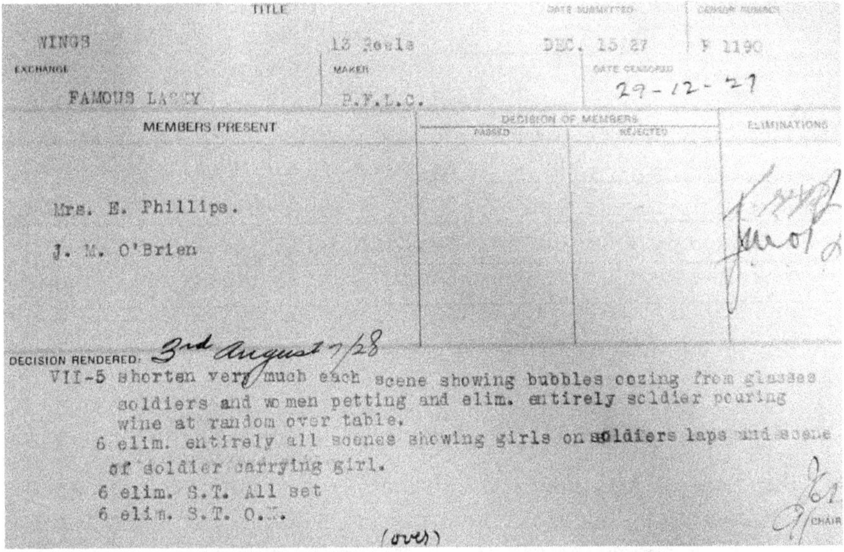

TITLE: WINGS — 13 Reels
DATE SUBMITTED: DEC. 15 27
CENSOR NUMBER: F 1190
EXCHANGE: FAMOUS LASKY
MAKER: F.P.L.C.
DATE CENSORED: 29-12-27

MEMBERS PRESENT

Mrs. E. Phillips.

J. M. O'Brien

DECISION OF MEMBERS: PASSED / REJECTED

ELIMINATIONS

DECISION RENDERED: 3rd August 7/28

VII-5 shorten very much each scene showing bubbles oozing from glasses soldiers and women petting and elim. entirely soldier pouring wine at random over table.

6 elim. entirely all scenes showing girls on soldiers laps and scene of soldier carrying girl.

6 elim. S.T. All set

6 elim. S.T. O.K.

(over)

CHAIR

Figure 13.7. Censor record for the film *Wings*, detailing cuts needed (Courtesy of author)

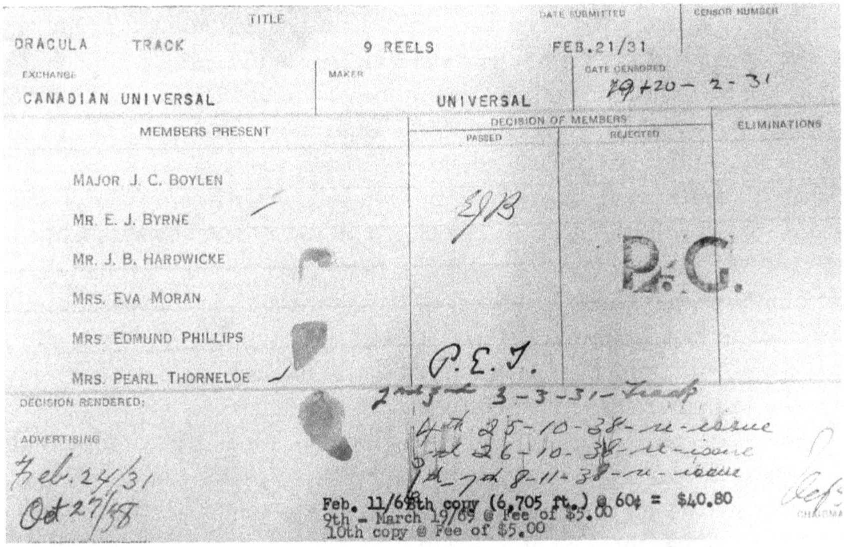

TITLE: DRACULA TRACK — 9 REELS
DATE SUBMITTED: FEB.21/31
CENSOR NUMBER
EXCHANGE: CANADIAN UNIVERSAL
MAKER: UNIVERSAL
DATE CENSORED: 20-2-31

MEMBERS PRESENT

MAJOR J. C. BOYLEN

MR. E. J. BYRNE

MR. J. B. HARDWICKE

MRS. EVA MORAN

MRS. EDMUND PHILLIPS

MRS. PEARL THORNELOE

DECISION OF MEMBERS: PASSED: EJB — REJECTED: P.G.

ELIMINATIONS

P.E.T.

DECISION RENDERED:

2nd 3-3-31 – Track

4th 25-10-38 – re-issue

26-10-38 – re-issue

7th 8-11-38 – re-issue

ADVERTISING

Feb. 24/31

Oct 27/38

Feb. 11/68th copy (6,705 ft.) @ 60¢ = $40.80
9th – March 19/69 @ Fee of $5.00
10th copy @ Fee of $5.00

CHAIRMAN

Figure 13.8. Censor record for the 1931 version of *Dracula*, demonstrating the notation of subsequent screenings (Courtesy of author) community and People of Colour, women, LGBT2Q+ and immigrant communities. Political, resistant, and community-based, counter-archives disrupt conventional narratives and enrich our histories.[31]

Significantly, the filmmakers, programmers and partnering organizations that Archive/Counter-Archive work with are the ones whose films would have been heavily censored, or more likely banned, by the Ontario Censor Board. A major example of an Archive/Counter-Archive partner that did protest the restrictions of the Ontario Censor Board is the Canadian Filmmakers Distribution Centre (CFMDC).[32]

While the records hold significant potential for project goals, Archive/Counter-Archive never intended to hold archival items permanently. The question is not whether to donate the collection, but where.

The Records as Teaching Collection

At this time, a suggested donation site is the Film & Photography Preservation and Collections Management MA programme at Toronto Metropolitan University (TMU). TMU is the only university that has any form of archival studies programme in Canada that specializes in film preservation. Hands-on work with physical materials, of which the Film & Photography Preservation and Collections Management programme already holds many, is a key component of the degree. Students of preservation could work on inspection, re-housing, repair and perhaps even digitization of the collection with a different focus than the Archives of Ontario. The material would become more accessible. Critical engagement facilitated by faculty could spur analysis that is politically conscious, and interrogative of the decisions made by the Ontario Censor Board. The preservation of the collection can also be taught in a way that allows students to analyse the wider contextual influence that censorship has on narratives of film screening and distribution in Ontario. The collection would help advance archival training at TMU as well. The records could be used to teach students archival description standards, cataloguing, metadata, how to handle archival objects, re-housing, scanning and so on.

There are several benefits to this approach. One is assistance with digitizing the collection for future research. This collection includes records of films that are long lost, particularly small independent Canadian pictures and silent films. These records give researchers who may never be able to access the original films information that may not exist elsewhere. Steps students can take to preserve the records include the following. The records should be re-housed into archival boxes for ease of access. Right now, these records are tightly fit into drawers, making their individual retrieval difficult.

Students would also remove the metallic staples binding multiple related cards, due to risk of rust staining, and replace with archival paperclips. Also of initial preservation importance is to clean for dust, pests and old rubber bands. Students would scan the records while maintaining original order, and sometimes restoring it when obvious cataloguing errors are evident— for instance, the record for a Mary Pickford film approved by the censors in the 1920s was found in the '8mm/Video' drawer. This would call for re-filing. How the collection would be worked into the curriculum would be up to the programme itself, perhaps through a series of workshops or working with the collection in a single course. There are often internships that students in such a programme need to complete. Students could perhaps work with the collection if they are not able to find a particular archival institution that meets their interests or needs.

These attentions to the materiality of the collection are important. Working with a physical collection enables a different way to browse. Often an online database requires a certain familiarity with the collection and search terms ahead of time. This may make looking for a particular title easier, but not necessarily the overall examination of the collection. In the context of a teaching collection, students could examine film censorship at the item level. Further inclusion of members from under-represented communities in archival training allows for a re-discovery of history lost due to racist, sexist, homophobic, transphobic and ableist censorship practices. This is where the support of faculty will be critical. Many of the records include outdated and outright offensive language. Working with such material can take a toll on the emotional health of the archivist. The slow introduction of future archivists to such material, if they so choose, in a controlled environment, allows for a space of discussion on how this sort of material exists. Students are quite likely to come across such material in their future internships and places of employment. Discussing it sensitively and respectfully while still in post-secondary education will help to prepare them.

A more pragmatic argument, directly benefitting the students, is that a collection such as this offers practice in preserving a medium that, while directly related to moving images, is not itself audiovisual. While jobs primarily working with moving images do exist, there is a realistic possibility that these students will be asked to work with a variety of media. Working with a collection such as this would give them that experience. Context is missed when a film archivist only works in preserving moving images. The archive is much more than merely a space to house objects. Archives are meant to preserve the history, culture and provenance of their contents. An effective archive is one that can acknowledge its gaps. Students engaging with the preservation of these censorship records will be able to work towards consideration of such archival silences. After all, one very important reason that many of these films are lost or were not preserved is because they were rejected by the Censor Board, and never screened or even destroyed.

Towards Engaged Preservation

Engagement with this collection is a way for the censors, and by extension the Ontario provincial government, to be held responsible for not only what was cut, but why. A big part of this censorship involves the racist, sexist, homophobic and transphobic language used in the records when referring to material that was deemed immoral. In preliminary observations, racist and homophobic slurs were used in the described language of material to be cut—even in records as recent as the 1970s and 1980s. To discard the collection would be to lose evidence that the narrative of Ontario cinema history includes bigotry. This is a major reason Archive/Counter-Archive took on these records. In recent years there has been more work dedicated to socially conscious archival practices.[33] The Archives of Ontario is also an entity of the same government responsible for the dissection of these films in the first place. So, if these records had stayed in the provincial government archive a certain narrative would have been followed, even if not a conscious one. This is by no fault of the archivists working at the Archives of Ontario, but an external body is able to look at such a collection with a more critical eye. A teaching collection, even within a major public university, is not as caught up in the same government restrictions.[34]

Future Research Directions

Working with the Ontario Censor Board collection allows students and researchers the opportunity to build off extant work on the topic, notably from Dean, Doyle and Sirove. Dean and Doyle's key works *Censored Only in Canada* and *A Chronology of Censorship in Ontario* were both published in 1981. At this time, information about the various censors was difficult to access, with a few exceptions. Access to the records would have been limited as the Ontario Censor Board was only beginning to peel back its organizational curtain. *Ruling Out Art* by Taryn Sirove, a 2019 book discussing censorship of video art, experimental film and film collectives in Ontario, is likely the last text published about film censorship in Ontario before the dissolution of the Ontario Censor Board. While Sirove refers to the early history of the Ontario Censor Board, the section is quite brief, with the majority of the text covering the activities of the Ontario Censor Board post the late 1970s. This is valid considering the specific media Sirove is engaging with but leaves a large gap in the history of banned films and under-represented populations. Sirove highlights the culture of censorship in Toronto. Using Sirove's themes as a framework, future scholars can build further conversation on the exclusion of various voices pre-1985, blending the earlier work done by Dean and Doyle with the latter writing of Sirove. The dissolution of the Ontario Censor Board may make this an easier endeavour.

The most important reason to preserve this material is to understand how the decision of each censor contributes to the contents of the collection itself. Each film record has a name, signature, and comments on what is being cut and why, allowing researchers to retroactively address deplorable language and decisions made by members of the Ontario Censor Board. Previous works mostly focus on the decisions made by the Ontario Censor Board and its history. No previous work deconstructs the language.

Conclusion

Ontario has a dark past with its treatment of under-represented communities. While underdiscussed, this history connects to film. For decades, the province's film censors pushed notions of 'normalcy' and 'decency' that had a detrimental effect on the growth and development of under-represented communities on the screen. Though it is not possible to travel back in time to change this, previous decisions and the censors themselves can be held responsible for their language and actions.

While it is disappointing that the Covid-19 pandemic of the early 2020s delayed working with this collection sooner, the card stock that these records were printed on is not nearly as vulnerable as motion picture film. Imminent deterioration is not as much of a worry, but the inability to engage with this collection due to Covid-19 highlights the importance of preserving it.

Housing the collection within a non-governmental body with no ties to the Ontario Censor Board is crucial. This distance would allow the archivist and future researchers to engage with the material with a more critical eye. A governmental archive may focus on the bureaucratic nature of the Ontario Censor Board over the social implications of the banned films and the language used in such censorship. Keeping the physical record at a distance from government archives combats the potential for images to be edited for the purposes of political propaganda.[35] The digital manipulation of documents is not the only worry when it comes to archival censorship. Intentional gaps in information are apparent and even exploited with the growth of digital archives, records and databases.[36] Discarding records, as attempted by the Ontario government, is an example of creating a similar gap in information, albeit a physical one. Keeping even very few of these censorship records in the Archives of Ontario creates a biased narrative of the Ontario Censor Board.

Even if the focus of an archive is on the previous censorship of political records, further analysis can be done on the archival practice of preserving censored material. A prominent example of this is provided by the work Sergio Lobejón Santos, Cristina Gómez Castro and Camino Gutiérrez Lanza have done with the records and documents at the Archivo General de la Administración (AGA) archive in Alcalá de Henares, Spain.[37] Santos, Castro and Lanza argue that while a lot of work has been undertaken studying censorship in Francoist Spain, more work needs to be done addressing how censorship data is collected and the role that the AGA plays in censorship research.

Keeping the Ontario Censor Board records in the Archive/Counter-Archive office is, however, only a temporary solution. The office is not an archive, and the project is of a finite length. Storing the material with a graduate-level archival programme would allow future archivists to engage with film censorship and records during their education. Early exposure to these records would allow them the opportunity to bring this awareness of censorship to any future archival employment, which is critical as material becomes more digitally accessible.

Notes

1   Taryn Sirove, *Ruling Out Art: Media Art Meets Law in Ontario's Censor Wars* (Vancouver: UBC Press, 2019), p. 5.
2   Ontario Board of Censors, 'Ontario Board of Censors Newsreel Cards', textual records, 1925–1955, series RG 56–2, Archives of Ontario, Toronto.
3   Sirove, *Ruling Out Art*, p. 18.
4   Ibid., p. 14.
5   Rob Ferguson, 'Ford Scraps Ontario's Film-Rating System to Save Money', *Toronto Star*, 27 September 2019, https://www.thestar.com/politics/provincial/2019/09/27/ford-scraps-ontarios-film-rating-system-to-save-money.html.
6   *[Forty Thousand Feet of Rejected Film Destroyed by Ontario Censor Board] (1916)* [online video], Library and Archives Canada, https://www.youtube.com/watch?v=bEyKLtdzg_g.
7   Malcolm Dean, *Censored! Only in Canada: The History of Film Censorship—the Scandal off the Screen* (Toronto: Virgo Press, 1981), p. 136.
8   'Here's to the Censors!', *The Goblin* 1.2 (1921): 18.
9   'Ontario Folk Well Guarded against Objectionable Films, Says Provincial Treasurer', *The Globe*, 16 September 1927: 13; 'The Censor Board's Work', *The Globe*, 14 January 1930; 'Pays Warm Tribute to Late Film Censor', *The Globe*, 22 April 1926; 'Censor Board Bans 8 Movies; Cuts 415 Others: Distinction Made Between "Adult" And "Infantile" Treatment', *The Globe*, 15 August 1936; 'Stop War for Smoke and Chat; Start Killing

Again', *Globe and Mail*, 17 April 1937; 'Legion of Decency Secretary Upholds Movie Censorship: Takes Columnist to Task for Criticizing Code Governing Films Says Need Shown', *Globe and Mail*, 23 December 1936; G.H. Robertson, 'Movie Censorship: The Scandal', *Maclean's Magazine*, 15 January 1952.

10   'Keep The "Talkies" Clean', *The Globe*, 26 November 1929; 'Movie Censors Call for Close Scrutiny of Talking Pictures: Objectionable Features Which Were Lessening in Silent Film, Reappear in "Talkies" in More Aggravated Form, They Find More British Items Urged in News Reels', *The Globe*, 25 November 1929.

11   'All-Family Films Bring Best Result to Their Theatres: Ontario Censor Board Encouraged in Keeping Standard High Types Are Reviewed', *The Globe*, 14 August 1931.

12   'Approve Women on Censor Board', 2 May 1949, *Globe and Mail*.

13   Judith Doyle, 'A Chronology of Censorship in Canada', *Impulse* (Fall 1981): 26.

14   Doyle, 'A Chronology of Censorship in Canada', p. 26.

15   Ibid., p. 27.

16   Dean, *Censored! Only in Canada*, p. 42.

17   Doyle, 'A Chronology of Censorship in Canada', p. 26.

18   Ibid, p. 27.

19   Ibid.

20   'Hepburn Lauds Offer', *Montreal Gazette*, 17 April 1937.

21   Ibid.

22   'Ontario Bars Film until after Election', *Lewiston Evening Journal*, 4 March 1940.

23   Ibid.

24   Frederick T. Birchall, 'Ontario Bars Film "Canada at War"', *New York Times*, 5 March 1940.

25   Ibid.

26   Mike Graston, 'ONTARIO CENSOR BOARD EDITING BOOTH', drawing, 26 January 1984, item number 2918906, box 10334, Mike Graston Fonds, Library and Archives Canada, Ottawa.

27   Phillip Mallette, 'CENSOR (Hooded men cutting up film)', drawing, undated, item number 2939827, box 20170, Phillip Malette Collection, Library and Archives Canada, Ottawa, LAC: 20170, 2939827.

28   Sirove, *Ruling Out Art*, p. 73.

29   *The Censor* [online video], 1980, dir. Gordon Lawson, https://www.youtube.com/watch?v=xkHSJrjOszI.

30   Sirove, *Ruling Out Art*, p. 3.

31   Archive/Counter Archive, https://counterarchive.ca/welcome.

32   Sirove, *Ruling Out Art*, p. 48.

33   Examples include: Marika Cifor, Michelle Caswell, Gracen Brilmyer, Anne J. Gilliland, Sue McKemmish.

34   Note that the records post-1985 are missing. This likely has to do with the transition of the Ontario Censor Board into the Ontario Film Review Board. At the time of this writing, it is unknown whether these records were scanned or if the material from the cards was transcribed. Digitizing the records for future use is important but there is something to be said for keeping the original objects. Even more so if the digitized records were to ever accidentally be deleted.

35 One prominent example of a government-affiliated archive digitally manipulating an image for political purposes involves the National Archives in Washington, DC. In 2019, the National Archives hosted an exhibition titled *Rightfully Hers: American Women and the Vote* that celebrated the centenary of the US women's suffrage movement. Included in the exhibition was a 49-by-69-inch photograph of a 2017 protest critical of then US president Donald Trump. The National Archives digitally altered the photograph so all signs criticizing Trump were blurred out before putting the image on display. See Joe Heim, 'National Archives Exhibit Blurs Images Critical of President Trump', *Washington Post*, 17 January 2020.

36 For example, Glenn D. Tiffert highlights how Chinese knowledge platforms actively remove information that contradicts their government's particular narrative. See Glenn D. Tiffert, 'Peering Down the Memory Hole: Censorship, Digitization, and the Fragility of Our Knowledge Base', *American Historical Review* 124.2 (April 2019): 550–68, https://doi.org/10.1093/ahr/rhz286.

37 Sergio Lobejón Santos, Cristina Gómez Castro and Camino Gutiérrez Lanza, 'Archival Research in Translation and Censorship: Digging into the "True Museum of Francoism"', *Meta: Translators' Journal* 66.1 (2021): 92–114.

14

Italian Film Censorship (1948–1976): A Quantitative Analysis

Mauro Giori and Tomaso Subini

Introduction: Contextualizing Film Censorship in Italy

The passage from fascism to the Italian Republic after the Second World War marked a fundamental shift in regard to the rights of free speech and the free circulation of ideas. This is particularly true for speech and ideas in opposition to government, as in the case of neorealist cinema which developed without restraint up to the beginning of the 1950s. Nonetheless, obscenity censorship continued to be enforced, as one of the few areas on which the Catholic Party (Democrazia Cristiana) and the Communist Party (Partito Comunista Italiano)—the two most important parties in post-war Italy—agreed while working on a general reorganization of society following a drafting of the constitution.[1]

The institutional and political post-war context offered an ideal background for a further development of censorship. As a result of the war, Italy became a Western democracy tied to the American model and led for the first time by a Catholic party. Catholics also led post-war modernization in Spain where a totalitarian state gave them unrestricted power. Unlike Spain, the intervention of Italian Catholics was constrained by a democratic model based on freedom of speech and pluralism, and on the free circulation of cultural goods, movies included. Therefore, post-war Italian censorship must be framed within the paradox of a 'clerical regime'[2] coexisting with a free capitalistic economy. Apropos the film industry, it was impossible to ban every troublesome movie

Mauro Giori and Tomaso Subini, "Italian Film Censorship (1948–1976): A Quantitative Analysis" in: *The Screen Censorship Companion: Critical Explorations in the Control of Film and Screen Media*. University of Exeter Press (2024). © Mauro Giori and Tomaso Subini. DOI: 10.47788/HIIB3780 by simply denying permission for production or for international import (as happened in Spain). Instead, the Italian Catholic government had to face the norms of a capitalistic market system and pluralistic society. In the paradoxical reality of post-war Italy, censorship served as a negotiating tool.

This paradox is also evident in the contrast between a constitution (the enforcement of which in post-war Italy was slow and not without resistance) that envisioned any intervention of censors only on the basis of obscenity, and the censorship law, which between 1949 and 1962 allowed the committees to intervene on a wide range of issues, including politics. After 1962, the censorship issue was overwhelmed by a growing sexualization of cinema and by the emergence of hardcore pornography as a consequence of the neo-capitalistic development of the country, once again through aspects that were peculiar to Italy.[3] In other Western countries the state considered it useful to negotiate and control the process, for example by giving special certificates to hardcore films as in France. Yet in Italy the containment of pornography was down to censorship intervention, in spite of its clear ineffectiveness. This is the reason why the Italian film censorship system was one of the longest-lasting among those working in Western countries. Because of this, the role of censorship in post-war Italy cannot be under-valued: its bureau faced an enormous amount of work (albeit decreasingly effective) during the 1950s and the 1960s, and it lasted until 2021 when the new 2017 law was actually applied so that movies could no longer be forbidden but just limited to adult viewers.

The social power of cinema in post-war Italy was regulated by a complex and peculiar system of surveillance, to which several institutions contributed at different times so that at the apex it was shaped by about five levels of intervention. Of these, state censorship was the most effective. It acted preventively, since it was meant to prevent a film from exerting any possible social damage when released. State censorship was also the form least exposed to libertarian criticism, as it was legitimated by the constitution. It encapsulated two of the levels on which the control system operated as a whole. The first level provided for the control of screenplays, mandatory during fascism and formally optional according to Andreotti's Law (1949), even if in fact still mandatory for accessing state funds and facilitating financing. At this level, a film's production could be adjusted (mostly through informal suggestions) or even totally discouraged by bureaucrats almost at liberty to intimidate film producers. At the second level, the censorship committee laid down the final form of a film text, which was the only one legally allowed to be released. We know of very few manipulations in the 1950s that violated such decisions,[4] but their number grew in the 1960s and even further in the 1970s (mostly in the case of porn movies), so that censorship became decreasingly effective.

Two other levels of censorship were related to ecclesiastical intervention. Their jurisdiction was confined to parish cinemas. Since Italy had a uniquely large number of such venues,[5] it resulted in the Church influencing the social power of cinema. On a national scale (third level) this was handled by the Centro Cattolico Cinematografico (hereafter CCC), which considered all films released in Italy and classified them on a moral basis. In the 1950s, ecclesiastical and state censorship were closely connected (according to the 'clerical regime' logic). Andreotti secretly arranged for two of CCC's representatives to illegally take part in the sessions of state censorship committees with the aim of letting them express their opinion to influence the judgement.[6] In the 1960s, also as a consequence of the sexualization of cinema and the rapid secularization of the country, the ecclesiastical censorship neither influenced nor recognized the judgements by state committees and began to manipulate the prints released (that is, to change the version already approved by the state) in the parish cinemas on a regional basis. This fourth level essentially involved cutting potentially problematic scenes such as those involving kisses or nudity, even when just evoked by dialogue or shown in the furniture of the set design. In so doing this intervention compromised the main function of state censorship, which is to fix the definitive version of the film text.

Finally, on the fifth level there was the magistracy's intervention. After the accidental seizing of *Zitelloni* (Giorgio Bianchi, 1958) in February 1959, the magistracy actually began to play a major role at the end of the following year, when prosecutor Carmelo Spagnuolo threatened to seize *Rocco e i suoi fratelli* (Luchino Visconti, 1960). Even if the procedure followed was irregular and controversial from a legal point of view (so much so that it was never repeated),[7] Spagnuolo's enterprise was effective enough to pave the way for about 500 actual seizures of films for obscenity in the following years.[8]

Although not always consistent with each other, these five levels participated in the general process of control through different roles. Political issues (the most debatable because illegitimate) were handled mostly at the first level, before any economic investment. The second level addressed both political and social issues (such as public insult to institutions) and the representation of sexuality. The third and fourth levels dealt with moral issues while the fifth mostly addressed obscenity.

Data Analysis

In this chapter we focus on the second level, which relates to the practices of the state censorship system, testing on the Italian case a new model of quantitative analysis. This approach is made possible not only by the availability of the files preserved at the Ministero della Cultura in Rome, but also by their indexing in the digital archive of the project Italia Taglia.[9] Thanks to this archive, it is now possible to improve the previous approaches necessarily limited to a sampling of case studies in order to build more systematic surveys.

Our analysis is confined to the period between 1948 (when the first republican government was established and the first post-war law concerning cinema was passed) and 1976, the year which marked the peak of the clash between censorship and the general sexualization of cinema, on the verge of the emergence of pornography.

Over this period, as with the majority of censorship systems within Western democracies, the committees could take three different decisions: 1) to approve a film for the general public, 2) to prohibit it from being shown to minors,[10] and 3) to forbid its circulation altogether. These different outcomes produce three kinds of data that can be analysed from a quantitative point of view, namely the frequency of each of them within the total number of movies judged by the committees each year. Additional data that can be extracted from the Italia Taglia digital archive include the number of films that were cut as a consequence of the negotiations prior to their approval or prohibition to minors.

These four kinds of data (see Figure 14.1) have been chosen because they can be followed throughout a long period, in a way that reflects the general trends in the development of censorship and highlights the main watersheds in its history. The opportunity of an overall perspective based on the total amount of data available compensates for the obvious simplification implied by a quantitative approach, and makes it possible to contribute new findings to the debate on Italian censorship.

From the chart, it is clearly visible that the total number of films evaluated by the state censorship committees (line 1) is not reflective of important changes. The number of films approved for all viewers (line 4) steadily falls and, as a compensation, the quantity of films prohibited for minors or cut (line 2 and 3, respectively) steadily rises. If these trend lines show a tension between censorship and the sexualization of cinema, the apex of which was reached in the 1960s, the chart also highlights at least three major watersheds which deserve attention and explanation. Firstly, there is a significant decline in the system around 1956 that can be explained in several ways. A decrease in the total amount of films, shown by the fall of line 1, is the consequence of a well-known crisis in the Italian film industry: in 1956, film production almost halved.[11] However, censors' less strict intervention may be explained not only as an attempt to facilitate an economic recovery but also as the result of a change in the political context after the election of a new President of the Republic, Giovanni Gronchi,

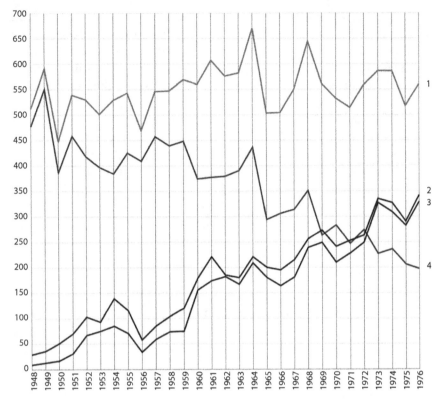

Figure 14.1. Main watersheds in the development of censorship in
Italy between 1948 and 1976 (Source: Italia Taglia database)

Key: 1. total films judged; 2. films forbidden to minors; 3. trimmed films; 4. films approved

who prepared the ground for a possible centre-left coalition.[12] A second
major change in censorship trends can be found in the late 1950s. It is now
common knowledge that after the Merlin Law (which in September 1958
closed brothels and established a new offence, the exploitation of prostitution), in the years of the so-called economic miracle, there was a first
radical clash between the Catholic cultural field and the sexualization of
media. This explains the steep rise of lines 2 and 3 between 1958 and 1962.
A third watershed comes ten years later. After 1968 there was a second
strong wave of sexualization which paved the way for the emergence of
hardcore pornography: this is clearly confirmed by the second steep rise
between 1968 and 1973. Of particular relevance is the fact that after 1968
the rising lines cross the falling one. Films which were cut or forbidden for
minors now outnumbered those approved. In this moment, the system was
on the verge of collapsing: metaphorically speaking, it was like a country
where the majority of the citizens were being put in jail.

A fifth result that can be extracted from the Italia Taglia digital archive and analysed from a quantitative point of view (Figure 14.2) is the number of films initially forbidden for all viewers (line 5), and whether they were eventually approved or not (the second outcome is counted by line 6). Each of the three relevant watersheds already discussed (1956, the late 1950s and the late 1960s) are confirmed, but in this case, there is also a sudden surge in 1963 which needs to be explained. It is even more surprising if we compare it with the trend of the other lines in the same year. This is the only moment in Italy's cinema censorship history when there is a contradiction between the different lines: lines 1 and 4 rise (that is, the total amount of movies and the number of approved ones), lines 2 and 3 fall (the films cut or forbidden for minors), while there is a significant peak in line 5—that is, the number of films forbidden for all viewers at least once. A possible explanation lies in the political situation: a new law about cinema had just been passed by

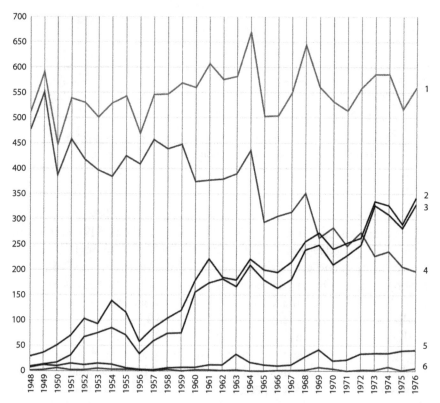

Figure 14.2. Total films forbidden on the background of the general development of censorship in Italy between 1948 and 1976 (Source: Italia Taglia database)

Key: 1. total films judged; 2. films forbidden to minors; 3. trimmed films; 4. films approved; 5. films forbidden to all viewers, at least initially; 6. films never approved

a centre-left coalition thanks to pressure from the left; yet the Ministry of Entertainment, led by a Christian Democrat, was strongly criticized for weakness over this compromise.[13] As a consequence, it could be argued that he found himself needing to prove to his electorate that censorship was as strong as before and still functioning properly, so he preferred to deny the certificates instead of starting negotiations. In conclusion, the quantitative analysis proves to be useful to point out the general trends as well as the minor changes. Generally speaking, it gives a reliable picture of the historical evolution of the phenomenon.

Conclusion

The literature on Italian censorship tends to devalue censorship's importance, describing it only as an anachronistic and repressive tool, already surpassed by modernity and meant solely to thwart artists' creative freedom. This approach, ideologically biased and typically embraced by the left, does not fully understand the social role and functions of Italian censorship. A quantitative analysis proves the one-sidedness of that traditional approach and offers insight into how institutions adopted a totally different perspective, increasingly investing in censorship as a privileged tool to negotiate with modernity. The model that we have tested on the Italian case, if properly adapted, could be applied to other national contexts (for example similar European Western democracies), allowing useful comparisons. We suggest, as a possible hypothesis to be verified by further research, that between the late 1940s and the 1960s, the Italian case shows data consistent with general international trends. In contrast, the second half of the chart, which maps what happened in the years of the gradual liberalization of pornography, is more surprising. We argue that in the 1970s the Italian case shows data probably inconsistent with general international trends, and that this discrepancy may depend on the peculiar approach chosen in Italy to confront pornography. In other words, the lack of a law regulating this challenge entrusted censorship with a frontline role in the battle for the defence of morality, thereby putting it under pressure with an excessively broad remit.

Notes

1   The paragraph of the Italian constitution which legitimates censorship was proposed by Aldo Moro as an amendment to the sentence: 'The law establishes adequate measures.' Moro proposed to add 'preventive and repressive' with the following explanation: 'I like fore and foremost to remind that the regulation of the last paragraph was proposed to the committee by us and by the communist colleagues, particularly the Honorable

deputies Terracini and Nobile. [...] I and these friends of mine were worried about the possibility that this expression would not be clear enough to the future legislator since it recalled only repression and not those measures of prevention that we consider vital. [...] We ask that, at least for obscene publications, entertainments and other events offending against public morals, not just a severe repression, but also an adequate and immediate prevention will be allowed' (Atti dell'Assemblea Costituente, session of 14 April 1947, p. 2820). All translations from Italian are the authors' own.

2   The historiographic category of 'clerical regime', as defined by Arturo Carlo Jemolo in *Chiesa e stato in Italia negli ultimi cento anni* (Torino: Einaudi, 1948) and *Chiesa e stato in Italia dalla unificazione agli anni settanta* (Torino: Einaudi, 1977), means an interpenetration of church and state after the Christian Democracy party won the elections in 1948, and has been confirmed by the most important historians who subsequently worked on the relationship between church and state in post-war Italy (see Andrea Riccardi, 'Chiesa di Pio XII o chiese italiane?', in Andrea Riccardi (ed.), *Le chiese di Pio XII* (Bari & Roma: Laterza, 1986); Pietro Scoppola, 'Chiesa e società negli anni della modernizzazione', in Andrea Riccardi (ed.), *Le Chiese di Pio XII*; Guido Verucci, *La chiesa nella società contemporanea: dal primo dopoguerra al concilio Vaticano II* (Roma & Bari: Laterza, 1988); Giovanni Miccoli, 'La chiesa di Pio XII nella società italiana del dopoguerra', in *Storia dell'Italia Repubblicana*, vol. 1: *La costruzione della democrazia* (Torino: Einaudi, 1994)). It seems to be particularly apt regarding church politics around public morality.

3   See Peppino Ortoleva, *Il secolo dei media: riti, abitudini, mitologie* (Milano: Il Saggiatore, 2009); Federico Zecca and Giovanna Maina (eds), *Sessualità nel cinema italiano degli anni sessanta: forme, figure e temi*, special issue of *Cinergie* 5 (2014): 5–118; Mauro Giori, *Homosexuality and Italian Cinema: From the Fall of Fascism to the Years of Lead* (London: Palgrave MacMillan, 2017); Tomaso Subini, *La via italiana alla pornografia: cattolicesimo, sessualità e cinema (1948–1986)* (Firenze: Le Monnier Università, 2021).

4   Between 1951 and 1959, we have found just eight cases of transgressions reported to the Direzione Generale Cinema: *O.K. Nerone* (Mario Soldati, 1951); *La mujer que yo amé* (*Fango*, Tito Davidson, 1952); *The Yellow Tomahawk* (*L'ascia di guerra*, Lesley Selander, 1955); *Sie* (*Lei*, Rolf Thiele, 1955); *Et Dieu ... créa la femme* (*Piace a troppi*, Roger Vadim, 1956); *Costa Azzurra* (Vittorio Sala, 1959); *La cambiale* (Camillo Mastrocinque, 1959); and *Caravan Petrol* (Mario Amendola, 1959). See the complaints by the Catholic Action's Segretariato per la Moralità preserved at Archivio Storico dell'Istituto per la Storia dell'Azione Cattolica e del Movimento Cattolico in Italia Paolo VI (ISACEM, Rome), PG XII.

5   As noted by the Catholic executives, a circuit of parish cinemas 'is a peculiarly Italian phenomenon' (Luigi Pignatiello, letter to Giovanni Battista Cavallaro, 24 May 1969, preserved at the archive of Associazione Cattolica Esercenti Cinema, ACEC). Around the mid-1950s, when in Italy there were between 4,000 and 4,500 parish cinemas (mostly equipped for 35mm), in France they were just 1,500 (mostly equipped for smaller formats), in Spain 1,000 (mostly equipped for smaller formats), in Germany 700 (mostly equipped for smaller formats). With 300 parish cinemas mostly equipped for 35mm, the Belgian circuit was the nearest to the Italian one in terms of the ratio of cinemas to citizens. See Commission Pontificale pour le Cinéma, la Radio et la

Télévision, *Le cinéma dans l'enseignement de l'église* (Città del Vaticano: Libreria Editrice Vaticana, 1955).

6   See Subini, *La via italiana alla pornografia*, pp. 28–31.

7   See Mauro Giori, *Rocco e i suoi fratelli: la vita amara di Luchino Visconti* (Torino: UTET, 2021), pp. 33–51.

8   The number results from the sum of the cases documented or just mentioned by several sources: the biweekly reports of the Italian Azione Cattolica's Segretariato per la Moralità (which by means of their local bases monitored complaints, seizings and trials) and the sentences collected at ISACEM; testimonies and/or complaints which form a consistent part in the traditional literature on Italian film history; the films enlisted in a document written for internal purposes only by Direzione Generale del Cinema (DGC: 'Elenco film sequestrati ed eventualmente dissequestrati', available at http://cinecensura. com); the information deducible from the files preserved at Archivio Centrale dello Stato (Fondo Ministero del Turismo e dello Spettacolo, Direzione generale spettacolo; Divisione Cinema, Concessione certificato di nazionalità, Fascicoli per film 1946–1965) and DGC (which often include copies of complaints and sentences), both in Rome.

9   The Italia Taglia website offers a large amount of data extracted from all the original censorship documents preserved at the Ministero della Cultura in Rome and partly available on the website http://cinecensura.com. See https://www.italiataglia.it/home.

10 This meant children under sixteen until 1962, when a new cinema law was passed which instead gave censors two options: to prohibit a film from being shown just to children under fourteen or to all children under eighteen.

11 See Barbara Corsi, *Con qualche dollaro in meno: storia economica del cinema italiano* (Roma: Editori Riuniti, 2001).

12 See Silvio Lanaro, *Storia dell'Italia repubblicana* (Venezia: Marsilio, 1992), pp. 235 and 327.

13 Such weaknesses were very obvious to some contemporaries. For example, referring to the economic bill that was being discussed in parliament just after the cinema law, the chairman of AGIS (Associazione Generale Italiana dello Spettacolo) invited the chairman of ACEC to 'a strict collaboration […] to prevent weaknesses or cracks in the majority party as happened in occasion of the debate about censorship' (Italo Gemini, letter to Francesco Dalla Zuanna, 15 May 1962, preserved at archive of ACEC).

15

Historicizing the Censor: Path-Dependent Patterns of Film Censorship in Turkey

İlke Şanlıer and Aydın Çam

Introduction

Within the long tradition of researching film censorship, it is critical to reflect on the latest challenges in censorship policies, strategies and practices both simultaneously and in various geographical and temporal contexts. This compiled volume includes a range of comparative approaches, which are reflective of different schools and generations in historiographical work. This chapter follows Edward H. Carr's line: 'when we attempt to answer the question "What is history?" our answer, consciously or unconsciously, reflects our position in time, and forms part of our answer to the broader question, what view we take of the society in which we live.'[1] Although Carr's projection is an internalized premise among historians or scholars chasing historical stories, we seek to understand a contemporary censorship practice in Turkey by following a more relational and processual route with a path dependency approach, which suggests that historical events and choices can shape and limit the future development of institutions, policies and technologies. This theory argues that once a particular path is established, it can become difficult to change course due to factors such as lock-in effects, institutional inertia and path-dependent processes.[2] Essentially,

İlke Şanlıer and Aydın Çam, "Historicizing the Censor: Path-Dependent Patterns of Film Censorship in Turkey" in: *The Screen Censorship Companion: Critical Explorations in the Control of Film and Screen Media*. University of Exeter Press (2024). © İlke Şanlıer and Aydın Çam. DOI: 10.47788/PRKT5596 path dependency theory highlights the importance of understanding how past decisions and events can have lasting and significant impacts on the trajectory of social and economic systems.

Historically, various institutions and legislation have been employed to control films in Turkey by different means, either through state regulations or market mechanisms. For example, in the Early Republican Period (1923–45), during the first half of the twentieth century, the state was at the very centre of control and censorship mechanisms. On the other hand, during the 1960–80 period, with the popularization of cinema, economic concerns also began to play a role in film control. As a result, distributors and exhibitors may have censored the parts of films they considered inappropriate to the values of the local population. In this chapter, we try to historicize all kinds of film censorship practices employed in Turkey, including film cuttings, bans, industry discouragements and involvements, age restrictions, self-censorial practices and other types of censorial interventions. We look at three major epochs from the 1930s until today and three corresponding categories of institutionalized censorship. In the course of our argument, we historicize our object of analysis, namely the film censor, within multiple temporalities,[3] and try to reflect on the path-dependent patterns and entanglements within the different epochs. Therefore, we aim to lay out a relational history of film censorship in Turkey regarding the institutionalization of the cinema/film censor by looking at the process of intercrossing. To achieve this, we employ Antonio Gramsci's conceptual framework of the historical bloc to trace a pattern. We adapt his initial concept of power structures that control the means of production through the shift of the mode of production to argue that historical power blocs may also be diverse throughout one way of production. The conception might be helpful as an analytical category to excavate 'the very process of intercrossing'[4] between political power, capital and cinema's relationship with censorship through various control mechanisms.[5] By examining the historical intercrossing of political power, capital and cinema in Turkey, we can gain a deeper understanding of the complex and often conflicting forces that have shaped film censorship over time. This can help to shed light on how censorship practices and policies have evolved in response to changing social, economic and political conditions, and how they continue to impact the film industry and wider society today. Such a perspective raises research questions that we try to answer in this chapter, such as: how can censorship mechanisms be compared through time? While trying to map a relational historical path, a relatively current issue is the role of social media in censorship debates. How do we define film censorship in today's world of content control on social media platforms? How is today's ideology of censorship connected to its inception during the establishment of the Turkish Republic?

Path Dependence: A Theoretical Trace of Understanding How History Matters

Although today it seems as if we are encountering a new form of censorship in contemporary media, it may be possible to reveal intercrossing in the history of censorship using common analytical categories and the same object of study following the path dependence approach. Drawing upon considered sources from various disciplines, including historical sociology, the path dependence approach delivers a historically based explanation for social, political or economic change. Put concisely, while path dependence methods theorize events occurring sequentially at one stage, this can limit the range of events possible at later stages in political processes.[6]

As James Mahoney outlines,[7] path dependence involves two types of analysis. The first is the analysis of self-reinforcing sequences that are characterized by the formation and long-term reproduction of a particular institutional pattern. The second enquiry into social phenomena is the study of reactive sequences, which looks at temporally ordered and causally connected chains. Mahoney argues that there are four rationales, each leading to a different kind of self-reinforcing sequence in institutional reproduction: 1) Utilitarian Explanations: institutions keep choosing the phenomenon because they benefit from it; 2) Functional Explanations: institutions are reproduced because they serve a particular function for the overall system in which they are ingrained; 3) Power Explanations: certain institutions may be reproduced in line with the dominance of particular power groups or actors; and 4) Legitimation Explanations: institutions are reproduced because actors believe it is appropriate and fits a particular system of ideas.[8] According to Dan Breznitz, in the institutional pattern approach, path dependence concerns formal institutions developing and legitimating 'a web of informal institutions and "rules of the game" around them. This web influences the future behaviour of said organisations and institutions and how new formal institutions are constructed in the future'.[9]

In a historicist manner, the legitimation paradigm explains that 'institutional reproduction is grounded in actors' subjective orientations and beliefs about what is appropriate or morally correct'.[10] Such a perspective suggests that the self-reinforcing sequences approach empowers agencies for social change. These changes may also encompass the transformation of lifestyle under an authoritarian rule or the internalization and institutionalization of self-control mechanisms over time, even if there are no legal sanctions. Examples of this include censorship mechanisms of non-state actors in Turkey during the 2000s in compliance with the status quo. Therefore, the legitimation explanation of self-reinforcing sequences provides a framework for analysing path dependence in the Turkish history of film censorship and its institutionalization both formally and informally.

A Short Review of Film Censorship History in the Turkish Context

At both macro and meso levels, earlier studies on film censorship in Turkey tend to assess censorship practices within a specific period and discuss their findings with policy changes and market regulations. Immediately after the arrival of cinema in the Ottoman Empire, the control started. While Özde Çeliktemel-Thomen studies the evolution of control to censorship in this early period,[11] Serdar Öztürk reviews the first censorship discussions with new documents.[12] The second period in which censorship and control mechanisms are explored is the era of nation-building after 1923, extending through World War II and even to the 1960s. Aydın Çam states that in the transition from the Ottoman Empire to the newly established nation-state, instead of institutional disjuncture, continuity can be observed in terms of censorship and control practices.[13] Again, in the same period, Ceyda Özmen discusses the relationship between dubbing and censorship as a particular field.[14] Looking at the dominance of Hollywood films before and just after World War II, Nezih Erdoğan and Dilek Kaya examine state intervention in distribution and exhibition practices in this period.[15] Dilek Kaya (Mutlu) examines in depth the censorship practices and methods of resistance against these practices in the 1960s and 1970s, when cinema in Turkey lived through its golden age.[16] In a recent three-volume compilation, Ali Karadoğan and S. Ruken Öztürk analyse the audits carried out by control commissions composed of representatives of various institutions between 1932 and 1988, based on different legislation, and categorize over 25,000 censor decisions from the removal of certain scenes to the banning of a film, based on the ninety-two decision reports archived by the Directorate General of Copyrights of the Ministry of Culture and Tourism.[17]

Although we try to cover the Republic's almost hundred years of history, the first epoch we want to discuss is the period of the 1930s and 1940s when the film market was formed. The ruling elite of the time can best be categorized as the military bureaucracy of the Ottoman legacy. This period introduces the first regulation of cinema venues, screening practices and films. Censorship was part of a large-scale/macro-level regulatory and control mechanism. Since there were not many national film productions yet, and those produced already had government approval, censorship was practised almost exclusively for imported films. During this period, imported films were checked and censored at the customs level of entry into the country. Until the Regulation for Control of Motion Pictures came into force in 1932, film control was carried out by the provincial governorships.[18]

According to the 1932 Regulation, films that include religious propaganda, violate the honour of military service, violate social decency, threaten social security and order, slander the country or disrupt political relations with allied states are not to be screened. For example, under the Regulation, *All Quiet on the Western Front* (Lewis Milestone, 1930) and *The Great Dictator* (Charlie Chaplin, 1940) were censored.[19] These examples represent the transnational political pattern of the day's government. Furthermore, there were news pieces announcing a new regulation was being prepared by the Ministry of Interior, which would enable the control of film scripts.[20] An addendum, issued in 1933, also subjected local films to inspection. For example, two films by Muhsin Ertuğrul, shown in the late 1930s, were found obscene and were banned after screening.[21] When the subject was discussed in the Turkish parliament, the government decided that a new censorship law was required. In particular, control over local films before production (i.e. the script) was needed. A similar pattern of authoritative control over films continued throughout the 1940s, further empowered by the introduction of the Regulations on the Control of Films and Film Scripts Act in 1939. Interestingly, in the same year, films were recognized as propaganda apparatuses through the adoption of the Regulations on the Control of Educational and Technical Films and promoting the ideals of the newly founded Republic, such as banning non-Turkish—primarily Arabic-language—songs in films. Ali Karadoğan and S. Ruken Öztürk review many examples of songs with Arabic lyrics being banned under the conditional admission decisions regarding films between 1932 and 1958, in their extensive study in which they examine the 'decision reports' of censorship commissions.[22]

Following Turkey's signing of an economic cooperation agreement with the United States in 1948 to participate in the Marshall Plan, a change in screening repertoire was observed due to the banning of Russian and Eastern European films by the Board of Censorship. This resulted in the dominance of Hollywood productions alongside a decline in European films after World War II.[23] In the meantime, the transition in Turkey to a multiparty parliamentary system in 1950 resulted from the seizure of power by a new historical bloc, namely the rural bourgeoisie. That power shift did not take long. With the rise of a bourgeoisie based on trade, a new epoch was begun in 1960, marked by a coup d'état. Our second epoch under discussion is the period between 1960 and 1980. Historically, it is the period in which film production, film consumption and the number of cinema venues were at their peak. Moreover, this period is accompanied by the transition to a multiparty system, military coups, the rise of the socialist movement, critical social shifts (such as migration and urbanization) and cultural transformations. In such an environment, film content changed. Even if the films were not directly political, they contained critical content. In this period, national censorship was centralized through İstanbul and Ankara commissions, and films were inspected before they were produced.[24] Controls were carried out over screenplays. Frequently, censorship was avoided by changing the names of the banned screenwriters, removing 'objectionable' content in the script, or sending completely different scripts to the censorship board with the same film's name. The films were still controlled by the police when they were released, but this time, only the copy to be watched during the audit (usually the premiere copy) was censored by the producers themselves; sometimes this control was circumvented through informal means such as bribery.[25] The Ministry of Culture proposed self-censorship to producers and directors as a softer authoritarian control. Some producers, members of actors' unions and critiques contested these political and legal practices. Protests included large gatherings and collective actions.[26] One criticism came through an animated short film, *Sansür* (*The Censor*, 1970), made by famous illustrator Tan Oral.[27] The film depicts censorship practices with fascist symbols, such as swastikas and fasces. Oral illustrates two modes of censorship, practised by state actors such as boards/commissions of censorship, and coercive powers such as the police and the military, which characterize the period's film control mechanisms (see Figure 15.1). The second epoch ended with a coup d'état in 1980 and reflects a shift in the historical power bloc, as with the rise of the industrial bourgeoisie and the neoliberal turn.

During the third epoch, from the 1990s until today, we observe for the sake of an analytical framework that there was an intense demand for films, especially those produced in the 1970s and 1980s. In the 1990s and early 2000s, with copyright and intellectual property issues not yet fully regulated, and even private channels illegal, films were screened on TV channels with

Figure 15.1. Screenshots from Tan Oral's film *Sansür* (*The Censor*, 1970), depicting the civil/institutional censor practices via scissors cutting the film reel, and the coercive powers as the police projected on the screen[28]

almost no censorship. The 1990s could be marked in a way as a period of freedom for TV broadcasting in Turkey, enabling the screening of every film format for each programme type. In the 2000s, the TV market became fully regulated, and the content of the broadcasts made on these TV channels was strictly controlled, formally by law and informally with the new conservative political power established in 2002. In films and TV series, this includes a process that extends from removing obscene scenes and censorship of scenes containing the consumption of alcoholic beverages and cigarettes, to the disappearance of low-cut dresses informally initiated by the practitioners working at the broadcasting companies.[29] Controlling media content in this period also involved the exclusion of dissident and oppositional content in both new films and the critical leftist films of the 1970s. Sonay Ban argues that eight types of censorship mechanism with political motivations in cinema occurred between 2000 and 2020.[30] Films were removed from festival programmes due to lack of a registration certificate; censorship was enacted at 'ministry-supported' festivals or screenings; films were censored because of objectionable subjects; registration certificates for theatrical release were denied; censorship was performed through rating practices; public screenings were prevented (by local municipalities or police officers); film shoots were prevented; and festival screenings outside Turkey were prohibited.

As Ban's typology exposing censorship cases makes clear, the past decade has witnessed various modes of censorship, self-censorship and control mechanisms practised on and by many film directors and producers, including internationally renowned and award-winning directors such as Nuri Bilge Ceylan and Emin Alper. Nuri Bilge Ceylan chose the path of making films with non-political or only implicit political content, whereas Emin Alper, while awarded a Golden Bear, made explicitly political and oppositional films, but ultimately faced state repression and was ignored for national funding programmes.[31] Kurdish directors were subjected to almost every mode of censorship and repression, which led to the enactment of a new law on the evaluation, classification and support of film production after 2015,[32] and expulsion from festivals.[33]

More recently, micro-level ethnographic studies examining censorship practices in the 2000s have come to the fore. Merve Tarlabölen Solmaz investigates from a self-reflexive perspective the actions in the units called 'Censorship' that many broadcasting groups, which host different television channels, created within their institutions in order not to be sanctioned after the regulations introduced in 2008 that prohibited the display of tobacco products on televisions.[34] Ban examines formal and informal pressures on film production, distribution and exhibition in her extensive study.[35] She argues that state and non-state actors increasingly practise (self-)censorship. These actors include festival organizers, non-governmental organizations tied to large corporate investors, art institutions and administrators, local authority officials, employee associations/film industry unions, and filmmakers and producers.[36]

Case Study: Re-Circulated Films on YouTube

Although these enquiries provide sound explanations with their analysis, limiting the study of censorship to a particular period seems to lack a relational approach for historical institutional tracing. In this chapter, with the specific case of screening old films on a new medium, we propose a more relationally historical dependency and intercrossing for a multi-temporal analysis. For example, some of the films produced during the 1970s and 1980s containing critical and dissident content have been moved to other channels, such as YouTube, which is not yet subject to extensive regulation. On the other hand, low-resolution films reproduced digitally from copies previously converted to video or DVD formats were shortened for technical reasons but never censored.[37] Since this medium's copyright and intellectual property rights are not yet regulated on a national scale, they are often circulated by various people overriding property rights. Recently, these films have been restored and re-circulated on official YouTube channels. During this restoration, we observe that the films are censored in two categories by their producers. These categories are the use of obscene scenes and scenes with political and dissident content.

Obscene scenes

In addition to the content rating regulation introduced by the 2004 regulation, by Article 8 of the Regulation on the Procedures and Principles of Broadcasting Services, under Law No. 6112 on the Establishment of Radio and Television Enterprises, it was decreed that television broadcasts could not be 'obscene'. In 2019, a regulation authorizing the Radio and Television Supreme Council to control broadcasts on the internet came into effect. With this regulation, films circulated on digital platforms such as YouTube are also considered within the scope of the ban. Moreover, with Article 8 of Law No. 5651 on the Regulation of Internet Broadcasts and Prevention of Crimes Committed through Such Broadcasts, adopted in 2007, broadcasts with 'obscene' content are subject to be 'removed and/or to block access' if there is an adequate reason for suspicion that the content constitutes a crime under the Turkish Criminal Code. This broadcasting regime, shaped by Turkey's authoritarian political climate, resulted in the producers implementing self-censorship practices for the films re-circulated on YouTube. For instance, self-censorship on the grounds of obscenity is clearly exercised in the film titled *Benim sinemalarım* (Füruzan & Gülsün Karamustafa, 1990). The film is about a young woman who lives in a suburb of İstanbul in the 1960s, taking refuge in cinemas during the golden years of Yeşilçam to escape from her life in poverty and her transition to adulthood. It was restored in 2019 by Gülşah Film. While the original copy released in 1990 had a runtime of 105 minutes, the version circulated by Film Atölyesi on YouTube is 92 minutes long. The version restored by Gülşah Film is 13 minutes shorter than the original, and all the obscene scenes in the film have been removed.

Political and dissident content

The second category of censorial practices on YouTube broadcasts of re-circulated films is removing political and dissident content. Examples include shots of graffiti depicting slogans from political organizations and the typical socialist slogans of the 1970s, which were initially unreadable in the low-resolution copies first uploaded to YouTube or screened on television broadcasts even in the 1990s and early 2000s. Subsequent restoration made the graffiti and slogans legible.

The most potent cases of (self-)censorship applied to films broadcast across different platforms on the internet are those involving political cinema, even though no law explicitly imposes the banning, limiting and monitoring of dissident content. Examples of 'social realist' Turkish cinema, which has been on the rise since the early 1970s, such as the films of Yılmaz Güney, Şerif Gören, Yavuz Özkan or Erden Kıral—despite being banned from movie theatres for a long time, up until the 2000s—are rarely shown on television channels. In addition, some comedy films with critical political content are rarely televised. An extreme example of this situation is the movie *Zübük* (Kartal Tibet, 1980). Adapted from Aziz Nesin's novel and criticizing the rise of a dishonest politician and his corrupt political relations, this satirical comedy film, despite its popularity, has not been televised or released online since 2014. From time to time, there is speculative news in the Turkish media that this movie remains banned and stripped of its screening rights.[38]

Within the scope of this research, we have studied comedies which reflect the social and political movements of the period, such as *Çöpçüler kralı* (Zeki Ökten, 1977), *Kibar Feyzo* (Atıf Yılmaz, 1978), *Neşeli günler* (Orhan Aksoy, 1978) and *Taşı toprağı altin şehir* (Orhan Aksoy, 1978). In these films, the slogans written on the streets and the walls were sometimes blurred or removed, and scenes of strikes, demonstrations or political marches were wholly removed. After these (self-)censorship practices, the duration of the 'restored' version of *Çöpçüler kralı* duration decreased to 79 minutes from 90 minutes on YouTube. Similarly, *Kibar Feyzo*'s duration dropped to 83 minutes from 91 minutes; *Taşı toprağı altın şehir*'s duration decreased to 85 minutes from 91 minutes, and *Neşeli günler*'s duration decreased by one minute. The most severe example of YouTube re-circulation of 'restored' and cropped versions through the removal of political content is the film *Maden* (Yavuz Özkan, 1978). *Maden* ('Mine' in English) narrates the struggle between workers and mine owners and the 'yellow' union that sides with the employer. It was screened briefly before the military coup that took place on 12 September 1980, and its duration was originally 159 minutes. There is also a 195-minute extended version of the film. The film has been restored several times and uploaded on YouTube. It became shorter after each restoration. The current version, uploaded in February 2022, is just 89 minutes long and now 70 minutes shorter than the original. As such, 44% of the film was self-censored.

As shown, it is evident that many restored films (even early movies) are censored, and the duration of some films is reduced by at least 25% due to the cut sequences. The most important feature of the control and censorship of this period is that these films were not censored by actors such as media owners or the government but by the producers themselves, who knew best how to avoid control and censorship during the 1960s and 1970s. The determining factor was market dynamics. Producers developed circumvention practices to avoid state censorship and meet audience demand in the 1960–80 period. The producers later encountered an intense demand after the 2000s. For example, the restored copy of *Kibar Feyzo* has been on the official channel of Arzu Film since June 2015. It has been watched 21.3 million times,[39] made possible via practices not subject to state control.

Regulated but not practised

Interestingly, new regulations on digital platforms prohibit the clear visualization of drinking alcoholic beverages and smoking, and the use of crass language and slang; we did not find evidence of producers practising self-censorship in these two categories. With the amendment made in 2018, the provision prohibiting the dissemination and broadcasting of images of tobacco products was added to Law No. 4207 on the Prevention and Control of Hazards of Tobacco Products:

> The use of tobacco products, including the display of images of tobacco products, in programs, films, series, music videos, commercials and promotional films, and in productions displayed in cinemas and theatres, as well as the use of tobacco products, including the display of images of tobacco products, on the Internet, in publicly accessible social media and similar media for commercial or advertising purposes shall be prohibited.[40]

In 2013, the provision that 'scenes encouraging alcoholic beverages cannot be included in TV series, films and music videos broadcast on television' was added to Article 6 of Law No. 4250 on Spirits and Alcoholic Beverages Exclusivity. In 2019, the regulation authorizing the Radio and Television Supreme Council to control broadcasts over the internet included digital platforms that broadcast films, such as YouTube, to be subjected to the ban's scope. After this date, short scenes of drinking alcoholic beverages and smoking in the restored films circulated on YouTube channels were visually censored by blurring or removing them entirely. But because the judicial system in Turkey is in crisis and enforcement is lacking, producers have not yet chosen to practise this kind of censorship, so as not to lose the few million views of the film on their YouTube channels.

One last category of control of films that has been regulated recently is the use of crass language and slang. Law No. 5224 on the Evaluation, Classification and Support of Motion Pictures dated 2004 and the relevant regulation introduced a novel content rating system and age limit regulation. Under this law, films have been classified according to the content of 'behaviours that may constitute a negative example such as rude behaviours and slang'.[41] Within the framework of the law, the Evaluation and Rating Board was established, in addition to the control commission that had been operating since the legislation of 1977 and later 1986. In Law No. 6112 on the Establishment of Radio and Television Enterprises and Their Media Services, which was adopted in 2011, it is specified that media services 'shall make sure that [the] Turkish [language] is used correctly, well, and comprehensibly without undermining its characteristics and rules; shall not make crude, inferior and slang use of the language'.[42] After these changes in the legislation, slang-based lines, shots featuring slang, rude speech and swearing used extensively in these films broadcast on television channels were either muted and beeped, or shots were excised entirely. In 2019, a regulation authorizing the Radio and Television Supreme Council to control broadcasts over the internet was published. With this regulation, digital platforms that broadcast films, such as YouTube, are subjected to the scope of the ban, but we have not yet seen the effect of this regulation on films posted on YouTube channels.

Concluding Reflections

In conclusion, we want to draw attention to the fact that authoritarian interventions such as coup d'états are milestones reflecting historical power bloc transformations. Therefore, we expect and indeed observe censorship practices to be re-formed or re-shaped within these transformations. Ontologically speaking, censorship is always a control mechanism practised either implicitly or explicitly. At the macro level, such control is structurally practised by power elites of any kind. But what is more interesting is that our most current cases show that even though there are no legal regulations backing this control, cultural producers such as festival organizers and art institutions and their administrators,[43] individuals such as film censors working for TV channels at the micro level,[44] or producers who re-circulate old Turkish films through channels such as YouTube at the meso level have still very much internalized this censorship as if already institutionalized not only by political or economic power elites but by almost all agents that are part of the cinema industry. This reactive dependency is similar to that of the early cinema period: 'among others, a positivist national project in social engineering solidified the westernised elite's class position through its reforms. In this respect, filmmakers and producers, who belonged to the elite (though to differing degrees), either controlled their texts or remained cautious about censorship'.[45]

The transformation of historical power blocs does not necessarily mean disjuncture. On the contrary, it contains the dialectic relationship of different agents transcending periods that reflect a path dependency. Therefore, we can see this as continuity rather than a break. Through internalized authoritarianism, censorship continues to *act* institutionalized, although actors may change. However, the legitimacy of the censorship practice goes beyond the institutional model because, as Tilly aptly puts it, 'once a process (e.g., a revolution) has occurred and acquired a name, both the name and one or more representations of the process become available as signals, models, threats, and/or aspirations for later actors'.[46] Therefore, institutional reproduction materializes when both state and non-state actors see an institution as legitimate and thus voluntarily choose to reproduce it. The consent of non-state actors to censorship in the face of the status quo when distributing old films on new media channels, which we examine in this chapter, results in the resilience of institutional configurations of censorship.

This is important not only because of the institutionalization of censorship but also because cinema culture and memory are interrupted. The lack of theatres that re-screen popular films of the 1970s, the fact that these films do not fit the interest of cinema clubs and cinematheques, and that they are rarely included in the programmes of film festivals mean that YouTube is the only medium where younger generations who do not watch television can connect with Yeşilçam cinema. Therefore, the films on YouTube channels that are censored while being restored are damaging the bond that young generations have established with the cinema of Turkey. At the end of the day, this bond is also broken because, in the cinema of the past, there is no longer any political criticism or way of life of which today's political power does not approve.

Notes

1   Edward H. Carr, *What Is History?* (Cambridge: University of Cambridge & Penguin Books, 1961), p. 5.

2   See Charles Tilly, 'Why and How History Matters', in Robert E. Goodin and Charles Tilly (eds), *Oxford Handbook of Contextual Political Analysis* (Oxford: Oxford University Press, 2006), pp. 417–37.

3   Helge Jordheim, 'Against Periodisation: Koselleck's Theory of Multiple Temporalities', *History and Theory* 51 (2012): 151–71.

4   Michale Werner and Bénédicte Zimmermann, 'Beyond Comparison: Histoire Croisée and The Challenge of Reflexivity', *History and Theory* 45 (2006): 30–50 (p. 31).

5   Antonio Gramsci, *Prison Notebooks II* (New York: Columbia University Press, 1992).

6   See James Mahoney, 'Path Dependence in Historical Sociology', *Theory and Society* 29.4 (2000): 507–48; Charles Tilly, 'Why and How History Matters', in Robert E. Goodin and Charles Tilly (eds), *Oxford Handbook of Contextual Political Analysis* (Oxford: Oxford University Press, 2006), pp. 417–37; and Dan Breznitz, 'Slippery Paths of (Mis)Understanding? Historically Based Explanations in Social Science', in Georg Schreyögg and Jörg Sydow (eds), *The Hidden Dynamics of Path Dependence Institutions and Organizations* (New York: Palgrave Macmillan, 2010), pp. 13–32.

7   Mahoney, 'Path Dependence in Historical Sociology'.

8   Ibid., p. 517.

9   Breznitz, 'Slippery Paths of (Mis)Understanding?', p. 21.

10   Mahoney, 'Path Dependence in Historical Sociology', p. 517.

11   Özde Çeliktemel-Thomen, 'Denetimden sansüre Osmanlı'da sinema', *Toplumsal tarih* 255 (2015): 72–79.

12   Serdar Öztürk, 'Türk sinemasında ilk sansür tartışmaları ve yeni belgeler', *Galatasaray Üniversitesi İleti-ş-im dergisi* 5 (2006): 47–76.

13   Aydın Çam, 'Türk ulus kimliğinin inşası sürecinde sinema politikaları', in *18: Uluslararası Altın Koza Film Festivali bildiri kitabı* (Adana: Altın Koza, 2011), pp. 133–38.

14   Ceyda Özmen, 'Mücadele, müdahale ve temsil alanı olarak film çevirisi: film kontrol komisyonlari, dublaj, sansür ve ulus inşasi (1939–1950)', *Dokuz Eylül Üniversitesi Edebiyat Fakültesi dergisi* 6.1 (2019): 300–28.

15   Nezih Erdoğan and Dilek Kaya, 'Institutional Intervention in the Distribution and Exhibition of Hollywood Films in Turkey', *Historical Journal of Film, Radio and Television* 22.1 (2002): 47–59.

16   Dilek Kaya Mutlu, 'Film Censorship during the Golden Era of Turkish Cinema', in Daniel Biltereyst and Roel Vande Winkel (eds), *Silencing Cinema: Film Censorship around the World* (New York: Palgrave Macmillan, 2013), pp. 131–46; and Dilek Kaya, 'Yeşilçam döneminde film sansürü: bir müzakere ve mücadele alanı olarak film sesi', *Kültür ve iletişim* 20.39 (2017): 12–34.

17   Ali Karadoğan and S. Ruken Öztürk, *Türkiye'de sinema sansürünün tarihi (1932–1988): sansür karar defterleri üzerine bir inceleme* (Ankara: Kültür ve Turizm Bakanlığı, 2022).

18   Çam, 'Türk ulus kimliğinin inşası sürecinde sinema politikaları'.

19   The film *All Quiet on the Western Front* (1930), which Mustafa Kemal Atatürk had watched at the Melek cinema in Beyoğlu (İstanbul), expressing that he liked it very

much, was banned for a long time because 'it offends the honour and dignity of military service and makes propaganda against military service'. Charlie Chaplin's *The Great Dictator* (1940) was also banned in Turkey until September 1944 due to the demands and pressure of Nazi Germany. The screening ban on the film is based on the 1939 Regulation on the Control of Films and Film Scripts. According to Article 7(3) of this regulation, 'films that offend the feelings of friendly states and nations cannot be produced or exhibited'. Giovanni Scognamillo, *Cadde-i Kebir'de sinema* (İstanbul: Metis, 1991), p. 36 and Ali Özuyar, *Faşizmin etkisinde Türkiye'de sinema* (1939–1945) (İstanbul: Doruk, 2011), p. 166. All translations from Turkish are the author's own.

20 'Filimlerin kontrolü', *Cumhuriyet*, 14 August 1936: 1, 3.

21 Alim Ş. Onaran, *Türk sineması*, vol. 1 (Ankara: Kitle, 1994), pp. 32–35.

22 Karadoğan and Öztürk, *Türkiye'de sinema sansürünün tarihi*, pp. 55–57.

23 Erdoğan and Kaya, 'Institutional Intervention'.

24 Kaya Mutlu, 'Film Censorship'.

25 Kaya, 'Yeşilçam döneminde'.

26 Ibid.

27 This seven-minute animated short film critiques the censorship of art in Turkey during the 1960s. Tan Oral, the creator of the film, draws a parallel between the censorship practices in Nazi Germany and those in Turkey. The film opens with a young director using his camera to capture images of nature, but he soon encounters a white rabbit that leads him to an image of a young revolutionary killed by fascists, with policemen standing over him. The director records the policemen and other images of violence against revolutionaries, ultimately producing a film that ends with a constitutional article prohibiting torture and cruelty. However, the police banned the film at its first screening, the censor broke the director's camera and the film was destroyed. Despite these setbacks, the film ends on an optimistic note. A sprout called 'revolutionary cinema' emerges from the roots of the art tree that was cut down by censorship. *Sansür* was awarded the Grand Prize at the Culture, Art and Science Awards organized by TRT (Turkish Radio and Television Corporation) in 1970, but it was never broadcast. In 1977, the film was published as a children's book under the same title, but the prosecutor's office banned its sale to those under the age of eighteen on the grounds that it was 'subject to restriction'. The film was not publicly screened until 2012, at the Antalya Golden Orange Film Festival, forty-two years after its production.

28 Screenshots are taken from the film *The Censor* (Tan Oral, 1970), https://www.youtube.com/watch?v=MYyED4i_LvQ&ab_channel=%C4%B0zmirTube [accessed 17 March 2023].

29 Merve Tarlabölen Solmaz, *Censorship and Self-Reflexivity: Censorship Practices on Films Broadcast Between 2018–2015*, Unpublished MA thesis, Marmara University, 2019.

30 Sonay Ban, *Banned Films, C/Overt Oppression: Practices of Film Censorship from Contemporary Turkey*, Unpublished PhD dissertation, Temple University, 2020, pp. 274–75.

31 Şenay Aydemir, 'Emin Alper: Ohal'de hissettiklerim kiz kardeşler'i anlamama çok yardim etti', *Gazete duvar*, 14 September 2019, https://www.gazeteduvar.com.tr.

32 Sevda Aydın, 'Kürt sinemasi da yikimdan payini aliyor', *Evrensel gazetesi*, 5 May 2016, https://www.evrensel.net.

33 Onur Aytaç, *Film festivallerinde belgeseller ve sansür: yeryüzü aşkin yüzü oluncaya dek ve Bakur*, Unpublished MA thesis, Marmara University, 2017.
34 Tarlabölen Solmaz, *Censorship and Self-Reflexivity.*
35 Ban, *Banned Films.*
36 Ibid., pp. 3–4.
37 Barry Salt, *Moving into Pictures: More on Film History, Style, and Analysis* (London: Starwood, 2006).
38 See Erkan Baş, 'Zübük filmi neden gösterilmiyor?', İleri haber, 17 December 2014, https://ilerihaber.org/; Esra Özgür, 'Kanal 7'nin 2006 yılında Zübük filminin haklarini satin aldiği ve gösterilmesine izin vermediği iddiasi', 22 September 2020, https://teyit.org/; and İrem Karagöz, 'Kemal Sunal'ın Zübük filmi neden yayinlanmiyor? RTÜK'ün cevap vermediği 'Zübük' sorusu!', *Aykırı haber*, 16 May 2021, https://www.aykiri.com.tr/.
39 *Kibar Feyzo*, https://www.youtube.com/watch?v=stOXnCPxOws [accessed 25 June 2022].
40 Law on Prevention and Control of Hazards of Tobacco Products, Article 3.
41 'The Regulation on the Principles of Evaluation and Classification of Motion Pictures, Article 10 (1)', *Official Gazette*, 25731, 18 February 2005.
42 Ibid., Article 8(m).
43 Ban, *Banned Films.*
44 Tarlabölen Solmaz, *Censorship and Self-Reflexivity.*
45 Savaş Arslan, *Cinema in Turkey: A New Critical History* (Oxford: Oxford University Press, 2010), p. 49.
46 Tilly, 'Why and How History Matters', p. 421.

Part 5

Disciplining Extreme Content

16

Don't Be Afraid, It's Only Business: Rethinking the Video Nasties Moral Panic in Thatcher's Britain

Mark McKenna

As prone as the British appear to be to moments of spontaneous moral panic it is important to recognize the forces that instigate, underpin and amplify these moments and to acknowledge that they are rarely benevolent, and the panics that result rarely spontaneous. One example of this occurred in 1982. Just as home video was finding a foothold, a 'moral panic' erupted about the nature of some of the video cassettes that were stocking the shelves of the newly established video rental shops appearing up and down the country. Criticism initially focused on the advertising that was being used to promote a handful of the more salacious titles, but this narrative quickly escalated into what the conservative Christian campaigner Mary Whitehouse called a battle for 'the soul of the nation'.[1]

The videos would become known as the 'video nasties' and the panic that surrounded them suggested that they presented a very real threat to society, particularly to children who were perceived to be most at risk from the harmful effects of horror films released on video. The video nasties quickly became a catch-all explanation for moral decline and were soon being blamed for all manner of social ills, from rape to murder and even the horrific sexual assault of a horse with bottles and sticks. All were attributed to the harmful effect of the video nasties.[2] Distributors and

Mark McKenna, "Don't Be Afraid, It's Only Business: Rethinking the Video Nasties Moral Panic in Thatcher's Britain" in: *The Screen Censorship Companion: Critical Explorations in the Control of Film and Screen Media*. University of Exeter Press (2024). © Mark McKenna. DOI: 10.47788/GTGZ8668 retailers soon found themselves targeted in a wave of prosecutions under the provisions of the Obscene Publications Act (1959) (OPA). The OPA made it an offence to publish obscene material intended for financial gain, and the panic that surrounded the video nasties would ultimately become the catalyst that would lead to the introduction of the Video Recordings Act (1984) (VRA). Perhaps the most significant piece of legislation governing film that was ever introduced in the United Kingdom. The VRA gave the British Board of Film Classification statutory powers to classify, censor and ban films that it deemed to be problematic with impunity. While the circumstances that gave rise to the introduction of the VRA are frequently described as a moral panic, imagined as a spontaneously occurring moment of public outrage through which the parameters of what was considered indecent, immoral and obscene were redrawn, scholarly interventions in this area have long contested the narrative of spontaneous outrage. As early as 1984, as the full effect of the video nasties campaign was still unfolding, Martin Barker highlighted the benefits that the 'moral panic' posed to key players who were instrumental to the success of the panic in the first place, most notably the Conservative Party who had faced a general election in 1983 after failing to deliver on the campaign promises of their previous election. While the political benefits to the Conservative Party are evident, the benefits to other key stakeholders have received far less attention, particularly those within the film industry who stood to benefit greatly from the narrative of moral conservatism.[3]

This chapter will explore the motivations that underpin the emergence of the 'video nasties' moral panic, with a particular focus on the benefits to those operating within the film industry. Most notably the British Videogram Association—the trade body for the video industry; the British Board of Film Classification—a non-governmental organization founded by the film industry in 1912 and responsible for the national classification and censorship of films exhibited at cinemas and latterly, on video; and the Motion Picture Association of America—the American trade association that represents the interests of the major film studios at home and abroad. Through an analysis of the overlapping and often competing interests of these organizations and a consideration of the role of the Department of Public Prosecutions, the National Viewers' and Listeners' Association and the Advertising Standards Authority, this chapter seeks to reconceptualize the moral panic, not as a naturally occurring and spontaneous event, but as a mechanism through which the various agencies involved wrested control of the video industry from the independent sector.

A Cultural History of the Video Nasties

To fully understand the opportunities that the moral panic presented to the key stakeholders listed above, it is first necessary to understand the popular history of the video nasties, and how that series of events led to a wave of prosecutions that forced many companies into bankruptcy and ushered in government-sanctioned censorship of video through the introduction of the Video Recordings Act.

Popular media have long been viewed with suspicion, and fears about the corrupting effects of the media can be traced all the way back to the introduction of the printing press. However, the idea that video should be viewed with suspicion and that horror videos specifically presented a new threat to society begins benignly enough, with an article that appeared in the *Daily Mail* on 12 May 1982, entitled 'The Secret Video Show'. In the article, Gareth Renowden, editor for *Which Video?* and video columnist for the *Daily Mail*, expressed his concern at the lack of a regulatory body or classificatory system governing video. He referenced a survey conducted by Scarborough schoolteacher Richard Neighbour, in which Neighbour observed that teenagers were accessing difficult and challenging films and that films such as *Scum* (Alan Clarke, 1979), *Zombie Flesh Eaters* (aka *Zombi 2*, Lucio Fulci, 1979), *The Exorcist* (William Friedkin, 1973), *Flesh Gordon* (Beneviste & Ziehm, 1974) and *The Texas Chainsaw Massacre* (Tobe Hooper, 1974) were among their favourites. Renowden argued that 'video gives the children access to something that the parents may not be able to control',[4] though, despite his misgivings, he was keen to clarify that this was not a call for censorship but simply a plea for stricter parental control in lieu of an industry-sanctioned classificatory system. This article is significant for a number of reasons, not least for its rhetoric centred on child protection, something that would feature centrally in the campaign that was building.

Renowden's warning seemed to resonate throughout the press and was soon reiterated in an article in the *Sunday Times* that would prove to be much more influential and far-reaching. 'How High Street Horror Is Invading the Home' by Peter Chippendale speaks of 'nasties', giving name to what would soon become a collective fear in an article that is cited by Julian Petley as the first time the term appeared in the national press.[5] Chippendale, significantly, singles out titles like *Snuff* (Michael Findlay, Horacio Fredriksson & Simon Nuchtern, 1976), *SS Experiment Camp* (Sergio Garrone, 1976) and *The Driller Killer* (Abel Ferrara, 1979) as archetypes of the catalogue of depravity, but the article is also significant because it provides the template for what would become the defining characteristics of the 'video nasties'. They are described by Chippendale as films that revelled in 'murder, multiple rape, butchery, sado-masochism, mutilation of women, cannibalism and Nazi atrocities'.[6]

The campaign against the video nasties would gain momentum when the press found an ally in Mary Whitehouse and the National Viewers' and Listeners' Association (NVLA) (the organization that she founded and led). Whitehouse and the NVLA had campaigned for years against what they felt was the steady creep of social liberalism in the mainstream British media, directing attention at a myriad of diverse programming. This ranged from the seemingly innocuous, such as Tom Baker's 1975 incarnation as *Doctor Who*, described by Whitehouse as 'teatime brutality for tots',[7] to the ostensibly educational, such as *Panorama*'s coverage of the liberation of the Belsen concentration camp, described by Whitehouse as 'filth' and 'bound to shock and offend'.[8] Whitehouse and the NVLA had systematically targeted what they felt were problematic media since the organization's incorporation in 1965. However, in 1982 Whitehouse took aim at the problem of video, and along with the press was quick to condemn what was increasingly being presented as a new threat—horror films released on video.

On 9 June and relying largely on the tabloid press for their intelligence, the Obscene Publications Squad, headed up by Superintendent Peter Kruger and acting in conjunction with the Director of Public Prosecutions (DPP), conducted raids upon the premises of the three video distributors most closely associated with the video nasties: Astra Video Ltd, Go Video Ltd and VIPCO Ltd, seizing *I Spit on Your Grave* (Meir Zarchi, 1978), *SS Experiment Camp* and *The Driller Killer* respectively.[9] Forfeitures numbered in excess of 1,000 cassettes, and were pending the preparation of a report for the Director of Public Prosecutions to determine whether prosecutions could be brought against the three companies.[10] These raids represent a significant turning point in how the police were approaching the problem of the video nasties—stemming the tide of videos at the source by removing the product entirely at the point of distribution. The Department of Public Prosecutions compiled a list of what they felt were problematic films and began targeting the distributors of those films. Coverage of the panic oscillated between attacking the industry that produced the video nasties, and an emphasis on the supposed detrimental effect that these films were having on society. The latter likened the effect of the video nasties to the effect of drugs and suggested that children were particularly at risk. Headlines suggested that the video nasties were 'Sadism for Six Year Olds' and that the films were facilitating 'The Rape of Our Children's Minds'.[11] However, following a test case at Willesden Magistrates Court which saw the successful prosecution of the company VIPCO, there is a noticeable shift in emphasis evident in the coverage of the moral panic. Headlines such as 'The Men Who Grow Rich on Bloodlust' named and shamed distributors directly,[12] while the article 'Fury over the Video Nasties: The Merchants of Menace "Get Off"' documented Mary Whitehouse's feeling that the ruling at Willesden Magistrates Court did not go far enough.[13] Distributors were increasingly depicted as comic book villains, to such a degree that even a charitable donation made to the children's charity National Children's Homes by the managing director of Astra Video (the company responsible for releasing the nasties *I Spit on Your Grave* and *Blood Feast* (Herschell Gordon Lewis, 1963)) was reported as the 'Charity Shock from the King of the Nasties'.[14] Reverend Michael Newman, Vice Principal of National Children's Homes, claimed that they 'would not have accepted the money had they known of the company's involvement in so-called "video nasties"'.

The Conservative MP for Luton South, Graham Bright, was approached by Mary Whitehouse, who suggested that he propose a Private Members' Bill that would tackle the issue of the 'video nasties' directly. When Bright's Bill was read to the House of Lords in June 1984, Lord Houghton of Sowerby highlighted that as early as December 1982, MP Gareth Wardell had attempted to progress a similar Bill through the house but was discouraged from doing so by the then Home Secretary Willie Whitelaw. Whitelaw reportedly said that 'there was a great deal more work which needed to be done on the matter before they could contemplate legislation' and remained steadfastly committed to the introduction of a voluntary scheme by which the industry could govern itself.[15] A figure who remained committed to the introduction of a voluntary scheme, Houghton suggested that the only thing that had changed in the interim period was the Conservative Party's manifesto. With the general election looming, the Conservative Party had decided to 'brush aside the attempts of the trade to get a voluntary scheme' and to instead introduce government legislation.[16] Martin Barker's account reiterates Houghton's suspicion, suggesting that following a series of political disasters including the Toxteth and Brixton riots in 1981, and the violence of the conflict in the Falklands that led to the sinking of the ARA *General Belgrano* and the battle for Goose Green in 1982, the Conservative government was clearly not fulfilling its campaign promises and was looking for something through which it could demonstrate resolve. It found this in the 'video nasties', swiftly acting on a largely fictitious problem that had been whipped up by moralists and the right-leaning press.[17] Despite Houghton's reservations, the bill passed through the House of Lords unchallenged, ably assisted by *Video Violence and Children, Part 1* (1983), a report that was compiled by sociologist and theologian Reverend Dr Clifford Hill and the Parliamentary Group Video Enquiry. Hill's report is significant in that he claimed that four in ten children had seen a 'video nasty', a statistic that would later be debunked as methodologically flawed and fraudulent.

Nevertheless, it was enough to give an imprimatur of credibility to the cause and helped propel Bright's bill through Parliament.

The prosecution of distributors would continue to gather momentum, and before the panic was over would see distributors serve custodial sentences for releasing horror films on video. This is seen to culminate on 3 February 1984, when the managing director of World of Video 2000, David Hamilton Grant, was sentenced to eighteen months in prison for being in possession of over 200 copies of an obscene article for publication for gain. Grant had released *Nightmares in a Damaged Brain* (Romano Scavolini, 1981), a film which had previously been granted a theatrical certificate from the British Board of Film Classification (BBFC). However, Grant's version was marginally longer than the BBFC-certificated release and was prosecuted on that basis. Grant served twelve months of the eighteen-month sentence and his company World of Video 2000 (and its parent company April Electronics) was put into liquidation.

While much was made in the press about the threat that the video nasties posed, beyond this rhetoric there is very little to suggest that parents were concerned about the threat of video nasties. In *Video Playtime: The Gendering of a Leisure Activity*, Ann Gray reflects on interviews she conducted with a cross-section of women from all social backgrounds, and suggests that while some of the women expressed concern about the possibility of their children accessing unsuitable videotapes surprisingly few mentioned the video nasties by name. This despite the interviews being conducted at the height of the moral panic in 1984.[18]

The Bill was given Royal assent on 12 July 1984 and was slowly phased in from September of that year, coming into full force by 1 September 1988. This three-year grace period was given to allow the BBFC, the organization that had been charged with categorizing films that were released in video, enough time to censor and classify the huge volume of films that had been released up until that point.

Towards an Industrial History of the Video Nasties

While for many the story of the video nasties begins with the newspaper articles cited above, there was some concern expressed from within the film industry about the problem that video posed long before it made headlines in the tabloid press. Though admittedly, this was for a range of very different reasons. Throughout this period, key stakeholders, such as the BBFC, the British Videogram Association (BVA) and even the Motion Picture Association of America (MPAA) were all engaged in a discussion about the future of the video industry and, in many ways, the video nasties moral panic provided them with an opportunity to reshape that industry.

To understand how the mainstream industry benefitted from the video nasties moral panic, it is first necessary to understand the origins of home video technology. Given the huge revenue streams generated for the film industry first by video, and then by DVD and Blu-ray, you would be forgiven for thinking that the film industry was somehow involved in the development of video. However, the reverse is actually true, and for almost a decade the film industry instead played an active role in trying to suppress the technology. Sony launched the Betamax video format in 1975 and was met with immediate resistance from the film industry. Much of the concern stemmed from the machine's ability to record programmes directly from television, an addition that Sony had made after the prohibitive costs of pre-recorded cassettes resulted in Sony's failure to successfully market the Betamax's predecessor (U-matic) as a home entertainment system.

The Walt Disney Company and Universal Studios were fearful that the technology had the potential to enable copyright infringement, and responded with a legal action that challenged the 'legality of the manufacture, sale and home-use of VTRs (VCRs) to record copyrighted motion pictures from television broadcasts without compensation to the copyright owners'.[19] Sony Corp. of America v. Universal City Studios, Inc., or the 'Betamax case' as it became known, continued up until 1984 with the Disney Corporation and Universal Pictures pushing for a decision that would nullify the recording capabilities of the technology. While Sony was embroiled in the court case, JVC had developed its Video Home System (VHS) to the point that it was ready to bring it to market; however, unlike Sony, they adopted an Original Equipment Manufacturer (OEM) model of dissemination, sub-licensing its technology to parent company Matsushita Electric Industrial Co. (Panasonic), who in turn approached RCA to distribute the machine in the United States.[20] In the United Kingdom, this meant that the VHS gained a lot of ground over its competitor in Radio Rentals and DER, who were both subsidiaries of Thorn EMI, a partner of JVC that had developed the format.[21]

Despite a continued investment in the lawsuit, video was impossible to ignore and Disney made tentative steps into the industry, establishing its own video distribution operation in 1980, Walt Disney Telecommunications and Non-Theatrical Company (WDTNT), while Universal established its own MCA Videocassette, Inc. However, it should be noted that these early releases were typically older titles and that the major studios were still suspicious of the video industry. The court proceedings continued until 1984, and infringement of copyright remained a concern throughout this period, shifting the focus from that of broadcast television to 'tape-to-tape' piracy, which was becoming a growing problem faced by all corners of the industry.

In 1982, Jack Valenti, the long-time President of the Motion Picture Association of America (MPAA), addressed the House of Representatives, Committee on the Judiciary, Subcommittee on Courts, Civil Liberties, and the Administration of Justice. Valenti was arguing in favour of a Bill that would allow the established film industry to either suppress home video, or profit from introduction of the technology by charging tech firms and videotape manufacturers a premium. Valenti argued:

> [T]he VCR is stripping [...] those markets clean of our profit potential, you are going to have devastation in this marketplace. [...] We are going to bleed and bleed and haemorrhage, unless this Congress at least protects one industry that is able to retrieve a surplus balance of trade and whose total future depends on its protection from the savagery and the ravages of this machine [...] I say to you that the VCR is to the American film producer and the American public as the Boston strangler is to the woman home alone.[22]

Deliberately provocative and hyperbolic it may be, but Valenti's statement needs to be considered carefully in the context of the time, and of the person delivering it. As President of the MPAA, Valenti held incredible sway over the film industry. The MPAA had been established in 1922 by the film studios themselves with the express aim of ensuring the viability of the American film industry by attracting investment and managing its public image at home and abroad. As President of the MPAA, Valenti is speaking with the full authority of the film industry, and his voice reflects the fear and concern that industry was feeling at that moment. However, despite Valenti's best efforts, in 1984 the Supreme Court of the United States found in favour of Sony and ruled that making individual copies of television shows for purposes of time shifting was fair use and did not constitute copyright infringement. Even as early as 1982 it was becoming clear that they were not going to be able to suppress the technology, so they began discussions with the industry and its representatives to begin reshaping the marketplace—namely, the BBFC and BVA.

The initial reticence of the major studios to adopt video had left a space for the independent sector to thrive. Though unable to access the mainstream cinema controlled by the majors, the independents had imported cinema from around the world and packaged them in what would later be described as lurid designs. In doing so they had unwittingly attracted the attention of the British press and given rise to the video nasties as a category. From May 1982 when the first articles began appearing in the press, to August of the same year, there was a visible increase in the number of articles addressing the problem that the video nasties posed. However, predating all of this in February of 1982, *Television and Video Retailer* magazine reported on a number of complaints made to the Advertising Standards Authority (ASA) about the nature of the advertising being used to promote the video cassettes of *The Driller Killer*, *SS Experiment Camp* and *Cannibal Holocaust* (Ruggero Deodato, 1980). These issues over the artwork predate anxieties over content by a matter of months. When the problem eventually spilled over into the popular press, Norman Abbott, Director General of the British Videogram Association (BVA), was forced to intervene, suggesting that 'it is a competitive situation, and everybody was trying to outdo each other and be more outrageous. But now the publishers have decided to put their own house in order'.[23] He announced the formation of a working party, in conjunction with the British Board of Film Censors (BBFC),[24] with the aim of tackling the issue of video nasties.[25]

Taken at face value, it is easy to imagine this as an organically developing situation in which the BVA are trying to manage the reputation of the entire video industry; however, the records of the Advertising Standards Authority are revealing. The ASA's records are extensive, containing hundreds of thousands of entries going back to its incorporation in 1962. These records are catalogued against a variety of criteria such as advertiser name, complaint type, media type, issue/code rule and complexity. However, despite numerous attempts, they were unable to locate a record of any complaint against any of the advertising used to promote any of the seventy-two films associated with the video nasties moral panic. The only mention of the video nasties comes from the 1982–83 Annual Report:

> The Authority has noted the action being taken by the British Videogram Association, in conjunction with the British Board of Film Censors, to establish standards and a classification for video tapes. The Association is rightly anxious about the standard of much of the packaging and many of the advertisements. The BVA sent us several complaints against advertisements for videos so revolting (as, for example, those entitled 'SS Extermination Camp' and 'Driller Killer') that we were appalled by their publication and took stern action to prevent a repetition. The Authority is pleased that the video trade is making efforts to ensure compliance with BCAP and will continue to use the full range of sanctions at its disposal to repress breaches of the Code. In addition, the Authority has welcomed the statement by the CAP Committee that it will expect the standards of BCAP to be observed by all advertisements carried on video tapes.[26]

What this seemingly innocuous report reveals is potentially of great significance when it comes to establishing the origin of the initial complaints and has far-reaching implications that problematize the entire received history of the video nasties. Most accounts of the 'video nasties' begin in the same way, with a series of complaints made to the Advertising Standards Authority about the advertising being used to promote certain horror video cassettes. The British Video Association then responds to these complaints publicly, concerned that 'everybody was trying to outdo each other and be more outrageous' but also suggesting that distributors 'have decided to put their own house in order'.[27] To assist in this, the BVA announces the formation of a working party with the British Board of Film Censorship to develop a classificatory system to help govern video and, in this narrative, the BVA present themselves as intermediaries and mediators endeavouring to advise their members on best practice and the best way to respond to these issues. However, in the report cited above, the complaints do not originate from the consumer but from the BVA themselves. These complaints are not the result of a public outcry, but of the BVA, the trade body responsible for the video industry, telling tales on sections of its own industry.

This is hugely significant, not only because it clearly demonstrates the division that existed in the industry at that time, but also because this predates any sense of concern that was later articulated in the national press and seems to be the original source of the concern. In subsequent interviews Abbott could often be heard making distinctions between the independents and what he described as the 'respectable' face of the industry, so it should perhaps come as no surprise that the BVA did not represent the needs of the entire industry and that their membership was not inclusive.[28]

In September 1986, only one year after the implementation of the Video Recordings Act, the British Videogram Association's membership consisted of precisely thirty full members.[29] Included in this were all the established Hollywood studios, forming what would have historically been understood as the 'Big Five' and the 'Little Three', the studios that shaped the industry in the formative years of cinema—Warner Bros; MGM (having recently merged with United Artists to release their works through the imprint MGM/UA); Paramount and Universal Studios (distributing through the imprint Cinema International Corporation (CIC)); 20th Century Fox (who merged with the CBS Corporation to form CBS/Fox); and Columbia (who licensed their catalogue to Granada Video through the imprint of The Cinema Club). Walt Disney joined the market in November 1982 with the release of *Pete's Dragon* (Don Chaffey, 1977), a film that was at that point already five years old.

Outside of the established studios, many companies that had begun life as music producers such as A&M Records, Chrysalis, Polygram, Virgin or Picture Music International (PMI)—a division of EMI—were all making inroads into the video market. What this demonstrates is that the overwhelming majority of the film companies that held full membership with the British Videogram Association in 1986 were either established distributors associated with major studios, mini-major studios, the imprints for regional and national television stations moving into the video arena, or the result of multinational record producers extending into the video market.

Clearly, by this time, the independent distributors that had established the marketplace and developed the networks and infrastructure had gone. This membership suggests a kind of oligopoly, though this is not without historical precedent, especially if we consider the British video industry an extension of the Hollywood film industry. Here, the Motion Picture Production Code offers the most striking parallel, which as Richard Maltby has argued should be seen 'not as the industry's reaction to more or less spontaneous outburst of moral protest backed by economic sanction, but as the culmination of a lengthy process of negotiation within the industry and between its representatives and those speaking with the voices of cultural authority'.[30]

While not always visible, the MPAA worked closely with the BVA and the BBFC to shape the future of the video industry. Together they devised a voluntary code that would be administered by the newly appointed Video Standards Council (presumably a precursor for the organization of the same name that would not officially come into being until 1989). Although voluntary in name, the mechanisms of the scheme were such that if implemented, distributors, wholesalers and retailers would have had little choice other than to join. The process was simple: a distributor would submit their video to the Video Standards Council for certification and the council would then determine whether it was suitable for release. If the film was later deemed to be suitable for release, it would be classified using a U, PG, 15 or 18 certificate and would then be made available to wholesalers and retailers. However, if a film was deemed to be unsuitable for release and then a retailer was found to be stocking that cassette, all distributors with an affiliation to the British Videogram Association—read the major studios— would stop supplying that retailer with their product, effectively preventing them from accessing mainstream Hollywood fare and squeezing them out of the industry. This is the proposal that was developed by the BBFC and the BVA, clearly working in partnership with the MPAA.

Not only does this proposal assume that major distributors would not be on the wrong side of this legislation, but it also constructs a binary between them as the moral arbiters and representatives of the 'official' film industry and the independents as other. While the majority of the industry were not consulted, the major studios played an active part of developing a solution to the perceived problem that video posed. Significantly, in the history section of their website the BBFC suggest that as an organization, 'we take care that the film industry doesn't influence our decisions, and that pressure groups and the media don't determine our standards'. Clearly this early collaboration suggests that this hasn't always been the case.

Conclusion

While the voluntary scheme proposed by the BVA, the BBFC and the MPAA did not come to fruition, the Video Recordings Act is in many ways its spiritual successor, naming the BBFC as the organization charged with certificating any commercial film released on video from that point on. The BVA's involvement in complaints against its own industry suggests an alignment with what Norman Abbott termed the 'respectable industry', couching his own industrial practice in starkly moral terms. However, more than that, his complaints reported in *Television and Video Retailer* magazine are the starting point for a moral panic. Similar interventions in the press from James Ferman, the Director of the BBFC, cast Abbott and Ferman as the moral stalwarts, protecting both an industry and a country from the enemy at the gates. In many ways, that enemy is globalization, and for a brief moment video democratized distribution. In doing so it provided a platform for global film, much of which had not been made available to the conservative British marketplace. This moment can be, and often is, romanticized by fans of cult film, when there is arguably a greater breadth of material available today than there ever was. Nevertheless, the moral panic needs to be understood as more than a moment of spontaneous concern and recognized for the benefits that it posed to the established film industry.

Notes

1   *Video Nasties: Moral Panic, Censorship & Videotape*, dir. by Jake West (Nucleus Films, 2010) [on DVD].
2   Tim Miles, 'Fury over the Video Rapist', *Daily Mail*, 28 June 1983: 1; Christopher White, 'A Video Nasty Killer', *Daily Mail*, 13 July 1983: 1; John Jackson, 'Pony Maniac Strikes Again', *Daily Mail*, 3 January 1984: 5.
3   Martin Barker, *The Video Nasties: Freedom and Censorship in the Media* (London: Pluto Press, 1984).
4   Gareth Renowden, 'The Secret Video Show', *Daily Mail*, 12 May 1982, p. 17.
5   Julian Petley, 'Are We Insane? The "Video Nasty" Moral Panic', in Chas Critcher, Jason Hughes, Julian Petley and Amanda Rohloff (eds), *Moral Panics in the Contemporary World* (London: Bloomsbury Academic), pp. 73–98.
6   Peter Chippendale, 'How High Street Horror Is Invading the Home', *Sunday Times*, 23 May 1982: n.p.

7   Anthony Hayward, 'Obituaries: David Maloney Director of "Doctor Who" Chillers', *The Independent*, 10 August 2006, https://www.independent.co.uk/news/obituaries/david-maloney-411226.html [accessed 6 July 2022].

8   Allison Pearson, 'Mary, Mary, quite contrary', *The Independent*, 28 May 1994, https://www.independent.co.uk/arts-entertainment/television-mary-mary-quite-contrary-1439331.html [accessed 6 July 2022].

9   John Martin, *The Seduction of the Gullible: The Truth behind the Video Nasties Scandal* (London: Stray Cat Publishing, 2007).

10 Anon., 'DPP Ponders the Case against "Horror" videos', *Video Business* 2.9 (Mid-June): 1.

11 See Tim Miles, 'Charity Shock from the King of the Nasties', *Daily Mail*, 16 July 1983: 8; Anon., 'The Rape of Our Children's Minds', *Daily Mail*, 30 June 1983: 5; Kate Egan, *Trash or Treasure: Censorship and the Changing Meanings of the Video Nasties* (Manchester: Manchester University Press).

12 Vivien Harding, 'The Men Who Grow Rich on Bloodlust', *Daily Mail*, 4 August 1983: 19.

13 Sun Reporter, 'Fury over Video Nasties: The Merchants of Menace "Get Off"', *The Sun*, 1 September 1982: 5.

14 Tim Miles, 'Charity Shock from the King of the Nasties', *Daily Mail*, 16 July 1983: 8.

15 House of Commons, Local Government (Miscellaneous Provisions) Bill (15 March 1982, vol. 428 cols 463–510) [online], http://hansard.millbanksystems.com/lords/1982/mar/15/local-government-miscellaneous-1#S5LV0428P0_19820315_HOL_396 [accessed 10 July 2022].

16 Ibid.

17 Martin Barker, 'Nasty Politics or Video Nasties', in Martin Barker (ed.), *The Video Nasties: Freedom and Censorship in the Media* (London: Pluto Press, 1984), pp. 7–38.

18 Ann Gray, *Video Playtime: The Gendering of a Leisure Activity* (London: Routledge, 1992), p. 134.

19 Frederick Wasser, *Veni, Vidi, Video: The Hollywood Empire and the VCR* (Austin: University of Texas Press, 2002), pp. 76–103.

20 Ibid., p. 73.

21 Brian Hindley, 'European Venture: VCRs from Japan', in David Greenaway and Brian Hindley (eds), *What Britain Pays for Voluntary Export Restraints*, *Thames Essay no 43* (London: Trade Policy Research Centre, 1985), p. 37.

22 House of Representatives, hearings before the Subcommittee on Courts, Civil Liberties, and the Administration of Justice of the Committee on the Judiciary, 'Home Recording of Copyrighted Works', Ninety-seventh Congress, second session, on H.R. 4783, H.R. 4794, H.R. 4808, H.R. 5250, H.R. 5488 and H.R. 5705, Volume pt. 2 (1984).

23 Martin, *The Seduction of the Gullible*, p. 14.

24 The Board would subsequently be renamed to the British Board of Film Classification, a name change designed to reflect the largely classificatory function of the organisation. Ironically, this came during a period in which the censorious function of the board had never been more pronounced.

25 Tim Dawe, 'This Poison Being Peddled as Home "Entertainment"', *Daily Express*, 26 May 1982: 7.

26 Matt Wilson, email to Mark McKenna, 2017.

27 Martin, *The Seduction of the Gullible*, p. 14.

28 *Ban the Sadist Videos*, dir. by David Gregory (Blue Underground, 2007) [on DVD].

29 Video Recordings Act Status Reports, British Videogram Association, September 1986.

30 Richard Maltby, 'The Production Code and the Hays Office', in Tino Balio (ed.), *Grand Design: Hollywood as a Modern Business Enterprise 1930–1939* (Berkeley: University of California Press, 1996), pp. 37–72.

17

The Ontario Film Review Board Meets the New French Extremity

Daniel Sacco

Film, like most forms of cultural production, is expected to be responsive to external social control. The character of such control dynamics is contextualized by specific national and regional factors. In Ontario, Canada's capital province, the relevant body had (until recently) been the Ontario Film Review Board (OFRB), a rotating committee of classification 'experts'. Prior to 2019, when the Ontario government began phasing out its regulatory film review system, all films required the approval of the Board before being distributed or exhibited in Ontario. This approval being mandated by law, any filmmaker refusing to comply could face legal consequences.

The legal dimension of the Ontario government's regulation of film content had the effect of equating certain forms of artistic expression with punishable criminality. Though rarely enforced, prosecution strengthened the notion that government power remained the ultimate arbitrator of cinema's bounds of acceptability. This idea was problematic in many senses, not least of which is reflected in the idea that political power exists in a state of perpetual flux. The criteria by which cinematic expression could be declared criminal were subject to change, while the penalty of failing to comply remained constant. The liberalization of Ontario's film regulation policies, which shifted towards classification-oriented practices in the early 2000s, would seem to address this problem: the principle of protecting vulnerable portions of audiences, grouped by age, remains intact while only

Daniel Sacco, "The Ontario Film Review Board Meets the New French Extremity" in: *The Screen Censorship Companion: Critical Explorations in the Control of Film and Screen Media*. University of Exeter Press (2024). © Daniel Sacco. DOI: 10.47788/HJES6116 the parameters defining which films should be excluded through banning are subject to modification. Such practice may seem like censorship only in an academic sense, since confrontational artistic strategies resulting in the criminal prosecution of their producers seem far-fetched in contemporary Canada, where political power is largely unconsolidated and subject to scrutiny.

What happens, however, when a review board can construe the content of a film as a violation of its government's criminal code? Such was the case in the OFRB's most high-profile controversy: its temporary refusal of classification to Catherine Breillat's coming-of-age film *À ma sœur!* (2001), released to English-speaking markets as *Fat Girl*. The case demonstrates a rare instance of narrative filmmaking strategies constituting punishable criminality, even though no part of the production process violated criminal law.

Fat Girl offers the story of two teenaged sisters who lose their virginity during a weekend vacation. It was critically lauded upon its Canadian premiere at the Toronto International Film Festival in September of 2001. However, by November of that year, the OFRB had voted against classifying the film unless the distributors, Cowboy Pictures and Lionsgate Films, made significant cuts to two key scenes. These companies unsuccessfully appealed the Board's objections, which, centring on the depiction of underaged characters in sexually explicit situations, were sufficient to prevent the film from being shown legally in Ontario until the decision was overturned in 2003.

While the OFRB was undergoing a structural renovation, changing its name from the Ontario Censor Board to the Ontario Film Review Board in the mid-1980s and prioritizing advisory ratings over traditional censorship, the *Fat Girl* affair highlighted the limit to which reform had thus far been carried. It ultimately led to the passing of the Ontario Film Classification Act in 2005, and to legislation that restricted the Board's power to ban 'mainstream' films and imposed a mandate to consider the general character and integrity of films reviewed. It is possible to gain a greater understanding of the shift from blocking to typifying films by exploring how the revisions of the OFRB's policies corresponded with the aesthetic strategies of *Fat Girl*.

The OFRB originates from the Ontario Theatres and Cinematographs Act of 1911, a statute that represents the first major attempt anywhere to implement social control of motion pictures. The broad evaluative criteria provided to the Board noted, 'No picture of an immoral or obscene nature or depicting a crime or reproducing a prize fight shall be exhibited'.[1] Given that it took until 2005 for the Board to legislatively limit the extent to which it could prohibit 'mainstream' films from entering the public market,

Ontario can be seen as serving Western cinematic censorship practices as both incubator and hospice.

The *Fat Girl* affair demonstrates the collapse of a long-lived model in which classification boards could persist in drawing lines between a film, its content, the intentions of its author and the potential effects of its release. Preceding significant revisions to its policies in the early 2000s, the Board ill-advisedly proclaimed it could excise *Fat Girl*'s 'potentially harmful' elements while simultaneously preserving the power of Breillat's intended message and upholding the value of free expression. Analysis of the film, and of the Review Board's objections, highlight the failure of this effort. While installing certain protections for filmmakers' right to free expression, the idea of a more 'liberal censorship' in Ontario brought significant complications when put into practice.

New Extremes and Classification Reform

Revisions to the OFRB's policies in the early twenty-first century seemed to coincide with the emergence of a trend in French filmmaking, in which new and abrasive forms of cinema were dealing frankly and graphically with the body. *Trouble Every Day* (Claire Denis, 2001), *Irréversible* (Gaspar Noé, 2002) and *Twentynine Palms* (Bruno Dumont, 2004) were labelled a 'New French Extremity' by critic James Quandt, who accused the filmmakers of exploiting shock tactics traditionally associated with pornography and horror.[2] Quandt's designation was pejorative, a lament upon the reliance of established arthouse filmmakers on visceral thrills to court attention. Tim Palmer offers a different way of approaching these films, not by singling out their transgressive elements as the basis of a new subgenre, but instead by suggesting the idea of a 'cinéma du corps', whose basic agenda, 'an onscreen interrogation of physicality in brutally intimate terms', offers an 'increasingly explicit discussion of the body through its sexual capacities and conflicts'.[3] His approach has less to do with genre markings than with atypical narrative, aesthetic and stylistic strategies.

A central influence on the 'New French Extremity', Breillat's readiness to engage in controversy dates to the release of her first feature, *A Real Young Girl* (1976). Her landmark feminist film, *Romance* (1999), used un-simulated sex to tell the story of a young woman's harsh sexual awakening, becoming one of the most debated French films of the 1990s.[4] *Fat Girl*'s scenes of teenaged characters engaged in sexually explicit activity, by contrast, contain no shots of un-simulated sexual activity, but effectively conjure scenarios that some read as child pornography, the distribution of which is a criminal offence in Ontario.

Initially reviewing *Fat Girl* in November of 2001, the Board requested substantial cuts, demanding the removal of approximately fifteen minutes of content. Asked to justify the Board's recourse to censorship, Chairman Robert Warren replied:

> There is a scene where a 15-year-old is shown in full frontal nudity in a sexual situation, and also a 13-year-old girl with partial nudity in a rape scene. That contravenes a section of the Theatres Act.[5]

Introduced in 1953, the Ontario Theatres Act legislated the establishment of licensing fees and the mechanisms for official approval of construction plans for theatres throughout the province.[6] In the mid-1970s, the Act was amended to forbid the public exhibition of hardcore pornography, meaning any such title would be subjected to cutting if submitted to the Board. Shortly thereafter, the Board cited the same section used against *Fat Girl* as grounds for banning *The Tin Drum* (Volker Schlöndorff), in 1979, featuring scenes in which eleven-year-old actor David Bennent appears to have intercourse with a sixteen-year-old girl.[7] Despite being awarded the 1979 Academy Award for Best Foreign Film, *The Tin Drum*'s banning by the Ontario Censor Board meant that its exhibition in the province would be a prosecutable offence under sections of the Criminal Code dealing with child pornography. The *Fat Girl* affair contained echoes of this controversy, with one key difference: unlike Bennent, both lead actresses in Breillat's film are merely *portraying* underaged characters.

The banning of *The Tin Drum* in Ontario demonstrates how, prior to the introduction of the Film Classification Act, the Board had little ability to ensure works of considerable artistic merit were afforded different review criteria than pornography. Their approach thus implied an understanding of film content as being entirely separate, in its power and potential effects, from the intentions and reputation of the author.

The 2005 Act defines 'pornography' in terms of a primary intention to arouse spectators.[8] Films designed with this purpose are, from a government standpoint, akin to drugs or gambling, requiring regulation to prevent the health and safety of audiences becoming subordinate to the financial motives of filmmakers. Such legislation obviously takes for granted the assumption that a film could compromise an adult's health and safety, but even if this conceit is granted, a filmmaker's intention remains difficult to ascertain. The Classification Act is less useful as a definitive guide to categorization of content than as a way of formally ensuring reviewers have some measure of discretion in deciding how to approach films on a case-by-case basis.

As a system of categorization, classification may serve the purpose of informing consumers about the content of films, dictating the suitability of imagery for portions of a larger audience, but the resulting categories serve regulatory interests by leading to the establishment of different rules for different kinds of films. In short, it remains a process of sharpening boundaries—between art and pornography, harmful and benign content, and so on. *Fat Girl* aims in the opposite direction—towards the dissolution of categorical boundaries. To approach the film as child pornography is to neglect the context in which the film's nudity appears—what Asbjørn Grønstad has referred to as Breillat's 'de-pornofied' poetics of looking.[9] Despite the film's reworking the conventions of pornography (and horror), critical analysis casts doubt on any suggestion that its scenes of sex and violence are intended to mimic the aesthetic strategies of successful porn or horror productions.

Sexuality and Sisterhood

Fat Girl opens with a conversation between two sisters on holiday. Elena (Roxane Mesquida), the more conventionally attractive of the two, describes her desire to lose her virginity and vows to pick up the next boy she meets. Her portly sister, Anaïs (Anaïs Reboux), accuses her of having loose morals, a charge that Elena contests, saying she is saving her virginity for a romantically appropriate moment. Anaïs claims she, by contrast, would rather lose her own virginity before finding romantic love.

Here, Breillat establishes one of the film's main thematic concerns, that Elena, despite being the presumably more mature of the pair, betrays naivete in her understanding of gender relations. She envisions her 'first time' as the perfect moment, infused with overwhelming romance, while Anaïs, despite her sexual inexperience, is better able to separate romantic love from sex. Already, Breillat is using genre to establish expectations that will be subverted. As a coming-of-age story, one might expect the film to show Anaïs overcoming her pessimism about the nobility of future male partners by meeting a worthwhile suitor. By the end of the film, her negativity is instead proven not only warranted, but essential to her emotional survival through a series of traumatic events.

Arriving at a café, the girls meet an Italian law student named Fernando (Libero De Rienzo). Anaïs watches Elena and Fernando engage in an overt mutual seduction. Her role as a spectator of Elena's 'romance' with Fernando becomes more dramatic when, a few scenes later, Elena sneaks Fernando into the bedroom of the family vacation home (a bedroom she shares with Anaïs). In a nearly twenty-minute sequence, Fernando attempts to seduce Elena with promises of love, coercing her into surrendering her virginity while Anaïs secretly bears witness. This theme of the third party (the viewer, by way of Anaïs) observing two people in lovemaking is essential to Breillat's treatment of sexual awakening.

The sequence provides a depiction of sexual interaction as a site of power struggle. Fernando is aggressive, removing Elena's clothes and caressing her body while professing his 'love' for her. Yet his demeanour shifts as Elena begins to display hesitation and reluctance. He grows despondent and acts uninterested, as Elena relays her concern that 'sleeping' with him might cause him to lose romantic interest in her. This seems to counter her faith in romantic love, but Elena too is engaged in an act of manipulation. She is attempting to elicit a particular response from Fernando, which will be sufficient to negate the fears she is expressing. Whether or not she believes his promises, she requires them if she wishes to retain any hope of placing her sexual desires in an appropriately 'romantic' context.

Elena proceeds to lift her nightgown, exposing her pubic area, as Fernando climbs on top of her. The camera shifts to a shot of Anaïs watching from across the room, again emphasizing her spectatorship. In the next shot, Elena becomes overwhelmed with emotion and stops Fernando. She explains that she is not ready. Fernando responds cruelly, accusing her of 'ruining everything'. In Elena's apologetic insistence that Fernando 'give her time' is the simultaneous expression of guilt for 'ruining' his plan and the fear of allowing him to continue. Having highlighted the moment as one of painful ambivalence for Elena, the scene continues for several minutes as Fernando caresses her partially nude body while requesting that she allow him to enter her anally. As Elena's will is eventually weakened, the camera returns to the image of Anaïs watching, where it remains for the rest of the scene (as the sexual activity is heard in the background).

In her analysis of the sequence, Tanya Horeck identifies as a key aesthetic effect the fact that although Elena is the one being seduced, the drama is played out on Anaïs's face.[10] Hearing her sister's moans, indeterminately indicating pain, pleasure or some combination of the two, Anaïs's reaction is also, fittingly, one of ambivalence. Still, her body language offers no suggestion that she derives voyeuristic pleasure from this act of spectatorship. Thus, any such pleasure for the viewer, as they have come to identify with Anaïs's gaze, becomes nearly impossible.

Elaborating on the formal design, Breillat stated that she decided to shoot Anaïs during its sexual climax because 'violation is more strongly felt from the other's perspective'.[11] Through this distancing, Breillat defines the moment as violation, whereas one is less certain of Elena's position on the matter. Instead of the viewer registering Elena's 'violation', we register Anaïs's registering of this event.

Linda Williams has identified two additional elements that separate this sequence from countless others representing the loss of innocence in cinema: its prolonged duration and relative explicitness.[12] Both are central to the New French Extremity's particular use of realist techniques to viscerally engage the spectator. Breillat has insisted that, in her work, duration and explicitness are tied to a concern for showing images in their fuller contexts: 'Porn films remove sex from human dignity [...] [My films] restore female dignity by showing sex acts in their entirety.'[13]

Critical discussions of these elements recall debates surrounding *Trouble Every Day*, *Irréversible* and *Twentynine Palms*. The prolonged scenes of graphic sex and violence in these films attract accusations of sensationalism. However, as Williams argues, in this case the explicitness and duration of the sexual content are combined for the purposes of allowing a battle over the loss of virginity to become a more psychologically and emotionally accurate ordeal.[14]

The sequence of Elena's seduction was one cited by Warren as having contravened the Theatres Act by containing 'full frontal nudity' of underaged characters. This basis disregards thematic concerns underlying the scene's use of prolonged nudity, which Breillat has designed not to arouse, but to generate discursive meaning. Arguably, the Board was simply following the criteria set forth in the Act, which contained no provisions for considering an artist's intent. However, Warren's assertion was complicated by additional comments justifying the Board's decision: 'We talked about whether (the scenes) were necessary for the picture. The feeling was that it could have been as powerful a picture without them.'[15]

While the comment signals a political difference as to what 'sex scenes' ought to be, Warren's reasoning indicates that the real challenge posed by such content is categorization. As Martine Beugnet has argued, negative responses to the explicit sexuality in the cinéma du corps suggest it is less the images themselves which attract disapproval, than the fact that these images cannot be fully assimilated in the generic categories that the films evoke.[16] That is, explicit sexuality is only gratuitous for an art cinema in which a relay of discourse and narrative is expected to at least counter-balance the presence of visceral effects. This is complicated, however, by the fact that the formal experimentation displayed in such films tends to result in the critical element of discourse being inseparable from the same strategies that complicate its decipherability.[17] The content of *Fat Girl* did not merely violate the policies of the Theatres Act—it confounded the criteria of controlled separation used to shape definitions of cinematic acceptability.

It becomes difficult to take seriously Warren's claim that removing fifteen minutes of content deemed objectionable would have no effect on the film's meaning. The comments fail to acknowledge that tampering with *Fat Girl*'s formal design is, invariably and fundamentally, altering its message.

In seeking to curb the affectivity of certain formal elements, the Board's own reasoning fell apart. The primary concern of reviewers was the presence of 'underage' sexuality. It seems unlikely they took exception specifically to the scene's duration, as other 'mainstream' films (such as *Kids* (Larry Clark, 1995) or *American Beauty* (Sam Mendes, 1999)) contained similarly prolonged scenes of minors involved in sexual situations yet were passed uncut in Ontario.[18] If the objections were rooted in the fragments of explicit sexual action, it should likewise be noted that nudity of underaged characters frequently goes unchallenged in mainstream comedies like *American Pie*. Breillat broke no laws in the filming of *Fat Girl*: Mesquida was herself over eighteen at the time of filming, as was De Rienzo, who wore a prosthetic erection during shooting.[19] The nudity is never presented in close-up, and the sex act itself takes place off-screen. Consideration of such factors did little to assuage the Board's concerns that *Fat Girl* carried the potential for social harm, as with the thematic context provided in the film's numerous inexplicit other sequences.

Fat Girl's second point of controversy occurs late in its running time in the form of a rape scene. Elena's mother learns of the affair between her daughter and Fernando, and cuts short the family vacation. On the drive home, the family car pulls into a rest stop where, in an abrupt tonal shift, a man smashes through the windshield, killing Elena with a blow to the head and strangling her mother. Anaïs exits the car, holding the gaze of her attacker, who proceeds to sexually assault her in a nearby woods.

Throughout the ordeal, Anaïs's body language betrays an ambivalence that has been highly debated. The British Board of Film Classification, for example, completely excised the sequence from home video releases, fearing it perpetuated the myth that rape can be sexually pleasurable for the victim.[20] However, as Horeck argues, to read Anaïs's lack of negative emotion as pleasure is to fatally oversimplify. Much as her sister was tempted to do when confronted with Fernando's aggressive seduction tactics, Anaïs is struggling to put the rape in the context of sentimental romance.[21] In the final moments of the film, two police officers guide her from the woods, one commenting, 'She said she wasn't raped.' Anaïs adds: 'Don't believe me if you don't want to.' It is a startling coda, but to say Breillat is suggesting rape as pleasurable violation is to disregard the thematic context she has designed the preceding action to establish.

The Appeals

Writing to the OFRB in support of *Fat Girl* and in condemnation of the ruling, David Cronenberg vouched for Breillat as an important artistic voice and for her film as a 'serious study of sisterhood and adolescent sexuality'.[22]

His letter was part of the written appeal submitted by Cowboy Pictures and Lionsgate, who vowed not to cut the film regardless of the Board's response. Five board members screened the film for a second time, and voted 3–2 in favour of upholding the refusal to classify its uncut version.[23] Since Ontario law required that all films be classified prior to exhibition or distribution, the effective ban was upheld. By this time, the film was playing to great acclaim in British Columbia, and in Quebec—where it was rated 16+.[24] Sarah Waxman, a member of the Ontario appeal panel who voted in favour of the film's release, expressed her disapproval of the Board's decision publicly: 'This intelligent handling of a controversial subject, adolescent sexuality, does not glorify or glamorize the subject [...] if anything, this is an anti-sex film'.[25] Cowboy and Lionsgate announced they would be taking the Ontario provincial government to court, to argue for the film's uncut release, but also to challenge the constitutionality of the Theatres Act and combat what they deemed an unjustifiable infringement on freedom of expression as guaranteed by the Canadian Charter of Rights and Freedoms.

Addressing the unsuccessful appeal, Warren cited the OFRB's regular consultation with psychologists and 'ordinary' Ontario citizens to represent prevailing community standards, and concluded:

> A lot of [*Fat Girl*] is based on potentially harmful activities which shouldn't be shown to vulnerable people in our society [...] We're in the business of drawing boundaries [...] based on community standards.[26]

Warren's envisioning of the Board's role as one of boundary delineation highlights its conflict with films of the New French Extremity, the stylistic strategies of which transgress most in their collapsing of boundaries. As Grønstad points out: 'The recurring problems of censorship with which Breillat's films have wrestled are in no small measure due to Kristevan blurring of categories held sacrosanct by the culture at large.'[27] Faced with criticisms of its inability to recognize artistic value in challenging artworks, the Board was retreating to the most well-worn and useful term in any contemporary censor's toolkit: 'harmful'. For vocal conservative crusaders, 'harm' functions as an effective substitute for 'evil' and 'wrong' in the wake of rapid secularization and social diversification in the second half of the twentieth century.[28]

The designation of the Ontario Film Review Board as responsible for the regulation of 'harmful' materials, however, raises perplexing questions. First, what qualifications of the Board members (drawn from a range of industry, educational and governmental occupation holders) constitute the ability to judge harm? Audience researcher Martin Barker has compared claims used by classification boards to regulate film content with surveys of actual audience responses to those same films, finding 'systematic differences between the experiences which regulatory bodies impute to viewers and those which engaged viewers say that they experience'.[29] As audiences and review boards clearly do not agree on 'social values', Barker demonstrates that film review processes function essentially as rationalizing camouflages for idiosyncratic moral judgements.

Further, in what sense might the ruling of the Board not be made redundant by more efficient mechanisms for the enforcement of moral judgements already in place (in this case, sections of the Canadian Criminal Code dealing with child pornography)? Concluding his nationwide survey of Canadian censorship history in 1981, Malcolm Dean labelled such practices as 'misguided attempts to deal with vital social processes and to place constraints on creative individuals' and suggested they were 'representing a process of judging the emerging present through a vision of the past'.[30] Dean's critique foreshadows the prevailing sentiment of reactions to *Fat Girl*'s banning, in artistic circles and in the Canadian press, where discussions of the distributor's right to exhibit the film became ensconced in language reflecting the rights of adult spectators to choose their own entertainment.

In November of 2002, Robert Warren announced his retirement from the Board 'for personal reasons'.[31] By 17 January of the following year, the Board approved a new policy of taking into account the 'General Character and Integrity' of any film considered for non-approval.[32] Less than a month after these revisions, Cowboy Pictures announced that the Government of Ontario had agreed to have the film resubmitted and approved, one month prior to a scheduled hearing before the Ontario Superior Court of Justice.[33] In a sudden reversal of the Board's verdict, Warren's replacement Bill Moody declared the scenes in question 'artistic and integral to the plot',[34] indicating a shifting of priorities in the Board's criteria and, more directly, measures to protect against the sort of rigidity that came under fire in the *Fat Girl* case.

Accounting for the reversal in the Board's decision, Craig Martin, who was set to represent the distributors in court, cited the government's reluctance to defend the constitutionality of its censorial powers.[35] It remains unclear whether Warren's departure was the impetus for, or a symptom of, revisions to the OFRB's policies. In either case, the Board was signalling its capacity for flexibility.

Conclusion

The challenges posed to the OFRB by the abrasive aesthetics of *Fat Girl* blurred long-standing demarcations between the cultural value of transgressive artwork and the highly arguable theorizations on which the Review

Board's claims of 'harmfulness' were based. Due to Breillat's risky artistic sensibilities, the OFRB was forced to take measures to limit its ability to censor works of artistic merit. The *Fat Girl* case thus represents a significant step forward in the privileging of serious cinematic projects as worthy of protection in Canada, however confrontational in their formal design and subject. Most crucially, the *Fat Girl* versus OFRB affair demonstrates that the idea of a review board simultaneously recognizing the cultural value of an artwork and nonetheless seeking to excise its allegedly 'harmful' moments is ultimately untenable, particularly when such moments are deliberate components of the film's formal design.

Notes

1 *Report of the Royal Commission on Violence in the Communications Industry*, vol. 1: *Approaches, Conclusions, and Recommendations* (Toronto: The Royal Commission on Violence in the Communications Industry, 1976), p. 484.

2 James Quandt, 'Flesh and Blood: Sex and Violence in Recent French Cinema', in Tanya Horeck and Tina Kendall (eds), *The New Extremism in Cinema* (Edinburgh: Edinburgh University Press, 2011), pp. 18–26 (p. 18).

3 Tim Palmer, *Brutal Intimacy: Analyzing Contemporary French Cinema* (Middletown, CT: Wesleyan, 2011), p. 57.

4 Ibid., p. 62.

5 Quoted in Andrea Baillie, 'Controversial Movie Featuring Teen Nudity Banned in Ontario', *Kingston Whig-Standard*, 14 November 2001: 30.

6 *Report of the Royal Commission on Violence in the Communications Industry*, vol. 1, p. 484.

7 Pierre Veronneau, 'When Cinema Faces Social Values: One Hundred Years of Film Censorship in Canada', in Daniel Biltereyst and Roel Vande Winkel (eds), *Silencing Cinema: Film Censorship around the World* (New York: Palgrave Macmillan, 2013), pp. 49–62 (p. 56).

8 Film Classification Act, 2005: Ontario Regulation 452/05, http://www.ontario.ca/laws/regulation/050452.

9 Asbjørn Grønstad, *Screening the Unwatchable: Spaces of Negation in Post-Millennial Art Cinema* (New York: Palgrave Macmillan, 2012), p. 10.

10 Tanya Horeck, 'Shame and the Sisters: Catharine Breillat's *À ma soeur! (Fat Girl)*', in Dominique Russell (ed.), *Rape in Art Cinema* (New York: Continuum, 2010), pp. 195–209 (p. 203).

11 Breillat quoted in ibid.

12 Linda Williams, *Screening Sex* (Durham, NC: Duke University Press, 2008), p. 281.

13 Horeck, 'Shame and the Sisters', p. 203.

14 Williams, *Screening Sex*, p. 35.

15 Warren quoted in Christopher Hutsul, 'Board Upholds Ban on Acclaimed Movie', *Toronto Star*, 21 November 2001: A02.

16 Martine Beugnet, *Cinema and Sensation: French Film and the Art of Transgression* (Carbondale, IL: Southern Illinois University Press, 2007), p. 37.

17 Ibid.
18 Gary Arnold, 'Fat Girl Tips Scales of Lewdness', *Washington Times*, 16 November 2001: 9.
19 Judy Gerstel, 'Breillat Plays Sex for Laughs; Fat Girl Takes a Shot At Ontario Censors', *Toronto Star*, 13 September 2002: C04.
20 Martin Barker, 'Watching Rape, Enjoying Watching Rape …: How Does a Study of Audience Challenge Film Studies Approaches?', in Horeck and Kendall (eds), *The New Extremism in Cinema*, pp. 105–116 (p. 105).
21 Horeck, 'Shame and the Sisters', p. 208.
22 David Cronenberg, 'David Cronenberg: [Ontario Edition]', *Toronto Star*, 23 November 2001: F03.
23 Jay Stone, 'Fat Girl Furore Proves Film Board's Irrelevance', *Ottawa Citizen*, 10 February 2003: B1.
24 Veronneau, 'When Cinema Faces Social Values', p. 56.
25 Hutsul, 'Board Upholds Ban on Acclaimed Movie', A02.
26 Ibid.
27 Grønstad, *Screening the Unwatchable*, p. 94.
28 Julien Petley, *Film and Video Censorship in Modern Britain* (Edinburgh: Edinburgh University Press, 2011), p. 9.
29 Barker, 'Watching Rape, Enjoying Watching Rape', p. 110.
30 Malcolm Dean, *Censored! Only in Canada: The History of Film Censorship—The Scandal off the Screen* (Toronto, ON: Virgo Press, 1981), p. 24.
31 Michael Posner, 'Chief of Censor Board Quits for Personal Reasons', *Globe and Mail*, 2 November 2002: R2.
32 *Annual Report 2002/2003* (Ontario Film Review Board, Report from the Chair: 4), 2003.
33 Jay Stone, 'Fat Girl Furore Proves Film Board's Irrelevance', B1.
34 Moody quoted in Murray Whyte, 'Censors Lift Ontario Ban on Fat Girl', *Toronto Star*, 30 January 2003: A29.
35 John McKay, 'Ontario Film Review Board Approves Previously Banned French Film Fat Girl', *Canadian Press Newswire*, 29 January 2003.

18

Invisible Censors, Opaque Laws and Surveilled Subjects

Julian Petley

Once, it was relatively easy to know who the 'official' censors of the moving image were, although it was usually much more difficult to ascertain exactly what they'd been doing and why. But today a 'legacy' censor such as the British Board of Film Classification not only details its activities in highly informative Annual Reports, but it has even permitted one of its senior staff to edit a detailed, candid and sometimes highly critical account of its past and recent activities.[1] On the other hand, the practices of the Classification and Rating Administration of the Motion Picture Association of America (now simply the Motion Picture Association), as documented and critiqued in, for example, *This Film Is Not Yet Rated* (2006) and Lewis, are still opaque and secretive.[2]

Such opacity and lack of public accountability are, however, disturbing characteristics of the new and 'invisible' censors of the online age. As Daniel Biltereyst and Roel Vande Winkel noted in *Silencing Cinema: Film Censorship around the World*, the renewed interest in film censorship today is

> part of a wider awareness of the importance of different types of control and surveillance in the field of media and communication. This is closely related to a wider set of transformations such as the growth of the internet and the availability of new sophisticated surveillance

Julian Petley, "Invisible Censors, Opaque Laws and Surveilled Subjects" in: *The Screen Censorship Companion: Critical Explorations in the Control of Film and Screen Media*. University of Exeter Press (2024). © Julian Petley. DOI: 10.47788/EUHI2366 technologies, along with the continued importance given to societal control within the new geopolitical world order.[3]

In this chapter I want to outline a number of these new control and surveillance mechanisms, and in particular to show how state and corporate actors frequently collude in censorship of one kind or another. In the case of the latter this may be for commercial reasons, such as the desire for access to lucrative markets in which media content is heavily regulated, as happens in China. And in the case of the online world, service providers may engage in self-censorship for fear of being accused of publishing images, both moving and still, which might be deemed to be illegal under a wide range of laws of which they may not be immediately cognisant—for example, those regarding terrorism or indecency—and by agencies whose censorship operations are unfamiliar and opaque, such as those carried out by the police. However, it is not only those who distribute images online who may self-censor out of caution in the face of a confusing and sometimes authoritarian regulatory environment, since there is now an ever-growing range of images which it is actually illegal to *possess* as well, and whose presence on people's computers can be traced by the increasing surveillance by the authorities of citizens' online activity. Since this practice is now widely known, it may well encourage overcaution on the part of those using the internet, particularly if they are unfamiliar with the legal position in their own country.

Many of my specific examples will be taken from the United Kingdom, but the processes that I describe here certainly have their equivalents and analogues in other democratic countries, such as the USA and Australia.

The Censorable Internet

It was once widely assumed that the internet is essentially un-censorable and thus should be treated differently from the legacy media by policymakers and law enforcement agencies. For example, David Johnson and David Post stated in the early days of online communication that the internet 'radically subverts a system of rule-making based on borders between physical spaces, at least with respect to the claim that cyberspace should naturally be governed by territorially defined rules'.[4]

However, it soon became clear that it is perfectly possible for national governments to regulate and indeed censor the internet in numerous ways. As Jack Goldsmith and Tim Wu noted in one of the early books that punctured utopian dreams of the internet as a censor-free zone: 'The last ten years have shown that national governments have an array of techniques for controlling offshore Internet communications, and thus enforcing their laws, by exercising coercion within their borders'.[5] For example, blocking, filtering, surveillance and threatening internet users with legal action.

Thus Freedom House's 2019 report notes that of the over 3.8 billion people globally who have access to the internet, 56% live in countries where political, social or religious content is blocked online, and 46% in countries where the authorities disconnect internet or mobile networks, often for political reasons. It lists twenty-one countries in which it defines the internet as 'not free', the worst offenders including China, Russia, Saudi Arabia, Turkey, Egypt and Iran.[6]

Of course, that undemocratic countries censor a form of communication that in principle allows their subjects to access material coming from outside their borders is hardly surprising, but this should not obscure the fact that democracies too have become increasingly keen to censor the internet, although they are more likely to refer euphemistically to what they are doing as 'consumer protection'. A particularly revealing example of the latter approach was provided by the May 2021 launch in the UK of the Draft Online Safety Bill, which the government hailed as a 'milestone' in its 'fight to make the internet safe', one which would 'protect children online and tackle some of the worst abuses on social media'.[7] On the other hand, the Open Rights Group called it 'a bloated Bill [that] contains so many risks to free speech that it's hard to know where to start',[8] a view widely shared by many organizations concerned with freedom of expression online.

Internet Governance

Internet regulation in democratic countries involves both corporate and political power, frequently acting in concert. This system is best understood as a form of governance as opposed to direct governmental regulation. According to the definition developed by the UN Working Group on Internet Governance, 'governance is the development and application by Governments, the private sector and civil society, in their respective roles, of shared principles, norms, rules, decision-making procedures and programmes that shape the evolution and use of the Internet'.[9] As Des Freedman puts it:

> The preferred mechanisms of contemporary governance regimes are increasingly self-regulation, where industry modifies its behaviour in response to a set of agreed codes, and co-regulation, where industry works in partnership with the state to design and enforce adherence to rules.[10]

And although governments of non-democratic countries routinely practise direct online (and indeed offline) censorship, companies, whether domestic or foreign, that wish to operate in such countries are frequently prepared to do their governments' bidding, which results in insidious, and frequently invisible, forms of self-censorship. This is particularly the case in highly lucrative markets, such as China. Take, for example, the case of American films in China, whether streamed or shown in cinemas. In 2020 and 2021, China actually outstripped the United States as the world's most lucrative film market. In 2019, American films screened in China earned $2.6 billion (£2 billion), even though there is a strict government-imposed annual quota on Hollywood imports (thirty-four at the time of writing) in order to protect indigenous productions. This may help to explain why no Marvel film was released in China after *Spider-Man: Far from Home* in July 2019.

Since 2018, media censorship has fallen under the remit of the Publicity Department of the Chinese Communist Party, which is better known as the Central Propaganda Department. This extension of Party control has also seen censorship become even stricter than it was previously. Within this structure, all forms of film regulation are carried out by the China Film Association (CFA). Naturally this exerts control over all Chinese film production, but it also regulates imported films, and takes a particular interest in Hollywood ones, since these are so popular. This is not simply a matter of banning or cutting American films which the CFA finds in some way offensive, but, as part of China's soft power strategy, also includes trying to ensure that Hollywood films project a positive image of the country.

It is because the Chinese authorities have such power over which Hollywood films are allowed to enter the Chinese market that, as a report by PEN America puts it, they can

> pressure Hollywood studios to cooperate with censors: play ball, and you will be rewarded with entry into the nation's cinemas, and possibly receive additional preferential treatment in the form of coveted release dates or preferential advertising arrangements. Refuse, and your movie's financial success will be deeply impacted. Studios that invest millions in their movies have substantial economic incentives to comply with requests from Chinese censors, particularly if such studios have additional business interests in China.[11]

As an article in *The Atlantic* sardonically observed: 'What critics might call censorship, Hollywood studios might label a market entry strategy'.[12] This practice is also discussed in Richard Maltby's chapter in this collection.

Consequently, Hollywood studios are frequently prepared to accede to the Chinese censors' demands, either by making cuts or by creating a version of a film for the Chinese market only. Problem areas for the censors include sex, LGBTQI+ issues, crime, violence, the supernatural, or portrayals of China that Beijing sees as negative. For example, three minutes of scenes in *Bohemian Rhapsody* (2018) depicting same-sex relationships were cut. *Pirates of the Caribbean: Dead Man's Chest* (2006) was banned for including ghosts and cannibalism. *Alien: Covenant* (2017) lost some six minutes for violence and a same-sex kiss between androids. When *Fight Club* (1999) was streamed on Tencent Video, China's largest streaming service, the ending, in which it appears that modern civilization is in the process of being destroyed, was replaced by a title card explaining that the plot was foiled by the authorities, and the ending of *Minions: The Rise of Gru* (2022) was also changed to make it more morally acceptable. A major Tibetan character was whitewashed out of Marvel's *Doctor Strange* (2016). The Taiwanese flag on Tom Cruise's bomber jacket disappeared from the trailer for *Top Gun: Maverick* (2022). And the release of *Nomadland* (2020) was cancelled when an eight-year-old interview with its director Chloé Zhao came to light in which she called China 'a place where there are lies everywhere'.[13]

However, the studios may be prepared to go further than acceding to cuts, and, in versions of films intended for global distribution, to set certain scenes in China or include popular Chinese actors in order to portray an image of China that will appeal to the authorities there. Furthermore, as the PEN America report explains:

> Hollywood's posture of cooperation with CCP censors is increasingly advancing into something more: proactive anticipation of the censor's objections, and corresponding self-censorship. To reduce the chances that reviewers will delay or reject their film, studios have developed informal feedback loops—with fixers, distribution partners, consultants, and even with the censors themselves—to ensure they stay within the lines that Beijing has drawn.[14]

It is at such points that self-censorship segues into invisible censorship, and the demands of an undemocratic country impact negatively upon what film viewers outside its bounds are able to view on their screens.

Returning to democratic states, in these self-regulation is favoured by online industry actors, since they prefer to operate in a lightly regulated environment. However, the extent to which self-regulation enables publicly accountable regulation is limited; furthermore, self-regulatory bodies are almost invariably dominated by the most powerful interests in the industry in question. Meanwhile governments, well aware of the importance of the internet for economic development, have generally adopted a pro-business approach to it, including in the matter of regulation. What, however, needs to be stressed here is that the codes and regulations which self-regulatory industry bodies devise and enforce have their origin in the laws of the land. Thus although governments to a considerable extent delegate internet regulation to powerful corporate intermediaries, they still exercise a significant degree of control over online structures and contents via the legislative process.

The Internet Gatekeepers

Chief among the intermediaries are the internet service providers (ISPs). As Goldsmith and Wu put it, these are

> the obvious first target for a strategy of intermediary control. It can be great fun to talk about the Internet as a formless cyberspace. But [...] underneath it all is an ugly physical transport infrastructure: copper wires, fibre-optic cables, and the specialised routers and switches that direct information from place to place. The physical network is by necessity a local asset, owned by phone companies, cable companies, and other service providers who are already some of the most regulated companies on earth. This makes ISPs the most important and most obvious gatekeepers to the Internet. Governments can achieve a large degree of control by focusing on the most important ISPs that service the majority of Internet users.[15]

What this means in practice is that governments can exert considerable indirect and delegated control over both the conditions in which the physical network is permitted to operate and the nature of the material which it is allowed to carry. This establishes what Freedman calls 'a new dynamic of regulatory power in which it becomes increasingly difficult to distinguish between public and private sources of regulation and between self- and co-regulation'.[16]

Absent a robust governance framework that is transparent, publicly accountable and committed to human rights principles, there is a very real danger that the intermediaries, or 'internet information gatekeepers' as they have also been described, become agents of what European Digital Rights call 'devolved law enforcement'.[17] Whereas in pre-internet days someone accused of infringing, say, the Obscene Publications Act could contest the case in both the courtroom and the court of public opinion, the role of the judiciary is being increasingly sidelined in the online age. This is because the intermediaries are frequently acting as 'police, judge, jury and executioner with regard to alleged infringements of either the law or of their own terms and conditions, which may be stricter than the law'.[18] And they are doing so in the absence of democratic, transparent and publicly accountable decision-making processes governing how they are exercising their powers. This 'leads to situations where private companies and their priorities establish which aspects of the law are enforced, how they are enforced and what sanctions are imposed in the event that a private company considers that a given action is illegal'.[19]

To describe this process as 'self-regulation' is seriously misleading given the number of instances in which intermediaries have been pressured by government into policing online communications, often with little regard for the relevant laws and for human rights considerations. Furthermore, as European Digital Rights argue, this has led to a situation in which intermediaries increasingly regulate the behaviour of their consumers at the behest and on behalf of government: 'Their Internet access is being increasingly blocked, logged, spied upon, restricted and subjected to sanctions imposed by the intermediaries, who fear legal liability for the actions of their clients'.[20] In such a situation,

> essentially every aspect of our online activity is subject to regulation by private companies, based on and motivated by—in various proportions at various moments—public relations concerns, business priorities, threats of strict regulatory interventions and worries about civil and even criminal liability.[21]

This poses a considerable threat to not only the democratic potential of the internet but indeed to citizens' fundamental right to freedom of communication, as enshrined in Article 10 of the European Convention on Human Rights and Article 19 of the Universal Declaration of Human Rights. These, it should be remembered, protect the right not only to receive but also to impart information, something which is greatly facilitated by the internet and which makes it a far more open medium than any of the legacy media.

The Internet Watch Foundation

The issue of how online censorship takes place invisibly, and who actually carries it out, can seem rather abstract, if not paranoid, so how this can operate in practice can be illustrated by examining the workings of particular bodies. To this end I will focus on the Internet Watch Foundation (IWF) in the UK.

In Britain, as in countries of the European Union, ISPs were originally regarded as publishers of the material which they carried, and thus as legally responsible for it, even though most of it originated with third parties. After being repeatedly threatened by the police (threats which were greatly amplified by the press, which already regarded the internet as a serious competitor) for carrying allegedly illegal material, the major ISPs set up the IWF (initially known as the Safety Net Foundation) in 1996, a self-regulatory industry body to which members of the public could report internet content which they deemed illegal, particularly in the area of child abuse material. However, after three years the government decided that the IWF was insufficiently effective, and its workings were reviewed for the Department of Trade and Industry and the Home Office by the consultants KPMG and Denton Hall. As a result, a number of changes were made to its role and structure, and it was re-launched in early 2000, endorsed by the government and the Department of Trade and Industry (DTI), which played a 'facilitating role in its creation' according to a DTI spokesman. At the time, Patricia Hewitt, then Minister for E-Commerce, gave it her blessing by stating that 'the Internet Watch Foundation plays a vital role in combating criminal material on the Net'.[22]

The IWF describes itself as 'an independent, non-profit charitable organisation working in partnership with a range of other organisations from the private, public and NGO sectors'.[23] According to a Memorandum of Understanding between the Crown Prosecution Service (CPS) and the National Police Chiefs' Council (NPCC):

> The IWF is funded by service providers, mobile network operators, software and hardware manufacturers and other associated partners. It is supported by UK law enforcement and CPS and works in partnership with the Government to provide a 'hotline' for individuals or organisations to report potentially illegal content and to seek out illegal content online.[24]

And in 2008 Professor Tanya Byron in her review *Safer Children in a Digital World* described it as 'lying at the heart of the Government's safeguarding strategy'.[25] As Emily Laidlaw has noted in a highly detailed study of the IWF,[26] there is clearly a relationship between the IWF and government, 'although it is not formally provided for in a legislative document'.[27] Although the IWF was originally set up and now operates with strong governmental support, its workings have never been subject to sustained parliamentary or public scrutiny or debate.[28]

However, after a human rights audit was carried out in 2013 by the former Director of Public Prosecutions, Lord Macdonald of River Glaven, the IWF accepted that it is a public authority under the Human Rights Act. It is also subject to an independent organizational external review, but this is not well publicized, and although this applies legal principles, it is not itself a legal process, and thus does not help the relevant laws to evolve via the accumulation of legal precedent.

As the IWF is a private company and charity, and not a body set up by the Crown, statute, a government department or a minister, it lacks freedom of information obligations. Under Section 5 of the Freedom of Information Act 2005, the Secretary of State can designate a private body a public authority if it performs public functions or is contracted by the government to perform otherwise governmental functions, but this has not been done. The IWF does have a complaints and appeals process,[29] and an independent legal expert to review its decisions on appeal, but there is a lack of information about how the process works, and in particular about how many decisions have been made and the reasons for them. Furthermore, the complainant takes no part, after making the initial complaint, in what is effectively an adjudicative process. Appeal findings are not made public. As Laidlaw puts it, 'the effect of this is to make the complaints procedure inaccessible, unpredictable and, arguably, illegitimate'.[30]

After the EU Electronic Commerce Directive came into force in 2000 (although not until 2002 in the UK), Internet Service Providers (ISPs) were classified as simply conduits, carriers of information rather like the postal services.[31] This recognized that an ISP is not a publisher, and that it does not have editorial control over material posted on its servers by third parties. However, if an ISP obtains knowledge (in this instance, notification by the IWF) of illegal content held on their servers and fails to remove it, then they render themselves liable to prosecution. This was spelled out by the 1998 DTI document *Net Benefit: The Electronic Commerce Agenda for the UK*, which stated that:

> Primary responsibility for illegal material on the Internet would clearly lie with the individual or entity posting it. Under UK law, however, an Internet Service Provider (ISP) which has been made aware of the illegal material (or activity) and has failed to take reasonable steps to remove the material could also be liable to prosecution as an accessory to a crime.[32]

According to the above-mentioned Memorandum of Understanding between the CPS and the NPCC, the IWF's first task in the case of potentially illegal content which is reported to it is to assess and judge that material on behalf of UK law enforcement agencies:

> If potentially illegal content is hosted in the UK the IWF will work with the relevant service provider and British law enforcement to have the content 'taken down' and assist as necessary to have the offender(s) responsible for distributing the offending content detected. In cases

where the potentially illegal content is hosted outside the UK, the IWF
will work where possible in partnership with hotlines across the world
and various Law Enforcement bodies at home and abroad to have the
content investigated.

The Code of Practice of the Internet Service Providers Association (ISPA)
notes that:

> ISPA membership does not automatically confer membership
> of the IWF but Members are encouraged to consider direct IWF
> membership, to take careful consideration of all other IWF notices
> and recommendations, and to provide ISPA with a point of contact
> to receive notices from the IWF.[33]

It would surely be a very foolhardy ISP that refused to avail itself of the
IWF's services, and the extent to which this system of regulation is actually
'voluntary' is clearly open to question.

The IWF is concerned with child sexual abuse material, which it
assesses according to the levels detailed in the Sentencing Council's *Sexual
Offences Definitive Guideline*.[34] The section headed 'Indecent Photographs
of Children' outlines the different categories of child sexual abuse material,
which it is an offence to possess, distribute or produce, as follows:
- Category A: Images involving penetrative sexual activity; images
  involving sexual activity with an animal or sadism.
- Category B: Images involving non-penetrative sexual activity.
- Category C: Other indecent images not falling within categories A
  or B.

The IWF operates a blacklist of about 5,000 URLs which depict
allegedly indecent images of children, or advertisements for or links to
such content, on a publicly available website.[35] This list is made available
to ISPs, mobile operators, search engine services and filtering companies,
who have agreed to block the material whilst steps to have it removed
are in progress. For example, BT has developed the Cleanfeed technology
for its broadband services which blocks any URL on the blacklist. Any
child sexual abuse content found on a UK website is typically removed
within hours of discovery, so this content is not added to the list. For
obvious reasons, the blacklist cannot be seen by members of the public,
but, as Laidlaw argues, the need for a certain amount of secrecy 'does not
obviate the need for a democratic, transparent and accountable governance
structure. If anything, it makes the need for due process more critical'.[36]
The IWF does recommend, although it does not insist, that users trying to
access a blocked URL encounter a 'splash page' which states:

Access has been denied by your internet access provider because this page may contain indecent images of children as identified by the Internet Watch Foundation.

Deliberate attempts to access this or related material may result in you committing a criminal offence.

The consequences of accessing such material are likely to be serious. People arrested risk losing their family and friends, access to children (including their own) and their jobs.[37]

We now come on to the specific laws which govern what kinds of material the IWF puts on its blacklist.

Indecency and Images of Children

Under the Protection of Children Act 1978 (as amended by the Sexual Offences Act 2003), it is an offence to take, make, permit to be taken, distribute, show, possess with intent to distribute, or advertise indecent photographs or derivatives of photographs of children under the age of eighteen (this was raised from sixteen in 2003).[38] The 'making' of such images includes downloading them on a computer; thus accessing such content online is a serious and imprisonable criminal offence.

To the problems of the IWF's ambiguous status and lack of transparency should now be added the problem of defining indecency when it comes to images which fall into Category C. Images showing the sexual abuse of real children are not exactly hard to recognize; they are clearly abhorrent and their making has involved the commission of an extremely serious crime. However, this third category of potentially indecent images complicates the matter considerably, raising questions about how the Protection of Children Act is interpreted by the IWF, and about the degree of legal certainty regarding their judgements and any subsequent actions taken by the ISPs, the CPS and the police. The IWF is careful to note that 'we refer to content as *potentially* criminal because a definitive legal judgement is a matter for the Courts' and that the content of the URLs that it blacklists is '*likely* to be an offence to view, download, distribute, or possess in the UK' (emphases mine),[39] but one of the problems with a formal legal process is that it is a time-consuming way of dealing with an issue that may well require a speedy resolution. However, the pressures to remove potentially illegal material of this kind are so great that the likelihood of an ISP refusing to block a URL on the IWF blacklist and challenging in court any consequent action by the Director of Public Prosecutions (DPP) and the police is vanishingly unlikely, given the torrent of negative publicity which would most certainly follow and which would constitute a PR disaster for the ISP in question.

In this respect, it is worth noting the ISPA's response to the House of Lords Communications Committee's Inquiry 'To Regulate or Not To Regulate' in 2018, which resulted in the report *Regulating in a Digital World*.[40] This is not only relevant to the matter of potentially indecent material online in the UK but engages in the much wider issue of the competency of ISPs *anywhere* to judge the legality of *any* sort of material which they carry. Thus in their response, the ISPA attests to

> the difficulty in accurately identifying illegal content without the assistance of a judicial process. Non-judicial competent authorities cannot be expected to have the same impartiality, legal expertise and interest in balancing competing rights as judicial authorities [...] ISPA maintains that intermediaries should not be asked to be judge and jury and that notices should be filed by competent authorities, ideally a court or other independent and impartial body qualified and with legitimacy to make these kinds of decisions [...] Furthermore, content control mechanisms should always respect due process and be backed by some form of statute, with removal-at-source as the default content control measure, with access blocking to be used as a targeted and temporary resort in certain circumstances. If trusted flagging mechanisms are used, clear standards and rules should be provided by the Government in order to avoid the infringement or [*sic*] rights.[41]

The CPS Legal Guidance on Indecent and Prohibited Images of Children states that whether an image is indecent

> is for the tribunal to consider the issue of indecency by reference to an objective test, rather than applying their wholly subjective views of the matter (*R v. Neal* [2011] EWCA Crim 461) taking into consideration the age of the child (*R v Owen* [1988] 86 Cr. App. R. 291).[42]

The question of what constitutes indecency in terms of the Protection of Children Act is clearly a complex and controversial one, and although it is one with which the IWF is centrally concerned, it also takes us usefully beyond their offices to consider the role of others, most notably the police and the Crown Prosecution Service, in the regulation of certain kinds of images.

'Recognised standards of propriety'

The offence of indecency (which had previously featured in the Customs and Excise Act 1952 and the Post Office Act 1953) is at the opposite end of the same continuum as obscenity, with the threshold for indecency being set at a lower level than that for obscenity. Briefly, obscenity involves an element of corruption, indecency a contravention of standards of taste and conventional morality. The *Stamford* judgement noted above by the CPS emphasized the key role played in indecency cases by 'recognised standards of propriety', and in *Knuller v. DPP* (1973) Lord Reid stated that indecency 'includes anything which an ordinary decent man or woman would find shocking, disgusting or revolting'.[43] In short, jurors are trusted to know indecency when they see it and expected to act as the custodians of recognized standards of decency. This is what, in the view of the CPS, constitutes an 'objective' test.

However, it's extremely difficult to understand what is meant by 'objective' in this context, and the case referred to above by the CPS, *R v. Neal*, is really of no assistance.[44] This concerned a successful appeal against a verdict in a case in which the defendant had been found guilty on five counts of possessing indecent images of children. Both the judge who had granted the appeal and Lord Justice Richards at the Court of Appeal agreed that the Recorder in the case, when instructing the jury, had failed to make clear to them that 'they were to apply the recognised objective standard of right-thinking people, not their own subjective view'. But the case also vividly illustrates just how slippery the concept of 'indecency' in this context actually is. As Lord Justice Richards pointed out in granting the appeal, all the supposedly indecent images were contained in books of photographs by the well-known photographers David Hamilton, Sally Mann and Jock Sturges, books which were available from WHSmith, Waterstones, Tesco and Amazon. One of the Mann images had also appeared in an article in the *Guardian* in May 2010 which was published in both its online and offline editions.

It is important to stress that these definitional problems are not confined to the UK, and that the problem of where to draw the lines when it comes to certain kinds of images of children is a common one across the globe.[45] Different countries have different levels of acceptability and consequently different laws, and the situation is made more complicated by the fact that in federal countries such as the USA and Australia, matters can vary from state to state. However, I want to concentrate here on how indecency has been interpreted by the authorities in the UK, as it illustrates in a particularly acute form the kinds of problems thrown up by any attempt legally to codify images of children. And the fact that Index on Censorship has felt the need to issue a detailed information pack on this issue shows just how fraught the legal situation in this area has become in the UK.[46] Those interested in wider global legal developments are recommended Gillespie and Ost,[47] and an authoritative historical overview of the situation in the USA is provided by Heins.[48] Well-informed and level-headed discussions of representations of children which some, in the UK and elsewhere, have found indecent include Newnham and Townsend, Steiner, Warner, Morrison, Higonnet and Ost.[49]

'A mess'

That the indecency provisions in the Protection of Children Act have proved to be so problematic is hardly surprising given the conditions of near-hysteria in which the original bill was rushed, largely unconsidered, through both Houses of Parliament in 1977–78.[50] This was on the back of a campaign by the pressure group ABUSE, led by moral reformer Mary Whitehouse, a flood of lurid and inaccurate press stories, and the intervention of the highly controversial Chief Constable of Greater Manchester, James Anderton, whose views on moral matters can be gauged by his infamous remark in December 1986 that people with AIDS were 'swirling about in a human cesspit of their own making'.[51]

One of the very few parliamentarians to oppose the Bill was Lord Houghton of Sowerby, who repeatedly made the point that children were perfectly well protected by already existing legislation, and argued that:

> There is no doubt that the whole law on indecency and obscenity is in a mess, but it is in a mess because of the difficulties of definition. Attempts are made to define what we mean by the use of certain words, and 'indecency' is not defined in this Bill any more than 'obscenity' is defined in the obscenity laws. It is bound to be a mess and therefore it is bound to be left to the judgment of juries and courts as to what is indecent and what is obscene. We know that there have been some quite surprising results from attempts to get convictions under existing law, and I believe that we may encounter the same problems again.[52]

And how correct he turned out to be, as the examples below demonstrate. It needs to be borne in mind here that none of these cases involved successful prosecutions, but the two main questions that need to be asked in the present context are: a) what would the IWF and the ISPs carrying the images have done had they been online; and b) what kind of a chilling effect have cases like these had on online users who are not in search of actual child abuse material?

'Transfixed by childhood sexuality'

The indecency provisions in the Protection of Children Act apply equally to moving and still images. Although it is the latter which have occasioned the most controversy, in the UK as elsewhere, a number of films have also raised concerns. For example, Jess Franco's *Women in Cellblock 9/Tropical Inferno* (1978) remains banned in Britain by the BBFC because one of the actresses who appears in it, Susan Hemingway, was under eighteen when the film was made, and is naked for much of the time and in some fairly steamy scenes. Similarly, the scenes in which she appears naked in Franco's *Love Letters of a Portuguese Nun* (1977) were cut out by the Board.

In March 1978, just as the Protection of Children Bill was passing through Parliament, Louis Malle's *Pretty Baby*, in which a ten-year-old Brooke Shields briefly appears naked in a couple of scenes, was submitted to the BBFC. It was seen by not only the Board's president, Lord Harlech, but also by representatives from the Home Office and the Director of Public Prosecutions. Opinions concerning whether it might fall foul of the new law were divided, and the Board's director, James Ferman, originally asked the distributors to re-submit it the following year, by which time he hoped that various test cases would indicate where juries would draw the line on indecent images of children. But the film was then seen by other members of the BBFC, Customs and Excise and the Williams Committee, which was discussing the reform of the Obscene Publications Act, and details of these screenings were leaked to the press. Thus Ferman decided to wait only until the Act passed into law in July 1978, and in August the Board asked the distributor to make two cuts to scenes in which Shields appears naked, one in a bathroom and one on a sofa. Malle agreed to the first, but objected to the second. In the end, it was agreed to darken the sofa scene in order to obscure the lower half of Shields's body, and the bathroom scene was cut by six seconds. The film was passed with an X rating, and the Attorney-General announced to Parliament that the DPP would not take any action against it. Nonetheless, Cardiff City Council banned the film from the city's cinemas.

Pretty Baby was released uncut on video in 1981, as at that time videos were not subject to BBFC classification. Following the passing of the Video Recordings Act 1984, the video was considered by the BBFC in June 1987. By now, the examiners felt that the initial censorship decisions had possibly been an overcautious response to the new legislation, and after the film had been viewed by the Board's presidents and vice-presidents, it was passed uncut in September 1987. In 2006 it was resubmitted to the BBFC for DVD release, and passed uncut with an 18 rating.[53]

What this episode demonstrates is the degree of uncertainty and caution that the notion of indecency introduces into the censorship process. A further illustration is provided by *Lolita* (1997), which starred fifteen-year-old Dominique Swain. In the USA this was censored by the MPAA to achieve an R rating, and this was the version distributed internationally. It was submitted to the BBFC in 1998, who passed it uncut. However, when the DVD was submitted in 2000, the BBFC insisted on the deletion of two extras, which were more explicit versions of two scenes, even though, as in all Swain's naked scenes, Dawn Mauer was used as a body double. As the BBFC announced:

> Our main concern with these highly eroticised scenes is that they might invite feelings of arousal towards a child. We have a particular concern in the context of DVD extras where the scenes in question can be readily accessed and replayed at any speed. The obvious sexualisation of a 14 year old girl with the use of such provocative detail must raise concerns about the potential misuse of this material by those predisposed to seek illegal sexual encounters.[54]

Thus even though an actor in a film may themselves be over eighteen, unlike the character they are playing, if they appear naked in a film then those scenes will not necessarily be immune to censorship, nor indeed to prosecution under sections 62 to 68 of the Coroners and Justice Act 2009 (see below).

On the other hand, films in which underage actors have appeared naked have escaped both censorship and prosecution—consider, for example, Jenny Agutter at sixteen in *Walkabout* (1971); Nastassja Kinski at thirteen in *Falsche Bewegung/Wrong Move* (1975), fourteen in *To the Devil a Daughter* (1976) and seventeen in *Così come sei/Stay As You Are* (1978); Brooke Shields—again—at fourteen in *The Blue Lagoon* (1980), although this uses a body double, and at sixteen in *Endless Love* (1981); and finally Phoebe Cates at seventeen in the *Blue Lagoon* knock-off *Paradise* (1982). That these films have been passed uncut by the BBFC and have not been subject to prosecution indicates just how slippery the concept of indecency is when applied to young people appearing naked in films, but anyone possessing an image or images from the relevant scenes, let alone distributing them online, could possibly render themselves liable to the threat of prosecution.

In 1991 Lawrence Chard was arrested and charged for taking around thirty pictures of his wife and children in their garden. The children, who had been swimming, were naked. The film processors tipped off the police, who arrested Chard in front of his children, who were then quizzed by social workers. When the case came to court fourteen months later he was unanimously acquitted, but by now the family's life had been wrecked; they were forced to change their names and move to a different part of the country. As a result, the magazine *Amateur Photographer* launched a Campaign for Common Sense, aimed at photographic processors, following which a whole string of similar cases came to light.

In November 1995 the ITN newsreader Julia Somerville and her partner were questioned into the early hours by police about photographs of their seven-year-old daughter naked in the bath. They had taken these to Boots to be processed, and the processing staff had called the police. One or other of these two parties then gave, or far more likely, sold, the story to *The Sun*, and the inevitable tabloid frenzy then followed. After four weeks the CPS announced that it was letting the matter drop.

Professional photographers have also been victims of police attention. For instance, Ron Oliver is a renowned photographer specializing in family portraits who has sometimes been asked by parents to photograph their children naked.[55] In January 1993 police raided his studio ('next door to a playschool' as the *Daily Mail* obligingly noted)[56] and seized his entire body of work—more than 20,000 prints. He was arrested and held for twenty-four hours, but when no charges were forthcoming after seven months he and his family decided to leave the UK and settle in the Netherlands. They still live abroad.

Two months later, Graham Ovenden, an internationally respected artist, art critic and photographer who specializes in pictures of children, sometimes naked, was arrested, along with Oliver and two others. He was alleged by the *Daily Mail* to be 'part of a porn ring' whose victims 'are believed to be aged eight and upwards' and which had been the subject of a 'secret two-month investigation by the Scotland Yard's Obscene Publications Squad'.[57] Many of the 2,500 works seized were part of Ovenden's extensive collection of Victorian photographs, including works by George Bernard Shaw and Lewis Carroll, and much of his own work that was seized was already in the public domain. In reality, the 'porn ring' was simply a loose association of artists which included Peter Blake, Graham Arnold and David Inshaw, all of whom had previously been members of the Pre-Raphaelite-inspired Brotherhood of Ruralists.[58] After a campaign by Sir Hugh Casson, David Hockney and Laurie Lee among others, and after what the *Mail* called 'months of often heated talks with detectives',[59] the charges against Ovenden were dropped and his property returned, although no apology was forthcoming.

In November 2006 Ovenden's house was again raided, and as a result he was charged with sixteen counts of creating indecent photographs or pseudo-photographs of children, and two counts of possessing 121 indecent photographs or pseudo-photographs of children. The case did not come to court until 2009, but on 22 October, after less than two days, the jury was discharged and a new trial date set. On 9 April 2010, after a five-minute hearing, the case was thrown out by the judge as two of the police officers who had searched his home in 2006 failed to turn up. The police declined to explain themselves and the CPS to launch an appeal; they also refused to disclose how much the investigation had cost the taxpayer. In the *Daily Telegraph*, Ovenden described the police as 'totally and utterly transfixed by childhood sexuality'.[60]

Robert Mapplethorpe's photograph of a three-year-old girl, 'Rosie', was removed from an exhibition of the artist's work at London's Hayward Gallery in September 1996 after its staff took 'advice' from the Clubs and Vice Squad of the Metropolitan Police. The picture's subject, Rosie Bowdrey, then twenty-two, was quoted in the *Independent* as saying 'I think this is all so stupid, everyone should see the picture'. She also described it as 'a very, very sweet picture, it captures childhood innocence'.[61]

In March 2001 the Saatchi Gallery in London, which had mounted an exhibition entitled *I Am a Camera*, was visited by the same police force. Clearly prompted by journalists from the *News of the World* (which fulminated against 'a revolting exhibition of perversion masquerading as art' and a 'degrading exploitation of child nudity for commercial gain'),[62] they tried to insist on the removal of two pictures which Tierney Gearon had taken of her children. They also threatened to prosecute the publisher of the exhibition catalogue unless he removed it from distribution, and voiced concerns about a picture by Nan Goldin. However, both the gallery and the publisher made it clear that they would defend any legal action, and they were strongly supported by leading figures in the cultural establishment (who, predictably, were then pilloried by sections of the press). Shortly thereafter the CPS instructed the police to drop the case, as there was insufficient evidence to provide a realistic prospect of conviction. According to the *Daily Mail*, the decision was made 'despite strong protests from the police', who feared that a 'dangerous precedent has been set which will help lawyers representing sex offenders' and made clear that they would be watching out for such exhibitions in future.[63] Highly significantly in the present context, the police argued with regard to one particular image that had it appeared on the internet, it would have 'automatically' led to indecency charges, which prompts one to wonder what a) the attitude of the IWF would have been in the circumstance; and b) whether the relevant ISP would have defended it as robustly as did the gallery.

In October 2007 the Nan Goldin photo about which the police had expressed concerns in 2001, 'Klara and Edda Belly-Dancing', was once again the subject of their attention. The Baltic Centre for Contemporary Art in Gateshead had intended to show it as part of an exhibition of Goldin's work owned by Elton John, entitled *Thanksgiving*, which had been shown without any problems in numerous other countries. However, in a clear demonstration of the chilling effect of the Saatchi incident, the gallery took advice from Northumbria Police, and, as a result, withdrew the picture the day before the exhibition opened. Nine days later Elton John insisted on its closure. On 26 October, Kerrie Bell, head of the CPS Northumbria South Unit, stated that in order to consider the photograph indecent, the CPS would have had to be satisfied that standards of propriety had changed so much since the Saatchi exhibition that it would be likely that a court would now conclude the image was indecent. In her view, this was not the case, but, of course, by now the damage had been done, and it is difficult to explain the actions of the police as anything other than an attempt to dissuade others from displaying such images in future.

Finally in this section, we return to the figure of Brooke Shields. At the age of ten, she had posed for the New York photographer Garry Gross, who was regularly employed by Shields's mother to photograph her daughter, then a model with the Ford agency. In one of his series with Shields, which was made in 1975 and was part of his project 'The Woman in the Child', a number of images show her naked in a bath. Her mother gave Gross full rights to exploit the images of her daughter, and a number of photographs from the series were published in 1975 in Gross's collection 'Little Women' and in 1976 in *Sugar and Spice: Surprising and Sensuous Images of Women*, a Playboy Press publication.

In 1981 Shields attempted to buy back the negatives, claiming that her mother had agreed to the images being published in one publication only, but after a lengthy legal battle the court decided that she was bound by her mother's contract with Gross, which made no such stipulation. She then argued that the publication of the images caused her distress and embarrassment—a difficult tack given the nature of her film appearances noted above—and although the court argued that the photographs were not sexually suggestive, provocative or pornographic they stipulated that they could not be shown in any pornographic magazine.

The contemporary artist Richard Prince then re-photographed and re-contextualized one of the images, which showed Shields standing naked in a bath, covered in body oil and made up in a fashion that caused her to resemble a Playboy 'Playmate', and gave it the title 'Spiritual America'. In 1992 he decided that he wanted to include the picture in an exhibition of his work at the Whitney Museum in New York, and bought the rights to it from Gross for $2,000. It was also shown in a retrospective of Prince's work at the Guggenheim Museum in New York in 2007.[64]

However, when in September 2009 Tate Modern in London attempted to include Prince's image in an exhibition entitled *Pop Life*, officers from the Obscene Publications Branch of the Metropolitan Police, prompted by press articles, warned the gallery that it could be illegal to show it. The Tate immediately withdrew it, and also the exhibition catalogue, which it then reissued without the offending item.

It is not particularly difficult to find online an uncensored image of both 'Spiritual America' and Gross's original, and indeed of the other pictures taken by Gross of Shields naked in the bath. This raises the key question of whether downloading them, and thus 'possessing' them according to the Protection of Children Act, might constitute a criminal offence. Notwithstanding the vagueness of the notion of 'indecency' with which the Act operates, the police have shown themselves all too eager to try to enforce it, as the above examples demonstrate. It might be argued that in a number of the cases discussed here they have been successfully seen off, in spite of the best efforts of sections of the press, but the fact remains that a lone individual targeted by the police does not have at their disposal the same forces as the Baltic Centre or the Saatchi Gallery. Unless advised by a solicitor well versed in the appropriate legislation (actually quite a rare being) and able to afford their services (difficult given the savage cutbacks in legal aid), someone arrested for an indecency offence is all too likely to accept a caution or simply to plead guilty—not least in order to avoid the embarrassment of a trial in a local court, with the police briefing against them in the local media, and possibly even at the national level too.

This chapter has repeatedly raised the question of what might have happened if these examples of alleged or potential indecency had been located online, and a possible answer is provided by the events following 5 December 2008. This is when the IWF decided to take on that bastion of free expression online, Wikipedia.

Following a single complaint, the IWF blacklisted a Wikipedia article containing an image of the cover of the Scorpions album *Virgin Killer*, which depicts a naked prepubescent girl; this it regarded as coming within the ambit of the indecency provisions of the Protection of Children Act. The decision was taken in consultation with law enforcement in the shape of the Child Exploitation and Online Protection agency (CEOP). In a dramatic demonstration of the censorship capabilities of the Cleanfeed system, the page almost immediately became unavailable to the vast bulk of British internet users. Furthermore, for related technical reasons, people found themselves unable to edit other parts of the site, and in some cases access to the whole site slowed to a crawl. Following this, the IWF also received a complaint about the same image being available on the Amazon website. However, rather than blocking the commercial online giant in one of its busiest weeks of the year, and following representations from Wikipedia, it reversed its original decision on 10 December on the basis of the 'contextual issues involved in this specific case and in the light of the length of time the image has existed and its wide availability'.[65]

This isn't exactly convincing, to put it mildly: either the IWF and CEOP thought the image was illegal, or they thought it wasn't. A rather more likely explanation for the IWF's volte-face is that, utterly unused to having its decisions challenged, it simply backed down before the situation spiralled out of control. But whatever the case, it is worth noting what Mike Godwin, chief counsel to the Wikimedia Foundation, said about the case, as it clearly relates to not simply the criticisms of the IWF raised earlier in this chapter, but to the more general concerns explored here about invisible and unaccountable censorship online. Of the appeals process he noted that when Wikipedia first challenged the blocking 'we were soon told that there had been an appeal of the block but that Wikipedia had lost. Who represented Wikipedia in that appeals process? I asked that question immediately, and discovered that, of course, no one had represented our side'. And secondly, he stated that:

> It's clear that IWF relies for its expertise on the question of whether content might be 'potentially illegal' by talking to pro-censorship law-enforcement entities. This is not the way to operate if you want to understand freedom of expression as an expansive rather than a cramped and restricted freedom. Policemen and prosecutors tend to think of all the ways they can view an act as criminal—you need civil libertarians (ideally lawyers trained in the theory of freedom of speech) to balance the perspective of law-enforcement personnel, if freedom is to mean anything in your society.[66]

Geoffrey Robertson, Britain's leading barrister in matters pertaining to freedom of expression, has stated that 'a bad law is never justified by the hope that it will be sensibly enforced'[67]—a hope which would appear to have been an entirely vain one in most of the cases discussed above, not least because of the malign and censorious role frequently played by papers such as the *Mail* and *News of the World* in encouraging and endorsing oppressive, ill-informed and heavy-handed policing. In the final analysis, however, it is the law itself which is the problem in these cases, and it is difficult to disagree with Robertson's judgement that 'a law which makes careful distinctions in every other criminal area abandons "indecent articles" to the aesthetic taste of random tribunals, reposing blind faith in subjective responses and mythical absolutes'.[68] Or as Roy Jenkins put it in 1974 when he was Home Secretary: 'The term "indecency" has no meaningful definition and should not be part of any criminal statute'.[69]

The Dangerous Cartoons Act

There is, however, another category of images of children which it is illegal to produce, distribute or possess, and this too falls within the IWF's remit. These are those covered by sections 62 to 68 of the Coroners and Justice Act 2009, which make it illegal to possess an image of a child if it is 'pornographic', 'grossly offensive, disgusting or otherwise of an obscene character', 'focuses solely or principally on a child's genitals or anal region' or involves the portrayal of a specific list of proscribed activities involving children.[70] However justifiable such a measure might appear at first sight, the problem is that the Act's definition of 'pornographic' is questionable ('of such a nature that it must reasonably be assumed to have been produced solely or principally for the purpose of sexual arousal'), and that 'grossly offensive' and 'disgusting' are highly subjective terms. Furthermore, it must be understood that the creation of the images with which the Act is concerned need not have involved actual, physical children in any way at all, since it covers moving or still images produced *by any means* and data stored *by any means* which is capable of conversion into an image. Moreover, the Act specifies that:

> Where an image shows a person the image is to be treated as an image of a child if—
>
> (a) the impression conveyed by the image is that the person shown is a child, or
>
> (b) the predominant impression conveyed is that the person shown is a child despite the fact that some of the physical characteristics shown are not those of a child.
>
> References to an image of a person include references to an image of an imaginary person.
>
> References to an image of a child include references to an image of an imaginary child.

This belt and braces approach to, some might say obsession with, images of children inevitably brings purely graphic images within reach of the law, which is why it has come to be known as the Dangerous Cartoons Act.[71] Particularly at risk here are manga images, as Abigail Bright, a barrister at Doughty Street Chambers, has pointed out:

> A vast body of commercially produced manga or manga-type, anime cartoon images depict images prohibited by English law. Consumers of mainstream manga images have reason to be circumspect about the lawfulness of exactly what is, or may come into, their possession. Whether still or moving content, this is true of mainstream manga as much as it is true of niche or specific sub-sets or genres of manga [such as Lolicon and Shotacon]. Law enforcement agencies and prosecuting authorities, national and cross-border, have flexed muscle in the investigation and prosecution of this type of offending.[72]

It is not only in the UK that the possession of certain kinds of purely graphic images of children is illegal, but very few countries have been so rigorous in attempting to draw up legislation that dots every 'i' and crosses every 't' in the lexicon of such material.[73]

Conclusion: 'We will track you down'

What is particularly notable about the laws discussed in this chapter is that they make the very *possession* of certain kinds of images of children a criminal offence, and in this they differ in a very significant respect from the Obscene Publications Act 1959, which criminalized only the production and distribution of certain kinds of material. This approach has now expanded to take in the possession of other kinds of materials, such as what Section 63 of the Criminal Justice and Immigration Act 2008 defines as 'extreme pornography' (which is why it has come to be known as the Dangerous Images Act). This no longer falls within the IWF's ambit, and as I have discussed it extensively elsewhere,[74] I won't repeat myself here. As Jacob Rowbottom has observed, the law now places much greater responsibility on the recipient of the content, but

> the responsibilities that can be expected of a possessor or viewer are distinct from those expected of a publisher. In some cases, there are concerns about the level of culpability that can be assigned to the recipient, for example, where possession resulted from a failure to delete an image that they did not seek or solicit. Clarity in the law is also particularly important so people know exactly what content to avoid. While a publisher may be expected to take legal advice to clarify how a law would be applied and to negotiate risk, an individual cannot be expected to go through such an assessment before viewing content on the internet (and such an assessment will not be possible where the specific image that will appear on screen is not known in advance).[75]

I want to conclude by stressing that the proliferation of possession offences (which also feature in the Terrorism Act 2000) has facilitated the increasing surveillance of internet users by the police and strengthened their powers to enter people's homes and offices, seize their computers and mobile devices, and search their online activity. That they have been increasingly active on this front is demonstrated by the rapidly rising number of prosecutions for possessions of indecent images of children in recent years[76]—although it is impossible to tell the proportions that fall into each of the Sentencing Council's categories cited above. It is also important to note the large number of cautions handed out by the police in this area. These are given to anyone aged ten or over for minor crimes if the person admits to an offence and agrees to be cautioned (they can be arrested and charged if they refuse). Cautions are placed on the Police National Computer, will form part of a person's criminal record and will show up if they apply for a job and their potential employer runs a check with the Disclosure and Barring Service,[77] as is standard practice in the case of jobs involving contact with young or otherwise vulnerable people. Furthermore, anybody cautioned for possessing indecent images of children, even at Category C, will be placed on the Sex Offenders Register,[78] which will have extremely serious personal consequences. The obvious advantage for the police of a caution is that it is a quick and useful mechanism that avoids the paraphernalia of a court case, and for the person cautioned it avoids the negative publicity attendant upon a court case which, as is evident from the examples noted above, the police will be only too happy to engineer.

Thus the internet user, particularly one who is unsure of the law, finds themselves in the same position as a prisoner in Jeremy Bentham's famous Panopticon, who, never certain when they are actually being watched, behaves all the time as if under surveillance, and so, as Foucault puts it, 'assumes responsibility for the constraints of power' and 'becomes the principle of his own subjection'.[79] Given the extremely serious consequences of committing the ill-defined offence of possessing indecent images of children, internet users are particularly subject to the 'chilling effect' of surveillance explored in various realms by David Lyon.[80] Indeed, it is interesting to note just how overt the threats of police surveillance have actually become in this area. Thus, for example, discussing the successful prosecution of a man arrested for using a forum containing child abuse images, Jim Gamble, Chief Executive of CEOP, stated: 'There is a simple message to those individuals [...] who think they can go to this website—or indeed any other space on the Internet—and discuss their sexual interest in children and share images. You leave a digital footprint. We will track you down and hold you to account', a comment that was obligingly reproduced widely in the press.[81] Similarly, in a response to the government's consultation on the possession of 'extreme pornography', Detective Inspector Ian Winton of the Nottinghamshire Police argued that any change in the law should be accompanied by a widespread publicity campaign which will 'inhibit from "surfing" the Internet for pornography and accessing it'.[82] We thus move ineluctably from invisible censorship to the most invidious of all forms of censorship: self-censorship.

Note: Given the consequences of publishing some of the kinds of images discussed in this chapter, it was decided not to include any illustrations herewith.

Notes

1   Edward Lamberti (ed.), *Behind the Scenes at the BBFC: Film Classification from the Silver Screen to the Digital Age* (London: BFI/Palgrave Macmillan, 2012).

2   *This Film Is Not Yet Rated* (2006); Jon Lewis, *Hollywood v. Hard Core: How the Struggle over Censorship Created the Modern Film Industry* (New York: New York University Press, 2000), pp. 42–45.

3   Daniel Biltereyst and Roel Vande Winkel (eds), *Silencing Cinema: Film Censorship around the World* (Basingstoke: Palgrave Macmillan, 2013), pp. 8–9.

4   David R. Johnson and David G. Post, 'Law and Borders: The Rise of Law in Cyberspace', *Stanford Law Review* 48.5 (1996): 1370.

5   Jack Goldsmith and Tim Wu, *Who Controls the Internet? Illusions of a Borderless World* (New York: Oxford University Press, 2006), p. viii.

6   Freedom House, *Freedom on the Net 2019: The Crisis of Social Media* (Washington, DC: Freedom House, 2019).

7   Department for Digital, Culture, Media & Sport, Home Office, and The Rt Hon Oliver Dowden CBE MP, 'Landmark Laws to Keep Children Safe, Stop Racial Hate and Protect Democracy Online Published', press release, 12 May 2021, https://www.gov.uk/government/news/landmark-laws-to-keep-children-safe-stop-racial-hate-and-protect-democracy-online-published.

8   Open Rights Group, 'Defend Democratic Expression: What's Legal To Say Should Be Legal To Type. The Online Safety Act Could Change That', https://www.openrightsgroup.org/campaign/stop-state-censorship-of-online-speech/.

9   *Report of the Working Group on Internet Governance*, June 2005, http://www.wgig.org/docs/WGIGREPORT.pdf.

10   Des Freedman, 'The Internet of Rules', in James Curran, Natalie Fenton and Des Freedman, *Misunderstanding the Internet* (Abingdon: Routledge, 2016), pp. 117–44.

11   PEN America, *Made in Hollywood, Censored by Beijing: The U.S. Film Industry and Chinese Government Influence*, 2020, https://pen.org/wp-content/uploads/2020/09/Made_in_Hollywood_Censored_by_Beiing_Report_FINAL.pdf, p. ii.

12   Shirley Li, 'How Hollywood Sold Out to China', *The Atlantic*, 10 September 2021, https://www.theatlantic.com/culture/archive/2021/09/how-hollywood-sold-out-to-china/620021/.

13   Helen Davidson, 'Nomadland references censored in China over critical comments by Chloé Zhao from 2013', *Guardian*, 8 March 2021, https://www.theguardian.com/world/2021/mar/08/nomadland-references-censored-in-china-over-critical-comments-by-chloe-zhao-from-2013.

14   PEN America, *Made in Hollywood, Censored by Beijing*, p. iii.

15   Goldsmith and Wu, *Who Controls the Internet?*, p. 73.

16   Freedman, 'The Internet of Rules', p. 138.

17   European Digital Rights, *The Slide from 'Self-Regulation' to Corporate Censorship* (Brussels: European Digital Rights, 2011), https://www.edri.org/files/EDRI_selfreg_final_20110124.pdf, p. 4.

18   Ibid.

19   Ibid., p. 14.

20   Ibid., p. 8.

21   Ibid., p. 36.

22   Quoted in Julian Petley, 'Web Control', *Index on Censorship* 38.1 (2009): 85, https://journals.sagepub.com/doi/pdf/10.1080/03064220802712266.

23   https://www.iwf.org.uk/about-us/who-we-are/.

24   *Memorandum of Understanding Between the Crown Prosecution Service (CPS) and the National Police Chiefs' Council (NPCC) concerning Section 46 Sexual Offences Act 2003*, 14 November 2022, https://www.cps.gov.uk/publication/memorandum-understanding -between-crown-prosecution-service-cps-and-national-police.

25   *Safer Children in a Digital World: The Report of the Byron Review*, https://webarchive. nationalarchives.gov.uk/ukgwa/20130401151715/http:/www.education.gov.uk/ publications/eOrderingDownload/DCSF-00334-2008.pdf.

26   Emily Laidlaw, *Regulating Speech in Cyberspace: Gatekeepers, Human Rights and Corporate Responsibility* (Cambridge: Cambridge University Press, 2015), pp. 123–71.

27   Ibid., p. 141.

28   On the status of the IWF see also C.J. Davies, 'The Hidden Censors of the Internet', *Wired*, 28 May 2009, https://www.wired.co.uk/article/the-hidden-censors-of-the -internet.

29   Available at https://www.iwf.org.uk/complaints/.

30   Laidlaw, *Regulating Speech in Cyberspace*, p. 163.

31   In spite of Britain's departure from the EU, and in spite of the passing of the Online Safety Act 2024, the situation remains the same.

32   Department of Trade and Industry, *Net Benefit: The Electronic Commerce Agenda for the UK*, October 1998, https://www.cyber-rights.org/documents/dti_net_benefit.htm.

33   ISPA UK, *Code of Practice*, https://www.ispa.org.uk/about-us/ispa-code-of-practice/.

34   Sentencing Council, *Sexual Offences Definitive Guideline*, https://www.sentencingcouncil. org.uk/wp-content/uploads/Sexual-offences-definitive-guideline-Web.pdf.

35   How this operates is described at https://www.iwf.org.uk/our-technology/our-services/ url-list/url-list-policy/.

36   Laidlaw, *Regulating Speech in Cyberspace*, p. 149.

37   Taken from https://www.iwf.org.uk/our-technology/our-services/url-list/url-blocking -good-practice/.

38   Protection of Children Act 1978, https://www.legislation.gov.uk/ukpga/1978/37.

39   At https://www.iwf.org.uk/our-technology/our-services/url-list/url-blocking-faqs/.

40   House of Lords Select Committee on Communications, *Regulating in a Digital World*, 9 March 2019, https://publications.parliament.uk/pa/ld201719/ldselect/ ldcomuni/299/299.pdf.

41   ISPA UK, *ISPA Response to Communications Committee 'The Internet: To Regulate or Not to Regulate' Inquiry*, https://www.ispa.org.uk/wp-content/uploads/180518-ISPA -Submission-to-Communications-Committee-Inquiry.pdf.

42   Crown Prosecution Service, *Indecent and Prohibited Images of Children*, 20 December 2018, https://www.cps.gov.uk/legal-guidance/indecent-and-prohibited-images -children.

43   Quoted in Geoffrey Robertson, *Obscenity* (London: Weidenfeld and Nicolson, 1979), p. 176.

44 The judgement is available at https://www.bailii.org/ew/cases/EWCA/Crim/2011/461. html.

45 For a very useful tabular account of these differences see https://en.wikipedia.org/wiki/ Legality_of_child_pornography.

46 Index on Censorship, *Art and the Law: A Guide to the Legal Framework Impacting on Artistic Freedom of Expression*, https://www.indexoncensorship.org/wp-content/ uploads/2015/07/Child-Protection_210715_interactive.pdf. Although it should be noted that Scotland actually has its own legal system.

47 Alisdair A. Gillespie, *Child Pornography: Law and Policy* (Abingdon: Routledge, 2011), pp. 64–97, 286–309; Suzanne Ost, *Child Pornography and Sexual Grooming: Legal and Societal Responses* (Cambridge: Cambridge University Press, 2009), pp. 192–233.

48 Marjorie Heins, *Not in Front of the Children: "Indecency", Censorship, and the Innocence of Youth* (New Brunswick: Rutgers University Press, 2007).

49 David Newnham and Chris Townsend, 'Pictures of Innocence', *Guardian Weekend*, 13 January 1996: 12–15; George Steiner, 'What Are You Looking At?', *Observer Review*, 13 September 1998: 15; Marina Warner, 'Outing of the Family Album', *Times Higher Education*, 4 December 1998: 25; Blake Morrison, 'No Place for This Moral Panic', *Independent*, 11 March 2001: 25; Anne Higgonet, *Pictures of Innocence: The History and Crisis of an Ideal Childhood* (London: Thames and Hudson, 1998); 'Pretty Babies', *Index on Censorship* 38.1 (2009): 105–16, https://www.eurozine.com/pretty-babies/?pdf; Ost, *Child Pornography and Sexual Grooming*, pp. 186–88.

50 Ost, *Child Pornography and Sexual Grooming*, pp. 155–64; M.A. McCarthy and R.A. Moodie, 'Parliament and Pornography: the 1978 Child Protection Act', *Parliamentary Affairs* 34 (1981): 47–62.

51 Quoted at http://news.bbc.co.uk/1/hi/programmes/panorama/4348096.stm.

52 His contribution can be found at https://api.parliament.uk/historic-hansard/lords/1978/ jun/28/protection-of-children-bill.

53 The BBFC case study of this film is available at https://www.bbfc.co.uk/education/ case-studies/pretty-baby.

54 Available at https://melonfarmers.co.uk/hitsl_ln.htm#lolita.

55 Richard Preston, 'A Question of Taste', *Independent Magazine*, 4 September 1993: 28–31.

56 Peter Rose, 'Fury as Porn Raid Artist Avoids Trial', *Daily Mail*, 7 July 1995: 37.

57 Peter Rose, 'The Porn Victims from High Society', *Daily Mail*, 13 March 1993: 8.

58 Nicholas Usherwood, *The Brotherhood of Ruralists* (London: Lund Humphries, 1981); Ian Gale, 'Portrait of the Artist as an Accused Man', *Independent*, 15 February 1994, p. 25; Jerrold Northrop Moore, *The Green Fuse: Pastoral Vision in English Art 1820–2000* (Woodbridge: Antique Collectors' Club, 2007), pp. 211–50.

59 Rose, 'Fury as Porn Raid Artist Avoids Trial', p. 37.

60 Anon., 'Artist Accuses Police of Being "Transfixed by Childhood Sexuality"', *Daily Telegraph*, 12 April 2010: 2.

61 Melanie Rickey, 'Revealed (Again): Mapplethorpe's Model', *Independent*, 15 September 1996.

62 Peter Rose and Amanda Evans, 'Child Porn They Call Art', *News of the World*, 11 March 2001.

63 Stephen Wright and David Williams, 'Gallery Escapes over Nude Child Photos', *Daily Mail*, 16 March 2001: 17.

64 The image can be viewed at https://www.christies.com/en/lot/lot-5792590. This also contains an insightful essay.

65 The statement is no longer available on the IWF site but is quoted at https://www.theguardian.com/technology/2008/dec/09/wikipedia-ban-reversed.

66 Godwin's full response is available at https://web.archive.org/web/20081217093048/http:/www.webmink.net/2008/12/why-iwfs-wikipedia-reversal-is-not.htm. Wikipedia's account of the case is available at https://en.wikipedia.org/wiki/Internet_Watch_Foundation_and_Wikipedia.

67 Geoffrey Robertson, *Media Law*, 5th edn (London: Penguin Books, 2008), p. 223.

68 Robertson, *Obscenity*, p. 206.

69 Quoted in ibid., p. 176.

70 Coroners and Justice Act 2009, https://www.legislation.gov.uk/ukpga/2009/25/contents.

71 Jane Fae, 'UK to Outlaw Cartoons of Child Sexual Abuse', *The Register*, 28 May 2008, https://www.theregister.com/2008/05/28/government_outlaws_pictures/.

72 Available via https://www.doughtystreet.co.uk/news. And https://www.doughtystreet.co.uk/childrens-rights-group.

73 For a very useful tabular account of different countries' legal approaches to such material, see https://en.wikipedia.org/wiki/Legal_status_of_fictional_pornography_depicting_minors#Australia.

74 Julian Petley, 'Pornography, Panopticism and the Criminal Justice and Immigration Act 2008', *Sociology Compass* 3.3 (2009): 420–29; 'Punishing the Peep Show: Carnality and the Dangerous Images Act', in Xavier Mendik (ed.), *Peep Shows: Cult Film and the Cine-Erotic* (London: Wallflower Press, 2012), pp. 257–63.

75 Jacob Rowbottom, *Media Law* (Oxford: Hart Publishing, 2024), p. 198.

76 Jacob Rowbottom, 'The Transformation of Obscenity Law', *Information & Communications Technology Law* 27.1 (2018): 26.

77 Details available at https://www.gov.uk/government/organisations/disclosure-and-barring-service.

78 Details available at https://www.nacro.org.uk/criminal-record-support-service/support-for-individuals/advice-prisoners-people-licence-sex-offenders-mappa/advice-people-convicted-sex-offences/.

79 Michel Foucault, *Discipline and Punish: The Birth of the Prison* (London: Allen Lane, 1977), pp. 202–03.

80 David Lyon, *The Culture of Surveillance* (Cambridge: Policy Press, 2018), pp. 57–83.

81 For example: Hannah Wood, '"Librarian" of Global Paedophile Ring Jailed', *Mirror*, 18 August 2008, https://www.mirror.co.uk/news/uk-news/librarian-of-global-paedophile-ring-jailed-328788; and Lee Glendinning, 'Internet Paedophile "Librarian" Given Indefinite Jail Term', *Guardian*, 16 August 2008, https://www.theguardian.com/uk/2008/aug/18/ukcrime.childprotection?gusrc=rss&feed=networkfront.

82 Quoted in Petley, 'Punishing the Peepshow', pp. 261–62.

19

What Is a Hard Core?
Obscenity, Pornography and Censorship

Linda Williams

So long as grossness had a *home* and stayed there—primarily in satire and comedy—it [obscenity] could be freely displayed to a select audience without inspiring much outrage. But [...] when it began to seem possible that anything at all might be shown to anybody, new barriers had to be erected against a threat that was probably already invincible.

Walter Kendrick[1]

Pornography as a regulatory category was invented in response to the perceived menace of the democratization of culture.

Lynn Hunt[2]

What Is a Hard Core?

If I ask Google to define the words obscenity and pornography in relation to one another, I receive this response: 'Obscenity refers to a narrow category of pornography that violates contemporary community standards and has no serious literary, artistic, political or scientific value. For adults at least, most pornography—material of a sexual nature that arouses many readers and viewers—receives constitutional protection.'

Linda Williams, "What Is a Hard Core? Obscenity, Pornography and Censorship" in: *The Screen Censorship Companion: Critical Explorations in the Control of Film and Screen Media*. University of Exeter Press (2024). © Linda Williams. DOI: 10.47788/TMRX1263

These intertwined definitions are surprising, yet they do describe a contemporary state of affairs: pornography is a genre aimed at sexual arousal that is readily available; obscenity is a small, censorable portion of that large category. This has not always been the case. In the sixteenth century, when the term obscenity first came into use, it was a broad term meaning anything offensive to the senses. It did not necessarily connote the arousal of sexual feelings; at that time the nineteenth-century neologism 'pornography' did not exist at all. This chapter asks how obscenity came to be such a small thing and pornography so large. The answer lies in the paradox of the quest to define, isolate and expel the offensive aspects of pornography through the specification of the 'hard core'. Through the quest to define a 'hard core of obscenity', censors of an increasingly mediated culture inadvertently enabled what they had originally set out to forbid: a deluge of what had previously been considered obscene.

To understand this process, it is helpful to consider the etymology of obscenity. Most scholars argue that it derives from Latin (*ob* 'onto' + *caenum* 'filth'). However, there is also a possible Greek etymology from *ob skene* meaning literally 'off scene'. On the classical Greek stage strong emotions or actions were deemed unseemly for public display on the scene (*skene*, meaning stage) before which citizens gathered for public performances. Obscenity thus either derives from unseemly filth or emotions not suitable for public display. Yet we know that many types of obscenity were readily tolerated in less public situations. For the purposes of this chapter I will speak of two overlapping eras: an era of obscenity in which many kinds of unseemly representations could be tolerated in certain non-public contexts—from symposia in Ancient Greece to gentlemen's clubs in Victorian England; and an era of widely available pornography in which we now live, for which I have coined the term 'on/scenity'.[3]

As Lynn Hunt's anthology on pornography amply demonstrates, obscenity in that earlier period was diverse.[4] It could include anything from Aristophanes to Ovid, from illustrated medical treatises to the anonymous novella *L'école des filles ou la philosophie des dames* (1655), to anti-clerical or anti-royalist depictions, including cartoons and lithographs of the period leading up to the French Revolution. Hunt calls this later, eighteenth-century period the 'zenith' of political pornography. However, her use of the term 'pornography', which had only just entered the French language in the late eighteenth century, and which as she admits in her own essay was not yet considered 'a distinct genre of its own', may thus be a touch anachronistic.[5] So, while there is certainly a tradition of works aimed at arousal in the early modern period, most of these works have only been named pornography retrospectively.

The pornography scholar Walter Kendrick has called what I call the era of obscenity the 'pre-Pornographic'. In this era, as he writes in my epigraph, 'grossness had a home and stayed there—primarily in satire and comedy', but to select audiences it also could be 'freely displayed [...] without inspiring much outrage'.[6] We know that these 'select audiences' were most often composed of men eager to protect the purity of women from what they themselves could freely enjoy. It would not be until the nineteenth century, as mass media became more accessible, that these same gentlemen would seek to define and prosecute a legally defined 'hard core' of obscenity that needed to be kept off the scene (i.e. obscene). Here is how Kendrick describes this elusive 'hard core': 'No clear statement has ever been enunciated, but over a period of decades the omnium gatherum called "obscenity" was steadily pared down, like some fleshy fruit with an indigestible stone at its heart, to lay bare what came to be known as the "hard core"'.[7] To Kendrick, pornography has never been a genre; it has always and only been an argument about a problem: how a dominant group (upper-class men) could keep certain works out of the hands of a less dominant group (upper-class women). I agree, but I also think pornography *is* a genre—a genre about an ill-defined problem whose very definition by censors importantly shaped that genre. As Western culture increasingly became mass culture, efforts to define obscenity in order to censor it narrowed its scope until pornography became the gigantic category of lust-inducing arousal it is today.

The word pornography itself had no prior existence before it was defined as a problem of whores. The self-proclaimed French pornographer Restif de la Bretonne created the word by combining the verb 'to write' (*graphein*) with the word 'prostitutes' (*pornei*). Restif wrote as a reformer about the problem of syphilis (and the prostitutes who spread it, not the johns who frequented them). His subtitle said it all: *A Gentleman's Ideas on a Project for the Regulation of Prostitutes, Suited to the Prevention of the Misfortunes Caused by the Public Circulation of Women.* His civic-minded solution was to develop whorehouses administered by the state, dedicated to 'lust and virtue', that would take prostitutes off the streets.[8]

The legal trials in the late nineteenth and early twentieth centuries heroically liberated true literature—from *Madame Bovary* through *Ulysses*—from the dross of prurient obscenity. However, I am interested in the 'dross' addressed in the trials of the second half of the twentieth century, which more often concerned moving images. These trials would determine the changing place of lust in the modern imagination. Here, I hope to show how the regulatory legal 'paring down' of diverse obscenities led to the notion of an indigestible, lust-inducing 'hard core' that we recognize today *and* to understand how that hard core subsequently dissolved. To do this

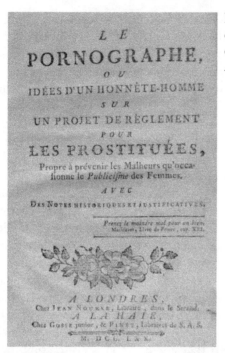

Figure 19.1. Cover of Nicolas Restif de la Bretonne's *Le pornographe* (1769)

I will isolate three distinct 'moments'—each briefly characterized by some minimal examples of the gradual shift from an era of obscenity to the on/scenity that prevails today:

> 1) an early 'moment' in which tacit toleration in the era of obscenity is still in full force but in which we can begin to glimpse a primitive version of an emerging genre;
> 2) a middle 'moment' in which, owing to the malleable metaphor of a supposedly indigestible 'hard core', moving-image pornographies would increasingly come on/scene;
> 3) finally, the contemporary 'moment' in which more incitements to lust via moving images than had previously been dreamed of in anybody's philosophy are now 'freely' available in that quasi-public/private marketplace called the internet.

Moment I: With the Arrival of Cinema, Obscenity Gradually Becomes a Genre about Sex, but Is Not Yet Called Pornography (*c*. 1907–1960)

This is a fairly long 'moment', extending from the invention of cinema to beyond mid-century, but one in which an incipient and still 'primitive' genre did not evolve much. Although dates for these anonymous, illegal films are uncertain, the first film I will mention is the earliest I have been able to locate in any country. Serge Bromberg's Lobster Film Archive in Paris gives it the approximate date of 1910, but I suspect it is a bit earlier, perhaps 1907. Entitled *Les cartes érotiques*, it begins when a small man with large sideburns wearing an apron enters what seems to be a café kitchen to show off his '*cartes érotiques*' to two female co-workers. Called 'French postcards' in Anglo-Saxon countries, such cards belonged to a familiar genre of photographed obscene sexual poses which circulated widely in Europe during the second half of the nineteenth century.

By any standard of the day, this film would have been considered obscene, as well as the kind of photographs it animates. 'Pornography', although coming into use in the aftermath of a type of literature associated with whores, was not yet a common name either for 'dirty photographs' or for films of this sort. Still, this particular film is worth mentioning because it is so early and because it so vividly foregrounds what moving-image pornography had to offer over the already proliferating photographs: movement itself. We know that some of the first public projections of the 'cinematograph' began with the projection of still images that initially disappointed blasé audiences already familiar with such magnified projections in magic

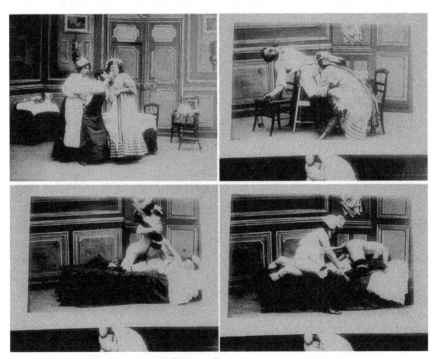

Figure 19.2. Frames from *Les cartes érotiques*

lantern shows. The real *coup de théâtre*, then, would occur when the still image began to move.[9]

Early cinema's primitive attractions were very often called obscene in the common sense of unseemly or offensive, or what Kendrick simply calls 'gross'. For example, in James Williamson's sixty-second *The Big Swallow* (1901), grossness lies in the fact that a man who resists the stare of a camera does so by seeming to swallow its prying eye, which momentarily disappears into the mouth's gaping orifice. Another example is Edwin S. Porter's *The Gay Shoe Clerk* (1903), where the spectator sees a close-up of the clerk buttoning a shoe on a young woman. In both cases the desire to see what is not supposed to be seen ends with the punishment (of the camera in the first instance and the clerk in the second).[10]

Les cartes érotiques grows out of the kind of appeal that Tom Gunning has called the 'attractions' of early, or 'primitive' cinema: a 'fascination with the thrill of display rather than the construction of a story'.[11] Foregrounded here by the device of showing the waiter's hand holding a card in semi-close-up *while it moves*, the attraction in this case is the display of an explicit and graphic sex act—much more of it than could ever be viewed on a French postcard. This display is connected to an epistemological urge inextricably connected to a new medium of vision that can see more of the world, more of the body than older media (painting, photography, even 3D photography) could see. It is the reason for the old adage that as soon as cinema was invented, so too was pornography.[12]

Obscenity in this very early film is channelled into an exclusively sexual form that develops out of the kind of scenarios that obscene 'cards' could generate. The portability of such small cards permitted their entry into more public places such as this kitchen. The scenario thus shows off what the new medium can do beyond the pose of a card, but its primitivity is evident in the way this example stops short of developing the attraction of movement into entire sexual acts. It is as if the film were flexing its obscene muscles but hasn't yet discovered the formula that might sustain them. The waiter, in showing the cards to the women, says, 'This is what I wish to do with you', and the cards then illustrate that wish—but not to the extent of permitting viewers to see its details in close-up and not yet to the extent of reaching a 'happy ending'. The achievement of this happy ending in at least one sexual act will be the limited destiny of this first moment of obscenity.

As primitive cinema grew to a reel in length (ten to fifteen minutes instead of the three and a half minutes here), it became possible to depict entire seductions leading to lustful frenzies of movement and 'happier' endings. By the following decade this crude beginning had found its basic formula: the seduction of a woman, or sometimes a man by a woman, into lust demonstrated by at least one full sexual act. A plumber might seduce a housewife, a doctor a patient, or a female prostitute a male client. The seduction might need to overcome initial resistance or, as in my next example, there might be none. The act will have a beginning, a middle and, instead of ending in punishment, some kind of satisfying end.

My second example from this still-primitive moment is the American film *A Country Stud Horse*, held in the Kinsey Institute with the (again approximate) date of 1920. While still early, the film constitutes a fully developed example of the genre as it would continue throughout the first half of the twentieth century. Such American films of this period were variously called 'smokers' or 'stags' because they were shown at parties for single men, or 'blue movies' (named for the bluish light emanating from projectors). A man arriving in the big city, and whom an intertitle calls George, is looking for amusement. He cranks a mutoscope (a viewing machine that animates still photos into movement) and we see what he sees in it: a writhing female stripper who goes well beyond the typical striptease to show a close-up of her spread labia. Genital close-ups are typically what the American stag films deliver that the earlier European films did not.[13] George continues to crank the machine but now also himself. A prostitute spies the erection and leads George (almost by the penis) to a bare room where they awkwardly undress (long underwear takes a long time). The second half of this single-reel film is the full display of the sex act, privileging close views of female genitalia, erect penis and penetration. 'Insert' is the name primitive cinema gave to a shot that would allow a viewer to see, from close-up, a fragment of an otherwise still theatrically conceived space—usually falling short of what would eventually be called 'classical' continuity editing. In this case, the characteristic 'meat shot' of primitive pornography is an 'insert of an insert'—proof that the sex is not simulated.[14] It is at this early stage, I argue, that the genre discovers its most important vocation: to provide 'maximum visibility' into those acts which have previously been hidden. The typical primitive stag film does not necessarily end with such a shot, but has little more to deliver after this, even having some trouble knowing when to end—when the reel of film runs out in the camera, or, as in this case, when a director, or someone(!), 'throws in the towel'.

There are 1,652 films in the stag archive at the Kinsey Institute at Indiana University—the largest and earliest collection of moving-image pornography in the world. The earliest of them appears to be from 1913. There are a few hundred more than that scattered in archives and private collections in Europe and South America. Few archives have been willing to preserve or restore these illicit films, and their history is not well documented. There has also been some confusion about how they were exhibited. Many French and American scholars have assumed that in France such films were projected in legally tolerated houses of prostitution (*'maisons closes'*, *'maisons de tolérances'*, 'bordellos'). However, the French scholar of early pornography Frédéric Tachou has convincingly put to rest this misconception, at least for France, insisting that such films were projected in clandestine cinemas in the backs of meeting rooms in less frequented cafés, so the two institutions were not linked.[15]

In the USA, however, the stag party or smoker was a more informal practice that could include prostitutes as guests to parties to which itinerant projectionists travelled with their films. So even if prostitution was not built into the architecture of the 'institution', it is significant that no other type of cinema presumed such specific bodily reactions on the part of viewers, nor did any other type build the mimicry of these bodily reactions into the space of screening; for even if they were not screened in actual *houses* of prostitution, prostitutes were often present at the screenings in both countries. It is worth speculating why these films arose when they did.

Most historians have assumed that the rise of a genre aimed at the elicitation of lust was simply an escalation of the 'indexical realism' of photography itself, as if the more realistic the new medium seemed, the more spectators were likely to mimic what they saw depicted in it. I had assumed as much when I wrote *Hard Core*. Now, I am less sure. Without going into the details of this argument,[16] I now think that the rise of moving-image pornography may have had as much to do with the rise of a new nineteenth-century regime of embodied vision, such as that explored by the 'philosophical toys' causing wonder at the illusion of motion like the mutoscope viewed by George in *A Country Stud Horse*, or the thousands of obscene stereoscopes creating the illusion of depth also popular in this period. These 'toys', playing with the physiological vagaries of vision either having to do with the persistence of vision over time or the ways of tricking the monocular body into perceiving depth of space when there is none, were at least as uncanny as they were 'realistic'.

In *Techniques of the Observer*, Jonathan Crary argues that the demise of the regime of the camera obscura and its monocular perspective, and the rise of a physiological regime of embodied optics took place over the course of the nineteenth century as part of the transition to more modern forms of vision. Crary associates this new regime of 'physiological optics' with the rise of modern art, as increasingly vision becomes a matter of seeing/feeling the observer's own body more intensely. In a recent article, I have related this insight to the rise of modern pornography as one important factor.[17] Where Crary argues that the new physiological optics turned the body into a 'surface of inscription' on which a 'promiscuous range of effects' could play,[18] I argue that this new form of promiscuity, found in the frenzy of the illusion of motion, contributed to the formation of a special genre aimed much more narrowly than other forms of obscenity at the arousal of lust. At any rate, it is important to keep in mind that realism, and what I have called 'maximum visibility', always reaches its limits; screening sex can never be the same as having sex and some level of the uncanny, the phantasmatic, will always come into play.

Perhaps the most striking thing about the incipient 'moment' of obscene pornography I have briefly described is that the genre did not continue to evolve or even to evolve cinematically. It 'stayed there', as Walter Kendrick notes in my epigraph, and did not aspire to larger audiences beyond the select few happy to view it when the occasion (perhaps a sexual initiation or 'stag party') demanded. It remained much the same as we see in *A Country Stud Horse* (silent, one or two reels in length, black and white), delivering close-ups of erect penises, the entrances of vaginas, better viewed perhaps with spread labia, and 'meat shots' of penetration while the rest of cinema developed sound, feature length, colour and widescreen. In other words, it remained insistently 'primitive' and 'apart' from the rest of cinema, while other genres (westerns, gangster films, musicals, etc.) continued to develop. It is fair to ask, then, what made things finally change?

Moment IIa: How Defining an Obscene 'Hard Core' Failed to Clarify the Law of Obscenity, but Shaped the Future of a Hugely Popular Genre (1957–1973)

The next 'moment' I want to examine in the history of the development of a genre about to be called 'hard core' begins with a famous anecdote. In 1964 Associate Supreme Court Justice Potter Stewart concurred with the majority opinion of Chief Justice William Brennan, regarding the non-obscenity of Louis Malle's *Les amants* (1958). Potter wrote: 'I shall not today attempt further to define the kinds of material I understand to be embraced within that shorthand description [of hardcore pornography], and perhaps I could never succeed in intelligibly doing so. *But I know it when I see it*, and the motion picture involved in this case is not that'.[19] These words have long been considered an embarrassment to Justice Stewart.

Had the Supreme Court been willing to define obscenity as lust-inducing and had it drawn the line at explicit depictions of un-simulated sex of the sort we have just seen, it might actually have stemmed a tide that Walter Kendrick calls 'invincible' in my epigraph. The exoneration of Malle's film was not an important Supreme Court decision. That film was not 'it'. But because the Court had already gone down the particular rabbit hole of specifying just what 'it' was in a detailed way that would try to specify a 'hard core' of sex beyond 'lust-inducing', in many subsequent rulings, the question of the obscenity or non-obscenity of pornography would have a great deal to do with the degree to which a quasi-acknowledged lust could be normalized or else demonized.

But let me backtrack a bit. Obscenity laws had not long been on the books. The first conviction for obscenity occurred in 1868, in *Regina v. Hicklin*, the first case in Anglo-Saxon law to devise a 'test' to measure the obscenity of those works not deserving the protection of free speech. 'Test' may have sounded scientific, but it was entirely hypothetical: might the work in question 'tend to deprave and corrupt those whose minds are open to immoral influences, and into whose hands a publication of this sort may fall?'[20] This was the kind of subjective judgement appropriate to an era of obscenity that had not yet isolated lust as its key source. The judge in this case, Lord Cockburn, ruled that an anti-clerical Protestant pamphlet, *The Confessional Unmasked*, might indeed 'deprave and corrupt'. Sold on the street corners of London, this pamphlet did not intend to arouse; its intention was to denigrate the Catholic religion, but it did so by describing the lewd behaviour of priests and nuns that did 'deprave and corrupt' their innocent confessors. This is not much different than the anti-clerical obscenity described by Lynn Hunt in the eighteenth century, which was also censored for political reasons. But in this case the transgression was called obscenity, and could be legally prosecuted as such. Called the 'Hicklin Rule', after the man who had tried to sell this pamphlet in London bookshops, it inaugurated an era of entirely subjective judgements as to the tendency of a given work to 'deprave and corrupt' an innocent vulnerable person, never oneself. Such was the reigning precedent throughout the English-speaking world for the next eighty-nine years.[21]

Not until 1957, in an appeal made to the Supreme Court on the conviction of another bookseller, Samuel Roth, did American courts devise a different definition of obscenity that would more squarely address, and thus help constitute, the more precise sexual content of obscenity. Roth had been convicted for mailing obscene pamphlets containing nude pictures, erotic stories and 'salacious photographs'. None of it was as explicit as the primitive films we have discussed, which no one would have dared to send through the mail in the USA.[22] Roth's conviction was upheld and the ruling that did so redefined obscenity through the emerging legal logic of the 'hard core'. The innovation of this ruling, the first to overthrow Hicklin, was that it did not consider obscenity to be a simple matter of representing sex. Indeed, sex 'itself' was not inherently obscene. The majority ruling as authored by Justice William J. Brennan went to great lengths to exalt sex as 'a great and mysterious motive force in human life' of 'absorbing interest to mankind' and one of the 'vital *problems* of human interest and public concern'.[23]

Brennan's new 'test' for obscenity was more specific than 'deprave and corrupt': instead it asked whether 'to the average person [no longer a vulnerable innocent], applying contemporary community standards, the dominant theme of the material appeals to prurient interest'. At last, the institution that would be judging obscenity in American courts named lust as an issue. Moreover, it clarified that it did not intend to frivolously censor any portrayal of sex, but only those 'utterly without redeeming social importance'. But there was a 'problem'. Prurience at that moment could either mean 'having a tendency to excite lustful thoughts' (presumably normal) or having 'shameful and morbid interest in sex' (presumably abnormal); how to tell the difference?[24] The problems multiplied: who was that average person? What were the standards of a community?

The word hardcore does not appear in the language of this ruling, but it had already emerged as a concept behind the scenes in legal manoeuvrings. A young lawyer in the office of the solicitor in charge of defending Roth's previous conviction created a special box into which he placed material that was more obviously obscene (still undefined) than the comparatively innocuous materials Roth himself had been convicted of mailing. It contained what the lawyer called 'hard-core pornography'—the truly 'filthy stuff' that *would be* permitted to be mailed if Roth's conviction was not upheld.[25] This new term, 'hard core', laid on top of the neologism of pornography itself, functioned as a kind of promise that even if obscenity had no clear definition beyond the contested meaning of 'prurience' and changing notions of an 'average person' and 'community standards', there was a box somewhere in which the filth (recall the first, Latin, meaning of *skene*) would be obvious and needed to be kept off the public scene (recall the second, Greek, meaning of *skene*).

Recall also that pornography had originally been defined by Restif de la Bretonne as a problem of prostitution. Now the problem was not the whores blamed for spreading disease, nor was it protecting the innocence of those easily corrupted (never the upright jurists themselves). Now, with the still-unspoken new concept, the problem was perhaps not even pornography but its phantasmatic 'hard core'—the projection of everything that might be the most filthy or unfit for public consumption. Samuel Roth served five years in prison for obscenity, but in the years following *Roth*, a surprising onslaught of films, books and magazines, much more 'hardcore' than what Roth had sent through the mail, was only rarely prosecuted and many past convictions were reversed. Indeed, historian Whitney Strub chronicles that in the 1960s especially, the Supreme Court overturned nearly every obscenity conviction that reached it 'as sex—even in its *prurient* form—was finally afforded access to the imagined marketplace of ideas'.[26] By the late 1960s and early 1970s storefront theatres were showing graphic sex acts and a range of documentaries about issues like sexual freedom in Denmark. Pornography, under *Roth*, had emphatically arrived on/scene.

Obviously, *Roth* was not working to stem the rising tide of 'sexual liberation' throughout the sixties. With the election of Richard Nixon and his appointment of four new justices, it seemed time for a new 'landmark' decision from a more conservative court. *Miller v. California* (1973) was that 'landmark', authored by Chief Justice Warren Burger. Essentially a clarification and augmentation of *Roth*, it forged the definition of obscenity that endures today. Like *Roth*, it upheld the conviction of a man, named Miller, who mailed unsolicited brochures advertising several graphic books and a film that depicted sexual activity. It reiterated some portions of *Roth*, and elaborated and 'clarified' it at greater length. Here a work was obscene if:

> 1. the average person applying contemporary community standards would find that the work, taken as a whole, appeals to prurient interest—unchanged from *Roth*;
> 2. the work depicts or describes, in a patently offensive way, sexual conduct or excretory functions specifically defined by applicable state law;
> 3. and finally, if the work, taken as a whole, lacks serious literary, artistic, political or scientific value. (*Roth* had said simply 'utterly without redeeming social importance'.)

Of course, obscenity still depended on whether the judges or justices 'knew it' when they 'saw it', how they defined 'prurient interest', 'community standards' and values which now must be 'serious literary, artistic, political or scientific'.[27] But the real difficulty in defining obscenity this time around was the fateful term 'hard core'. Burger's ruling added, as if for reassurance, that '*no one* would be subject to prosecution for the sale or exposure of obscene materials unless these materials depicted or described patently offensive "*hard core*" sexual conduct specifically defined by the regulating state law, as written or construed'.[28] Though the Burger Court was more conservative than the one that ruled in Roth, its effort to further specify and to disparage obscenity as a form of deviance—as opposed to mere explicitness—would have the unintended consequence of educating judges and juries on the niceties of proliferating sexual discourses in the ongoing sexual revolutions of the sixties and seventies.

Sexual forms of obscenity, which the Court was only now, retroactively, naming pornography, had always been a form of sex education in their limited proliferation in the era of obscenity in the early half of the century. Now, 'movie days' at the Court, as described in Bob Woodward and Scott Armstrong's *The Brethren*, were beginning to play their part in educating the justices. These were the days in which several of the justices and most of the clerks watched the films that were exhibits in the obscenity cases under appeal.[29] This closer scrutiny of sexual representation in context inevitably engendered greater specificity. Consider, for example, how Burger embellished the original 'patently offensive' with 'excretory functions'.

Consider as well that when Burger attempted to elaborate his three-pronged definition by offering some 'plain examples' of hardcore depictions that were 'patently offensive', he muddied the waters considerably by introducing the wild card of 'perversion' into the mix of examples. These were: '(a) patently offensive representations or descriptions of ultimate sexual acts, normal or perverted, actual or simulated' or '(b) patently offensive representations of descriptions of masturbation, execratory functions, and lewd exhibition of the genitals'.[30] He thus went to the very heart of the problem—the conundrum really—of sexual desire: that its hard core is *not* a mere explicit showing of normal 'ultimate sexual acts' but a hodgepodge of associations and fantasies, some of which, 'like lewd exhibition of genitals', were not even explicit sexual acts. In some cases, then, the very lack of explicitness could be perverse in the literal sense of swerving away from 'ultimate sexual acts', as any reading of Sigmund Freud's *Three Essays on the Theory of Sexuality*—a work much read in the early 1970s—would show.[31]

The ruling thus did not claim that the depiction of explicit sexual acts constituted a 'plain example' of an indigestible 'hard core' that could be the essence, or kernel, of censorable obscenity. Rather, while allowing that visual depictions of heterosexual intercourse might be obscene, Burger chose to itemize a wide variety of sexual practices, some of which, like 'flagellation' and 'sado-masochism', did not necessarily involve sexual organs at all, but which—along with other practices including 'fellatio, cunnilingus and the like'—were considered perverse. Presumably, these 'other sexual practices' would turn the 'normal' juror off. That turn-off was a gamble, for as the rise of pornography on the public scene was already beginning to show, what was patently offensive to one person might be a turn-on to another. And if sexuality itself was actually 'a great and mysterious force in human life' as well as a 'vital problem', as Brennan had originally written in *Roth*'s initial attempt to specify obscenity, it is no wonder that Burger's 'clarifications' were less than clear. They shifted obscenity from mere explicitness in the representation of 'ultimate sexual acts'—for example, heterosexual intercourse—to a paradoxical lack of the 'ultimate'—an absence of an end goal or direct gratification—that is often the hallmark, and the literal meaning, of perversion.[32]

Burger's examples clarified one thing: obscenity is not limited to explicit sexual acts (typically but not exclusively male and female genitals in coitus; think of the 'meat shot' in the stag film), but actually leans towards more 'deviant' sexualities. These are the sexualities which 'prevailing community standards' do not want to admit to being arousing but which, as standards were inevitably in flux in this period, as women's, gay and lesbian liberation movements were showing, might prove so. In the intervening years it would often be *these* perverse sexual acts that would be targeted as the most important obscenities. However, targeting and naming them, as the courts were beginning to see, did not necessarily remove them from public view. Quite the contrary: by naming such a variety of them, judicial sexual discourse had joined the many other forms of sexual discourse to put them on/scene as never before.

Moment IIb: 'Diff'rent Strokes for Diff'rent Folks': The Pornographic Hard Core Explodes On/scene (1972–1973)[33]

According to laws that have only recently been struck down, fellatio is one of the possible meanings of sodomy, defined before the courts got more deeply into the business of defining obscenity, as any 'abnormal' form of sexual intercourse. In John Updike's 1968 novel *Couples*, a wife asks her husband if he wants her to 'take him' in her mouth. 'Good heavens, no,' he answers. 'That's sodomy.'[34] But in the late 1960s and early 1970s diverse sexual acts once considered abnormal were acquiring more specific names and thus becoming familiar. The year 1972 saw the big debut of fellatio, first in a film called *Deep Throat* (Gerard Damiano), and again when mentioned by name in *Miller v. California* as one of several other 'perverse sexual practices' defining the 'hard core' of obscenity. There is no greater proof of the failure of the Court's attempt to specify and censor obscenity than the fact that *Deep Throat* represented the moment that feature-length, hardcore pornography, with sound and colour, (briefly) entered the mainstream of American movies. The film would certainly be prosecuted and, depending on where, it would often be convicted, but it was the emblematic title that became a household phrase that presaged what some wanted to call the 'end of obscenity'.[35]

Fellatio had always been one of the possible sexual acts depicted in the short, silent primitive films of the 'era of obscenity' (we glimpsed it briefly in *Les cartes érotiques*). But you would think it had just been discovered given its epic treatment here, replete with theme-song and extraordinary narrative motivation. Recall that in *Roth* Justice Brennan had written that sex was one of the 'vital *problems* of human interest and public concern'. In the narrative of *Deep Throat*, sex itself, the assumed pleasure of it, *was* a problem. Just prior to the clip we have seen, the protagonist Linda Lovelace has confessed to her doctor that sex was disappointing, she only felt little tingles, no bombs bursting or bells ringing. When the doctor discovers her clitoris in her throat, the solution to the problem is obvious, providing narrative motivation to the 'deep throat' fellatio that follows.

Figure 19.3. *Deep Throat* (Gerard Damiano, 1972) (publicity still)

The laughter generated by this bad joke served to alleviate the nervousness of the first mixed-gender audiences watching hardcore sex together in a public theatre. But the stunt of deep throat fellatio 'solved' other problems as well: Alfred Kinsey in the 1950s and Masters and Johnson in the 1960s had identified the problem of the relative lack of female orgasm as due to the overrating of vaginal orgasm. Women had been faking pleasure because their clitorises were often ignored. *Deep Throat*'s 'solution' did not really address that problem, though it did indicate that the genre was acutely aware of it. Its 'solution' was actually a diversion. The exaggerated spectacle of the male's external ejaculation tried to compensate for what the evolving genre had not figured out how to deliver: convincing, involuntary and visible female pleasure on a par with male orgasm which, when external, produced visual evidence. With this trope standing in for the more problematic female pleasure, hardcore pornography invented what after this film would become its most valued staple: the 'come shot or money shot'—so called because actors were paid a premium for delivering them.

By placing a pretty, smiling female face so near the ejaculating 'star performer' of the film, director Gerard Damiano lent a visible expressiveness to the inherently less visible act of coitus while also providing a dramatic, highly visible climax and ending to individual sex (not to mention foiling unwanted procreation). With the 'money shot', the genre now had a true spectacular ending, if not to the narrative as a whole, at least for each of its many diverse sexual acts. 'Plan on at least ten separate come shots', writes one advice manual for the frugal pornographer published in 1977.[36] There was no more need to 'throw in the towel'.

If sex was a problem, then *more* sex, *different* sex, or what Chief Justice Warren Burger called '*perverse*' sex, was the genre's obvious solution. Solutions to these problems were rarely discovered in the missionary position. After the enormous success of *Deep Throat* (1972) the genre took great pride in exploiting spectacular perversions, sometimes offering S/M or anal variations as the solution, as if hardcore pornography were actually taking its cue from the 'deviant' varieties of sex acts named by *Miller*.

Michel Foucault's notion of the historical 'implantation of perversions' in which 'scattered sexualities rigidified, became stuck to an age, a place, a type of practice' may not fully explain the popularity of *Deep Throat* fellatio,[37] but it does allow us to see how the public awareness of previously 'gross' or 'obscene' sexual practices could change once pornographies came on/ scene. The British playwright and barrister John Mortimer, writing about Linda Lovelace's death, recalled a 1970 obscenity trial for a novel entitled *The Mouth*, in which the judge asked a witness for the defence why anyone needed oral sex when 'we've gone without it for a thousand years'.[38] Had that judge been speaking after 1972, it is unlikely he would have been so misinformed.

Joel Tyler, who presided over the New York obscenity trial of *Deep Throat* in the winter of 1973, was another judge who learned a lot. Ignorant at the beginning of the trial about the meaning of the term *missionary position*, after the testimony of five expert witnesses he was eagerly instructing others of its meaning. Constantly at stake in this often hilarious trial was the question of the obscenity or non-obscenity of the display of fellatio and the perversity or non-perversity of the much discussed, though rarely shown, clitoral orgasm.

Judge Tyler learned a great deal about the respective arguments of Freud, Kinsey, and William Masters and Virginia Johnson concerning the practice of fellatio and the relative merits of clitoral versus vaginal orgasm. Arguments for the defence centred upon the instructional and liberatory value of explicit sex acts on the screen in improving the sex lives of individuals and couples. Arguments for the prosecution centred upon the inherent perversion and obscenity of such acts. In a famously long and vehement decision, Judge Tyler pronounced the film obscene and fined the theatre $3 million, concluding, 'This is one throat that deserves to be cut'.[39]

Obscene or not? Judgements could go either way in the many trials throughout many states over the next decade. Conviction would often depend upon the venue of the trial, since one of the repercussions of *Miller* had been to shift from national to 'local community standards'. However, hardcore pornography was now an established genre and *Deep Throat* had become so familiar that it even became the alias of the man who secretly informed on the Watergate burglars. The fact that there was so much sexual speech, for or against hardcore pornography, was proof enough that the shock of on/scenity was wearing off.

Moment III: Lust Finds a Home: The Contemporary Example of Pornhub

In the first two 'moments' of this chapter I described a waning era of obscenity with two brief examples of primitive 'pornography' in which obscenity still 'had a home and stayed there'. This obscenity, as we have seen, did not much change or even proliferate for there was little public discourse about it. The unwritten and unclarified laws of obscenity remained in force, perhaps because they were unwritten. It was in the second moment when those laws *were* written, and needed to be clarified, that the genre began to diversify and change.

Though I have tried to characterize this second 'moment' with a single example, this example was meant to be emblematic of the perverse and diverse expansion of 'other' sexual practices over the next two decades. In hardcore pornography this meant the exponential growth of gay, lesbian, BDSM and racially fetishized niches. The popular song 'Every Day People' with its tag line 'Diff'rent Strokes for Diff'rent Folks', referred to explicitly in *Deep Throat*, joined the repertoires of celebrated, often identity-forming sexual 'perversions' on offer. Of course, new laws attempting to censor an expanding hard core continued to be passed and these more minoritized niches were usually the more easily prosecuted. But without a national consensus regarding obscenity's definition, increasingly localized interpretations of community standards meant that individual states and localities might prosecute a work, but convictions were often reversed in higher courts. Not only did the definition of obscenity in *Miller v. California* (1973) increasingly seem irrelevant, but its enumeration of the true hardcore obscenities uncannily seemed to anticipate and define the growing on/scene genre.

Although the 1970s are often referred to as the 'Golden Age' of on/scene pornography in the literal public space of movie theatres, it was really the adult video era which brought the 'diff'rent strokes' ideology its greatest diversity and most sustained economic success, and that consumption of on/scenity would take place very much in the privacy of the home. By the mid-1980s, hardcore pornography had crept into the home in the form of rented videotapes, first as copies of films, later as more cheaply produced videos. In fact, pornography was the market force that pioneered the commercial viability of all forms of home video. Remarkably efficient porn studios, such as Vivid and Wicked, carried forward the popular model of the 'all American girl who liked sex' begun by Linda Lovelace into the 1980s.[40] Building their success upon the ingratiating and sexy personas of mostly female 'pornstars', some of whom, like Ginger Lynn or Jenna Jameson, gained a remarkable deal of autonomy in their careers, studios modelled on the Hollywood studio era built lucrative empires eventually leading the charge into digital production and distribution. Smaller, more artisanal companies, like Candida Royalle's Femme Productions, brought female-centred pornography to the fore. Many new 'niches' were created: Fatale Video promoted lesbian pornography with titles like *Suburban Dykes* (1991); instructional videos like *Nina Harley's Guide to Anal Sex* (Adam and Eve, 1996) or Carol Queen's *Bend Over Boyfriend* (1998) offered good-humored how-to lessons; independent performers like Annie Sprinkle mixed conventional porn with performance art. A thousand flowers bloomed and many auteurs flourished.[41]

By far the biggest niche was gay pornography. Like the heterosexual mainstream it was all about arousing and satisfying the lust of male viewers, with the important difference that its pornstars were men who had sex, at least on-screen, with other men. Though there were only a handful of male–male couplings in the archives of the primitive era of obscenity, gay pornography actually pioneered the popularity of on/scenity in the Golden Age. In 1971, a year before *Deep Throat* seized the (hetero)sexual imagination of the nation, a modest but infinitely better made and more imaginative film called *Boys in the Sand*, directed by the former dancer Wakefield Poole, anticipated the impact of *Deep Throat* for the narrower but also trendsetting loyal audience of an emerging gay community, and was the first work of hardcore pornography to reap giant returns on a small investment. Other important auteurs and pornstars followed in a smooth transition to video.[42] By the late 1980s gay hard core was instrumental in modelling safer sex practices to its fans.

Gay and straight adult video initially continued the fictional narrative tradition begun by *Deep Throat*: a pretty woman (or man) seeks more or better sex in ways that would arouse and gratify viewers. But two new interrelated subgenres would begin to transform the industry by the late 1980s and 1990s: amateur and gonzo. *Amateur* began with non-commercial swapping of home movie sex tapes, and grew into myriad imitations for which participants were paid (thus technically becoming professional), leaving only an 'amateur' aesthetic. *Gonzo* was a commercial genre that

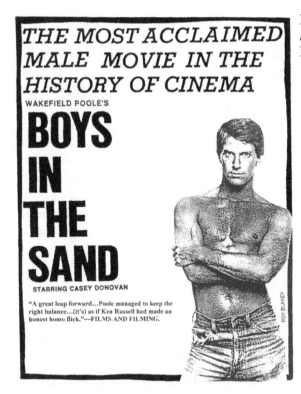

Figure 19.4. *Boys in the Sand* (Wakefield Poole, 1971) poster

mimes amateur style, attempting to place the viewer in the scene through a crude caught-on-the-fly aesthetic. Both new trends actively countered the polished professionalism of studio-produced pornography, sometimes adding the new element of first-person point of view (in which the sex act is experienced from the point of view of the, inevitably male, performer, attempting to immerse the viewer 'in' the act itself. Sometimes this subgenre would combine with certain preferred fetishes (more often butts than breasts). Whether distributed on videotape or DVD, these subgenres would become even more popular in online pornography eager to appear more user-generated.

It was during this period that hardcore pornography actually became the $8 billion business of many a scandalized exposé.[43] The sacrosanct American value of privacy—in what one reads, watches or does in the home—trumped obscenity law and women finally became economically significant customers, enjoying like everyone else the new control over rewind and fast forward. But privacy was not total because video stores were still brick and mortar, and customers still had to physically go into and out of them.[44] Once hard core went online, it became the 'invincible' force that Walter Kendrick had predicted in my epigraph.

This is not to say that laws have not been written to censor pornography in the home. The Communications Decency Act (CDA, 1996) threatened stiff fines to anyone transmitting obscene or indecent communication online, and the Communications Child Protection Act (COPA, 1998) attempted more specifically to target online obscenity that might be made available to persons under the age of eighteen. However, both were found overbroad and unconstitutional by the Supreme Court because they did not require screening or accessing in a public place. Though these laws had little efficacy in curtailing the spread of online pornography, they had a profound effect upon the new forms the genre would take in this new 'moment' of hardcore on/scenity.

To make sure that sexual speech did not fall into the wrong hands, the websites that hosted pornographic content offered up credit card verification as a means of assuring that no minors could access their content. Ostensibly to protect children—but really to protect themselves—non-commercial websites, many of whom had previously functioned as exchanges for the swapping and sharing of home-made (genuinely) amateur videos, instituted credit card purchases. If a 'content provider' required purchase through credit cards, then, as new media scholar Wendy Chun puts it, 'they could seem responsible rather than greedy […] for charging for something that was freely accessible elsewhere'.[45] Most websites in the mid-1990s were not yet 'monetized'. This seemingly inadvertent monetization, in obedience to laws that were written but never enforced (because found unconstitutional), was a crucial turning point in the entire history of the World Wide Web, which in 1996 began to become the credit card-driven enterprise we recognize today. Just as hardcore pornography had driven the rise and profitability of home video, so it now drove the leap into online consumption.[46]

Today, one can legitimately ask if an elusive hard core of obscenity legally functions at all, now that hardcore pornography is both accessible to and consumed in the privacy of the home. Returning to the Google definition of obscenity that so confounded me, we can perhaps better understand how it is that 'Obscenity refers to a narrow category of pornography that violates contemporary community standards and has no serious literary, artistic, political or scientific value', and how it is that 'For adults at least, most pornography—material of a sexual nature that arouses many readers and viewers—receives constitutional protection.' Obscenity, and the legal quest to define it via the malleable metaphor of indigestible 'hard core', has today become so narrow as to have almost disappeared altogether. In the privacy of the home, what is obscene? Now it is the hard core that is the capacious category accessible on computers, cell phones, iPads, anywhere and everywhere, even at work, if you want to risk it. The indigestible hard stone at the core of pornography that jurists sought to pare down and discard has grown as a genre into the most lucrative part of the 'enter-tainment' industry. It is on/scene and off/scene on the World Wide Web, a place that is everywhere and nowhere. It is a community whose 'standards' aim to 'build rich interactive experiences, powered by vast data stores, that are available on any device'.[47] But who makes it? Who is responsible for it? The World Wide Web is not a producer of content but a way to link up different content sites with users. Is it a genre? How to describe it?

The following attempt to characterize the experience of watching hardcore pornography online will necessarily be incomplete, idiosyncratic and cheap. It will be incomplete because databases carry inherently more information than any mortal can ever deal with. It will be idiosyncratic because I am a scholar of hardcore pornography in its celluloid and adult video incarnations, a feminist who has been both interested in and critical of hardcore pornography for its masculinist subjectivity, and am now an older person grown impatient with many of the 'interactive' pretensions of new media. I had hoped to determine quickly and easily what a genre I have lost touch with has become now that it is consumed online. Quick and easy this has not been. Finally, my sampling will be cheap because I did not pay for what I saw. Apparently very few people do, although those who do pay enough to permit the rest of us to freely 'lurk'.

My sampling is of Pornhub,[48] the website that hosts the largest amount of hardcore video content at the time of writing. Because of my general aversion to online experiences, I had never previously visited this or any other online porn site, and in this research I was aided by a younger and more expert guide.[49] The home page is a Halloweenish orange and black, announcing the current number of videos to be accessed on the site: a phenomenal 11,700,127 searchable videos as of April 2020.[50] I am accessing this site during the second month of the Covid-19 pandemic in the USA; a banner invites me to 'Stayhome hub' (an alternative name?) and to 'Help Flatten the Curve'. The eroticized risk of human contact thus pervades the site on my first visit, and many of the more extreme videos I will sample, as if my vicarious visit will keep me safe from the very real danger of human contact.

Pornhub's masthead offers me seven options:

1. *Home* (where I am);
2. *Porn videos*, which allows me to filter through all videos on the basis of whether they are professional or home-made, how long they are and their price;
3. *Categories*, a bewildering array of types of videos;
4. *Live Cams*, which are real-time 'interactions' (prostitution at a distance) that are tedious to me since I don't pay;
5. *Pornstars*, which organizes videos via the named 'stars' in them;

Figure 19.5. Pornhub's navigation

6. *Community*, which only tells me what's 'New in the Pornhub Community', and features only new product;
7. *Photos and Gifs*: still photos and tiny 'animations of still images' that are organized into files and provide tiny illusions of movement, like flip-books, when combined.

Because I am not ready for the confusing onslaught of *Categories* and want to understand the rules of the game and the democratic presumption of a site that invites the community to 'partner' with them, I go to the second column on the left, 'Work with Us', and click on 'Content Partners', and then on 'Content Partners Program'. There I learn that if I become a content partner my videos will reach over 100 million daily users with 'high quality adult traffic' already used by many studios. I am also given advice as to what kinds of videos to make. This is where I begin to learn the nitty-gritty of the genre as now reformulated for online 'traffic'.

In 1977, *The Filmmaker's Guide to Pornography* offered a checklist of necessary ingredients in the pre-video era: ten separate money shots in combinations with the following sexual numbers: masturbation; 'well-lit close-ups of genitalia'; 'straight sex' in a variety of positions; 'lesbianism'; 'oral sex', either fellatio or cunnilingus (noting the advantage of 'blow jobs' over cunnilingus in terms of visibility and facilitation of the money shot); 'ménage à trois' with two women and one man; 'orgies', which the book cautions can be expensive; and 'anal sex', in which the recipient is always female.

No comparable checklist is offered to the aspiring 'Content Partner', but it is immediately apparent here too that there are basic rules and advice to be had, such as: length of videos ('minimum duration of five minutes' but 'ten minutes or longer will achieve optimal viewing results'); good types of title (*Busty School Teacher Capri Cavalli Fucks Big Dick Student During Detention*); bad types of title (*Big Tit Teacher Pornstar Hardcore Sex*); the necessity for 'thumbnails' (illustrating the range of hardcore acts in a given video) and 'tags' (words to describe the same range: rimming, scissoring, doggystyle, anal, etc.); sexual settings (kitchen, library); sexual objects (dildo, handcuffs); and sexy attributes (petite, trimmed). Each video can have up to sixteen tags.

Thumbnails and tags are a classificatory improvement over the formulaic checklist for a film, the covers of well-stocked video stores of yesteryear. Even the covers of those big boxes could only fit so many glimpses of what might be inside the box. A renter might find some surprises among the 'diff'rent strokes' on offer. Now there are many 'diff'rent strokes' but unless you are new to the site there will be few surprises, for even the titles tell you what to expect: not so much a feature-length narrative but a variety show of sex in which a restless attention-deficit consumer can always click on the newest and more daring act. Indeed, the recommendation of a duration of five to ten minutes is a throwback to the primitive cinema of attractions era that measured films by ten- to twelve-minute reels. And even when a video *is* longer (some 'compilation orgies' can last many hours), there is a marked reversion to the fundamentals of the primitive era of obscenity of our first 'moment'.

Both the Golden Age and the video era of hardcore on/scenity (our Moment II) assumed that viewers wanted more elaborate narratives from which particular varieties of sex act might be generated. Today it seems that the value of 'diff'rent strokes for different folks' manifests less in the variety of sex acts in a given video and more in the totality of the database to which any thumbnail, only a click away, allows us to navigate. 'Categories' are the primary way to navigate the totality of 'diff'rent strokes'. There are a bewildering array and Figure 19.6 is only a tiny sampling, each type illustrated by a single thumbnail.

Categories can indicate types of sexual act (Gangbang, Creampie, Squirt, Bondage), types of body or combinations of bodies (Mature, Transgender, Old/Young, Big Breasts, Big Dicks, Big Ass), racial types (Ebony, Interracial, Japanese), and subgenres of hard core (Amateur, Cartoon). Race is almost never a matter of indifference; indeed, it is always named and fetishized if at all possible; size *always* matters; and age itself can be a fetish (Mature, MILFs). Some categories are as old as the genre itself (Cartoon), others (like Transgender) are new to webporn. There are many more categories than I can fit on a page, and I can only explore a few. If I take the plunge and click on 'Japanese', I am taken to a huge array of videos of differing, but short lengths all featuring Asian, not just Japanese, female 'pornstars'. When I click on 'Chinese Webcam', which is not a webcam site but a pre-recorded video, I'm treated to a Japanese-looking woman who spreads her labia, much as the woman in the mutoscope did in *A Country Stud Horse*.

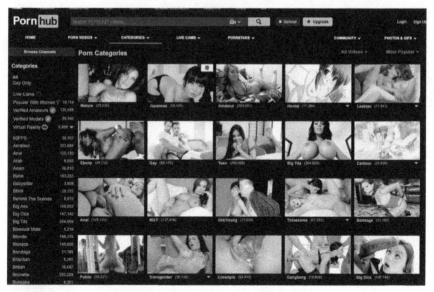

Figure 19.6. Pornhub's categories

The rest of the thirty-minute video includes a long monologue in Chinese, presumably spoken to the viewer in webcam-style, and several solo masturbations in which the woman dons various masks. This video has received 1,800 views and an 82% thumbs up rating. Like all others there is no telling when it was made. Should I get bored, I can always click on the many alternative possibilities to the side. Returning to 'Categories', I also note that the sidebar on the left has some *meta-categories* such as 'Gay Only', 'Virtual Reality' and 'Popular with Women'—alternative ways of accessing categories. 'Gay Only' gets me to the alternative universe of gay porn, which has many of the same features of straight but is kept quite separate. It is worth noting that once I am in it, it is always immediately possible to switch back to 'STRAIGHT' at the upper left-hand corner.

Figure 19.7. Pornhub's Chinese Webcam

I will come back to this universe in a moment, but first I want to discuss what Pornhub thinks is popular with women. The name of the meta-category itself is a dead giveaway: in the grand scheme of database pornography, women, of whatever persuasion, are a mere niche; the primary audience for Pornhub is heterosexual males.[51] 'Popular with Women' informs me that 'real women' prefer pornography ranging from 'passionate softcore porn' (of which there are no apparent examples) to 'hardcore gangbangs' (no examples of that either). If I am being catered to, it is not according to my presumed preferred object choices, whether heterosexual men or homosexual women. For example, I can only find one lesbian film on offer ('Hot Lesbians 14'). What *is* on offer is an abundance of low-budget, sometimes rather sweet gay couplings with very nasty-sounding titles such as *Boyfriend Wanted Dick So I Fucked Him Silly for 20 Minutes*, which lasts exactly twenty minutes, or the nastier-sounding *The BF Fucking Me Bareback Late at Night (Filled with Cum)*. Here Pornhub is not wrong. I *am* a real woman who does prefer to watch gay male porn. And perhaps the fact that I am in no way implicated in the first-person speakers of these titles frees me from any worries about my sexual identity. I'm just enjoying gay male sex.

Looking for some of the 'passion' I am supposed to want, I find my way to a subcategory within 'Popular with Women' called 'Passionate Sex'. Here again, although the coupling is heterosexual, the subjective point of view is male, as signalled by the title (*Passionate Sex with My Neighbor's Wife*) as well as by all the conventions of mainstream heterosexual pornography, including loud, faked orgasms. In some of these shortish videos (twenty

Figure 19.8. Pornhub's Gay Porn categories

minutes is again typical) the sex acts are embellished with romantic music, upscale decors and some of the bigger 'pornstars' of the moment (Lana Rhoades, currently ranked #1). Some of these seem to be from a studio labelled 'Metart Films'—the very word *films* here signalling a higher class of porn, an absence of the usual 'nasty' language, if not actual celluloid. I cannot help but remark that there seems to be nothing here that wasn't done better, and with better acting, in the 1990s on feature-length video by Femme Productions.

On the more 'amateur' side of the spectrum, but still in 'Popular with Women' and still exhibiting a pronounced male subjectivity, is a sixteen-minute video titled *How to Get Your Girlfriend Squirt Orgasm* [*sic*]. It shows a woman with spread legs in position for a gynaecological exam as only the hands of a faceless 'boyfriend' reach their fingers into her shaved vagina to manipulate her genitals, eventually producing the 'squirt' of the title. This video is all about exploring the space of the female 'hole'—the 'absence' that the penis 'fills' during 'normal' coitus. But as part of the genre of hardcore pornography it is also about the compulsion to make visible what may not be so visible in 'sex'. 'Squirting' (female ejaculation) is not new in sex or even, as we shall see, in pornography, but it has recently come into greater vogue as hardcore has become so much more visible to all. It first appeared in hardcore pornography in a justly famous film 1981 film written, directed and performed by Annie Sprinkle.[52] Entitled *Deep Inside Annie Sprinkle*, the film offered the kind of female counterpoint to the insistent male subjectivity I find so lacking in the 'Popular with Women' meta-category of Pornhub. In a soothing, seductive voice, Sprinkle instructs the men in the film, whose muscular bodies she admires and has sex with, in how to explore new pleasures by explaining what *she* likes, including stimulating them anally. Her 'squirt' is one of many diverse sexual acts and positions, thus challenging in subtle ways the usual hierarchy in with the performance of pleasure is for the man and by the woman.

In contrast, *How to Get Your Girlfriend . . .* is a clinical, wordless demonstration of how a woman's body might be disciplined and *manipulated* to achieve something comparable to a money shot. It is performed by the man 'on' the woman. The hands occasionally slap the pussy as if to warm it up, inserting fingers deep into the cervix and anus, and, like a magician doing tricks in a hat, produces various liquids, pausing each time some new kind of liquid appears as if to say 'ta da!'. These liquids are: first, a whitish viscous substance like male ejaculate that is probably female ejaculate, which women's bodies do produce (though not all women and it is not necessarily associated with orgasm);[53] second, and much more 'squirt'-like, the more forceful ejection of a clear liquid; and third, some rather large quantities of also clear liquid also forcefully ejected that is easily mistaken for urine because there is so much of it.[54] The point is not to argue that long ago Annie Sprinkle was the true pioneer of the 'female money shot'. Rather, it is to argue that she pioneered it on her own terms in ways that might believably be 'Popular with Women'. She also taught the presumptive heterosexual male spectator of hard core something about female pleasure, none of which is evident on Pornhub.

My last sampling of Pornhub is from the separate universe of the category 'Gay'. The 'perverse' sex acts privileged in *Boys in the Sand* were quite similar to those in straight hard core: fellatio plus anal sex followed by money shots as confirming proof of pleasure. But because of the male–male context these acts were *more* taboo, more perverse. For this same reason, early gay hard core was a powerful assertion of proud gay identity. It helped that Poole introduced a new atmospherics of wonder and fantasy not common to the more in-your-face maximum visibility of early straight hard core. The dappled sunlight of his Fire Island setting, in which fantasy lovers could be conjured from the sea like Botticelli's Venus, did not insist upon seeing everything there was to see all the time, though certainly one knew it when one saw it.

Fast-forward to 2020 and gay pornography is still seeking its perverse edge, a greater element of taboo. But the 'diff'rent stokes' of gay hard core have since undergone an epidemic that has indelibly marked many of the 'categories' of gay hard core on Pornhub. The history is this: as early as 1984, AIDS began to show up at alarming rates among both gay and straight segments of the industry. The straight segment began instituting tests, while the gay segment responsibly instituted condoms and 'safe', or at least 'safer', sex practices. The very lethality of unprotected anal sex meant that it was extremely taboo. And if we have learned nothing else from our legal history of the 'clarification' of hard core, it is that taboo practices can be especially alluring. During the AIDS epidemic gay hard core acted responsibly. However, when testing for seropositivity became routine in the industry, condoms became the last thing you will see on Gay Pornhub.

For example, *Cute Nico Leon Getting Rawfucked at the Pool* begins with an announcement about the importance of seropositive testing and a note that the performers in this eighteen-minute scene have done so. But because it has become almost de rigueur to suggest the eroticizing riskiness of *any* gay sex, the 'bareback' (condomless) sex that ensues, actually quite sweet and respectful, nevertheless wants to connote all the cowboy macho risks of riding without a saddle. Since it is Nico who is the bottom, he is taking the biggest risk, with 'rawfucked' in the title there to suggest it. Exhaustive tags are listed in alphabetical order (Bareback, Big Dick, Blowjob, Cumshot, Gay, Hand Job, Jock, Latino, Twink). According to Pornhub's own stats, there are 88,620 gay videos on the site and 21,836 of these are Bareback.

Cute Nico ... is a modestly popular 'twink', meaning a handsome and not excessively muscular young bottom. He is also Latino, though not much is made of that here. Race, however, will always factor into the phantasmatic overtones of sex acts when power differentials are scripted into the scenarios, sometimes going with, sometimes going against stereotype.

At the opposite extreme from the simplicity and friendly intimacy of *Cute Nico* ... is a fifty-six-minute non-stop orgy that also begins with the tag Bareback. It opens with three guys in a sun-dappled clearing in a wood that initially seems to echo some of the 'erotic in nature' effects of *Boys in the Sand*, filmed on Fire Island. Because this film is entitled *Fire Island Sex Party*, it could be the rare example of a work on the Pornhub site that is self-consciously aware of its own genre traditions, perhaps even an homage to Poole's celluloid classic. Like everything else on the site, there is no pretence that performers inhabit a 'normal' world in which sex is inhibited. Three men enter a wooded clearing mostly naked and already hard. Soon they are six and form a coordinated daisy chain in combinations of fellatio and anal.

The sex is noisy, vigorous and semi-choreographed. Like all the matching white women in a Busby Berkeley musical, they all look remarkably alike. Frequent, brief pauses to swap positions occur, as do occasional ejaculations, but unlike the convention established in *Deep Throat*, as well as in

Figure 19.9. *Fire Island Sex Party* (screenshots)

most gay pornography, money shots do not signal climax. This is an orgy; its fantasy is duration and insatiability. In its last third, it shifts to a tented structure more protected from the elements with slightly tighter framing. But how to end an orgy? With a grand coordinated climax? That might be predictable but it would end the pleasure. Instead, there is no climax, only a diminution of activity as couplings cease and twelve hard, horny men slowly walk off, ready to continue the party in another place on another day. *Fire Island Sex Party* has 91% thumbs up but only 177,547 views (compared to *Nico*'s 237,088). But without dates of posting there is no telling what this means. This video does not announce that its performers have been tested, though that does not mean they were not. Orgies are not new to on/scene pornography, but to see a sexual number performed and choreographed with verve and imagination on Pornhub is, unfortunately, novel.

On the continuum of hardcore perversities, *Cute Nico …* and *Fire Island Sex Party* are rather tame. More 'raw' and risky is *Daddy Screams in Ecstasy as He Breeds His Young Asian Twink Boy Raw*. Here too the sex is bareback, but now the racialized hierarchies are pronounced ('Daddy' is white and a top; 'Asian Twink' is a bottom, and that bottom is all we ever see of him). The ejaculation is internal, hence the verb 'Breeds' in the title. To 'breed' is to not use a condom (already called bareback) but also to not withdraw for the money shot: a perversion that perverts the original perversion. In the heterosexual context this is to 'swerve away' from the normal pleasurable feeling of procreative sex (coming inside) towards the visual pleasure of seeing 'it' (sharing it visually with another of an audience). In the homosexual context, it is to 'swerve away' from the normal pleasure of coming inside the orifice of another, feeling enclosed within that body's warmth. The money shot, which since both *Deep Throat* and *Boys in the Sand* had become so conventional in both straight and gay pornography, had long been considered to be in need of something new to spice it up.[55] That new thing arrived on/scene with the risky gay practice of 'breeding'. Consider for a moment how a heterosexual couple might fantasize the memory of that fateful night they neglected 'protection' and 'got pregnant' with sex acts that were imagined to be more intensely felt, more memorable than usual, saying 'they just got carried away'. In much the same way, some gay partners may also memorialize the intensely felt moment a powerful top 'bred' a powerless 'twink'. In both instances a phantasmatic desire to believe in the consequential nature of the particularly 'hot' sex colours the experience for both. In both cases risk is crucial. Does this mean that gay sex is mirroring heterosexual sex by suggesting that 'breeding' a virus is like conceiving a baby? Perhaps a little.[56] But hardcore pornography seeks the impossible: to render through sight and sound the feelings of the lust of others, as experienced as much as possible in our own bodies. The utter violence of the titles of so many of the videos on Pornhub, gay and straight, speaks to a certain escalating frustration with this impossibility. There is really nothing very 'raw' about the way 'cute Nico' is 'fucked' in *Cute Nico Leon Getting Rawfucked at the Pool*. That is a sweet coupling trying to convey the danger of transgression. There *is* something more 'raw' about *Daddy Screams in Ecstasy as He Breeds His Young Asian Twink Boy Raw*. In this video it is not only that there is no demonstrated affection or respect for the 'Young Asian Twink' being 'bred'. Respect and affection are not necessarily what hard core is all about. But there does seem to be an escalating logic at work in the perverse dynamic that demands visual and aural evidence of one dominant person's effect upon another, less dominant, person.

This logic operates to popularize the gesture of 'breeding' by offering, once again, a compensatory substitute for what can't be seen. It is thus perhaps not surprising that many other 'Bareback', 'Breeding' videos find a way to make the Daddy's power more visually evident in yet a new trope: pushing out from the anus the visual evidence that was missing during the invisible internal ejaculation. (If this does not all happen in a single take, 'semen substitutes' can be faked, but one is likely to be looking for the fake; reality counts for the fantasy.) This is what happens in a great many videos with the tag 'Creampie' (the noun alluding to the visual evidence of the milky ejaculate extruded, sometimes quite forcefully, from the anus). The 'Creampie' (aka 'reverse money shot'[57]) has not replaced the ordinary 'money shot' in hardcore pornography, but it has become quite common since the millennium (during my visits there were 2,381 videos with this tag on Gay Pornhub). What is surprising, however, is how popular it has also become in straight videos (56,360 videos in default Straight Pornhub) referring to anal or vaginal orifices. In the latter, the gay metaphor of breeding reverts back from women not using birth control, to the original sense of conception. Ironically, such is the new risk now working to eroticize the taboo of straight hard core: the old-fashioned, original risk of pregnancy.

Watching hardcore pornography on Pornhub has for me become an exercise in discovering at what point I will draw the line. I suspect this is a common experience, with the difference that many people would just say 'Yuck' and stop there. But I also understand the fascination of discovering my own limits and of furthermore discovering, quite unpredictably, that my limit might also be a turn-on. This is what has kept me coming back. As a scholar of pornography, I have an excuse. However, I want to end my sampling of Pornhub with one more video in a subgenre of hard core that is new to me, and that simply and unproblematically pleases me. It belongs to a subgenre of animation (aka Cartoons, Hentai) that I actually dislike intensely in its straight incarnation, but one particular thumbnail catches my eye when I switch to 'Gay'.[58] I have to wonder, though, why am I so consistently drawn to 'Gay', an identity that is not my own? Perhaps that's why: perhaps as the one type of hard core that implicates neither my gender nor my sexual identity, I feel less concerned about who might be harmed? In the case of animation, I am freed from the limits of what human bodies can do, but also from the worry about the infections that might plague real human bodies, so when I sight a thumbnail of a muscular red-headed man and click on the title, I go for it.

The scene begins ominously, like a horror film with epic music and the sucking sounds of primeval slime. A naked man (I learn later he is called 'Ginger') climbs out of the slime as if just born, à la Arnold Schwarzenegger in *The Terminator*. On unsteady feet he is nevertheless equipped with a full erection. He then falls slowly, weightlessly down a hole filled with a forest of gigantic penises. Halfway through his fall he begins to enjoy his surroundings. When he lands astride one of these penises (bareback! with his backside backed up against another), he proceeds to have impossible, phantasmatic and somehow also 'realistic' sex with these two oversized organs (see Figure 19.10). Though he himself is never penetrated he does 'dock' his own penis inside the uncut head of the one in the foreground, while being 'penetrated' from behind. The sex that follows observes the entirely predictable formula of pre-barebacking gay porn, ending in visible ejaculation from the two giants, and then the 'human' penis.

In the topper to that climax, he falls in a weightless backflip to an eventual soft landing—we don't yet know where. A phone rings and a camera pull-back reveals a real man half Ginger's size who hands him a cell phone, which he answers in the first words spoken in the video, 'Hey,

Figure 19.10. *Antechamber 2* (screenshots)

Figure 19.11. *Antechamber 2*'s antechamber (screenshot)

hi, what do you mean?' A further pull-back reveals the whole set. He has landed on the set of the very 'porn shoot' that has created him.

Prop giant penises line the walls; technicians, including one with a computer, are wrapping up. *Antechamber 2* is eleven minutes fifty-two seconds long and is both the most imaginative and the most erotic video I have seen yet in my sampling of the site.[59] Why? I could say it is because it is witty, fun and self-reflexive, or that it makes a smart pun on 'barebacking' without risking the transmission of any disease; it also fetishizes disembodied penises in a way that does not weaponize them. Size matters to the point of a parody that is also erotic. But I know that these reasons are too politically, even aesthetically, correct. Perhaps I just like fantastic penises. Frankly, I don't know.[60]

Conclusion

The story up until arriving at this most recent 'moment' has been one in which hardcore pornography has triumphed over a censorship that not only failed to keep what had once been deemed obscene off-(ob)scene, but actively shaped a genre whose forward march towards proliferating on/scene perversions has proved both invincible and lucrative. Censorship, we have learned, becomes more vulnerable the more it clearly names what is obscene. As Judith Butler writes, 'by rehearsing and proliferating the very terms that they seek to bar from discourse', censors fail.[61] For this reason, Butler distinguishes between the kind of censorship that comes after speech, which wants to forbid what has already been spoken, and a more 'implicit' kind of censorship that produces the potentiality of what can be spoken. This is the more internalized censorship we activate when we knowingly negotiate what might be considered obscene in more productive, formative ways. Because the barring-from-discourse naming of specific obscenities has been so dominant in American jurisprudence, hard core has been determined by this jurisprudential naming of 'deviance'. It has not had the luxury of producing the potentiality of what might be spoken about the 'hard core' so overwhelmingly determined by the courts. Yet this kind of internal, implicit censorship is what hardcore pornography needs to flourish as the cultural expression it could be.

So while I have been pleased to see foiled the paternalism of the censors, who are the inadvertent creators of the 'hard core', and much as I believe any adult should be able to enjoy whatever a Pornhub or any other hardcore website has to offer, I am not pleased with the cultural outcome of this triumph as evidenced by my sampling of Pornhub. My (porn)utopian dream of this triumph would have been something lighter, more playful and more diverse than most of the oh-so-similar videos I have just sampled. It would have produced more videos like *Antechamber 2* and fewer *Daddy Screams in Ecstasy as He Breeds His Young Asian Twink Boy Raw*, or more like Annie Sprinkle than what is 'Popular with Women'. But my judgement regarding the roughness of Pornhub should not be taken as an argument in favour of softening the hard core. Annie Sprinkle once defined a difference when she said 'Eroticism is where you use a feather and pornography is where you use the whole chicken.' My point has been that in a 'realistic' film or video moving-image medium, even the chicken is not the whole thing. 'Maximum visibility' can never see all there is to see, and fantasy will always play a part. When it comes to Pornhub, excepting the few examples I have cited, it seems that less is (almost never) more, which is to say that concealment rarely enhances or dramatizes revelation: on/scenity is on/scene all the time. Many sex acts actually now begin at the moment of penetration and one does not need to even see the faces attached to sexual organs. Penises are always already hard in this hard core; there is no time for, or interest in, the process of seduction into lust.

In 1999, in an 'Epilogue' to the first edition of *Hard Core*, I rather hopefully concluded that it was time for feminists to move beyond 'sweeping generalization about the phallic mastery of a disembodied 'male gaze' [...] to consider the quality and kind of its visual—and visceral—pleasures'.[62] Twenty years later, I better understand the escalating logic of perversity in today's visual and visceral hard core. Though I do not condemn it, I do wish there were more alternatives to this mainstream and I emphatically wish to promote the few female-friendly, genderqueer and alternative forms of LGBTQ pornography in this note.[63] But it has always been the case that the market for hardcore pornography has never needed to heed its critics; it has always been immune to its critics, and no more so than now.[64]

Now that the legal category of pornography has lost its teeth, now that it is difficult to point to *any* undigestible hard core that *some* community does not find acceptable, as long as sex acts are legal and performed by consenting adults and no one is hurt, all niches of perversity are welcome, and they should be. But must they always be bigger, better, longer, rawer and nastier than the last? Is there no room for subtlety, delicacy, nuance, artfulness and artistry within this economy of desire? I originally coined the term on/scenity to indicate how pervasive hard core has become, to play with the ironic fact that the obscene has become on/scene. But if hard core were *really* on the scene of public discourse like the kinds of movies that generate public discussion every day, then the slash signalling the perpetually liminal status would not be there at all. It would just be 'on the scene'.

The only time 'mainstream' hard core has received anything like constructive criticism beyond the 'peter meters' of *Hustler* magazine was in the pre-online adult video era in the pages of *Adult Video News*, and later in the reviews of pioneer lesbian feminist porn film critic Susie Bright.[65] Looking back now, this period was a cultural high-water mark in the on/scene cultural history of hard core. Apart from this, few voices that care about the health, longevity and aesthetic quality of the product have been heard apart from their ability to speak to their separate niches. More crucially, there has never been a real archive of hardcore pornography where its history might be studied and from which historians, critics and makers could learn.[66] Without an 'on the scene' history, without the force of real cultural critique, the crude instrument of the first kind of censorship Butler describes will continue to be the primary shaper of the genre, with or without teeth. Pornographers themselves, not to mention their encouraging critics, will not have the opportunity to cultivate the more implicit forms of censorship needed to speak what has actually become speakable within the genre of hard core.

Acknowledgements

This chapter has benefitted from editorial oversight by Damon Young, who also presented the paper's earlier draft at the *Screening Censorship Conference* (Ghent and Vancouver, online, 16–17 October 2020). Thanks also to Jack Wareham for his editing and assistance with the original production of the manuscript.

/>

Notes

1   Walter Kendrick, *The Secret Museum: Pornography in Modern Culture* (Berkeley: University of California Press, 1987), p. 57. Emphasis mine.

2   Lynn Hunt, *The Invention of Pornography: Obscenity and the Origins of Modernity, 1500–1800* (Princeton, NJ: Princeton University Press, 1993), pp. 12–13.

3   Linda Williams, 'Proliferating Pornographies On/Scene: An Introduction', in Linda Williams (ed.), *Porn Studies* (Durham, NC: Duke University Press, 2004), pp. 1–23.

4   Hunt, *The Invention of Pornography*.

5   Ibid., pp. 302–03.

6   Kendrick, *The Secret Museum*, p. 57.

7   Ibid., p. 196.

8   Ibid., pp. 18–26. According to Paul Preciado, Restif's was the first architectural proposition to reform prostitution in European cities. Entirely fanciful and never realized, it was the forerunner of a great many nineteenth-century biopolitical schemes for the disciplinary management of sexuality throughout the century. Paul B. Preciado, 'Restif de la Bretonne's State Brothel: Sperm, Sovereignty, and Debt in the Eighteenth-Century Utopian Construction of Europe', https://www.documenta14.de/en/south/45_restif_de_la_bretonne_s_state_brothel_sperm_sovereignty_and_debt_in_the_eighteenth_century_utopian_construction_of_europe.

9   Tom Gunning, 'An Aesthetic of Astonishment: Early Film and the (In)credulous Spectator', in Linda Williams (ed.), *Viewing Positions: Ways of Seeing Film* (New Brunswick, NJ: Rutgers University Press, 1995), p. 119; Linda Williams, 'Motion and E-Motion: Lust and the "Frenzy of the visible"', *Journal of Visual Culture* 18.1 (2019): 1–35.

10   Noël Burch tells us that these punitive endings were inherited from the circus; see Noël Burch, *Life to Those Shadows*, trans Ben Brewster (Berkeley: University of California Press, 1990), pp. 193, 220–23.

11   Gunning, 'An Aesthetic of Astonishment', p. 101.

12   There is no evidence of this actual immediacy but the compulsion to see more of … whatever … is obvious, and the 'attraction' of the forbidden things of sex, to the view of the interiority of bodies, the secrets of pleasure, is evident.

13   Note that although *Les cartes érotiques* seemed to offer its cards for close view as held in the hand of the waiter, the views from this earlier period were full shots allowing no close views of the sexual acts.

14   Linda Williams, *Hard Core: Power, Pleasure, and the 'Frenzy of the Visible'* (Berkeley: University of California Press, 1999 [1989]), p. 72.

15   Frédéric Tachou, *Et le sexe entra dans la modernité* (Paris: Klincksieck, 2013), pp. 197–212, 205. American scholars stand corrected by Tachou. It seems possible that Americans, beginning with Di Lauro and Rabkin (Al Di Lauro and Gerald Rabkin, *Dirty Movies: An Illustrated History of the Stag Film 1915–1970* (New York: Random House, 1976)), up to and including myself (Williams, *Hard Core*), have applied our own history of stag parties and smokers, where prostitutes were paid invited guests, to the French with their more legal tradition of *maisons closes*. However, Tachou shows that although many scholars such as Georges Sadoul and memoirists like Marcel Pagnol have assumed that

projections of pornographic films took place in the *maisons closes*, and though many films seem to be addressed to the 'Messieurs' and their clients to function as 'warm-ups' for business, these *maisons closes* were highly regulated institutions with no spaces for screening (Tachou, *Et le sexe entra dans la modernité*, p. 205).

16 Williams, 'Motion and E-Motion'.

17 Crary argues that by the nineteenth century vision was no longer understood to operate, as Newton once thought, as particles travelling in straight lines, but as rays or waves that affected the human senses in distinctly different ways. The sensation of light, for example, was just that—a *sensation* produced by stimuli in various parts of the body. If sensations could be so capricious and did not arise from an objective source 'out there' in the world, then vision itself was being redefined as 'a capacity for being affected by sensations that have no necessary link to a referent'. The world 'out there' could be reinterpreted to mean the arousal of feelings 'in here'. Jonathan Crary, *The Techniques of the Observer: On Vision and Modernity in the Nineteenth Century* (Cambridge, MA: MIT Press, 1990), p. 91.

18 Ibid., p. 93.

19 Courts were only slowly learning how to distinguish art from dross, so the case of *Jacobellis v. Ohio*—a theatre manager who had been convicted for showing *The Lovers* (as *Les amants* was known as in the USA)—was relatively easy for the Supreme Court. The 'motion picture in this case' was not by any stretch of the imagination obscene. It was already becoming an arthouse classic.

20 Kendrick, *The Secret Museum*, p. 120.

21 Ibid., pp. 120, 123.

22 *Roth v. U.S.* (1957). This is not to say Comstock laws did not prosecute such works. They did—much of the archive of the Kinsey Institute is composed of 'obscene' films and pamphlets donated by police departments. It is just to say that judicial rulings had not been pressed to define the objectionable obscenity in them.

23 Kendrick, *The Secret Museum*, p. 201. Italics mine.

24 See Donald Alexander Downs, *The New Politics of Pornography* (Chicago: University of Chicago Press, 1989), p. 14; Whitney Strub, *Obscenity Rules: Roth v. United States and the Long Struggle over Sexual Expression* (Lawrence: University Press of Kansas, 2013), p. 167.

25 Edward de Grazia, *Girls Lean Back Everywhere* (New York: Random House, 1992), pp. 297, 571.

26 Strub, *Obscenity Rules*, p. 201.

27 Downs, *The New Politics of Pornography*, p. 17.

28 De Grazia, *Girls Lean Back Everywhere*, p. 571 (italics in original).

29 Burger himself never went, nor did the libertarians Douglas or Black, who believed nothing should be banned. Justice Harlan, nearly blind, would need his clerk to describe the action. But Thurgood Marshall, Williams Brennan and Byron White and most of their clerks were in attendance. Some clerks would joke by mocking Potter Stewart's infamous 'That's it ... I know it when I see it'; see Bob Woodward and Scott Armstrong, *The Brethren: Inside the Supreme Court* (New York: Simon & Schuster, 1979), 239–40. The clerks developed a shorthand for how each of their bosses defined obscenity: apparently Justice Brennan would accept penetrations and oral sex as long as no erections were visible; for Justice Byron White no erections and no insertions equalled no obscenity.

Although this 'test' of erections surely referred to those visible *in* the films, they could equally have referred to those on the bench. (See FindLaw Attorney Writers, 'Movie Day at the Supreme Court, or "I Know It When I See It": A History of the Definition of Obscenity', https://corporate.findlaw.com/litigation-disputes/movie-day-at-the -supreme-court-or-i-know-it-when-i-see-it-a.html.)

30   De Grazia, *Girls Lean Back Everywhere*, p. 567; Downs, *The New Politics of Pornography*, pp. 17–18.

31   Sigmund Freud, 'Three Essays on the Theory of Sexuality', in *The Standard Edition of the Complete Psychological Works of Sigmund Freud*, vol. 7, trans. James Strachey (London: Hogarth, 1953–66 [1905]).

32   Downs, *The New Politics of Pornography*, p. 17.

33   Portions of this section are adapted from Chapter 3 of my book *Screening Sex* (Durham, NC: Duke University Press, 2008).

34   John Updike, *Couples* (New York: Knopf), p. 248.

35   *The End of Obscenity* was a book by Charles Rembar that celebrated the liberalization of what Damon Young has called the 'liberal sexual subject'. Rembar was a tad premature in his celebration—for liberalization, as Young, writing much more recently, points out, is not a simple matter of an autonomous pleasure-seeking agent seeking freedom but a further politicization when it immediately comes into conflict with notions of the heterosexual family as constitutive of the social. See Charles Rembar, *The End of Obscenity: The Trials of 'Lady Chatterley', 'Tropic of Cancer' and 'Fanny Hill'* (New York: Random House, 1969); and Nicholas Bahr, 'The Liberal Sexual Subject: A Conversation with Damon R. Young'), *Film Quarterly* 72.2 (Winter 2018): 8.

36   Linda Williams, *Viewing Positions*, p. 93.

37   Michel Foucault, *History of Sexuality*, vol. 1 (London: Allen Lane, 1978), p. 12.

38   Daphne Merkin, 'The Lives They Lived; Pop-porn', *New York Times*, 29 December 2002: section 6, p. 30.

39   Richard Smith, *Getting into 'Deep Throat'* (Chicago: Playboy, 1973), p. 284.

40   Peter Alilunas, *Smutty Little Movies: The Creation and Regulation of Adult Video* (Berkeley: University of California Press, 2016), p. 123.

41   See Williams, 'Epilogue', in *Hard Core*, pp. 300–15 where I summarize this period of 'Electronic On/Scenities'.

42   Fred Halsted, Joe Gage and Jack Deveau, and Gerry Douglas are directors who followed. See Williams, *Screening Sex*, 143–54, in which I compare *Deep Throat* to *Boys in the Sand*.

43   There is a caveat attached to these numbers and estimates. See: Eric Schlosser, *Reefer Madness: Sex, Drugs and Cheap Labor in the American Black Market* (Boston: Houghton Mifflin, 2003), pp. 112–15.

44   Alilunas (*Smutty Little Movies*, pp. 117–18, 196–200) puts the percentage of brick-and-mortar video stores at 63% of the market by 1986; in tandem, production companies began to acknowledge their influence in the market. As Alilunas puts it, adult videos remained liminal—located between dirty and respectable, between the store's curtained-off back room and the rest of the store (p. 200).

45   Wendy Hui Kyong Chun, *Control and Freedom: Power and Paranoia in the Age of Fiber Optics* (Cambridge, MA: MIT Press, 2006), p. 120.

46   Ibid., pp. 77–127.

47   See https://www.w3.org/standards/.

48   There are others: YouPorn, RedTube, etc., but they are also part of the MindGeek conglomerate. Pornhub is not even the most popular site, but it appears to host the largest number of videos available on the internet. (This information is courtesy of an outdated (2009) Wikipedia article that Wikipedia itself announces is 'written like an advertisement'. All subsequent information is taken from the Pornhub website itself in the month of April 2020.)

49   Thanks to Jack Wareham, who helped me understand many important aspects of website navigation.

50   This was the number listed on 17 April 2020; the next day there were more. Most of the examples I cite are from the second half of April and the first week of May.

51   According to the 2018 Analytics Pornhub blog post, women make up 29% of Pornhub visitors: https://www.pornhub.com/insights/2018-year-in-review.

52   See Linda Williams, 'A Provoking Agent: The Pornography and Performance Art of Annie Sprinkle', *Social Text* 37 (Winter 1993): 117–33.

53   This ejaculate seems to be extraordinarily visible in Pornhub pornography emerging from both vaginas and anuses these days, in the practice called 'creampie'. Because of its abundance, I suspect that some of it may come out of a tube, especially when takes are interrupted.

54   According to shockingly recent research, 10–50% of women do ejaculate at least some of the time during sex but because ejaculation of the milky sort is not necessarily associated with orgasm, it is sometimes not even noticed. Ejaculation of the colourless and odourless 'squirting fluid', which occurs in large quantities, accompanies orgasm and emphatically is noticed. It is obviously what *How to Get Your Girlfriend …* was shooting for. Researchers have determined that this liquid is not urine, because experimental bladders were empty both before and after the orgasm. Amanda Barrell, 'What Is Female Ejaculation?', 20 January 2020, https://www.medicalnewstoday.com/articles/323953. Annie Sprinkle's squirt was also mistaken for urine and thus subject to increased censorship because considered to be in the category of 'golden showers'—recall that Chief Justice Warren Burger's list of hardcore perversions included 'excretory functions'.

55   For a further exploration of the use of the money shot, see https://www.thedailybeast.com/is-it-time-for-porn-to-retire-the-money-shot.

56   See the chapter 'Representing Raw Sex' in Tim Dean, *Unlimited Intimacy* (Chicago: University of Chicago Press, 2009). Dean argues that barebacking is a subculture that seeks witnesses, documentary evidence and communal bonds: 'everything must be shown, nothing regarded as obscene' (p. 104). In this book, Dean gives serious attention to bareback videos made before 2008 by renegade studios that were not part of the established mainstream still then committed to safer-sex practices. At that time barebacking was a distinct minority practice. Dean's argument at that time, with which I disagreed, took the films as ethnographic documentary evidence of the subculture and not enough as part of the genre of hard core which combines documentary evidence with fantasy. See Linda Williams, 'Pornography, Porno, Porn: Thoughts on a Weedy Field', in Tim Dean, Steven Ruszczycky and David Squires (eds), *Porn Archives* (Durham, NC: Duke University Press, 2014), pp. 29–43 (p. 41). Today on Pornhub it is even more phantasmatic, but still risky.

57 Dean, *Unlimited Intimacy*, p. 144.

58 What displeases me especially is the horror aspect of the straight animations: the Japanese Hentai's tentacle penises with ugly titles like *Daemon Girl Titfuck Animation 3D*, or horrific 'Growth Animations' where body parts, not just penises, grow to grotesque proportions.

59 There are many other animations like this one, none longer than fifteen minutes: *Priapus of Milet, Priapus of Milan, Ad Fundum, The Seventh Circle*, …

60 There is much more that I could explore: MILFs, Cams (not really videos but 'live' 'interactions'), the utter hollowness of the term pornstar. (If everyone can be a star, then there are no stars. The point is not simply that today there are no stars of the magnitude and longevity of a Marilyn Chambers, Georgina Spelvin, Seka, Ginger Lynn or Jenna Jameson, who all had managed careers without overexposure or burnout, but that a 'pornstar' like Lana Rhoades, who is currently ranked #1 'Pornstar' with 1,922 videos, cannot help but be used up fast.) But my tour has taught me enough and I'm finally satisfied to have found a fantasy of unprotected sex that I like. I didn't want to be a spoilsport!

61 Judith Butler, 'Ruled Out: Vocabularies of the Censor', in Robert Post (ed.), *Censorship and Silencing: Practices of Cultural Regulation* (Los Angeles: Getty Research Institute, 1998), pp. 250, 248–51.

62 Williams, *Hard Core*, p. 315.

63 Though they represent the tip of the iceberg of the mainsteam, and some must resort to Kickstart or Crowdfund campaigns to produce their videos, they deserve serious encouragement for their assertion of female subjectivities and pleasures. For some of these alternatives see https://www.bustle.com/p/the-best-sites-for-lgbtq-friendly-porn-7428306 and look especially for Shine Louise Houston whose *Crash Pad* series and Pink and White Production has been a big hit, and Erika Lust, a Swedish producer based in the UK. See also https://www.marieclaire.com/sex-love/advice/a509/female-friendly-porn-for-women/. For some current reviews written from a feminist perspective, see http://femporn.blogspot.com/?zx=8423bc931ea840c4.

64 Though many feminist critics have come to the defence of hardcore pornography in the face of the censorships that would eradicate it, they have often done so less to defend the industry that is and more often to make room for the pornography that might be.

65 Peter meters were little cartoon caricatures of penises alongside capsule 'reviews' published in *Hustler* magazine. They were not real reviews but publicity for the films designed to sell the 'hotness' of the film, measured by the degree of erection of the penis. *Adult Video News* began in 1982 as a newsletter to inform adult video renters about which tapes were the best; when it later became a free trade journal informing distributing outlets about which tapes to stock on their shelves and accepting advertising from adult video producers, it took on greater influence, moving from a fan-oriented discourse to a more critical voice (see Alilunas, *Smutty Little Movies*, pp. 104–16). While it still exists, the shift to online distribution has considerably lessened its taste-setting influence. Pioneer feminist porn critic Susie Bright, on the other hand, has indefatigably written about and encouraged alternative lesbian critique and production for the last several years. She writes that the first 'limp dick' she saw in *Hustler* proved to be an enthralling moment. She rushed to see the film and found it enthralling; it launched her career as

a reviewer of hard core and publisher of female 'herotica'. See Susie Bright, 'The Birth of the Blue Movie Critic', in Tristan Taormino, Constance Penley, Celine Shimizu and Mireille Miller-Young (eds), *The Feminist Porn Book: The Politics of Producing Pleasure* (New York: City University of NY Press, 2013), pp 33–40.

66 Except for the Kinsey Institute at Indiana University which suffers from perpetual funding problems there is no hardcore archive, and archivists warn us that digital preservation is not up to the task of saving the celluloid, the analogue video or the more recent digital past. See Linda Williams, 'Pornography, Porno, Porn'.

Index

Page numbers in *italic* refer to illustrations; page numbers in **bold** indicate tables.

path dependency theory, Turkish film
  censorship 255–69
PCA. *See* Production Code
  Administration
PCI. *See* Italian Communist Party
PEN reports 21–2, 303
'Perspektywa' Film Unit 208
perversion/perversity
  and hardcore pornography 339, 355,
    359, 360
  and obscenity 339–40, 342
Pettijohn, Charles 38–9
Petzet, Wolfgang, *Verbotene Filme*
    pamphlet 101–20
  career of Petzet 105–6
  photograph of Petzet *105*
philosovietism, and Italian film culture
  49–64
Pinochet dictatorship, film censorship in
  Chile 139–52
Poland
  anti-Semitic campaign 123, 128,
    133–4
  arthouse cinemas 210, 211
  Artistic Evaluation Committee 203
  'Carnival of Solidarity' period 202
  Catholic Church 123, 124, 126–7,
    128, 129–30
  Chief Board of Cinema 121
  Chief Office for Film Culture 66,
    67
  Cinema Programming Council
    67–9, 73–4
  de-Stalinization 121, 135
  Film Approval Commission 122,
    124
  film censorship, communist period
    121–38, 201–14, **206**
  Film Club society 210, 211
  film industry 52, 121, 122, 123, 128,
    129, 130, 133–5, 203–4
  Film Rental Office 67, 68, 69
  foreign film censorship 65–76
  Gomułka regime 121, 123–4, 134–5
  Irzykowski Film Studio 202–11

Main Office for the Control of Press,
  Publications and Performances
  66–9, 71, 73–4, 203, 204, 205,
  209
martial law period (1981–83) 74,
  202–11
Passion play performance 129
Pre-Release Review Committee
  203–4
Programme Department of
  the Supreme Board of
  Cinematography 203, 208,
  209
purchasing and distribution of films
  66
Script Assessment Commission
  122, 124, 128, 130
Silence (Kutz, 1963), case study
  124–7
Soviet invasion/occupation of 57,
  58, 59–60
See also Polish …
Police National Computer 322
policing
  of indecent content 316–17, 319, 322
  of internet users 321, 322
  of obscene content 276, 315, 317
Polish Army 57, *59*, 131
Polish Film School 131, 201
Polish Filmmakers' Association, Young
    Filmmakers' Circle 202
Polish Socialist Youth Union 207
political cartoons 233–4
political censorship
  Canada 233
  Chile 146
  France 179
  Germany, Weimar period 101, 103,
    107–8, 111
  Hollywood 22–7, 28, 39
  Poland 201–14
  Turkey 261, 263–4
political pornography 328
politique des auteurs 183
Poole, Wakefield 344

Exeter Studies in Film History

Previous titles

Parallel Tracks: The Railroad and Silent Cinema, Lynne Kirby (1997)

The World According to Hollywood, 1918–1939, Ruth Vasey (1997)

'Film Europe' and 'Film America': Cinema, Commerce and Cultural Exchange 1920–1939, ed. by Andrew Higson and Richard Maltby (1999)

A Paul Rotha Reader, ed. by Duncan Petrie and Robert Kruger (1999)

A Chorus of Raspberries: British Film Comedy 1929–1939, David Sutton (2000)

The Great Art of Light and Shadow: Archaeology of the Cinema, Laurent Mannoni (2000)

Popular Filmgoing in 1930s Britain: A Choice of Pleasures, John Sedgwick (2000)

Alternative Empires: European Modernist Cinemas and Cultures of Imperialism, Martin Stollery (2000)

Hollywood, Westerns and the 1930s: The Lost Trail, Peter Stanfield (2001)

Young and Innocent? The Cinema in Britain 1896–1930, ed. by Andrew Higson (2002)

Legitimate Cinema: Theatre Stars in Silent British Films 1908–1918, Jon Burrows (2003)

The Big Show: British Cinema Culture in the Great War (1914–1918), Michael Hammond (2006)

Multimedia Histories: From the Magic Lantern to the Internet, ed. by James Lyons and John Plunkett (2007)

Going to the Movies: Hollywood and the Social Experience of Cinema, ed. by Richard Maltby, Melvyn Stokes and Robert C. Allen (2007)

Alternative Film Culture in Inter-War Britain, Jamie Sexton (2008)

Marketing Modernity: Victorian Popular Shows and Early Cinema, Joe Kember (2009)

British Cinema and Middlebrow Culture in the Interwar Years, Lawrence Napper (2009)

Reading the Cinematograph: The Cinema in British Short Fiction 1896–1912, ed. by Andrew Shail (2010)

Charles Urban: Pioneering the Non-fiction Film in Britain and America, 1897–1925, Luke McKernan (2013)

Cecil Hepworth and the Rise of the British Film Industry 1899–1911, Simon Brown (2016)

The Appreciation of Film: The Postwar Film Society Movement and Film Culture in Britain, Richard L. MacDonald (2016)

The Lost Jungle: Cliffhanger Action and Hollywood Serials of the 1930s and 1940s, Guy Barefoot (2016)

Celluloid War Memorials: The British Instructional Films Company and the Memory of the Great War, Mark Connelly (2017)

Silent Features: The Development of Silent Feature Films 1914–1934, ed. by Steve Neale (2018)

Film, Cinema, Genre: The Steve Neale Reader, ed. by Frank Krutnik and Richard Maltby (2021)

Decoding the Movies: Hollywood in the 1930s, Richard Maltby (2021)

The B&C Kinematograph Company and British Cinema: Early Twentieth-Century Spectacle and Melodrama, Gerry Turvey (2021)

Cinema on the Front Line: British Soldiers and Cinema in the First World War, Chris Grosvenor (2021)

Screening Europe in Australasia: Transnational Silent Film Before and After the Rise of Hollywood, Julie K. Allen (2022)

Picturegoers: A Critical Anthology of Eyewitness Experiences, Luke McKernan (2022)

Bill Douglas: A Film Artist, ed. by Amelia Watts and Phil Wickham (2022)

John Hamrick's Blue Mouse Cinemas: Independent Exhibition and Influence in the Studio Era, Michael Aronson (2024)

UEP also publishes the celebrated five-volume series looking at the early years of English cinema, *The Beginnings of the Cinema in England*, by John Barnes.

Printed in the USA
CPSIA information can be obtained
at www.ICGtesting.com
LVHW090328111124
796031LV00001B/1

9781804130667